MADAGASCAR

VISITORS' GUIDE TO MADAGASCAR

VISITORS' GUIDE TO MADAGASCAR

HOW TO GET THERE · WHAT TO SEE · WHERE TO STAY

Marco Turco

SOUTHERN
BOOK PUBLISHERS

This book is dedicated to Emma (Mamy) Rahantaharimanana, who took me dream-walking. Misaotra!

Copyright © 1995 by the author

All rights reserved. No part of this publication may be reproduced or transmitted in any form or by any means without prior written permission from the publisher.

ISBN 1 86812 585 8

First edition, first impression 1995

Published by
Southern Book Publishers (Pty) Ltd
PO Box 3103, Halfway House 1685

While the author and publisher have endeavoured to verify all facts, they will not be held responsible for any inconvenience that may result from possible inaccuracies in this book.

Cover photograph by Gavin Thomson/ABPL
Cover design by Insight Graphics
Maps by Colin Stevenson
Set on 10/11.5 pt Palatino
by Kohler Carton & Print, Pinetown
Printed and bound by Kohler Carton & Print, Pinetown

ACKNOWLEDGEMENTS

Researching and writing the *Visitors' Guide to Madagascar* was the most exciting, satisfying yet frustrating thing I have ever had to do as a writer. Without the steadfast encouragement, support and assistance of many people – too many to mention all by name – this book is unlikely to have reached fruition. Those who are not mentioned here are certainly not forgotten. All of you, from the affectionate Antakarana tribe with whom I stayed on the fringes of the Montagne d'Ambre rainforest, to the nomadic Antandroy who gave me shelter, food and comfort in their encampment west of Ifotaka, I thank you from the depths of my soul. The following people played significant roles in the compilation and completion of this guidebook; to them I am truly grateful:

Sahondra Solofoarivelo Razafindrakotohasina, Janet McCloughan; Elyane Rahonintsoa; Jan Wijnen, Mireille Ramarozaka; Anita and the Sofia Satrana Hotel; Josephine Mamie; Hakim Allouani; Derek Schuurman; Miss Jeannine; Robin Harris and Glynis Jackson; Ian Sinclair; Emma Rahantaharimanana; Louise Grantham; Jody Turco; Colin Stevenson; Dick and Pat Denham; my beloved parents, Graziano and Norma. Finally, to those beautiful people of Madagascar, who opened their hearts, homes and lives to me, I thank you all.

CONTENTS

Introduction 1
How to use this guide 3

1 FACTS ABOUT THE COUNTRY 5
History 5
Geography 11
Climate 12
Population 13
Culture 14
Economy 15
Religion and holidays 18
Wildlife 19
Language 24

2 FACTS FOR THE VISITOR 26
Visas 26
Embassies and consulates 27
Malagasy embassies and consulates abroad 27
Customs 29
Money 30
Costs 31
Tipping 32
Beggars 32
Tourist information 32
Post office 33
Telephone 34
Time 34
Electricity 35
Business hours 35
Media 36
Health 37
First aid 42
Clothing 43
Women visitors 44
Photography 45

Security	46
Places to stay	48
Camping	50
Food	51
Drink	52
Books	53
Maps	54
Things to buy	55
Things to do	57

3 GETTING THERE ... 61

Air	61
Sea	62

4 GETTING AROUND ... 64

Air	64
Bus	65
Taxi	65
Boat	67
Train	67
Car rental	68
Bicycle	69
Motorcycle	69
Hitchhiking	70
Tours	70

5 ANTANANARIVO ... 73

Getting there and around	73
Tourist information	76
Things to do	81
Things to buy	85
Accommodation	85
Places to eat	88

6 SOUTHERN MADAGASCAR ... 90

Tolanaro (Fort Dauphin)	93
Lac Anony	102
Betanty (Faux Cap)	103
Tanjona Vohimena (Cap Ste Marie)	103
Lokaro peninsula	104

Manafiafy (Ste Luce)	105
Toliara (Tulear)	105
Grotte de Sarondrano	112
Anartsogno (St Augustin)	113
Anakao	114
Tsimanampetsotsa Nature Reserve	115
Miary	116
Ifaty	117
Ihosy	119
Ranohira	121
Massif de l'Isalo (Isalo National Park)	122

7 CENTRAL MADAGASCAR 127

Ilafy	129
Ambohimanga	130
Ambohijanaka	134
Ambatolampy	135
Antsirabe	138
Lac Andraikiba	145
Lac Tritriva	146
Betafo	147
Ambositra	148
Fianarantsoa	149
Sahambavy	156
Ranomafana	158
Parc National de Ranomafana	160
Ambalavao	163

8 EASTERN MADAGASCAR 167

Toamasina (Tamatave)	170
Maroantsetra	179
Navana	181
Mananara	182
Manompana	184
Mahavelona (Foulpointe)	185
Andasibe (Périnet)	186
Mananjary	189
Manakara	192
Vohipeno	196
Farafangana	198
Nosy Boraha (Île Ste-Marie)	199

9 NORTHERN MADAGASCAR 207

Antsiranana (Diego Suarez) 209
Montagne d'Ambre National Park 217
Lac Antanavo 220
Ankarana Reserve 221
Ambanja 222
Nosy Bé and surroundings 223
Islands around Nosy Bé 233
Sambava 236
Vohemar (Iharana) 239
Andapa 240
Antalaha 241

10 WESTERN MADAGASCAR 243

Morondava 245
Kirindy Nature Reserve 252
Analabe Nature Reserve 253
Belo-Tsiribihina 254
Tsingy de Bemaraha 256
Morombe 257
Mahajanga (Majunga) 259
Katsepy 268
Mitsinjo 268
Tsingy de Namoroka 269
Marovoay 269
Ankarafantsika Nature Reserve (including Ampijoroa Forestry
    Station) 270
Cirque Rouge 272
Grottes d'Anjohibe (Zohin Andranoboka) 273

INDEX 275

INTRODUCTION

Situated between the bulk of Africa and the equatorial regions of the south-western Indian Ocean, Madagascar is thought by many, notably the legendary psychic Edgar Cayce, to be the fabled "Land of Mu", a remnant of Atlantis. It is easy to see why this island continent has reached into the realm of myths. Madagascar is a country of secrecy and sorcery, where creatures and plants have existed since the supercontinent of Pangaea, and later the southern landmass of Gondwanaland was formed. For those with a sense of adventure, a thirst for traditional places and a love of the wild, Madagascar is undeniably the ultimate destination.

This mystical country will tantalise, bemuse and enthral all who venture to her shores. Visitors must go soon though. Where once primary rainforests and tribal culture thrived, there is now the scream of chain saws and the noise of modern construction. The World Wide Fund for Nature (WWF) claims that already over 85% of the natural forest cover is gone. Each day nearly 22 species of life form are rendered extinct, many of them unrecorded, lost forever to the earth. All travellers through this alluring yet tragic country should feel compelled to stop the destruction in whatever way they can. Scattered across Madagascar you will encounter environmental organisations battling to stem the rape of the wilderness areas and halt the culture-destroying advance of Western influence. Madagascar is a storehouse of amazing creatures and medicinal plants. No one who journeys there is left unaffected, either by the warmth and hospitality of the Malagasy people, or the sheer majesty of the island's wilderness.

Madagascar is not a typical Indian Ocean tropical island. The tourism infrastructure is weak, transport is generally uncomfortable and time-consuming, while only two hotels can be classed as five-star: the Hilton and Radama. There are indeed beaches, palm trees and crystal-clear lagoons, but these are not the reasons for visiting Madagascar. The reality of a visit here is best perceived by leaving the cities, tourist hotels and tarred roads. You need to get out into the rural areas, to stay with villagers in their ancestral lands and walk the paths through dripping rainforests to isolated communities and yield to the adventure and experience that are Madagascar.

Flora and fauna abound on the island. Many of the species are endemic and found nowhere else on earth. This fact alone is usually enough encouragement to visitors. From the 31 species of lemur, to colourful moths and giant chameleons, from the six species of baobab to the delicate beauty of over 1 000 orchid species, Madagascar is a walk through the last corner of Eden. Most visitors return home with a commitment to save the endangered environment and vanishing tribes of this island.

Go with an open mind, seeing eyes and listening ears. Get immersed in the country, and slowly the mysteries and riddles will be revealed to you. The Malagasy still believe, and faithfully follow, their timeless proverb, "The soul makes the man" (Ny fanahy no olona).

HOW TO USE THIS GUIDE

Nothing can ever adequately prepare you for a visit to Madagascar. However, it is always good to have some idea of what to expect, where and how you wish to go, sights to see, accommodation and places to eat. Madagascar is an adventurous destination. It is a far cry from the well-organised tourism infrastructure on other south-western Indian Ocean islands. In view of this, prior planning becomes a necessity. The island is enormous, considered by many geographers to be an island continent. Unless you have unlimited time and loads of money for flights, it is unlikely that visitors will be able to see all regions of the island on one visit. This in itself is an excellent excuse for return trips to this marvellous, mystical island.

Start off by getting hold of a detailed map of Madagascar. You can use the one in this book for your planning, but it is recommended that you also obtain the free Carte de Madagaskara from La Maison du Tourisme de Madagascar, BP 3224, Antananarivo 101, Madagascar, tel. (261) 325.29, fax (261) 325.37. This fold-out map will prove most useful for finding suitable routes and will be ideal to use when travelling the country. Once you have some idea of the region you wish to visit, refer to the relevant chapter in this book. As soon as possible after deciding where you are going to travel in Madagascar, commence all the pre-trip arrangements. Make certain your passport is current, have at least eight passport-size photographs printed, get your immunisation certificate updated by having all the required vaccinations and prepare a first-aid kit. It is always a good idea to have a complete medical and dental checkup before venturing off to visit a Third World country.

Chapter 1 offers prospective visitors a brief introduction to Madagascar, that while not professing to be definitive, will provide a base from which to build once you arrive on the island. Chapter 2 details the nitty-gritty things which can make the difference between the best or worst trip of your life. Still enslaved in the endless red tape enforced by previous colonial administrations, Madagascar has enough official forms, requirements and pitfalls to baffle and frustrate even the most widely travelled visitor. This chapter is arguably the most important in the planning and pre-trip stages of your tour. Read it carefully and make use of the suggestions, gleaned from several months' research and travel around the country. Chapter 3 is useful for fixing travel arrangements to Madagascar. Chapter 4 is another vital chapter for travellers. There is certainly no shortage of choice of public transport on Madagascar. It can, however, be rather daunting to the inexperienced, and I have included numerous suggestions and advice for those visitors wishing to make use of taxis, buses, airlines, boats and sometimes, in those few places where it is feasible, hitchhiking.

Chapter 5 describes the fascinating capital of Antananarivo, commonly referred to as 'Tana. For most visitors, this will be their first stop on arrival in Madagascar. It is a baffling city that frequently confuses tourists and leaves them a little apprehensive about the rest of the country. There is a road map of 'Tana in this book, and everyone should use it while walking about exploring the enchanting lanes, alleys and markets of the capital. Chapter 6 takes visitors through southern Madagascar. It is a dry region of spiny deserts, runiform canyons, the oldest and newest European settlements on the island and is home to several tribes and clans. Chapter 7 covers central Madagascar, including the most beautiful city in the country, Fianarantsoa. Also in this chapter are routes for visitors who have limited time and are therefore restricted to 'Tana and its environs. Chapter 7 will lead travellers to some of the most remote and protected areas of this highly threatened island, and gives information on the magnificent Parc National de Ranomafana. Chapter 8 takes visitors into the secluded valleys, primary rainforests, deserted beaches, touristy islands and mist-shrouded hills of eastern Madagascar. Chapter 9 concentrates on northern Madagascar, and also provides details on the north-western isles, such as famous Nosy Bé and Nosy Komba. Travel in northern Madagascar is not for the faint-hearted, and unless you use aircraft, it will take considerable time to visit all the intriguing districts that comprise this magical region. Chapter 10 focuses on the remote, hot and dry provinces of western Madagascar. This area is home to the once powerful Sakalava tribe. Many visitors claim that the Sakalava are the most traditional, hospitable and friendly people on Madagascar. Any visitor who makes the effort to reach western Madagascar will be graced with a unique view of a culture that, while threatened, still manages to maintain its roots, and in doing so encourages hospitality and assistance to all travellers.

Take this book along as a working guide. Where you find changes – and Madagascar is changing at an alarming rate – scribble the information down, and when you return home, please write and tell me, care of my publisher. All information will be filed away for use in updated editions of this book.

1 FACTS ABOUT THE COUNTRY

HISTORY

No one knows for certain who the first inhabitants of Madagascar were. The negroid and Asiatic features found in the present ethnic groups have led to a multitude of speculations and heated debates. The most popular view held by anthropologists and archaeologists is that Malayo-Polynesians travelled around the edge of the Indian Ocean and landed on the west coast of Madagascar. But writer and sailor Bob Hobman has proved that it is just as feasible that the Malayo-Polynesians made a single, long crossing from Java or Sumatra. Taking a traditional wooden sailing craft, named the *Sarimanok*, Hobman crossed almost 6 500 km of Indian Ocean, following the seasonal south-east trade winds. On this epic voyage it was shown that early sailors, using the sun and stars for navigation, most likely landed near Antsiranana, on northern Madagascar, nearly 2 600 years ago.

Arab seafarers definitely came ashore on Madagascar. In the north-eastern forests, typically Arab, circular stone graves lie sad and forgotten in the lush vegetation. Similar graves on other Indian Ocean islands indicate that Arab seamen, while not settling, had explored this entire region by the early 15th century.

Whoever the first inhabitants were, enough myth and legend surround them that even the fabled "Land of Mu" has been ascribed to Madagascar. From those mysterious ancestors grew the modern Malagasy nation. In a series of expansive waves tribes developed and spread, until today there are 18 main ethnic groups and countless clans, all speaking Malagasy, but with a variety of local dialects.

Equally frustrating are the sketchy records of early European arrival. It was not until 1487 that official, written documents describe the landing by Portuguese navigator Bartholemeu Diaz on Madagascar's northern tip. The Portuguese found a harsh, arid countryside of scrub, red sand and little water. They did not stay.

When or why the name Madagascar was given the island is also unknown. Both the Arabs and Indonesians have been credited with naming the island. Yet, after years of research by the museum in Antananarivo, nothing definite has been found. Whatever the reason, the

6 Madagascar

fourth largest island in the world has remained Madagascar throughout its often turbulent history.

Despite coastal landings by the Portuguese, Dutch, French and British, no permanent settlement was established by any of these European visitors. The clans populating northern and eastern Madagascar were a fierce, and far from hospitable, bunch. Oddly, it was buccaneers who were able to reach the first agreement with the local chiefs. From the thickly wooded shores of the east coast, and safe bays in the north, these adventurers plundered the slow-moving merchantmen of the British, French and Dutch East India companies. Hiding their rich caches on isolated islands, they soon became hunted by the British and French navies. It was off Madagascar that the richest and most famous of all Indian Ocean pirates, Olivier le Vasseur (La Buse), was finally captured by the French in 1730.

Living in remote communities, the clans had never been a cohesive people. Feuds, raids and abductions occupied their lives for decades. That is until about 1787, when the chief of the highland, Imerina tribe, Andrianampoinimerina, undertook a massive military offensive. Seeking to build an empire, Andrianampoinimerina declared himself king of all the Imerina and started a policy of conscription. In 1799 he moved a garrison of over 1 000 troops to Antananarivo, establishing his capital 25 km away at Ambohimanga. The king launched his prepared and highly trained armies at the lowland and coastal tribes, literally colonising Madagascar for the Imerina. Resistance, in general, was weak. His toughest foes were the predominantly negroid Sakalava clans along the west coast. With his soldiers stationed throughout the land, he publicly proclaimed himself king of Madagascar in 1801.

A mere five years later, in 1806, the warrior king died. Replacing him on the throne was his capable and wise son, Radama I. He too was determined to build a united and strong Madagascar. European interest, meanwhile, had started to grow, notably from the colonising French. Surprisingly, it was to the British that Radama I turned for the formation of an alliance. British Royal Marine and Navy officers exchanged official documents with the young king. Therein it was stated that the British Crown acknowledged and accepted the sovereign state of Madagascar and her king.

Following the declaration, British advisors and investors poured into the country, hoping to reap a rich harvest from the bountiful land. One good thing that did result from the European arrival was that for the first time, the Malagasy language was presented in written form. Until then, oral traditions and drawings had preserved the communication.

After the death of Radama I, the throne remained vacant for eight months while the wives from his polygamous marriage disputed the right to rule. In September 1827, theცruellest ruler in Malagasy history seized the throne; Queen Ranavalona I. In early 1828 she banned all Christians from the country, giving them three days to leave. She then set about executing anyone still clinging to the Christian faith. For 33 years she controlled her subjects by force and terror. Happily, in December 1861 she died of some unspecified disease. In the towns and villages across the land there was rejoicing. In her place now sat Radama II. A shrewd, fair man, he re-admitted Christians and sought to re-open links with Europe. It was, however, not the British who were once again in favour, this time the French were given the invitation.

France had no desire to remain just a trading partner. Her ambition was to annex Madagascar and proclaim it a French colony. Within the ranks of the ruling Imerina there was now considerable dissent. Many of the ministers wanted the British back, fearing the "hidden agenda" of the French. Just seven months after ascending the throne, Radama II was murdered by unknown assailants as he walked around the gardens of his summer palace at Ambohimanga. His wife, Queen Rasoherina, took over and moved to Antananarivo in 1867. There, she had the Rova palace built high above the narrow, cobbled streets of the town. (This magnificent building should be toured by all visitors to the capital.)

France had gained a valuable foothold in Madagascar and was not prepared to relinquish her holdings. However, the Imerina prime minister, Hononaire Rainilaiarivony, was more interested in building ties with the obviously more powerful British. Britain, however, had found more lucrative places in the Indian Ocean on which to build settlements. The damage had been done and the French started the process of annexing Madagascar to the French Crown. Ignoring any claims or disagreement from the Malagasy monarch, the British and French signed a peace treaty that acknowledged French rule in Madagascar. The colonisers could now start exploiting the country. Things were not to be that easy though. Demanding the surrender of the Imerina queen and all her ministers, the French were surprised to have their envoy publicly executed. Furious, they sent artillery, cavalry and infantry against the poorly armed Malagasy. Using spies and false reports, they launched their attack from Mahajanga – totally the opposite to what the Imerina generals had been led to believe. In the late afternoon of 30 September 1895, the final Malagasy defence fell and the French marched into a city riddled with death, disease and starvation.

With no choice, and no allies, the queen signed over her country to the French in January 1896. Astute generals allowed the queen a degree of autonomy, thereby quelling any possible mutiny. In April 1896, General Joseph Galliéni arrived as the first governor of Madagascar. An administrative man, one of his first efforts was to remove all power from the Malagasy. He expropriated land and gave concessions to French settlers. The Malagasy had become slaves in their own country. Galliéni's hatred of the British pushed him into discrediting Protestants, banning the use of English and trying to remove all English-based education and Malagasy words. His *coup de grâce* came in 1897 when he exiled Queen Ranavalona III to Algeria, and destroyed all records of the local monarchy.

Seeing the potential of Madagascar, France invested huge sums of money in trying to develop a business and military infrastructure on the island. Building roads, bridges, farms and industry, she was soon exporting to France and other French colonies. While the French prospered, the Malagasy grew poorer. Secret societies were formed, and subversion was fomented by ousted ministers. It was not until 1942 that the chance for liberation came.

Back in Europe, the Germans occupied France and were supported by the Vichy government. For reasons still unclear, the majority of colonials on Madagascar supported the German occupation and refused to allow access to the Free French, who were fighting for the liberation of France. Seeing the danger in the Indian Ocean, the British rushed marines and battleships to the area. In the bay of Antsiranana, a bitter battle ensued as the British caught Vichy warships at anchor. The result: the Vichy French surrendered and the Royal Marines landed. Pushing inland, they encountered no resistance from the locals. Instead, tribesmen joined the ranks and gladly marched on all Vichy French-ruled towns, businesses and farms. Britain stationed troops on the island until 1943, when enough Free French were available to hand the island to them. The Malagasy were shocked. Promises made by the British were summarily broken and Madagascar returned to the status of a colony.

Now, opposition parties started to show themselves publicly. Demonstrations and cries of "Fanafahana" (liberation) occurred more frequently. Nothing concrete was done, and in early 1947, an attempted revolution was violently crushed by French troops. For days following the attack, the bodies of Malagasy people littered the streets, mute testimony to the determination and savagery of the colonial French. All had not been in vain. In France, the citizens began to question the cost of keeping their colonies. Pressure mounted, and in 1958, De Gaulle allowed a referendum to be held in Madagascar. Unanimously, the Malagasy voted for independence. In a meagre acceptance of the public mood, France agreed to allow limited independence, but retained overall rule. Philibert Tsiranana, leader of the Parti Social Démocrate, became the country's first elected president in 1960.

Change was slow. For almost 12 years Tsiranana was little more than a lackey for the French government. His weakness and hesitancy resulted in his popularity plummeting. Tired of the vacillating of the West, a growing number of Malagasy looked to the East bloc countries for support in their search for full independence. The economy worsened, strikes became a regular occurrence and all fingers were pointed at the French and Tsiranana. Finally, in late 1972, the people could take no more, and after a protracted strike and street demonstrations, Tsiranana resigned. France said nothing, waiting to see what the new military junta would do.

As expected, the military immediately sought assistance from China and Russia. Things did not go as planned, and once again the Malagasy citizenry expressed its displeasure in coup plots, bombings and work stoppages. Power was handed over to another military officer; Ramantsoa. Ramantsoa ruled from 1972 to 1975, was forced to step down and replaced by Col. Ratsimandrava. His rule lasted less than a week, before his body was found, shot 12 times, in his car on the outskirts of 'Tana (Antananarivo). In 1975 the ex-navy admiral Didier Ratsiraka became president. He too was in favour of Marxist ideologies, and steered his country on that finest of lines between communism and socialism. Continuing to nationalise large corporations, as his failed predecessors had, Ratsiraka propelled Madagascar towards further economic decline. In his later years, up to 1992, he slowly started turning the country towards a market-orientated economy. As so often happens, although he was the instigator of change, it was left to another to carry the country onto the new road.

In 1992, Didier Ratsiraka took a gamble that failed. He insisted on a national election to prove his popularity. The results astonished analysts. The overwhelming majority of Malagasy voted Albert Zafy into office. Zafy is a radical among traditional Malagasy politicians. He has made huge strides in bringing the country towards capitalism. His ministers are vibrant and dynamic, determined to push Madagascar into a First-World position before the year 2000. Their hopes and dreams are admirable, but the reality is a long way off. Further than the year 2000 for sure. But, the start has been made. There is still dissatisfaction among the non-Imerina tribes. Huge differences between the upper and lower classes continue to plague the government. The tiny middle class staggers under high taxation, inflation and corruption.

The present government is made up of a cabinet of 25 members, including the president of the republic. Each minister has a portfolio and is responsible directly to the president for his or her particular ministry.

GEOGRAPHY

With a total land area of 590 000 sq km, 2% of the African landmass, Madagascar is the fourth largest island in the world. From the northernmost point, at Tanjona Bobaomby, to Tanjona Vohimena in the south, the island is 1 573 km long. Across its widest point, from near Lac Mandrozo on the west coast, to Mahavelona in the east, the distance is almost 600 km. Lying 412 km east of mainland Africa, Madagascar was once part of the supercontinent Gondwanaland. About 150 million years ago, as the huge tectonic plates shifted, Madagascar came adrift and settled. Along the coasts, sedimentary rock wore down quickly, leaving expansive deltas and vast deposits of richly coloured lateritic soils. Inland, in the hills, plateaus and highlands, crystalline bedrock lifted mountains and sculpted gorges that continue to amaze and baffle geologists and tourists alike. In the north, volcanoes spewed forth lava and then collapsed, leaving only calderas as reminders of their existence. Madagascar remains a geological anomaly. Still very much in the evolutionary process, this primal land is home to an amazing variety of topographies.

There are four distinct regions, although many other sub-regions exist within each classification. The centre is marked by the highlands. Ranging from between 800 m to 1 500 m in height, the highlands are cold yet dramatic. Falling away from the highlands, the wide valleys and gentle hills of the midlands roll down to the hot lowlands. While the highlands are windswept and covered in a carpet of green, the southern reaches of Madagascar are characterised by semi-desert and staggering rock formations. Along the central and north-east coast, threatened rainforests are the island's lungs. The highest peak, Maromokotra, reaches 2 880 m into the tropical sky on the 14° south latitude line.

12 Madagascar

The ancient landscape yields a bounty of gold, precious and semi-precious stones and recently discovered oil supplies. Sadly, many precious stones are ripped from the earth by unscrupulous dealers and sold on the streets of 'Tana and Antsiranana.

Numerous rivers, natural lakes and waterfalls continue to mould Madagascar. Caves, coralline islands and runiform cliffs in the south near Toliara testify to a unique geomorphology that intrigues all who visit this island.

CLIMATE

In the highlands and midlands the seasons are strikingly obvious. Spring, summer, autumn and winter each take their place on the revolving stage of Mother Nature's play. However, in the lowlands and along the coast, the changing of the seasons is less obvious. The rain in particular is a source of constant bewilderment to visitors. Definite wet and dry seasons do occur across Madagascar, albeit in different places at different times. As a result, very seldom will travellers experience similar weather patterns when flying between destinations over 300 km apart. Derek Schuurman, in his *Traveller's advisory* for Air Madagascar, sums it up when he writes, "Travelling through Madagascar is more like visiting different countries than just adjacent parts of a single island."

As a rule of thumb, the following guide has been given by the Malagasy Weather Bureau:

Cold and dry season in the highlands is between April and October. From June to late August is the driest period of the year in the highlands, but also the coldest. During June and July, temperatures of between 0 °C and 5 °C in the early morning are quite common in places like Antsirabe and 'Tana. Very rarely, reports of light snow in the high mountains are received. The hot, wet period extends from November through to March, with almost daily showers falling from mid-November through to early March. The recommended time for visiting the highland areas of Madagascar is therefore from early May until late October.

In the western lowlands, March to October is the dry season. The rains arrive in November and continue to fall until late April. During the rainy season, regular low-pressure cells hover in the Mozambique channel and off north-east Madagascar. This is the time of the southern cyclone season in the Indian Ocean. Temperatures are warmer than in the highlands. Summer day-time temperatures can go as high as 38 °C, and even in winter the mercury seldom drops below 23 °C.

On the east coast, wet humid weather is a feature of the climate. March is the only month that can be termed dry. Between September and January rain does fall, but intermittently. Humidity along the east coast is high throughout the year. In February and April, and from June to August, torrential downpours occur regularly. The rain is not cold though and most people simply continue with normal routines. Along the Masoala Peninsula, rain exceeds 3 500 mm each year – a good reason for taking wet weather gear no matter what time of the year you visit. Every year the east coast is lashed by tropical cyclones roaring down from the equatorial seas. Although small cyclones are experienced almost yearly, it is the large cyclical tropical storms that wreak most havoc. The east coast of Madagascar is warm all year. Occasionally, in the far south-east, around Tolanaro, temperatures during mid-winter drop to around 12 °C late at night if it rains.

In the south-west January to October is the dry period. The sky becomes tinged with ochre-coloured dust, creating the most magnificent sunsets. For just two months, November and December, short, heavy rain squalls quench the land's thirst. Summer rages from January to early May. Winter, such as it is, occurs between late June and the end of August. Midday temperatures in the south and west are between 24 °C and 34 °C for most of the year.

POPULATION

Ethnographers and anthropologists have divided the people of Madagascar into 50 ethnic groups. Of these, 12 are considered primary tribes, and six root tribes. The primary tribes are: Antaifasy, Antaimoro (of Arab descent) and Antaisaka in the south-east, Antonosy in the south-east and south-west, Mahafaly and the African-featured Makoa in the south-west, Antambahoaka, Bezanozano and Sihanaka in the east, the Tsimihety in the north-east, Antankarana in the north-west and the Tanala in the rainforests.

The root tribes are considered the original stock from which all other tribes developed. These root tribes are: Imerina in the central highlands, Betsileo in the midlands and Betsimisaraka along the east coast. To the west live the Sakalava, while in the south are found the Bara and Antandroy.

Travellers will, however, notice that within each tribe are numerous sub-tribes, or clans, each with subtle feature and pronunciation differences. The Imerina are noticeable by their almond-shaped eyes, straight black hair and high cheekbones. The more Indonesian Betsileo have the striking characteristics and behaviour of Asians. In the east and south, the obviously negroid and Arab crosses of the Betsimisaraka often blend with the more African Bara and Antandroy. Along the central and north-west regions live the Sakalava, a rich mixture of Arab, African and southern Asian.

At present, the population of Madagascar is nearing the 12,6 million mark. By 2025, conservative estimates place the populace at a staggering 28 million. The most obvious thing about the people is the number of children. At the last census taken in 1991, it transpired that almost 53% of the nation was under 18. UNICEF and EU programmes have recently begun to be backed by the new government, and moves are afoot to promote birth control. Sadly, the problem already seems out of control as urban centres burst under the sheer weight of numbers that flock daily to larger cities such as 'Tana and Toamasina.

Although united by a common language, Malagasy, regional dialects, traditions and social orders serve to keep each region refreshingly unique. The people are collectively known as Malagasy. Spend enough time in the country and astute visitors will begin to discern the subtle undertones of unspoken apartheid that exists. The predominantly Asian people hold key positions, seldom marry across racial lines and have a noticeably superior attitude when it comes to other tribes. The negroid and Arab tribes, in turn, have only disdain for the large immigrant populations of Indians, Chinese, Pakistanis and Comorians. This has several times erupted into violent demonstrations. Rest assured, however, that wherever you may travel in Madagascar, you will be greeted only with kindness and warmth.

CULTURE

With their varied ancestry, the culture of the Malagasy is complex and confusing to foreigners. Remember that Madagascar is their country, and while you may not always understand, show respect for their ways.

Taboos play a central role in the lives of the tribal Malagasy. While in cities and large urban areas, taboos (known as fady) are disappearing rapidly, even city folk observe certain rules. To avoid offending the locals, simply watch what they do and where they go. It is not expected that foreigners practise the rituals, but respect is required, and often demanded.

In the southern regions, magnificent ornate tombs occur in remote areas. These are the ancestral tombs of the Mahafaly tribe. Their mystical carvings and ornaments must not be touched or tampered with. You should even get permission before taking photographs of these sites. The famadihana ceremony is a major event. After several years of burial, the grave is reopened, the skeleton exhumed, clothed again and, before being reburied, taken on a tour of the village and supplied with local gossip. A feast always follows, and should you be fortunate enough to be invited to one, every effort should be made to attend.

Music is a part of Malagasy culture. Using drums, bamboo and string, valiha, guitars, accordions and flutes, the people make music that reflects the beat of Africa and the spirituality of Asia. From balladeers, through reggae to musical theatre, music and dance form an integral piece in the jigsaw of Malagasy tradition. Tourist resorts often put on shows of traditional dancing and music for guests, but it is in the remote villages that the most beautiful dances and music are found. Spend enough time exploring the country and you are certain to encounter at least one such display. Mpihira Gasy (traditional singers and dancers) put on joyous pantomimes, intricate swirling sequences and tell tragic stories.

In the cities, nightclubs and discos are all the rage. Go to one of the nightclubs that perform live Malagasy music. At Hell-Ville, on Nosy Bé, the Vieux Port dance hall features local bands. Modern pop music is played at the discos, but no evening is complete without some Malagasy music. Top of the Malagasy charts is Jaojoby, who play wonderful Salegy dance music. Their cassettes are available from Prisunic in 'Tana.

There is a technique to dancing to a Malagasy song in a disco. Everyone faces forward and links arms, then takes two steps forward and two back. Sometimes you all move around the floor in a circle, at others you form rows that move backward and forward. This form of dancing is open to foreigners and inevitably ends in much laughter and sweat.

ECONOMY

Agriculture is Madagascar's main employer and earner of foreign revenue. An estimated 84% of the adult population work the land and in affiliated industries. During the colonial period, the country's agriculture prospered, reaping rich rewards for the French plantation and ranch owners. Since they left, and because of the disastrous policies of Philibert Tsiranana – the newly liberated country's first president – the Malagasy have been in the shameful position of having to import much of their staple diet, rice.

Rice is still the main crop, but the government is now looking to other, more lucrative crops. It is the slash-and-burn (tavy) agriculture of the rice growers that is the major factor in the rapid annihilation of the rainforests. Cutting and burning tracts of forest to plant rice, cassava and, lately, maize, they are destroying the oxygen-producing capacity of the area.

Coffee and vanilla used to be large revenue earners, but these crops too have crashed. Madagascar is the world's largest producer of vanilla. The invention of vanillin, a synthetic flavour similar to vanilla, has dealt a severe blow to both the predominantly Chinese landowners and the workforce of the north-east coast. For the first time in decades, unemployment has reached double figures and the future looks bleak. In the south and west, sisal production and allied factories barely manage to keep operating. Visitors can tour these facilities near Tolanaro and Mahajanga.

Cotton, sugar cane and spices are potentially lucrative crops. Visitors to Toamasina will be struck by the scent of cloves, which lies like a fragrant blanket over the town. Anyone with the slightest business acumen will note that marketing these products seems to be the main problem. Outside Antsiranana, a German food company is putting up a factory for the processing, marketing and export of spices, coffee and vanilla to Europe and North America. Some tea is also grown, but due to the poor quality – it can only be used for blending – and the competition from the extensive tea gardens in capitalist-orientated Mauritius and now the Seychelles, Madagascar cannot hope to keep pace.

Perfumed flowers and plants, most notably the captivatingly scented ylang-ylang, are cultivated. Travelling to Nosy Bé from Antsahampano, you will smell the fragrance of ylang-ylang long before reaching the island. Despite low labour and production costs, few of the perfumed flower plantation owners are wealthy.

Crops which the government is now looking at producing on economically viable scales are oil palms, copra, coconuts and cocoa. The Ministry of Agriculture is having a tough time trying to re-educate farmers, accustomed to subsistence farming, to take an economic view of their work. Beef ranching, forestry and extensive cereal cropping are being encouraged by the limited foreign interest in the country. France and the USA send advisers to assist in rural development, and even the World Wide Fund for Nature (WWF) has now become involved in the projects.

Beef ranching has for many years been the way of life for many of the southern and western tribes. But it is not the production of beef that is the drawcard. Rather it is the amassing of wealth in the form of cattle. Forestry in Madagascar is the reason for much heated debate and speculation and the subject around which rumours of corruption centre. Concessions have been granted to certain logging companies, who are not interested in exotic plantations, but are quite content to tear down indigenous hardwoods such as ebony, pallisandra and rosewood, without any thought to replanting where they harvest.

Madagascar is also rich in minerals. For many years the locals have mined family-operated claims, using their finds for both personal use and sale. Until recently, little large-scale mining occurred, but that is soon to change. Desperate for foreign investment and income, the government is on the point of handing out several exploration and development permits to multinational mining companies. Soon the landscape will be disfigured with the grotesque shapes of mining gear as the obviously vast mineral wealth is exploited. Not only minerals are attracting investment; oil too has been found. Continually in search of new reserves to feed an oil-hungry world, oil companies have already sent geologists and engineers to Madagascar.

Fishing has been a way of life for the coastal clans for generations. Using wooden pirogues and fabric sails, their techniques have changed little in 200 years. Fed by the warm, south-flowing Mozambique Current in the west and the equally warm South Equatorial Current in the east, the waters around Madagascar offer a bounty of fish. Actively engaged in the growth of the fishing industry and fish exports to supply the exhausted resources of Europe and North America, the government of Madagascar has started a programme to purchase factory ships, trawlers, long-liners and drift-netters. Its control of its territorial waters, however, is far from ideal: a legacy from the French that still lingers. An increasing number of deep-water trawlers from Spain, France and Asia hunt the rich fish banks off Madagascar.

Tourism is the newest and fastest growing of all Malagasy industries. The demand and rate of growth far exceed the infrastructure. Tourism is the "boom" industry, seen as a cure-all for the country's short-term economic ills. Unfortunately, things have also got out of control, the biggest offenders being Italian, French and German hotel and vacation consortiums. On Nosy Boraha and Nosy Bé, secondary-growth forests are disappearing at the rate of almost five hectares a day, to be replaced within months by luxury tourist resorts providing employment for the locals.

RELIGION AND HOLIDAYS

Influenced by Eastern philosophy, Islam and Christianity, the Malagasy still include animism in their lives. It is this odd mixture that will excite visitors who look for the real Madagascar. With the Polynesians came the profound, timeless teachings of the great spiritual masters of the East. Arab sailors brought the beliefs and laws of the Koran, while European missionaries arrived bearing the relatively new religion of Christianity. As the ages passed, Africans were forced to Madagascar as slaves and brought their ancient faiths of ancestor worship and the occult, which also found its way into Malagasy culture.

On the surface, the diplomatic islanders accepted the Christian teachings. First Protestants, then Catholics, found favour with the monarchy, except when Queen Ranavalona I carried out her purges to rid Madagascar of Christians. Today, the major religion is Roman Catholicism, followed closely by Protestantism; there is a minority of Muslims and a sprinkling of Buddhists and Hindus.

Animism (ancestor worship) continues to play an important role in the lives of the tribal people. As a result, ceremonies at certain times of the year are attended by lively crowds. Seldom are foreigners allowed, but, if you are fortunate enough to get invited, do not miss the opportunity. In the east, around Mananjary, Ifanadiana and Manakara, the mass circumcision of small boys takes place every seven years, during October. Known as Sambatra, the exact reasons for this ritual are now vague, lost in the oral traditions of the Antaimoro and Antambahoaka people.

Public holidays revolve around the Christian calendar, and a few other days are set aside as national days. This is not to say that there are no other holidays. In the rural villages, travellers will find that, as well as the government-sanctioned holidays, there is a host of local holidays, ceremonies and celebrations. Each region has its own events and interested visitors should enquire about them from elders and headmen.

Public holidays

1 January – New Year's Day
29 March – National Day. Commemorates the 1947 uprising by Malagasy nationalists against the colonists, when almost 77 000 islanders were massacred by the French military
Late March or April – Easter
1 May – Labour Day
May – Ascension Day
26 June – Independence Day
15 August – Assumption Day
1 November – All Saints' Day
25 December – Christmas Day
30 December – Republic Day

WILDLIFE

The 18th century naturalist and explorer, Alfred Russel Wallace, wrote that Madagascar was, "the naturalist's Promised Land." Today, without any doubt, Madagascar should be the number one conservation priority in the world. Of hundreds of thousands of square kilometres of rainforest and natural wilderness, less than 25 000 sq km remains. Erosion, monoculture, tavy agriculture and poor environmental practices are reducing Madagascar's flora and fauna at an alarming rate. In 'Tana the pollution from motor vehicles and industry will leave visitors, literally, gasping for breath.

Madagascar's varied terrain and topography have resulted in several specialised environments. From tropical rainforests, through grasslands to semi-desert, the diversity will astound travellers. Among its plant and animal species are some of the world's most intriguing and baffling biological specimens. Developing in relative isolation, most of the island's wildlife "root-stock" took hold about 60 million years ago. Evidence of dinosaurs is found throughout this mysterious country. A thousand years ago, the elephant bird walked the southern coasts of Madagascar. Its fragmented bones and shattered eggshells lie exposed on many remote beaches south of Tolanaro.

Note that a permit is required to visit any protected area in Madagascar, except private reserves. Permits are obtainable from any ANGAP (Agence Nationale pour la Gestion des Aires Protégées) office, where a green waterfall poster will be displayed.

Flora

With nearly 10 000 botanical species, of which 80% are endemic, Madagascar is a wonderland for tourists interested in botany. The one plant that all visitors will see, whether in its natural state or represented as the country's national symbol, is the ravinala. Known as the traveller's tree – due to its wide-based stems which trap water for drinking – it is related to the bird-of-paradise flower and herbaceous banana. Should you travel the road between 'Tana and Toamasina, you will pass through forests of these elegant, whispering trees.

Six species of baobab tree are found on Madagascar. Along the west coast, an avenue of baobabs has grown along the road near Morondava. In the south-east, the magnificent *Adansonia za* baobab grows in isolated groups. At Mahajanga, in the north-west, a 700 year old baobab can be seen near the coast on Avenue de France. Other baobab species grow in the spiny deserts of the far south, notably the *Adansonia fony* variety.

Perfumed and colourful flowers are another endearing characteristic of the island. Madagascar captivates visitors with everything from yellow and green ylang-ylang blossoms, with their heady scent, to over 1 000 species of orchids. In the eerie darkness of the eastern forests, snow-white comet orchids send out a fragrance on the night breezes. Few orchids have strong scents, relying more on their bright colours to attract pollinators, but the comet is joyfully different. The Madagascar Tourist Bureau is able to arrange botanical tours for interested groups. Contact La Maison du Tourisme de Madagascar, BP 3244, Antananarivo, Madagascar, or visit them on Place de l'Indépendance, Antananarivo, tel. 325.29, fax 325.37.

A unique species of plant is the *Didereas* family. Although resembling cacti in the Americas, it is absolutely no relation. Another highly specialised plant found only on Madagascar is the succulent kalanchoe, found in the arid reaches of the southern massifs. Sunflower species have also bemused many botanists. On Madagascar, developing to suit their environment, many of the species grow into tall trees, their huge, colourful blossoms cascading from leafy boughs. Two varieties of the flesh-eating pitcher plant (*Nepenthes* spp.), also found in southern Asia, grow in secret locations in Madagascar.

In the lowland forests, visitors will find most of the plants to be almost evergreen. These forests have the greatest diversity of plant species in Madagascar, especially deciduous trees. It is these forests which are under the greatest threat from timber companies, for in them are the prized hardwood trees sought for the Far East market. Lianas hang from branches, and high up in the canopy, epiphytes parasitise other plants.

Madagascar's montane rainforests have flora very different from those in the lowlands. The canopy is lower, lichens and moss are more prolific, and both orchids and bromeliads grow in abundance. Although there are fewer species, their colours and forms are fascinating. Junipers (*Juniperus* spp.), bamboo and conifers occur, as do wild mushrooms and exquisitely shaped fungi.

Marine life

Brushed by the warm equatorial currents, the seas around Madagascar are filled with marine life. In the shallower waters, along the reefs, brightly coloured soft and hard coral reflect filtered sunlight. Dazzling tropical fish swim languidly through the coral formations. Offshore, in the cooler deep water, giant manta rays, cruising sharks and migrating whales entice scuba divers. The waters around the island are a living aquarium. There is little danger for the experienced diver or snorkeller. Sharks, of course, are always a potential problem, but very few reports have ever been received of a diver being attacked.

Around the islands of Nosy Bé and Nosy Boraha, tour package operators and beach resorts have mushroomed. Offering basic scuba courses, they promise tourists a unique experience. It is recommended that visitors qualify – at least to NAUI Openwater 1 – before arriving. The short introductory resort courses cannot possibly adequately prepare you for the range of problems that may be encountered. If unqualified, stick to using a snorkel, mask and fins in the shallow water and pools of the shoreline. The variety of life in these waters is just as exciting as that out in the deep sea.

Perhaps the most curious of all Malagasy sea life is the small mudskipper fish. They live in shore pools, and spend as much time out of the water as in. Breathing through their skins, they use their front fins as arms to hop along rocks, searching for food. Well camouflaged, they are difficult to see unless they are moving. With their bulging eyes, enlarged head and amphibious ways, they were considered for many years to be the link between land and marine creatures.

Fauna

For many visitors, the fauna is the reason for travelling to Madagascar. The island continent boasts the oldest living mammal, smallest primate and, of course, the famed lemurs. Animals in Madagascar developed in relative isolation. Zoologically grouped as relicts, many of these creatures have evolved little in thousands of years. There are 260 species of reptile, including boas and crocodiles. Madagascar is the ancestral home of the chameleon; 36 species live here, ranging in size from 5-50 cm.

There are 70 species of land mammal, plus 220 species of bird, of which 118 are endemic. Butterflies and moths, too, are evident in wild profusion. Many of these moths are day fliers. As brightly coloured as butterflies, they can reach enormous sizes, as evidenced by the *Urania* moth. However, the most unusual member of the order Lepidoptera is *Xanthopan morgani praedicta*, with its 35 cm long proboscis. Using its tongue, this moth sucks moisture and nectar from the rare and beautiful Christmas tree orchid.

Progeny of the earth's first small insect-eating mammals also still live on Madagascar. Known as tenrecs, their ancestors first appeared almost 100 million years ago. Resembling hedgehogs and armed with equally sharp quills, the tenrec has changed little over the millennia. The burrowing tenrec has the dubious reputation of having a prolific birth rate, an average of 25 per litter. It lives almost exclusively in the drier parts of the country, excavating grubs and other soft-bodied insects for food.

It is the lemurs which attract most tourist attention. A fairly modern creature on the evolutionary list, lemurs were first identified by early Portuguese explorers. The name means "ghost" in Latin, an apt reflection on these animals that appear and vanish just as quickly. Primates, they nevertheless have developed a lot slower than their African and Asian cousins. The size and functioning of their brains, in particular, are far behind those of other primates. There are 31 species of lemur inhabiting Madagascar. Sadly, the giant lemur, flying lemur and another 10 species are now extinct; victims as much of their changing environment as of man. Early Arab, Portuguese and Dutch seamen wrote of these creatures, whose meat they considered a delicacy.

Within the 31 species, zoologists have classified four groups: typical, monkey-like, mouse and dwarf, and aye-ayes. Noted for their shrill, almost human-like calls, lemurs are found throughout the treed wilderness areas of Madagascar. The most common are the friendly ringtailed and brown lemurs. The smallest primate, the mouse lemur (*Microcebus rufus*), achieves a length of no more than 10 cm, and weighs on average a mere 50 g. Another strange lemur is the black and white ruffed lemur (*Varecia variegata rubra*), which builds a nest high in the forest canopy. The most attractive of all lemurs is the sifaka lemur. With beautiful amber-coloured eyes, jet black facial hair and a mane of pure white, it resembles the work of an imaginative artist rather than something alive. Madagascar's most vocal creature is the tailless Indris lemur. Its series of shrieks, grunts and chattering will be heard by all visitors to the remote lowland rainforests.

In 1986 the rarest of all primates, the golden bamboo lemur, was discovered in the Ranomafana rainforest. This secretive lemur eats giant bamboo, a plant filled with sap containing lethal quantities of cyanide. The poison has no effect on the golden lemur, and researchers have made little progress in finding out why. The largest of all lemurs, the indri, which can weigh over 10 kg, is often seen standing upright, using its front paws as hands to hold, peel and eat berries, leaves and fruit.

Madagascar's largest carnivore is the ferocious fossa, related to the mongoose family. Seldom seen by humans, the fossa feasts on insects and small animals and has even been known to attack calves and kid goats.

Birdlife

Ornithological tours have become increasingly popular in Madagascar. Well-known birding experts such as Ian Sinclair regularly lead tours to the island. Bird evolution is very much in evidence in Madagascar. The flightless elephant bird is now extinct, but several other birds exhibit varying degrees of flying ability. The mesites have weak wings, that although flapped occasionally, cannot lift the bird into flight. Rails can but seldom do fly, preferring instead to run across the ground, even when pursued by predators.

The list of birds to be seen on Madagascar could fill volumes. There are 118 species that live nowhere else in the world. Among the shrike family alone, there are 12 Vanga shrike sub-species. Despite the lack of songbirds, gaily coloured flamingoes, kingfishers, sunbirds and flycatchers provide visual beauty. The asities birds are entirely without fear. This is most likely due to their isolation and lack of contact with humans or predators. Few visitors get to glimpse them, but once you have seen their brave attacks on possible intruders, these little birds are unforgettable.

LANGUAGE

The Malagasy language is often difficult for visitors. It has its origins in southern Asia, with words assimilated from African tribal tongues, the Arab world and Europe. Malagasy and French are the two officially recognised languages. Recently, however, English has become more prevalent, especially among high-school scholars and college students. In urban areas and tourist resorts, visitors will find that apart from Malagasy and French, Italian, German and English are also spoken. In the port city of Antsiranana, Spanish is taught at school level.

The first step in learning something of the language is to get hold of a reputable dictionary. These can be bought for a few thousand francs at any large librairie. In 'Tana, good places to try are FLM Librairie on Avenue Grandidier, opposite the Radama Hotel, and La Librairie de Madagascar on Avenue de la Libération (soon to be changed to Araben ny Fahaleovantena), to the left of the Jean Ralaimongo monument if walking towards the station. A number of teaching books for beginners can also be bought from these shops.

The letter O is pronounced as in the English word too. OA is spoken as U in the north and O in the south. If a word ends in A or Y, the letter is not pronounced. Words that end in NA also change. The A is ignored and the N is pronounced as M.

Here then are a few words on which to build:

Good day	Salama or Manao ahoana
In the northern areas and islands:	Baolatsara
Goodbye	Veloma
Name	Anarana
My name is . . .	. . . no anarako
Yes	Eny
No	Tsia
Thank you	Misaotra
I	Aho
Hungry	Noana
Breakfast	Sakafo maraina
Very good	Tsara dia tsara
Help	Fanampiana
Accommodation	Hotely misy fandriambahiny
Rate	Tarify
Agreed (okay)	Ekena
Tomorrow	Rahampitso
Price?	Ohatrinona?

Expensive	Lafo
Where?	Aiza?
Street	Lalana
Market	Tsena
Pretty	Tsara tarehy
Station	Gara
Island	Nosy
Beach	Morona
Forest	Ala
Address	Ladiresy
I will return	Haveriko aho

2 FACTS FOR THE VISITOR

VISAS

All visitors to Madagascar must have a valid passport and visa. A number of idiosyncrasies concerning the visa regulations and supply have appeared in the last few years. For example, anyone who travels to Madagascar via South Africa is able to get a seven-day "transit" visa on arrival at Ivato Airport. No photographs are required, and payment for the visa may be made when leaving the country. This, however, does not apply to tourists arriving by sea.

Foreigners arriving directly from countries in Europe, the Americas and Asia are expected to have validated visas when arriving. It is recommended that even if travelling from South Africa, you get a visa for the duration of your visit – up to 30 days – prior to departure. Not only is this more convenient, but it also avoids the hassle of getting a visa extension once in Madagascar.

Visas may be obtained through a visa service, travel agent, tour operator, or directly from a Malagasy embassy or consulate. Should Madagascar have no representative in your country, apply to: Ministère des Affaires Étrangeres (L'Immigration), Anosy, Antananarivo, Madagascar. Register your passport, and if possible, use a reliable courier service such as DHL. It takes four to six weeks for the document to be returned.

Visitors using the "transit" visa option will need to apply for an extension after seven days. This is done either at the Ministère des Affaires, Anosy, Antananarivo, or at the Commissariat of Police in any urban centre. Here again, there are vagaries in the process. While the ministry in 'Tana demands four passport-sized photographs, forms filled in in triplicate, a letter in French stating why you want the extension, revenue stamps, copies of your air ticket and accommodation confirmations, many district police offices ask only one photo and one application form. The government offices in 'Tana are poorly staffed and unbelievably slow. A visa extension here can take anything from two days to a week to process. The biggest problem in being without a passport for any length of time is that you cannot travel by road; there are frequent roadblocks where identity documents must be presented. Neither can you do any banking transactions. Conversely, the district police offices are usually efficient and pleasant. Visa extensions must be paid for upon collection, the amount being written on your visa stamp.

EMBASSIES AND CONSULATES

Few countries keep diplomatic missions in Madagascar, and apart from the French government, which still views the country in a patriarchal way, keeping "officials" in most large urban centres, the countries represented all have their offices in Antananarivo.

Embassy of France
3 Rue Jean Jaures, BP 204, Antananarivo, tel. 237.00.

German Consulate
101 Rue Pasteur Rabeony, Ambodirotra, tel. 252.33.

Japanese Embassy
37 Rue Docteur Theodore Villette, tel. 261.02.

Embassy of the United Kingdom
67 Immeuble ny Havana, Antananarivo, tel. 277.49.

Embassy of the United States of America
14-16 Rue Rainitovo, Antsahavola, Ambohidahy, tel. 212.57.

MALAGASY EMBASSIES AND CONSULATES ABROAD

Australia
Consulate of Madagascar
19 Pitt Street, Sydney, New South Wales 2000, Australia, tel. 2-252-3770.

Austria
Consulate of Madagascar
Potzleindorferstrasse 94-96, A-1184 Vienna, Austria, tel. 47-4192.

Belgium
Embassy of Madagascar
276 Avenue de Tervuem, 1150 Brussels, Belgium, tel. 770-1726.

France
Embassy of Madagascar
4 Avenue Raphael, 75016 Paris, France, tel. 1-45.04.62.11.

Germany
Embassy of Madagascar
Rolandstrasse 48, 53000 Bad Godesberg, Postfach 188, Bonn, Germany, tel. 228-33-1057.

Italy
Embassy of Madagascar
Via Riccardo Zandonai 84/A, Rome, Italy, tel. 327-7797.

Kenya
Consulate of Madagascar
Hilton Nairobi, PO Box 41723, Nairobi, Kenya, tel. 26-494.

Mauritius
Embassy of Madagascar
6 Queen Mary Avenue, Floreal, Mauritius, tel. 65-016.

Réunion
Consulate of Madagascar
Corner MacAuliffe and Juliette Dodu streets, 97461 St-Denis, Réunion, tel. 21.05.21.

Switzerland
Consulate of Madagascar
Birkenstrasse 5, 6000 Lucerne, Switzerland, tel. 211-2721.

Tanzania
Embassy of Madagascar
135 Margaret Street, PO Box 5254, Dar es Salaam, Tanzania, tel. 29-442.

United Kingdom
Embassy of Madagascar
16 Lanark Mansions, Pennard Road, London, W12 8DT, UK, tel. 081-746-0133.

United States of America
Embassy of Madagascar
2374 Massachusetts Avenue NW, Washington DC 20008, USA, tel. 202-265-5525.

Where there is no Malagasy embassy or consulate, prospective travellers may find assistance at the French embassy.

CUSTOMS

On arrival at either the international airport or one of the coastal ports, all visitors are required to report immediately to the passport and customs control authorities. Each tourist is permitted to bring in 1 ℓ of spirits, 1 ℓ of wine, 500 cigarettes, 25 cigars and 25 ml perfume. You are restricted to two cameras, 12 spools of film, one video camera and three video cassettes.

Visitors will also be required to fill in a form declaring all the money they are bringing into the country. You may be required to show the customs official this money. This form is then stamped and returned to you. Remember, it must be produced when departing Madagascar (see "Money" section of this chapter). At present, nonresidents cannot take more than FMg25 000 (Malagasy francs) out of the country.

Desperately trying to protect its dwindling wilderness and wildlife, the Malagasy government has clamped down on people trying to smuggle goods out of the country. It is expressly forbidden to export lemurs, crocodiles, tortoises, all endemic plants and items of historical or anthropological significance.

Certain articles may be taken out of Madagascar providing you have first obtained written and stamped permission. These include:

Fresh produce – contact Service Phytosanitaire: Tsaralalana post office.
Precious and semiprecious stones – permission from Ministère du Commerce, Ambohidahy.
Seafood and meat – clearance certificate from Service de l'Élevage, Mahamasina.
Unprotected plant species – Direction des Eaux et Forêts, Antsahavola.

Your luggage, including hand luggage, will most likely be searched when you leave the country. Woe betide anyone caught trying to sneak out things considered valuable by the government. You are guaranteed a short visit to the local jail, a hefty fine and having "Undesirable alien" stamped in your passport.

MONEY

The printing, distribution and flow of money in Madagascar are strictly controlled by the government's treasury department. Visitors are expected to declare all the currency they bring in, spend and remove from the country. Although it is illegal, many travellers do not declare all their hard currency. This enables them to make use of the extremely well-organised and financially enticing black market that flourishes in the capital and all other towns. US dollars, French francs, German marks and sterling are very much in demand, often fetching up to three times the official bank rates.

The Malagasy franc (FMg) cannot be re-exchanged when leaving Madagascar. This means that budget control is vital if you are not to be left with money that must be left behind. If you do have money spare, the street children of 'Tana are a good cause. The FMg has a low value against most currencies, the French franc and Italian lira being the worst.

At customs and passport clearance all tourists are issued with a currency declaration form. Each time you change money officially, this form must be signed and the exchange rate entered and dated by the bank clerk who deals with the transaction. It is also advisable to keep as many sales receipts as possible. When you leave Madagascar, visitors must present their currency declaration form and show any remaining money (both foreign and local). Often, tourists are also required to show how the money was spent; hotel and restaurant bills, internal flight receipts, bus and taxi dockets can be used.

Traveller's cheques and credit cards can be used for purchases at many curio shops and boutiques in 'Tana, on Nosy Bé, Toamasina and Toliara. In large urban centres, MasterCard, Visa, American Express and Diners Club cards can be used to draw cash from banks. Outside these areas, a credit card becomes useless and even cashing traveller's cheques can be a problem. The best way to take money is hard cash in dollars, francs, marks or pounds sterling. Other currencies are viewed with suspicion and rarely accepted. While all banks will change hard currency into Malagasy francs, several refuse to handle traveller's cheques. The Banque Malagache de l'Océan Indien in particular does not cash traveller's cheques at its branches outside 'Tana.

As tourism blossoms, the government now encourages tourist-class hotels and tour operators to charge their clients in foreign currency. Paying in foreign currency can obviously be done with a recognised credit card. Visa, MasterCard, Diners Club and American Express are all accepted, EuroCard less so. American Express is represented by Madagascar Airtours, which has offices in 'Tana at the Hilton Hotel; Antsiranana opposite Air Madagascar; Toliara; Fianarantsoa at Hotel Moderne; and Nosy Bé near Air Madagascar.

There are four main banking institutions in Madagascar:

BFV – Banque National pour le Commerce (Banky Fampandrosoana ny Varotra)
BMOI – Banque Malagache de l'Océan Indien
BNI – Banque Crédit Lyonnais
BTM – Bankin' ny Tantsaha Mpamokotra

Most of these banks have facilities in the larger towns and agencies in rural communities.

An exchange counter is open at the airport when international flights arrive. Tourist-class hotels will also cash traveller's cheques, but charge a high commission, as do certain banks, notably BMOI.

The Malagasy franc is comprised of both notes and coins. The notes come in 25 000, 20 000, 10 000, 5 000, 1 000 and 500 denominations. You will find the ariary in denominations of 50, 20, 10 and 5. One ariary is equal to FMg5. Franc coins come in denominations of 20, 10, 5, 2 and 1.

COSTS

Compared to other Indian Ocean islands, Madagascar is cheap. Certain items are, however, expensive. Deciding on a budget for a visit is dependent on several factors. Among these, your personal preferences and demands will obviously need to be considered. It is safe to say that a three-week visit to Madagascar will cost 50% less than a similar visit to either the Seychelles or Réunion.

Nearly all tourist-class hotels require payment in foreign currency, as does Air Madagascar for nonresidents. Where hotels demand this, visitors can expect high prices for accommodation and meals. If you prefer to mix with the Malagasy, and are prepared to endure a certain amount of roughing it, then payment is made in FMg and is pleasantly low.

Curios in craft shops are always high priced. Rather spend time scouring the local markets for things. The Zoma market in Antananarivo has vast displays of handicrafts and Malagasy goods for sale, all at negotiable prices. Bargaining is a way of life in the markets, and visitors should not disappoint the vendors. Let them start the bidding. Your opening offer should be less than half their price. If language is a problem, they simply pick up a pencil and paper, which you both then use until an acceptable price is reached. Outside the Air Madagascar offices in 'Tana, be prepared for protracted periods of wheeling and dealing, as the hawkers start with really high prices.

Public transport is also cheap. Even long-distance taxi-brousses and buses charge negligible fees for the journey. Private transport, on the other hand, is costly. Food prices, away from de luxe restaurants, are low. Many travellers find themselves eating filling, cheap meals at Malagasy cafés and hotelys (local eating establishments).

At the time of writing, tourists who stay at top hotels, eat at de luxe restaurants and take part in organised tours, can expect to spend at least US $300 per day. Budget travellers, who stay in Malagasy hotels, eat with the locals and use public transport, will quite easily manage on about US $30 a day. Most visitors' spending falls between these extremes. Staying at medium-tariff hotels, eating breakfast and dinner and using both public transport and tour operators, you should comfortably get by on about US $60 per day.

TIPPING

Tipping is expected practice. In restaurants and hotels visitors should leave a suitable tip for the waiter, porter or clerk who assists you. There are no definite rules though and the amount you leave is at your discretion. It does go a long way in improving the already enviable service. Visitors are certain of personal attention if they provide tips.

BEGGARS

Begging is becoming a major problem in the large towns; 'Tana is probably the worst. Tourists will be bothered by street children, old people, women with babies and the disabled. The struggle for survival among the poor of Madagascar is a heartbreaking sight. They are, however, not as tenacious as beggars in India or Egypt.

TOURIST INFORMATION

The main tourist office in Madagascar is on Place de l'Indépendance: La Maison du Tourisme de Madagascar. Contact it during the planning stages of your visit: BP 3244, Antananarivo, Madagascar, tel. 325.29.

It has several booklets, maps and brochures available to the public. Rather high prices are charged for the literature if you call to collect. Postal queries are answered with information free of charge. Apply for information from this office at least six weeks ahead of your departure. A booklet that is highly recommended is *Madagascar: a practical guide*. Oddly, it has no detailed street map of 'Tana, but does have of other provincial centres. The tourist office has an information counter at Ivato Airport, which is open whenever international flights are due to arrive or depart.

Limited tourist information can be obtained from your nearest Malagasy embassy or consulate. Write to it requesting details on the area you wish to visit. By far the best source of pre-trip information for tourists is Air Madagascar. It has offices and agents in several countries, all of whom are efficient, helpful and highly knowledgeable about Madagascar. A number of Air Madagascar offices have even brought out brochures in the language of the country in which they are located. These brochures contain recommended itineraries, practical information and contact numbers. The Air Madagascar office in South Africa has the reputation of being the best for tourist information. Air Madagascar, 3 Willow Street, Kempton Park 1619, South Africa, tel. (011) 394-1997, fax (011) 975-4634. You could also visit or write to its head office in Madagascar: 31 Avenue de l'Indépendance, BP 437, Antananarivo, tel. 222.22.

Further information can be found at top hotels, notably the Hilton and Radama in 'Tana, Motel Gina in Tolanaro, Motel Capricorn in Toliara, Marlin Club on Nosy Bé and Hotel Sofia Satrana in Mahajanga. Tour operators are another source of information. Madagascar Airtours has an amazing selection of brochures and items of interest to tourists. You will find its office in the Hilton Arcade, Hilton Hotel, Antananarivo. Alternatively, write and ask for general information on the country. Madagascar Airtours, BP 3874, Antananarivo, tel. 241.92. Other tour operators tend to be biased, leaving you little choice from the limited information. The exception is SETAM, which willingly supplies as much information as possible. It can be contacted at 56 Avenue du 26 Juin, Analakely, tel. 329.09.

POST OFFICE

The main post office is on Araben ny 26 Juin 1960 in Antananarivo. It is the tall cream-coloured building opposite the market police station. On the ground floor are the counters for stamps, parcels and bills.

Upstairs, you will find the telecommunications division. From here, telegrams, telexes and faxes may be sent. It also has a good poste restante service. The postal service is generally slow, but eventually you will receive mail.

Supposedly open Monday to Saturday, it doesn't always work to that schedule. It does however open promptly at 8h00. Lunch times vary a little, but count on the sales counters being closed from about 12h00-14h00. At about 18h00 the ground floor doors are closed, but customers left inside will still be served.

Visitors can make use of the telegram, telex and fax facilities every day of the week from 7h00-19h00, including Sunday from 8h00-12h00.

TELEPHONE

Tourists can make overseas telephone calls from hotels and the post office. The second floor of the main post office in 'Tana has several public phones for international phone calls. Hotels invariably charge a high service fee, while the post office has a fixed rate, irrespective of whether you are a resident or not. If phoning overseas from one of the regional capitals, you may have to pre-book your call about three hours ahead. There are massive construction programmes underway around the country, and it is expected that soon, instant linkups with other parts of the world will be a lot easier.

It is simpler making an international call than a local one. Lots of static and frequently being cut off are the norm with local calls. Trying to send a domestic fax is virtually impossible. Plagued by monsoon rains, cyclones and severe storms, many of the rural areas are left without telephones for days at a time. Wherever you travel in Madagascar, you will see men working on the telephone lines. To circumvent the poor phone service, more and more Malagasy businessmen are changing to satellite-linked cellular phones. At international hotels, guests are given this option whether calling locally or abroad. It is fairly safe to say that the telephone system in Madagascar is frustrating, expensive and archaic.

TIME

Madagascar is three hours ahead of Greenwich Mean Time. That puts it an hour ahead of South African time, and two hours ahead of Europe. Government offices follow a prescribed time schedule, with small variations of up to 20 minutes each way. In shops, on the streets and in rural communities, expect to have only a vague idea of operating times. In the country villages, the day commences at sunrise, with a break at about noon, and the end of the working day comes when the sun sets. Hotels are surprisingly efficient regarding wake-up calls, meal times and providing courtesy transport to and from the airport. Public transport usually leaves within 30 minutes of the stated time. Remember, though, that the time written on your ticket is the recommended time that you arrive, not the time when the transport leaves.

ELECTRICITY

Standard 220 volts is used throughout the country. If you are arriving from the Americas, note that few hotels outside the capital will be able to supply you with a transformer. Guests arriving with appliances such as hair driers or shavers should bring along their own adaptor plug. "Black-outs" are not uncommon, even in the cities. Driven by huge diesel generators and occasionally hydroelectric turbines, the electrical grid across Madagascar is prone to failure. Take along a torch, batteries and consider a candle with some matches.

BUSINESS HOURS

Banks are open Monday to Friday 8h00-16h00. Smaller agencies sometimes close from 13h00-14h00. Banks close their doors at 12h00 on the day prior to a public holiday. Government offices open Monday to Friday 8h00-12h00 and 14h00-16h00. They might open at that time, but it is recommended that you only call from about 9h00. Administrative business offices start work at 8h00, shut for lunch from 12h00-14h00, and close for the day at 18h00. Numerous offices also open on Saturday morning from 8h00-12h00.

Cafés open early, from about 6h30, and only close at around 18h00. Markets operate from 6h00-18h00 Monday to Friday, with a few stalls open on Saturday morning until 11h00. The Friday market in 'Tana, which swells the daily market to twice its normal size, starts to close at about 19h00.

Restaurants are usually open for lunch from 11h00-15h00, then close until dinner, which usually starts from 19h30 and ends around midnight. Nightclubs and discos open their doors Monday to Saturday from 21h30 to 5h00.

In some towns, such as Toliara, taxis are not permitted to operate after 18h00, starting their day at 6h00 the next morning. This peculiarity does not seem to affect other places, and you will usually find a taxi available throughout the 24 hours.

MEDIA

Two national newspapers are published daily. Both have material in Malagasy and French. *Midi Madagasikara* is available in the morning until 13h00, while the *Madagascar Tribune* is on sale most of the afternoon. Concentrating on subjects regarding Madagascar, they do carry a fairly comprehensive coverage of world news, especially relating to international sport. Newspapers are available from tourist-class hotel reception desks. You can also buy the newspaper at any librairie, and from the newspaper vendors in the streets.

The Malagasy media has for several years been under severe constraints. State-controlled, the media has often been accused of pandering to government practices. Things have now begun to change. A greater degree of leniency towards the press has encouraged journalists to question and investigate more, and to publish their findings without fear of recriminations. This is not to say that all is well. There is still censorship, and until freedom of the press is granted, the public will remain ignorant of many policies that affect it and its future.

Foreign newspapers are sold on the streets of 'Tana within three days of their publication. They are available from England, Germany, France and the USA. The international Sunday papers are usually obtainable by Tuesday of the following week.

Magazines are in short supply, English ones in particular. However, visitors can buy the latest issue of *Time* from the street vendors near Hotel Colbert in 'Tana. Monthly glossies are imported from France and include *Le Monde, Paris Match* and *Vogue*.

Malagasy television has grown in leaps and bounds over the last few years. Its documentaries, sports coverage and international affairs broadcasts are well done and supported by those few of the population who have television. Visitors who stay in medium-class hotels will often see groups of locals watching the hotel's television. Réunion television (RFO) is also shown, and its films are widely watched by the Malagasy. The price of even a portable black and white television set is prohibitive for most islanders.

HEALTH

Although it is unlikely that you will fall ill in Madagascar, it is possible that if you do the problem could be of a serious nature. Madagascar is a Third World country, with all the associated medical complications. Get as fit as you possibly can before you go. Have your teeth checked and any problems sorted out. Don't forget to pack an emergency dental kit. It is recommended that you undergo a complete medical check and have all your immunisations done at least six weeks prior to leaving. Contact your local department of health for the latest medical information on Madagascar.

While many travellers omit it, some sort of health and travel insurance is recommended. One of the best is with a company called Travel Assistance. It has a whole range of policies, at various prices, covering a multitude of possibilities. Its International Leisure Travel policy is the one that you should consider. Travel Assistance, PO Box 4352, Johannesburg 2000, South Africa, tel. (011) 838-6311, fax (011) 834-2633.

On Madagascar there is a fine selection of well-stocked pharmacies and highly trained hospital and clinical staff. Should you find yourself unwell, and none of your first aid remedies is working, you may quite confidently visit a hospital or clinic. Most of the foreign embassies keep lists of recommended doctors and dentists used by their staff. In rural areas, visit the local clinic or mission station. Large urban areas are well supplied with qualified medical practitioners. The "Cabinet Medical" sign indicates a private surgery.

Occasionally, visitors arriving from Africa and Asia are required to show an International Certificate of Vaccination. This is a booklet verifying that you have had the prescribed vaccinations. Even if you are arriving from continents other than Asia or Africa, it is recommended that you enquire which immunisations are necessary. Their period of validity is indicated below. The following diseases occur in Madagascar:
Yellow fever – valid for 10 years
Cholera – valid for six months
Tetanus – valid for five years
Typhoid – valid for three years
Hepatitis A – valid for 10 years
Hepatitis B – valid for 12 months
Polio – Usually administered when a child, but a booster every five years is recommended.
Smallpox – Usually administered when a child, with life-long immunity.

Immunisations against yellow fever, cholera, polio and smallpox are available at your local department of health.

Problems that may affect your health in Madagascar are discussed below. Visitors who use common sense, have their inoculations and follow basic health rules are unlikely to fall prey to any afflictions. If you do feel ill and are uncertain what the problem is, contact a doctor immediately.

Bilharzia

Bilharzia is common in the midlands and the coastal rivers and fresh-water lakes of Madagascar. Fresh-water snails that carry the infected larvae cause bilharzia in humans. Once they have entered the body the blood flukes inhabit the veins, large intestine and bladder, where they lay more eggs. Be careful about swimming in any fresh water on Madagascar. Obviously, the sea is quite safe. Bilharzia is a serious disease that needs specialised treatment immediately. Symptoms are blood and stained mucus in the stools, and a general debilitation.

Diarrhoea

This is the most common affliction suffered by travellers to Madagascar. Those arriving from Africa seem to succumb less than do visitors from Europe. Usually, it is just the change in diet that causes a loosening of the stomach. This normally clears up within a day or two. Restrict your food to bland meals. Avoid dairy products or anything which contains spices. However, make certain to keep your liquid intake high. The heat and humidity of Madagascar quickly dehydrate visitors. Drink lots of purified water, tea without milk and "flat" cola. If after two days you are still ill and getting weaker, try taking a course of Lomotil or Imodium tablets. Should these not work, you obviously have something worse than diarrhoea, and should consult a doctor as soon as possible.

Dysentery

In the heavily populated urban centres, dysentery is a worsening problem. Both amoebic and bacillary dysentery are prevalent. Amoebic dysentery is the worse of the two, and is a lot harder to treat. Symptoms of dysentery are "stringy" mucus and blood in your faeces, agonising cramps and a rapid deterioration in your health, accompanied by a feeling of weakness and nausea. If Lomotil has not cured the problem within a few days, you should approach a chemist and ask for Flagyl. However, rather than try to cure yourself, visit a doctor and mention that you have started taking Flagyl. Limit your intake of rich food and all dairy products, but remember to keep taking lots of fluid, preferably fortified with vitamins and electrolytes.

Hepatitis

There are two types of hepatitis: infectious hepatitis and serum hepatitis. Both can prove fatal, and both attack the liver. Madagascar has a high incidence of this contagious viral disease and all visitors should pay particular attention to what they eat and drink and with whom they have sex. Remember that even sharing clothing, towels or toothbrushes can transmit this disease. If you are uncertain whether fresh food has been washed in polluted water or not, rather avoid eating it. Foods deep-fried in oil are the safest to eat.

Symptoms of this awful illness are a high fever, lethargy, pain around the base of the ribs and a continual feeling of nausea. There is a discolouration of the skin to a yellow colour. This is most noticeable in the mucous membranes. The urine changes to a dark orange and occasionally red colour. There is not really much that doctors or hospitals can do for someone infected with hepatitis. Just get yourself home as quickly as possible and plan on a long rest when you do arrive.

Malaria

Malaria is endemic to Madagascar. The disease is spread by the female anopheles mosquito, which is a blood-parasite. These little terrors usually confine their forays to the hours of darkness. A single bite from an infected mosquito is enough to induce the disease. The medical profession fights a continuous battle in developing anti-malarial drugs, but just as quickly, the mosquitoes develop an immunity. Make certain to check with your doctor on the current programme. At the time of writing, the recommended anti-malarial programme, according to the South African Department of Health and Welfare, consisted of chloroquine plus Proguanil. Chloroquine (Nivaquine tablets or Plasmoquine capsules) 400 mg (adults) once per week, on the same day each week. Proguanil (Paludrine tablets) 200 mg (adults) daily. Another frequently used prophylaxis, mefloquine (Lariam tablets) should only be followed with medical prescription and monitoring. Start taking your anti-malarial medication about five days before departure, and continue for a minimum of four weeks after returning. Despite the high cost of antimalarial programmes, this is one thing no visitor should skimp on.

Symptoms of malaria include shivering, fevers and severe headaches. The diagnosis must be confirmed as soon as possible. Medical advice on malaria can be obtained from all clinics, missions and hospitals in Madagascar. Should you find yourself in some remote area, where there is no medical facility, the recommended treatment consists of four chloroquine tablets, all at once, followed by two tablets six hours later, with two tablets to be taken on each successive day. In those areas where the mosquitoes have built up an immunity to chloroquine, take one dose of three Fansidar tablets. Make certain to take along smouldering mosquito coils and sufficient insect repellent. It is now possible to purchase mosquito nets for campers. These are ideal for visiting the more humid, wet regions of Madagascar, where malaria is prevalent. The nets fold up into little sachets that fit easily into a pack or bag. You will usually find them on sale at outdoor and camping retailers.

Sun

The intensity of sunlight often takes foreigners completely by surprise, and they suffer severe **sunburn**. Apply liberal amounts of high-factor sun cream, especially during the first few days' exposure to the tropical sun. As your body gets accustomed to the sun you may reduce the protection factor of the cream you use, but continue wearing a hat and sunglasses. Pay particular attention to children. Even when it is overcast, the reflected sun rays can cause severe sunburn. Areas most prone to painful sunburn are the feet, the back of the legs and the top of the head. When hiking, it is advisable to wear long-sleeve, collared shirts and apply extra amounts of factor 35 sun cream to your nose and the back of the neck.

Heat exhaustion is caused by a loss of body salts and electrolytes due to excessive sweating and failure to keep fluid intake high enough. The first indications of heat exhaustion are a general listlessness, muscular cramps and severe headache. The best method of preventing this is to drink lots of liquid, try not to overdo physical exertion during the first few days and include salt in your meals or take salt tablets.

Heatstroke is the most serious of all afflictions caused by the severe Malagasy heat and sun. If not treated it can lead to death. The first indication that the body's thermostat has stopped functioning is when all sweating stops. A raging fever follows soon after, accompanied by painful headaches and a loss of coordination. There is a noticeable personality change and the skin turns bright pink or red. The victim must immediately be taken to a hospital. En route try to keep him or her as cool as possible, by splashing the body with cold water and removing as much clothing as is acceptable.

There is not a great deal you can do to prevent the internal heat regulatory system from breaking down. To reduce the possibilities, take it easy during the first few days. Allow your body to acclimatise gradually to the change in temperature and humidity.

Prickly heat seems to affect visitors from northern European climes the most. Perspiration is unable to escape via the pores and forms blisters beneath the skin. The first sign that you are suffering from prickly heat is an itchy rash, usually on the arms and back. Avoid scratching. Take large doses of vitamin A and calcium, and dust the burst blisters with talcum powder.

Sexual diseases

Numerous foreign travel agents, notably those in Germany and France, are trying to sell Madagascar as a "sea, sun and sex" destination. With high unemployment, large families and an increasing tourist trade, many young women have turned to prostitution to supplement the family's income. As a result, there has been an explosion of sexually transmitted diseases. Be aware of the dangers, use condoms and take the necessary precautions during sexual contact. The safest solution is still abstinence.

Typhoid

Take your course of tablets prior to departure; typhoid is not something you want to go down with in Madagascar. It is one of the most serious medical problems in the country. The illness is introduced by eating infected food or drinking polluted water.

Women's health

The change in diet and climate often has a negative effect on women's health. The most common medical problem encountered by women is yeast and fungal infections. These are usually noticed by a slight discharge, itchy rash and burning on urination. Keep the genital area as clean and dry as possible. Wear loose-fitting, natural fabric clothing and apply a light dusting of talcum powder to your underwear. Tampons are only available from the large department stores in 'Tana and a few supermarkets in other urban areas. Rather take along all your own gynaecological requirements, including an adequate supply of contraceptive pills.

Insects

These are a feature of travel in Madagascar. Apart from the ubiquitous mosquitoes and flies, on the coast you will encounter biting sandflies, and in the forests, the ferocious sweat bees. Insect repellent works well when staying in hotel rooms or settlements, but becomes a bit useless when you are walking through the enormous rainforests. Sandfly bites are best treated with kowloon oil. Sweat bees inflict a nasty sting. Although it may take a concerted effort, avoid swatting at these black bees. They are only after the salt in your sweat.

Budget travellers may find themselves discovering a whole range of interesting insects in low-cost accommodation. Of these, the most common are bed bugs and lice. Lice can be dealt with by keeping yourself as clean as possible and washing with a medicated soap and shampoo. Coal-tar soap and Lorexanne shampoo are recommended. Bed bugs, on the other hand, are a real nuisance. They hide during the day and only venture out at night to bite sleepers. There is not a great deal you can do. One Italian traveller claimed that burning a mosquito coil under his bed during the day had some effect. I tried it and was still bitten. Rather change accommodation.

In the forests, hikers are going to find leeches. Leeches attach themselves to you and suck your blood! During the wet season – most of the year in the eastern rainforests – leeches hang on blades of grass and bushes, waiting for some unsuspecting human or animal to pass by. At day's end, it is a good idea to spend a few minutes examining yourself or have someone do it for you. Getting them off is rather difficult. Whatever you do, never try to pull them off, as their point of attachment nearly always becomes infected. Rather, apply a sprinkling of salt or burn them off. Once they have fallen off, apply a medicated salve to the bite.

FIRST AID

Every visitor to Madagascar should take along a personal first aid kit. If you wear glasses, then a spare pair should be included. Travellers taking prescription drugs are advised to have a signed copy of the script

and sufficient medication to last the trip. Below is a list of what every first aid kit should contain. Add your own requirements to this list:
- A course of broad-spectrum antibiotics. Amoxil is recommended.
- Antihistamine tablets and cream for insect bites and allergies.
- Antiseptic lotion and cream to wash wounds, bites and stings.
- At least two rolls of bandages, and one triangular bandage. Include clasps and a selection of plasters as well.
- Calamine lotion for mild sunburn.
- Electrolyte and glucose powder to keep your body chemistry balanced and to replace lost fluids due to heat or exertion.
- Zinc, sulphur and talcum powder to use on rashes and help in keeping areas of your body prone to moisture build-up dry.
- Tablets to reduce fever and ameliorate pain.
- Diarrhoea remedies such as Lomotil or Imodium.
- Sun preparations and sun protection creams. Start with a factor 35 and work your way down to a minimum of factor 10.
- Scalpel, scissors, tweezers, thermometer, syringes and needles.
- A small mirror, knife, suture kit, water purification tablets and a course of multivitamins are also highly recommended.

CLOTHING

As for most Third World countries, take as little as possible. Clothing is cheap and easy to find in Madagascar. In the larger urban markets, visitors will have a staggering selection of clothing from which to choose. Bargaining is expected, and although the quality of goods is not particularly high, they are suitable for travel around Madagascar. The best place to locate casual clothing is in the Zoma of Antananarivo. The real bargains are found in the tiny stalls around the alleys off the main road. In these narrow lanes, tourists can select from imported clothing and shoes, at prices at least 70% lower than those asked in regular shops.

A good idea is to get yourself an item made by one of the tailors found in smaller towns. The ones in Ambanja and Ihosy are really good. A pair of trousers or a blouse can be run up in a few hours.

A recommended list of clothing for a visit to Madagascar would look something like this: one pair jeans, two pairs shorts, four changes of underwear, swimming costume, two T-shirts, one short-sleeved collared shirt, one set of smart clothes, one light jersey, one windbreaker, one pair sneakers, one pair walking boots, one pair sandals (Bio-tribes are especially suitable), rain gear, hat, towel, lamba oany (to wear, lie under, sit on, erect as a shelter from the sun, or use as a sheet).

If you plan to hike, include a lightweight sleeping bag, portable mosquito net and gaiters. In addition to this list of clothing, remember to include those sundries that make every trip a little easier: multifunction knife, sewing kit, sunglasses, toiletries, two small padlocks and spare keys, torch, barrier cream and an elastic clothesline with a few pegs.

When packing your gear, first pack it all into plastic dustbin liners. Take along a few spare ones as well. A backpack is the ideal luggage to carry to Madagascar. If you are travelling on a tight budget, then this is definitely the way to carry your belongings. Even tourists who are visiting on an organised package tour or staying at top-class accommodation should forego cumbersome suitcases and rather opt for a far more practical "Travel Pack". These soft carriers are suitable for the rigours of Malagasy travel. Made by Backpacker in South Africa, the "Travel Pack" is an ingenious cross between a backpack and a suitcase. Contact Backpacker Products for further details: tel. (011) 885-2391, fax (011) 887-2268.

WOMEN VISITORS

Although very few women ever travel about Madagascar alone, or independently, those who do are in for a marvellous experience. There is none of the pestering and annoying advances which are characteristic of many African and Asian countries. Obviously, it still makes good sense to adhere to a few rules, to avoid any undue trouble.

In the cities and large urban areas it is prudent to avoid walking around the streets alone after sunset. If you must be out, arrange to be accompanied, or have a taxi waiting for you. Once into the rural, tribal regions, women travellers will be quite safe moving around at night. Despite the increasing reports of rapes in towns such as Fianarantsoa and Toamasina, there has yet to be an incident involving a foreign woman. In villages, women will be received with the same courtesy as male visitors, and are generally more readily accepted, in a cultural sense, than foreign men are.

Dress codes are not strict. Despite the African influences, no women wander about topless. Suntanning without a costume or top is common practice at beach hotels, but not advised on public beaches. Wearing miniskirts, short shorts or going braless is not frowned upon; many Malagasy women dress in this way. When attending a disco or nightclub, you will be amazed by the amount of bare skin around. Look to the locals for appropriate dress codes.

As a general rule, women visitors should stay in medium-tariff accommodation, avoiding the cheapies, which often double as brothels, especially in 'Tana and Toamasina. Don't walk down the narrow alleys that crowd the Zoma near the train station in 'Tana, and if you do go to a nightclub, arrange to go in a group.

Take along all your own tampons and other feminine hygiene products, including contraceptives.

PHOTOGRAPHY

The most important thing about taking photographs in Madagascar is that you respect and observe local taboos, known as fady. Always ask before taking a photograph of people, especially children. If you are refused, avoid the temptation to sneak a picture. This causes untold harm for future travellers. Airports, harbours and both military and police installations are definitely off the photo list. Should you be caught, not only will all your film and camera equipment be confiscated, but there is virtually no chance of your ever getting it back. If you are in any doubt about a building or area, ask at the local police station.

Two of the biggest problems that photographers in Madagascar face are the intense light and dirt. Lying mostly in the tropics, Madagascar has a degree of light intensity that baffles most visitors. This is particularly so along the coast, where the beach and sea throw up harsh glares and long shadows. Inland, you will have to contend with the perpetual haze that hangs over the mountains and reflects the sunlight, creating mirages and images that are difficult to get into focus. To reduce the effect of the strong light, limit your photography to sunrise and late afternoon. The softer light during these times produces subtle shadows that make for mesmerising photographs.

Madagascar is a poor, overpopulated country, surrounded by the vast expanse of the south-western Indian Ocean. Expect lots of dust, sand, humidity, rain and dirt. No photographer should even think about visiting Madagascar without a comprehensive cleaning kit. Cleaning must be done daily on all the equipment you have used. A can of compressed air is ideal for getting to those awkward nooks and crannies.

Keep your camera inside its bag as much as possible. Extended lengths of time in direct sunlight will affect both your equipment and film.

Most visitors to Madagascar are not that interested in turning their holiday into a photographic expedition. However, I doubt whether any travellers will arrive without wanting to take some memorable photographs. Serious photographers should have two SLR (single lens reflex) camera bodies – make certain that they have the same lens capabilities. This prevents a disaster if one of them should fail. In addition to the camera bodies, add as many of the following lens lengths as possible: 28 mm, short zoom 35-75 mm, 55 mm lens and macro lens, 80-200 mm fast zoom lens. Stay away from heavy, extra-range zoom lenses. Most of them are cumbersome and frustrating to work with in the high heat and humidity of Madagascar.

To the above list add a folding tripod, bounce flash unit and both 30A and 80M filters. It is easy to find colour print film in 'Tana and on Nosy Bé. Most tourist hotels carry a limited range of colour film. The best place to try in 'Tana is in the lobby of the Hilton Hotel. Photographers using colour slide or black and white print film are advised to bring all their own supplies. The best colour film for travel photography is a low 64 ASA. Any film above 100 ASA often proves unsuitable for exotic pictures, by increasing its grain and losing the sharpness of the subject. Camera batteries are available everywhere. This, obviously, excludes specialised batteries, like those found in video cameras or the new range of battery-driven lenses.

Although many film manufacturers insist that their film is impervious to the effects of airport x-ray equipment, still ask that your film (both exposed and unexposed) be hand checked. The customs officials are helpful and cordial in this regard. Should you be staying longer than three months in Madagascar, it is wise to send your exposed rolls of film home for developing. It is now acknowledged that as soon as film is exposed it starts to lose colour saturation until developed. If you send film home, tape it into a lead-lined anti-x-ray bag and put that inside a plain manila envelope.

SECURITY

Escalating unemployment, overpopulation and homelessness have all contributed to an increase in crime in Madagascar. The worst places for tourists are Antananarivo, Nosy Bé and Nosy Boraha. Travellers, especially those touring alone, are extremely vulnerable to attack and mugging. While it is highly unlikely that you will experience any security problems in rural regions, it is prudent to follow a few simple rules in urban areas.

Keep your supply of traveller's cheques safe by splitting them up. Carry some of these on your person, hide some for emergency use and leave a few in the hotel's safe-deposit box. Visitors with American Express traveller's cheques are well cared for. Should you lose or have your traveller's cheques stolen, immediately contact the American Express office in the nearest large urban centre. In Madagascar, American Express is represented by Madagascar Airtours. The head office is in the Hilton Hotel arcade in 'Tana, tel. 241.92. It also has offices in Antsiranana, Fianarantsoa, Nosy Bé and Toliara.

Carrying cash always presents a problem. Many tourists wear waist-pouches for this purpose. The obviousness of this type of wallet limits its suitability. Instead, choose a money pouch that either hangs around your neck and inside your shirt, or one that fastens on the inside of your belt. Another alternative is to sew some pockets inside your clothing. Never carry large amounts of cash around with you.

Carry your important documents, passport, airline ticket and contact telephone numbers with you at all times. If you stay in a dubious part of town, lock your door with your own padlock or speak to the management about getting a guard for your room while you are out. At night, always lock your door, and in ground floor accommodation, the windows as well. Never leave anything lying around when you are not in the room. Camera equipment should be securely hung around your neck; never just one shoulder, and unless absolutely necessary, avoid carrying a day-pack. These nylon bags are ideal candidates for the "slit 'n snatch" technique favoured by thugs in crowded markets.

Taxi and bus drivers are energetically conscious about their passengers' belongings. At stops both the driver and his assistant will get out and inspect the luggage being unloaded. Each item is securely strapped to the roof rack, and whenever possible a tourist's baggage is carried inside the vehicle. If you still feel a little insecure about theft, carry a length of chain and padlock to attach your bags to the roof rack. While on this topic of luggage; buy bags that can be locked, or sew on extra grommets which can take small locks.

All visitors will be approached at some stage by someone offering gemstones, gold or drugs. Be wary of stories that gemstones can be sold for huge profits in your home country. Few people are knowledgeable enough about gemstones to authenticate those on sale. The opportunity to sell a fake to an unsuspecting tourist is tempting. Those of you who really want to buy precious and semiprecious stones are advised to visit a registered dealer; ask at jewellery shops. Gold is of high quality, but its export from Madagascar by unlicensed traders is illegal. Drugs are sold nearly everywhere. Remember that drugs use is punishable by law in Madagascar. Cannabis and hashish are freely available, and the police turn a blind eye to personal use. Opium and cocaine, however, are viewed in a serious light. If caught with these substances you will be imprisoned. There is little most embassies can do to get someone released from a drug offence. It's not even worth thinking about trying to smuggle drugs or gold out of the country; the sentences are just too heavy.

Avoid walking about the streets of Antananarivo and Fianarantsoa at night. Rather arrange for a taxi to transport you if you need to go out. Most taxis then wait for you anyway. If cornered and mugged, do not resist; give your assailants what they want and then report the matter to the police. Criminals are wary of attacking tourists in busy areas. Crime is not tolerated in Madagascar. Should something happen, it is likely that those who see what is going on will immediately rush to your assistance. Staying with villagers in remote districts is probably the safest way of seeing Madagascar. Tribal law is inflexible, all crimes are unforgivable, and often retribution includes some form of corporal punishment. The hospitality which you will be accorded includes caring for your belongings. There has yet to be a theft complaint from a traveller staying in isolated traditional communities.

Be aware of what is going on around you, practise basic safety, but do not become paranoid about theft, and Madagascar will remain one of the safest places that any foreign traveller can visit.

PLACES TO STAY

There are noticeable differences between what is classed as tourist accommodation and Malagasy accommodation. The Malagasy Tourist Board has carried out classifications of the places it presumes islanders would stay at. You will notice that Malagasy hotels recommended by the board have a circular white plaque, with blue writing, at their entrances. Tourist accommodation has for some time been left to the discretion of the owners and management. However, there have been moves to grade all tourist accommodation on Madagascar, irrespective of whether it is intended for Malagasy or foreigners. The biggest advantage of staying at a place that is Malagasy tourism-graded is that the bill is paid in FMg, usually meaning that it is a lot cheaper than a resort where payment must be made in foreign currency.

Top-class hotels are limited to places popular with tour operators, travel agents and their clients. Thus, on places such as Nosy Bé and Nosy Boraha, and in 'Tana, Tolanaro and Toliara, you will find hotels that compare favourably with similar accommodation in Europe or America. Without doubt, Madagascar's best hotel is the Madagascar Hilton in Antananarivo, opposite Lac Anosy. Although a lot smaller, the Radama Hotel, also in 'Tana, on Avenue Grandidier, is not far behind in terms of comfort, service and quality. In the south, at Tolanaro, Le Dauphin is the best and most expensive hotel. In the coastal city of Toliara, there is nothing to compare with the Motel Capricorn. In the north, at Antsiranana, there is the somewhat dilapidated and overpriced Hotel de la Poste. On Nosy Bé, the recommended hotel for up-market travellers is the exclusive Marlin Club resort. For those going to Nosy Boraha, the only place worth considering is Soanambo.

Mid-level hotels are recommended. Not only are they a great deal cheaper, but there is little to differentiate between service in them and expensive top-class hotels. These hotels are not always advertised by travel agents and visitors may have to ask taxi drivers or locals for directions. The police are another good source for finding medium-tariff accommodation. Air Madagascar will provide tourists with a list of recommended medium-priced hotels.

In 'Tana, try the Hotel la Muraille de Chine, opposite the station on Avenue de la Indépendance. In Toamasina, the once grand Hotel de la Plage is comfortable, well placed and reasonably priced. Tolanaro has the well-known Motel Gina, which now has an annexe. Mid-level accommodation in Toliara is almost nonexistent, and apart from the Hotel Central in the CBD, there is little choice. In the busy town of Fianarantsoa, travellers will find the legendary Hotel Cotsoyannis opposite Le Panda restaurant. The Hotel de la Gare outside the Andasibe (Périnet) Nature Reserve is used by most people visiting the area. In the far north, at Antsiranana, try the Hotel Valiha on Rue Colbert, near La Vahinee snack bar and nightclub. Nosy Bé will prove more difficult for visitors looking for medium-tariff accommodation. The abundance of tourist resorts has almost pushed many of the Malagasy hotels out of business. Hotel de la Mer, on Rue du Doctuer Mauclair, has rooms with ocean views and a restaurant, and fits into the mid-level category. In the dusty city of Mahajanga, the best and most reasonably priced hotel is the Sofia Satrana, just off Avenue Philibert Tsiranana, near the stadium.

Budget travellers are in for a treat. There are countless cheap hotels scattered across Madagascar. Be warned; take along a plastic sheet, sandals for the showers and insect repellent.

Here too, taxi drivers, bus drivers and street vendors are the best source of information on where to find cheap accommodation. In the capital, walk along Arabe Andrianampoinmerina, east of the train station. Numerous cheap lodgings can be found along here. La Regina, in the market area of the street, is clean, conveniently situated and full of university students. On the coast, at Mahajanga, in the gravel alleys north of the port, you are bound to find a room in any of the hotels that serve seamen and travelling salesmen. Both the Tropic Hotel and Hotel Boina on Rue Flacourt are recommended. Nosy Bé is obviously a problem. In Hell-Ville however a few low-tariff hotels are available. The Venus Hotel and Restaurant on Boulevard Raymond Poincare is a favourite with budget visitors. At the northern end of Boulevard Raymond Poincare is the low-priced Sambatra Hotel. More of a guesthouse, it has a delightful manager who cooks the most amazing seafood dishes. Antsiranana has Le Paradise du Nord and the Royal Hotel, opposite the basketball hall on Rue J Bezara. Toamasina has several hotels which fall into this classification. For the lowest prices, cross the Pangalanes Canal west of town and simply wander around the sand streets asking the locals where you may find a hotel. It will not take more than 10 minutes before someone will personally lead you to one. The places seldom have name boards and are usually family run. Tolanaro has little budget accommodation. Your best bet is to ask for one of the old grass-mat rooms at Motel Gina. Visitors to Toliara will find cheap rooms at the Hotel Sud, opposite Glace des As. In Fianarantsoa, the cheapest place to stay is Hotel Escale. It is situated between the wooden shanties and stalls that line Nouvelle Route Antananarivo and Route MDRM.

CAMPING

Madagascar has no official camp sites. Visitors may pitch their tents virtually anywhere, provided they have permission either from a village elder or the local police. Avoid camping on Nosy Boraha, Nosy Bé or too close to a large town, as theft is a possibility. With the high unemployment it is unfair to place temptation in the way of people struggling to survive. It is forbidden to camp alone in the national reserves.

To camp, you must join a tour group. There are numerous other areas of the country that make for wonderful camping. In the rainforests of the east coast there are no restrictions on where you may camp. This is one experience campers must try. Camping in a primeval forest cannot be described, it must be experienced. Campers should take along their own food and water.

FOOD

The staple food of Madagascar is rice. Outside of tourist resorts you will be given it for breakfast, lunch and dinner. Eaten with virtually everything, it is filling and cheap. Most Malagasy hotelys serve rice on the main plate, accompanied by a smaller bowl of meat or vegetables. You will also be given a soup dish of opaque hot water filled with boiled green leaves. This is not soup, it is meant to be spooned over your rice.

The dishes which accompany rice are a diner's delight. From fried seafood, grilled steak to spiced vegetables, there is something for every palate. Meat eaters are in for a feast. With the vast zebu herds in Madagascar, thick juicy steaks are common, as are thick gravies, beef and vegetable stews. Be careful of eating meat sold from the open-air butcheries. The Western constitution often cannot cope with the bacteria on this meat. Vegetarians will need to shop around. Fresh produce is always available at the local markets. Cassava is tasty when roasted and eaten with a dish of rice, chili, tomato and fried vegetables. At tourist-class hotels vegetarians must inform the management of their dietary habits when checking in.

Tropical and subtropical fruit is on sale in abundance. Depending on the season, visitors will find lychees, mangoes, avocados, citrus and bananas, coconuts, dates and an unpronounceable berry, which looks like a gooseberry and is sold by the tin full.

Along the coast, fish and shellfish are widely eaten. Tiger prawns, calamari, shad and barracuda are offered. Big game fish are also regularly eaten. Environmentally-aware travellers need to question the ethics of this practice, given the declining populations of these rare species. Inland, at Fianarantsoa, enormous fresh-water lobsters are on the menu of most Chinese restaurants. At Toliara, crayfish are on even the smallest of eateries' menus.

Chicken is another favourite of the Malagasy. You will see chickens running about everywhere, even through the rush hour traffic of Antananarivo. For such active creatures, Malagasy chickens are surprisingly tender. A regular dish in hotelys is chicken and sauce (poulet et sauce). This is possibly the safest dish to eat for foreigners with sensitive stomachs.

French baguettes are sold each morning at cafés, shops and by street vendors. Anyone going on a long taxi-brousse or bus journey should buy themselves one or two of the loaves. Usually heavy and dry, they can be made into long sandwiches, filled with cheese, tomato and onion. Pastries are a speciality of Mahajanga. In the salons de thé and patisseries, travellers will find an Aladdin's cave of cakes, buns, sweets and pies.

Chinese, Indian, Italian and French restaurants are prolific all over 'Tana. Visitors will not have to walk more than two blocks to find a suitable restaurant. Budget travellers should occasionally spoil themselves with a large meal. Ask for the *plat du jour* (dish of the day). The helpings are usually large and the price low. The Acapulco Restaurant and Piano Bar on Lalana Ratsimilaho has a reasonably priced *plat du jour* and good à la carte menu. If you are a little wary of eating at a Malagasy hotely, but still keen to taste traditional food, book a table at the Radama Hotel at 22 Avenue Grandidier. It has an extensive Malagasy menu, prepared by local chefs. The Hilton Hotel puts on a Malagasy buffet once a week. Contact reception for exact dates and times, tel. 260.60.

Snacks are sold in most of the villages along main routes and in local markets. Avoid eggs and dairy products in rural areas. The specialities vary with each region and should be tried by foreigners. On the road to Toamasina, sliced smoked eel is sold. In coastal areas grilled fish with a tomato and pimento sauce is common. At stalls in the grassland villages, zebu stew and roasted beef kebabs are available. Street vendors in communities of the west coast with a strong Hindu and Muslim influence sell delicious samosas and roti rolls.

DRINKS

Drinking water from rivers and taps is not recommended. Pollution is getting worse throughout the country, and sadly the rivers are also now affected. Eau de Vive is the bottled water which can be bought from supermarkets, hotels and a few cafés. It costs about the same price as a large beer. Perhaps this is why so many Malagasy drink beer! The locally manufactured beer is, quite simply, atrocious. There are two brands, Three Horse beer and the more bitter Gold Star. Both are made by the same company, Brasseries Star Madagascar. At tourist hotels there is usually a good selection of imported beers and malts.

Splendid wines are produced around Fianarantsoa, south of 'Tana. The dry red, Lazan'i Betsileo, is especially good. Red, rosé and white wines are available at all bars, restaurants and mid to high-tariff hotels. Make an effort to get down to the vineyards and winepresses of the region. Hotel Cotsoyannis, Hotel Modern and the Sofia Hotel in the city can organise day trips to the farms and cellars.

Spirits, notably rum (rhum), are brewed for export and local consumption. The place to visit for rum is the Sirama Rum Distillery on Nosy Bé. Rum connoisseurs will be able to try the finest of all rums, white rum, all the way through to toaky gasy: home-brewed dark rum. "Old Dzamandzar" rum must be tried. It is obtainable at hotels on Nosy Bé. Many restaurants also flavour and age bottles of rum for their own use. The Papillon restaurant, in Hell-Ville, has the reputation of having the best vanilla, coffee and citrus-flavoured rum liqueurs in Madagascar. One sip is enough to captivate any rum-drinker. The owners are loathe to part with an entire bottle, but occasionally do for an unexpectedly low price.

Coconuts, rice and maize are also used to concoct the most diabolical drinks. Village women are responsible for making these. Travellers who wander into the remote regions are likely to be invited to at least one party where the local brew is drunk. Again, beware, the stuff is highly intoxicating.

Alcohol made from coconuts is called "trembo". That made from fermented sugar cane is known as "betsabetsa". "Ranovola" used to be a popular traditional drink. Made by pouring boiling water over slightly burned rice in the bottom of a pot, its popularity however is waning as the Malagasy become more Westernised.

Cold drinks are widely available. Coca-Cola and Fanta have made big inroads, and are popular with the youth. Local cold drinks include the low alcohol beer shandy, Fresh, and Bon Bon Anglais lemonade. Fresh fruit juice is sold by street vendors and artificially flavoured ice lollies are good thirst quenchers.

BOOKS

Current literature on Madagascar is limited. The best books are those written by Hilary Bradt. Derek Schuurman is another veteran whose numerous articles, especially on wildlife in Madagascar, make for excellent pre-trip reading. You can obtain copies of his articles by writing to him directly at: PO Box 11583, Vorna Valley 1686, South Africa, tel. (011) 805-4833/4.

For a general introduction to travelling budget-class around the country, get yourself a copy of Dervla Murphy's book *Muddling through in Madagascar* (Hutchinson Travellers' Series, London, 1987). This is a personal account of her journey around Madagascar. As a pre-trip primer on the varied natural splendours of Madagascar, David Attenborough's thoughtful work *Journeys to the past* has a detailed chapter on the country entitled Zoo Quest in Madagascar (Penguin Books, London, 1981).

Although long out of print, if you can find a copy of the great 19th century naturalist Alfred Russel Wallace's book, *Madagaskar*, the hunt will be worth it. Published in the early 1900s, this work, which has detailed information on the country and its early people, was written by Wallace on his solo journeys through Madagascar in the 1860s. It will be inspirational and enlightening. Read it again once you have returned home, and note how little change has occurred in the remote villages since then.

A dictionary is more of an investment than an expense. Possibly the most suitable, although it lacks numerous words, is that compiled by K Paginton (Trano Printy, Antananarivo, 1970). While working for the Red Cross Society in Madagascar, Paginton compiled a practical dictionary for everyday use. It is pocket sized, cheap and will go a long way in giving you confidence to converse with the locals.

Several bookshops can be found in Antananarivo. Librairie de Madagascar, on Avenue de l'Indépendance, has the widest selection of literature. Worth visiting is Librairie Mixte, also on Avenue de l'Indépendance. Bibliomad, along Rue de Nice, has a number of books, dictionaries and magazines on sale. The quiet FLM Librairie on Avenue Grandidier, opposite the Radama Hotel, has dictionaries, educational books and a three-set series of books for English speakers on how to speak Malagasy.

'Tana's municipal library is next to Patisserie Suisse on Avenue Grandidier. There are virtually no books in English, but the staff are pleasant and will go to great lengths to assist tourists.

MAPS

A map of Madagascar is vital to travellers. Those sold by La Maison de Tourisme de Madagascar in 'Tana may initially be baffling. The Malagasy names of towns are shown in capital letters, while the names by which they are known to tourists and travel agents are in brackets below. To clarify any confusion regarding the main towns, these are the changes:

Tananarivo – Antananarivo (usually called 'Tana)
Toamasina – Tamatave
Antsiranana – Diego Suarez
Mahajanga – Majunga
Toliara – Tulear
Tolanaro – Fort Dauphin

This tourist map (Carte Touristique de Madagasikara) has a scale of 1:4 000 000. National parks, reserves and places of tourist interest are all clearly detailed. This is possibly the best map for general use and planning. You can get a copy by writing to the Ministry of Tourism (see Tourist information section).

Many tour operators put out a small map with their itineraries. If you are unable to find anything else, these can be used for planning. Contact your nearest travel agent for Madagascar brochures.

Should you be planning to hike the country or perhaps explore a particular area, then you must obtain a topographical map. You can buy these at bookstores in 'Tana, or order a copy directly from the cartographers: Foiben-Taosaritanin' i Madagasikara (FTM), BP 323, Ambanidia, tel. 229.35.

City maps are hard to find. Most of the travel guides have small maps of the main towns. The Hilton Hotel has a few available at reception. Tour operators in Madagascar usually keep maps of the island and road maps of the principal towns. Try asking Madagascar Airtours in the Hilton arcade. Voyages Bourdon, 15 Rue P Lumumba, are pleasant and will give you an A3 map of Madagascar, plus a street map of 'Tana.

THINGS TO BUY

From precious stones, through pottery to wooden carvings, Madagascar has an amazing selection of things to buy. Prices are low, bargaining is expected and the quality of workmanship is high.

Most curios are available from the Zoma market in Antananarivo. The handicraft stalls are located near the Air Madagascar offices and the Honey Salon de Thé. Much of the work has been brought in from rural communities, but the items containing semiprecious stones are done in local workshops.

Out in the country districts, visitors will be able to find items that are not sold in the capital. These include intricately carved totem poles, rough-hewn animist masks and brightly painted grasswork. In Ambalavao, the craftspeople make handmade paper and then decorate the sheet with dried flowers. These pieces are unique to Madagascar and make the ideal lightweight gift. On the north-east coast, travellers will find vanilla, spices and coffee for sale in the markets. One of the most expensive flavourings in the world is vanilla. On Madagascar, shoppers can buy packets of quills and statues made with damp vanilla.

Two items that should seriously be considered are a lamba oany from Mahajanga, and ylang-ylang perfume from Nosy Bé. There is a factory in Mahajanga that manufactures the coloured cotton shawls (lamba oanys) worn by north-west coast women. The length of cloth can be used for a variety of purposes. Budget travellers will find them useful on long taxi-brousse and bus rides, both for sitting on, and wrapping yourself up in as night temperatures drop. Pronounced "lumber one", the wraps come dyed in bright colours and interesting designs and are quite cheap. On Nosy Bé, no visit is complete without a tour of the ylang-ylang distillery. It is about 3 km north-east of Hell-Ville. To buy a bottle of the essence or perfume you will need to go into Hell-Ville. Chez Abud on Rue Raymond Poincare has a good selection of this and other Nosy Bé crafts.

Those interested in musical instruments will find themselves well catered for. Using bamboo, wood and other local material, Malagasy musicians have, for years, been making their own instruments. On Place de l'Indépendance in 'Tana, every foreigner is approached by at least one vendor selling instruments. The bamboo and gut valiha is a favourite and makes a typically Malagasy dance sound. Wood and hide drums are sold in the Zoma. The African influence is obvious when these drums are played. Wooden flutes and reed whistles produce soft sounds that are hauntingly Andean. The Malagasy flute is simple to play and fits easily into a day-pack.

Jewellery-making is another thriving industry. In a hundred lapidary workshops in the highlands, jewellers create exquisite pieces of delicate art. All urban centres have jewellery shops, known as *bijouteries*. Silver and brass are used for making finely crafted bangles. These bangles are worn by nearly all Malagasy. Few visitors return home without at least one embossed bangle. The jewellery shops along Araben ny 26 Juin 1960 and up Lalana Paul Dussac in 'Tana are the best for silver bangles. At the stalls around the main post office, tourists will find brass and copper bangles.

Silk-screening, silk paintings and sculpture are sold at Atelier Dera in Amboditsiry, tel. 400.16.

Madagascar is known for its magnificent stamps. Tourists can purchase sets or individual stamps from the Service Philatélique, Antaninarenina, on Lalana Printsy Ratsimamanga across from Hotel Colbert.

In the cattle-ranching parts of the country, leatherwork is the main craft. Belts, handbags and a few shoes are offered at most larger settlements in the region.

Do not try to smuggle out items made from turtle shell or other endangered species, such as crocodile.

Antiques may not be removed from the country without permission. The theft of the Malagasy heritage is alarming. Sacred sites have been desecrated, ancestral burial grounds robbed and valuable cultural artefacts stolen from museums.

THINGS TO DO

As tourism grows in Madagascar, so too do the number and variety of activities offered. Until now, the most common pursuits for tourists were scuba diving, deep-sea fishing and hiking, but other equally exciting things are becoming available for the adventurous. Caving, rock climbing, parasailing and sailing are gaining popularity among visitors and islanders.

Scuba diving

This is offered at most tourist resorts on Nosy Bé and Nosy Boraha. Although beginner courses are run, it is recommended that you qualify before arriving. The best organisation to contact if you are interested in scuba diving is the Nosy Bé Subaqua Club. It has gear for rent, qualified divemasters and offers a selection of dives. South Africans should contact Rita Bachmann for more information, tel. (011) 805-4833/4, fax (011) 805-4835. Nosy Bé Subaqua Club also caters for tourists who want to experience the excitement of parasailing. Prices are high, but this highly addictive pursuit should be tried.

Top-class resorts, such as the Marlin Club on Nosy Bé, can arrange for guided dives and equipment rental. Call its activities manager on the island for current details, tel. 206.50. Elite Nautique offers a luxurious vessel and all scuba diving equipment. Its qualified staff know the numerous islands, reefs, bays and coves well, guaranteeing you a memorable dive each time. You do, however, need to be part of its tour group. Elite Nautique, PC Box 1700, Durban 4000, South Africa, tel. (031) 22-3096, fax (031) 22-2591.

Around the island of Nosy Tanikely, off Nosy Bé, is a marine reserve that abounds with fascinating fish and plant species. Your best chance of seeing sea turtles while scuba diving is off Nosy Iranja, south-west of Nosy Bé. The best way of scuba diving in Madagascar is to arrange for what the Ministry of Tourism calls a "Discovery of the virgin islands around Nosy Bé". Sleeping in tents and eating seafood on isolated islands, scuba divers will thrill to night dives and exploring seldom visited reefs. For bookings and information about this tour, contact the Ministère du Tourisme, BP 527, Antaninarenina, Antananarivo, tel. 255.15.

Snorkelling needs little expertise and equipment. Mask, snorkel and fins can be hired from most island hotels. Put on a pair of shoes – to protect yourself from spiny urchins – and go drifting over the shallows in places like Hell-Ville on Nosy Bé or in the strait between Nosy Boraha and Nosy Nato.

Fishing

The favourite sport of South African and German tourists, game fishing is facing stiff opposition from "green" groups. Resorts arrange boats and skippers for interested guests. The skipper will usually supply the tackle and bait. Be prepared for high prices. Environmentally-conscious visitors who still want to try fishing, can also approach the local fishermen. Toliara is a good place to try. Go down to the fishing harbour at about 5h30. You will have no trouble finding a fishing pirogue to take you out for the day. No special fee is expected, as the trip will not be specifically just for you. Do take along something for lunch, and something to drink. Expect to be out until about 17h00. The Vezo fishing community at Anakao village, near Toliara, love having a vazaha (foreigner) along on one of the boats.

Hiking and rock climbing

The geological wonder of Isalo Massif, near Ranohira in the south, is an ideal destination for hikers and climbers. Proclaimed a national park, Isalo Massif has strange runiform cliffs and empty valleys. Hikers may need a guide, who can be hired by speaking to the Chef du Parc at his office in Ranohira.

A hike over 58 km to the Zohin' i Tenika (Caves of the Portuguese), will take hikers through the park's most impressive sites, including the Canyon des Singes, where sifaka lemurs can often be seen. Rock climbers will find challenging unclimbed cliff faces throughout the park. The sandstone is obviously dangerous due to its being so brittle.

Across the main Toliara to Ihosy road outside the boundaries of the national park are literally hundreds of cliffs edging the Imaloto River. Recently a group of French climbers put together a pamphlet showing routes up several of these cliffs. The only copy I could find was from a tour operator. You could try writing to him: R Biazarivelo Albert, Lot 04.K.715 Ambohimena 110, Antsirabe. The climbs are exciting and in many instances technically difficult. You will need some specialised equipment if tackling these cliffs.

There are two hikes which will involve a great deal of effort in return for the experience of a lifetime. The first is through the lowland rainforests between Maroantsetra and Andapa. Carry all your own food, tent and equipment for about eight to 10 days. There are few settlements in the forest, but at those that do exist you can be certain of a warm reception. A guide is imperative if you venture into this wild, fragile area. Tropical Touring, 41 Rue Ratsimilaho, Antananarivo, is able to arrange guides for this trip.

The second hike is in the same area, a 59 km walk from Sambava to the small forest reserve of Marojezy, which should take four or five days. Accommodation will invariably be in village huts en route. You do not need a guide along this hike, as a lot of the time the path follows the main road towards Andapa.

It is quite safe to hike and climb anywhere in Madagascar. Provided you extend common courtesy and get permission from chiefs or elders, visitors will encounter only friendship and welcome. There is no need to follow prescribed trails, simply set off armed with a map, compass, a sense of adventure and a respect for the locals.

Caving

This relatively new activity is now becoming popular in Madagascar. Caves are a feature of the central and western areas of the country, with their sedimentary rock base. Up in the Ankarana region, south-west of Antsiranana, is what writer Derek Schuurman terms "a lost world within a lost world". Visit the famed Crocodile Caves of the area. North-east of Mahajanga, on Baie de la Mahajamba, are the Grottes d'Anjohibe. Other caves worth exploring are in the far south, near Lac Tsimanampetsotsa. They are known as the Grotte de Mitaho, while further south are the Grotte d'Andavaka. Madagascar's most famous caves are not actually caves but cavities caused by wind eroding soft sandstone. These are the famed Grottes des Portugais in Isalo National Park.

Potholers who want to do a comprehensive exploration of Malagasy caves are advised to contact the tourist board and ask about its guided speleological tour.

Canoeing

Another activity gaining popularity among tourists is canoe trips down the Betsiboka and Tsiribihana rivers. The Betsiboka trip takes about three days, while the other lasts up to 10 days, depending on river conditions. Both take travellers through gorges, forests, valleys and over a few rapids.

Boating

Sailing down the Pangalanes Canal, along the east coast of the country, is not for the five-star tourist. You will travel mostly in wooden canoes – traditional dugouts, or ageing dhows and motorboats. The experience is unsurpassed. Visitors will sleep in village huts, so take along a sleeping bag, eat with tribesmen and for a while live at the pace of the rural Malagasy. If you have the time – the whole trip takes about 17 days – this is one trip that should not be missed. It starts about 5 km south of Toamasina, and continues for nearly 520 km south to the coastal town of Farafangana.

3 GETTING THERE

AIR

This is the most practical and the simplest way of reaching Madagascar. Although Air Austral, Aeroflot and Air France make scheduled stops in the country, Air Madagascar is the busiest of all the incoming carriers. Air Madagascar's reputation for service and passenger care is unsurpassed among Indian Ocean airlines. Travellers with specific dietary needs should mention this when making their reservations.

International flights connect Madagascar with Comoros, Djibouti, Johannesburg, Mauritius, Moscow, Nairobi, Paris, Réunion and Zurich. For the latest flight schedules and fares contact a travel agent or an airline representative in your own country.

Air Madagascar has several offices abroad:
Comoros: Magoudjou Street, opposite Volo-volo market, Moroni, tel. 73.02.90
France: 29-31 Rue des Boulets, 75011 Paris, tel. (1) 43.79.74.74
Kenya: Hilton Arcade, Nairobi Hilton Hotel, Mama Ngina Street, tel. 26-494 or 25-286
Réunion: Rue Victor MacAuliffe, St-Denis, tel. 21.05.21, fax 21.10.08
South Africa: 3 Willow Street, Kempton Park 1619, tel. (011) 394-1997, fax (011) 975-4634

The airline's agents are available in the following countries:

Australia: 1931 Pitt Street, Sydney, NSW 2000, tel. (02) 252-3007
Switzerland: 1-3 Rue Chantepoulet 1, 201 Geneva, tel. (22) 32-4230
Switzerland: 8152 Glattbrugg, 8035 Zurich 35, tel. (01) 810-8584
USA: c/o Cortez Travel, 117 Lomas Santa Fe Drive, Solana Beach, California 92075, tel. (619) 792-6999

Alternatively, write to the sales manager in Madagascar: Air Madagascar, BP 437, Antananarivo, tel. 222.22, fax 337.60. Tariffs and schedules do vary slightly according to high and low season. Contact the airline's nearest agency or the local Malagasy diplomatic representative for more information on its specials which include incentive packages, reduced rates for approved passengers and numerous other deals that will suit budget travellers.

All international airline reservations must be confirmed at least 72 hours before departure. Visitors can either do this themselves, by taking their tickets into one of the numerous Air Madagascar offices scattered around the country, or through a hotel. The hotels will do the confirmation for you free of charge, but it is advisable that you make certain of the confirmation. There have been several reports of visitors arriving at the airport to find their places given to someone else, as the hotel "forgot" to make the telephone call.

Airport tax must be paid by all people leaving Madagascar on a flight. Immediately after baggage weigh-in and seat reservation, go to the "Caisse" counter where, once you have paid the departure tax, a receipt is stapled onto your air ticket. This will be checked at customs. At the time of writing the tax for a "Passager Regional" was FF80 or FMg60 000. Note that all nonresidents must pay international departure tax in a recognised foreign currency, preferably French francs.

SEA

Getting to Madagascar by sea involves a considerable amount of research. A few shipping companies do make the voyage, but the recent laws pertaining to the carrying of passengers may make it difficult finding a berth. The Mediterranean Shipping Company (MSC) has a regular cargo service between South Africa and Madagascar. Occasionally it has berths for paying passengers. Visitors can contact it at its offices in Durban, South Africa. Mediterranean Shipping Company, 54 Winder Street, Durban 4001, South Africa, tel. (031) 360-7911, fax (031) 32-9297. From East Africa, Europe and Australia adventurous travellers will just have to visit the docks in places like Mombasa, Marseille and Perth.

Starlight Cruises' luxury passenger liners visit Nosy Bé in northern Madagascar during their summer season cruises in the Indian Ocean. The voyage to Nosy Bé usually departs from the South African port city of Durban in January. The ship's next visit to Madagascar is towards the end of February, when it sails from Durban to Tolanaro. You do not need to make a round trip on these vessels; an increasing number of passengers make a one-way trip only. Contact Starlight Cruises, 2nd Floor, Norwich Life Towers, 13 Fredman Drive, Sandton 2199, South Africa, tel. (011) 884-7680, fax (011) 884-7505.

Elite Nautique has a luxury motor yacht that occasionally travels between Nosy Bé and South Africa. Although many of the trips across the Mozambique Channel are for repairs and supplies, you may be able to get an expensive trip if there are no tourists aboard. Contact Bev Balusik, tel. and fax (01205) 51456.

Madagascar has, for many years, not been included in the seasonal sailing routes of yachts. However, as exciting destinations become overcrowded with vacationers, yachtsmen are now spending time in the bays and tranquil harbours of Madagascar. Finding a crew position is not difficult, especially if you are willing to carry your own expenses. Some sailing knowledge is preferred, and you can better your chances by attending a yacht hand or similar course before setting off. The seasonal yachting routes follow a fairly rigid pattern that avoids tropical storms and cold weather. From Australia, ocean-cruising yachts leave for Madagascar from early July through to mid-October, when the southern cyclone season commences. In South Africa, most yachts going to Madagascar depart from Durban from the end of April until early July. From the east coast of America, the yachts usually pass through the Panama Canal from April to June and then follow the route and timetable of yachts leaving Australia.

4 GETTING AROUND

Travelling around Madagascar is a challenge. Apart from the comfortable and efficient flights, all other travel will demand endurance. The problem is not so much the actual transport, it is the assault course roads that make land travel a test of both courage and patience. It will not make any difference whether you are driven in a luxury 4x4 or hire your own vehicle. Should you opt for public transport, you will need to be fit both physically and mentally. Rest assured that a trip around Madagascar will be an experience and a memorable adventure. While planes are regular and punctual, taxi-brousses and buses are known for delays and breakdowns. Tourists with limited time must choose the quickest mode of travel around the country – flying.

AIR

Air Madagascar serves 60 internal airports and airfields. Prices are lower than for most First World domestic flights, and packages with reduced rates are also offered. Its Twin Otter, single-engined Piper and Boeing jets fly a regular shuttle service between the capital and regional centres.

There are numerous other flights to isolated airstrips. The frequency depends on demand, and visitors hoping to fly to a remote destination should go to Air Madagascar at 31 Avenue de l'Indépendance in 'Tana. It also provides telephonic or faxed information, tel. 222.22, fax 441.02.

Remember to confirm your flight at least 48 hours ahead of a scheduled domestic flight. As with international flights, an airport departure tax must be paid when flying internally. Once you have your boarding pass, go to the "Caisse" counter and pay. You will then get a receipt stapled to your air ticket. This must be given to the ground hostess before entering the departure lounge. At the time of writing, the tax for internal flights was FMg6 000.

Often a boarding card will have a seat number allocated for a domestic flight, but don't rely on it. It's everyone for themselves when the doors open. There is no need to rush, the domestic flights on the larger aircraft are seldom full. Another quirk of Malagasy officialdom is the baggage ticket. When you check in, a numbered sticker is put onto your ticket. This number must be produced when claiming luggage on arrival at your destination. The airport police are quite strict about this and will not release baggage without verification.

BUS

Buses are the most crowded but cheapest and most exciting way of travelling around Madagascar. Known as "auto-buses", they provide the local Malagasy with transport for themselves, livestock and an amazing variety of luggage. Long-distance bus trips should be booked the day before you intend leaving. You will be allocated a seat on the day of departure. The time written on your ticket is only a vague indication of what time you should be there; 30 minutes on the far side will barely raise an eyebrow. Proper buses, albeit in third-class condition, mainly travel the long routes from regional capitals to 'Tana and back. You must not be in any great hurry if you use Malagasy local transport. Consider the experience part of the holiday. Daily buses travel between 'Tana and Toliara, Tolanaro, Toamasina, Morondava and Mahajanga. The 'Tana-Toliara journey takes about 30 hours. From 'Tana to Tolanaro is roughly 40 hours, depending on road conditions. Antananarivo to Toamasina is completed in a quick nine hours. To Mahajanga and Morondava involves an overnight journey.

TAXI

Two types of taxi are used in most of Madagascar: taxi-be and taxi-brousse. In the remote rural districts of the east coast, there is a third form known as taxi-ambanivohitra, which is a 4x4 pick-up fitted with parallel seats in the back.

The taxi-be occurs in towns and seldom travels long distances. Invariably they are exhausted little Renaults with highly decorated interiors. An official tariff is supplied to each driver, but as there is no fare meter, negotiation is the norm. Visitors can safely count on the driver's first bid being between FMg3 000 and FMg6 000 over his rate. Make certain to get the price sorted out prior to setting off. If you ask a taxi-be to wait for you, expect to pay an additional fee. To avoid this, especially if you have gone to a nightclub or restaurant, loudly announce what time you intend returning. Visitors will then, almost certainly, find the same taxi-be waiting.

Competition for business is fierce among the taxi-be drivers. Should you consider one too high even after bargaining, simply ask another.

By the third driver most travellers will have been offered a reasonable fee. A warning: the taxi-be operators on Nosy Bé are notorious for overcharging tourists. Ask for the tariff card when you get in; the distances and fees from the harbour or airport to all the hotels and lodges on the island are listed. Taxi-be drivers are a mine of local information. They can organise you virtually anything and know where to find hotels and restaurants to suit every budget.

Most visitors using public transport in Madagascar will travel in taxi-brousses. They are either station wagons (familial), minibuses (autobus) or panel vans (bacchee). Station wagons are the most comfortable, followed by minibuses and then the most uncomfortable, panel vans. At all large towns there is at least one public transport depot. Several companies operate vehicles. The biggest are Sonatra, Mafio and Kopfmad. Getting a reservation means going to the depot the day before you intend leaving. Find one of the wooden huts in which the ticket clerks sit. Their company names are painted on the outside, so they are not difficult to find. You will be required to write down your destination and name and pay for the journey. If you are taking a station wagon, a number will be written on your ticket. This number is your seat in the vehicle. Insist on either number two, three or six. These are window seats and the most comfortable.

Once the taxi-brousse is fully booked, all the luggage is strapped onto the roof and squashed into the back. Passenger names are called and seats are taken. Eventually you will depart. Be prepared for breakfast, mid-morning, lunch, mid-afternoon and dinner stops, plus numerous relief halts. Travellers must have their passports and valid visas on these journeys, as there is inevitably a police check somewhere along the route.

Minibus taxis have gained in popularity, but are always overcrowded and painfully slow. The same companies that run station wagon taxis also run minibuses. The procedure for obtaining a ticket is the same as for a station wagon taxi. On a long night journey, for example from Mahajanga to 'Tana, a minibus is a lot more comfortable than a station wagon, but the trip can take up to four hours longer.

Panel van taxi-brousses serve most rural areas. Apart from riding a horse or bicycle around Madagascar, this is the most uncomfortable way of getting around. Mostly antiquated Peugeots, they severely test your ability to focus outwards. There are a few tricks to making the experience a lot more comfortable and enjoyable. The problem seems to arise as much from overloading as the wooden planks or tyres on which you sit. Take along something soft to sit on. Carry a raincoat during the wet season and keep your dictionary handy. The best place to sit, if you get there early enough, is about three places away from the cab's rear window. Here, you will be sufficiently squashed in not to bounce about, within range of the music speaker, far enough away from the rain that will wash in over the cab roof, and ideally situated to talk to all the other passengers.

BOAT

Getting around Madagascar's long coast by boat is uncommon. Getting from one island to another, or from the mainland to an island, occurs more often. A ferry service is available to Nosy Boraha from both Toamasina and Manompana. It is far more exciting to get a local fisherman to take you across on his sailing pirogue. The trip may take up to nine hours depending on the tide and weather conditions. At Ivongo, Fenoarivo and Mahambo, the local fishermen are willing to make the crossing if you arrange it the day before. Make certain to get to the beach by at least 5h30. To get from Nosy Boraha to the surrounding islets, visitors will either have to join a tour group or convince the fishermen that taking them out for the day will be more lucrative than going fishing.

Getting to Nosy Bé by boat first means getting to Antsahampano, west of Ambanja. Old landing craft are used for the daily crossing. The best place to sit is not on the rows of seats on the foredeck, but as high up as possible, ideally on the roof of the bridge. The exact schedule is changed each month, according to tides, winds and season. You can obtain current sailing times and prices from the barman at the Hotel Patricia in Ambanja.

TRAIN

Train enthusiasts will be disappointed if they hope to see the whole country by train. Railroad tracks only extend from 'Tana to Ambatondrazaka (Lac Alaotra) in the north, Toamasina to the east and Antsirabe in the south. There is another strip of railway between Fianarantsoa and Manakara. The train journey from Antananarivo to Toamasina must surely rate as one of the most spectacular in the world. It does not always run though. Storms often wash away sections of the track, and repairmen are seldom in any great hurry.

The timetable is as follows:
'Tana to Toamasina: Monday, Wednesday, Friday and Sunday. Leaves the main station in the capital at 7h00 and takes about nine hours to reach the coastal city. On Sunday it returns the same day, but during the week it returns the day after arrival.
'Tana to Ambatondrazaka: Wednesday, Friday and Saturday. Departs 'Tana at 7h00 and takes around seven hours to reach the lake shore.
'Tana to Antsirabe: Wednesday, Friday and Sunday. Starts from 'Tana station at 6h30 and arrives in Antsirabe six to eight hours later.

Travellers may obtain current information from the Réseau National des Chemins de Fer Malagasy, BP 259, Antananarivo, tel. 205.21. Details can also be obtained at the enquiries counter of the main train station in Antananarivo. This is the grandiose building at the northern end of Araben ny Fahaleovantena. The difference between first and second class is negligible from a comfort point of view, but tourists using first class are sometimes asked to pay in foreign currency.

CAR RENTAL

This is an exceedingly expensive way to get around Madagascar. Aware of the road conditions, agents have wisely added in all sorts of clauses and insurances to their contracts. Read each contract carefully, and make sure you understand what you are expected to pay for and how you are covered in the event of an accident. If you intend going off-road, then your only choice is a 4x4 vehicle. These are even more expensive than cars and guzzle fuel. Should you elect to use a 4x4, ensure that the contract specifies the supply of jerry cans for spare petrol. Once out of the larger towns, fuel may become a problem.

Six car rental agencies are recommended by the Malagasy Tourist Board:
Air Route Services, Route de Majunga, Antananarivo, tel. 444.53
Aventours, 55 Route de Majunga, Antananarivo, tel. 317.61
Société Rahariseta et Cie, Lot IV E 92 Lac de Behorrika, Antananarivo, tel. 257.70
Madagascar Airtours (Avis Rent-a-Car agent), Hilton Hotel, Antananarivo, tel. 241.42
Voyages Bourdon, 15 Rue Patrice Lumumba, Antananarivo (101), tel. 296.96
Société Auto Express, Route Circulaire Ampahibe, Antananarivo, tel. 210.60

Euro Rent has now moved into Madagascar and offers several package deals for tourists. The longer you keep the vehicle the cheaper the daily rate becomes. Euro Rent will deliver a vehicle to the airport and collect it from your final destination. Contact it at BP 959, Antananarivo, tel. 260.60, fax 260.51.

Drivers must be in possession of a valid international driving permit, or, if from France, a current driver's licence. Age is often queried, and visitors who want to hire a car must prove that they are over 23. It is safe to say that driving yourself around Madagascar is not recommended.

BICYCLE

South African and French adventure tourists have been mountain-biking around Madagascar for several years now. It is no problem transporting a bicycle to Madagascar by air. Physical fitness is a priority for those planning a cycling journey of the country. The favourite routes are along the east and west coasts. As there are few locals who ride bicycles you are certain of an exciting visit. Spares are difficult to find outside of 'Tana, so take along your own requirements. Punctures are repaired quickly and cheaply at Solima fuel stations and local workshops – look for the sign "Vulcan" outside wooden stalls. The Malagasy word for puncture is "tsindrona".

MOTORCYCLE

This is the best way of travelling in Madagascar with your own transport. In 'Tana and Antsiranana, you will see the latest model scrambler motorcycles used by expats. As a great many of the roads are gravel, it is inadvisable to tour on a road bike, because high ground clearance is needed. Provide yourself with a detailed knowledge of motorcycle repairs if tackling the remote areas. Take along your own spares and change the regular fuel tank for a long-range one. You can get your motorcycle to Madagascar by air if it falls within the specified weight allowance. If not, bikers may have to resort to sending their vehicle by sea.

Motorcyclists must be over 21, be in possession of an international driver's licence and have both proof of ownership and acceptable insurance. The automobile association in your country will be able to

70 Madagascar

supply motorcyclists with a Carnet du Passage for taking a bike into Madagascar.

Helmets are not required, but are advised in the cities, where traffic is congested.

HITCHHIKING

Hitchhiking in Madagascar is almost impossible. Few Malagasy have their own cars, and aid organisations will not stop for foreigners. Go to the large Solima fuel depots in 'Tana, Antsiranana, Toamasina, Tolanaro, Toliara and Mahajanga. Trucks sometimes give travellers lifts. It appears that truck transport companies actually forbid their drivers from picking up hitchhikers. Still, on the long trips from the coast to the capital, trucks do stop. Apart from this, the only other people likely to pick up hitchhikers are taxi-brousses or buses that have seats available. You will, of course, be expected to pay for the ride.

TOURS

This is the way 87% of all foreign visitors to Madagascar travel. Independent travel is demanding, time consuming, and while certainly worth the effort, needs some previous experience. Two recommended tour operators, based in South Africa, work with several overseas agencies, who recognise their expertise and use them frequently.

Unusual Destinations. Known as the premier Madagascar specialist, it runs numerous tours and assists in planning itineraries. Its packages include:

Beach and water sport tours: Lasting between seven and 14 days, these flexible trips take in Nosy Bé, yacht charter for voyages to surrounding islands, scuba diving and deep-sea fishing. This tour can also be changed to include a trip to the east coast island of Nosy Boraha.

Business package: A seven day tour that takes in Antananarivo, Mandraka Reptile and Butterfly Farm, the botanical and zoological centre, yet leaves time for you to attend to business matters.

The east tour: This journey, of between seven and 14 days, travels to Andasibe (Périnet) Nature Reserve for a sight of lemurs, the gracious harbour city of Toamasina and a short hop across to Nosy Boraha.

The company is presently considering an eco-tour of the ecologically threatened Presqu'île Masoala (Masoala peninsula). Other tours take visitors to the sparsely populated west coast, to Morondava and the surrounding delta area. In the south, at Tolanaro, they are able to arrange for tourists to travel to Berenty private nature reserve, into the scenic and bewildering Isalo National Park, and on to the bright lights of Toliara. In the north, around Antsiranana, Unusual Destinations will devise itineraries that allow visitors to see the Montagne d'Ambre montane rainforest, hike across the wilderness of Tsaratanana Massif, or clamber through caves into the mysterious lost world of Ankarana Reserve.

Tourists who want to see natural beauty, should ask about this tour agent's nature tours to Madagascar.

These tours take about 14 days and have been designed with the assistance of leading experts in the field. Notable among these is Ian Sinclair of ornithological fame. His birding tours, which can last up to 24 days, have become world famous. The excursion takes in the Zoological Park in 'Tana, Lake Kinkony, Nosy Iranja, Lake Tsimanampetsotsa and Berenty. There are also visits to the major towns around the country, and time for entertainment.

The Zoological Tour run by Unusual Destinations begins in the vanishing eastern lowland rainforests, then moves south to the semi-desert regions before returning to 'Tana. From 'Tana, participants fly west to encounter deltas and savannas, then north to Sambirano Domaine or further to Tsaratanana.

The Botanical Tour takes clients to see orchids, trees, succulents and some of the staggering amount of endemic plants. The tour goes to Andasibe, Nosy Boraha, Maroantsetra, Sambava or the small reserve at Lokobe on Nosy Bé.

Unusual Destinations, 13 Gustav Preller Street, Vorna Valley 1686, South Africa, tel. (011) 805-4833/4, fax (011) 805-4835.

The other international standard tour operator based in South Africa is **Elite Nautique**. Its speciality is luxury motor yacht tours of Nosy Bé and the surrounding islands on the north-west coast. A typical itinerary lasts 10 days and nine nights. The prices are high, but the service is five-star and the degree of comfort offered is unrivalled in the Malagasy tourist industry. The first night in Madagascar is always spent at the Hilton Hotel in Antananarivo. Included in the 'Tana visit is a guided trip to the Zoma market and the Rova palace, ending with supper at Le Pave restaurant. Tourists are then flown to Nosy Bé and transported to the motor vessel *L'Étranger* in the port off Hell-Ville. This is their home for the duration of the holiday. Daily cruises take guests snorkelling, scuba diving and exploring the small islands in the area. Visits are made to the "Island of lemurs" at Nosy Komba, the marine reserve around Nosy Iranja and to Nosy Sakatia, to dine on barbecued seafood. Other cruises, depending on weather conditions, are to explore the Mitsio archipelago, to dive off Nosy Ankarea and to relax on the beaches of Nosy Tsarabanjina. Naturally, there is time to explore the bustling town of Hell-Ville. If you like, a rubber dinghy will transport you ashore in the evening for a meal or a visit to the Vieux Port dance hall on a Friday night. The tour ends back in 'Tana, again at the Hilton Hotel.

Reservations must be made at least three months ahead of departure, or even sooner over the festive season and during European school holidays: Elite Nautique, PO Box 1700, Durban 4000, South Africa, tel. (031) 22-3096, fax (031) 22-2591. Its contact in Gauteng is at telephone and fax number (01205) 51456.

In Madagascar, several tour agents and operators can arrange tours for visitors. Whether you only want to see lemurs, experience the semi-desert regions of the south, explore the northern reaches or simply sail along the east coast, these agents can organise the entire journey. Their specialised itineraries include caving tours and mineralogical excursions. Organisations sanctioned by the Malagasy Tourism Ministry are:

Madagascar Airtours, BP 3874, Antananarivo, Hilton Arcade, Hilton Hotel, opposite Lac Anosy, tel. 241.92

Transcontinents, BP 541, Antananarivo, 10 Avenue de l'Indépendance, Antananarivo, tel. 223.98

Tropica Touring, BP 6073, Antananarivo, 41 Rue Ratsimilaho, Antananarivo, tel. 222.30

Liounis Voyages, BP 425, Antananarivo, COROI, Antsahavola, Antananarivo, tel. 238.26

Julia Voyage, BP 3179, Antananarivo, 7 Rue Patrice Lumumba, Antananarivo, tel. 268.74

Tourisma, BP 3997, Antananarivo, 15 Avenue de l'Indépendance, Antananarivo, tel. 287.57

Sambava Voyages (specialists in tours of the north-east region), BP 28A, Sambava, tel. 110 Sambava

Top tour operators according to a strict Ministry of Tourism grading are:

SETAM, 56 Avenue du 26 Juin, Analakely, Antananarivo, tel. 329.09

Geckomad Madagascar, Lot IV 45 Bis Antanimena, tel. 201.41

Madagascar Evasion, 8 Rue Rajhonson Emile Tsaralalana, Antananarivo, tel. 328.47

5 ANTANANARIVO

Madagascar's capital city, Antananarivo, commonly referred to as 'Tana, is a paradox. Burnt-sienna medieval houses, cobbled alleys and street markets compete for space with austere modern office blocks, traffic jams and supermarkets. Nothing can prepare you for the city you will encounter. Travellers who have been to Kathmandu and Lhasa will find a striking similarity between architecture there and in 'Tana. But it is the people who make this bustling, colourful city such an experience.

Founded as a military encampment by the great Imerina king Andrianampoinimerina in 1794, 'Tana was for many years a strategic site for soldiers, artillery and horses. Then, as Imerina rule became more accepted, and garrisons were set up across the country, the importance of 'Tana seemed to wane. That is until 1867, when Queen Rasoherina moved to her new palace in 'Tana. Holding court in Antananarivo meant that supporting ministries also needed to be developed. Within five years, 'Tana was the undisputed capital of Madagascar. The French invaders tried, for a few years, to insist that Toamasina be the capital, mainly because of its port facilities, but they never succeeded, and 'Tana remains the nation's capital and economic hub.

It does, however, have its share of typical city problems. Continuing drought, unemployment and devaluation of the currency have resulted in thousands of rural people flooding in. They sleep under plastic or in cardboard boxes on the cold, dark streets. Street children are everywhere. Their sad eyes and sick bodies are an aching reflection on a country that has the natural resources and potential to be among the wealthiest in the southern hemisphere. Crime too has increased. It has not yet reached the proportions of Johannesburg, Nairobi or Miami, but the signs are already there. Avoid walking through dark areas after 20h30, or flashing bills when paying for something.

GETTING THERE AND AROUND

Most visitors arrive at the international airport. Known as Ivato, the airport is about 15 km from the city. To reach 'Tana, tourists have the option of taking a taxi or catching the bus. Taxi drivers wait in the airport building. As you pass through customs and passport control,

74 Madagascar

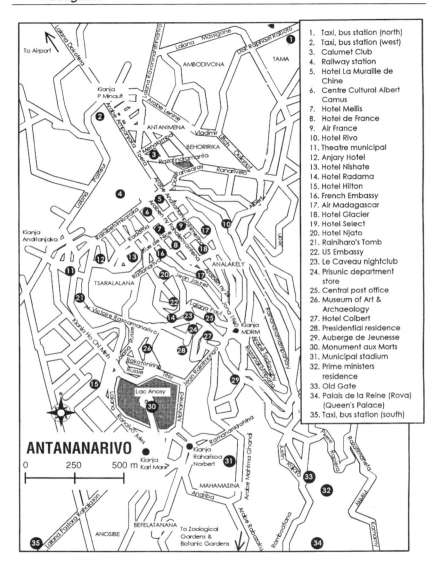

you will be confronted by a wall of touts and taxi drivers. Rule number one, remain calm. If you have no idea of the average fare, ask at the information counter or at the bank. Although official taxi drivers carry a card, they also tend to charge a higher fee than their tariff cards. The taxi touts are your best bet. Their taxis are always cheaper than official ones. If the police at the airport gate stop the vehicle and ask whether it is running as a taxi, you too will have to deny the fact and claim friendship with the driver. The difference in price however is a great incentive to using this transport.

To catch the bus, which is less than a quarter the price of a taxi, means leaving the airport grounds. Walk out the main gate and turn left. The Tana-Ivato bus stops outside the airport. It is always crowded and is an immediate introduction to Malagasy ways. This bus will drop you in the city, usually on Arabe Ampanjaka Toera, near the train station. From here it is a short walk into the city's main road, Araben ny Fahaleovantena.

The city is draped over 12 hills, the most important areas for visitors being restricted to three of the 12. Getting around 'Tana is best done on foot, provided you are fairly fit.

You could of course always flag down one of the many taxis that shoot about the city. They are expensive when you compare the prices to the distance travelled. The Ministry of Tourism claims that the fares are high because of the number of traffic jams and hills the taxi must endure. The taxis that wait for custom outside the expensive hotels always try to overcharge passengers. Bargain for a price or ask to see their tariff card.

A far more interesting and cheaper alternative is to take the local bus. These are always filled to bursting, with passengers hanging out of windows and clinging to doors. The local buses start their routes either around Kianja Ambiky, east of the train station, or from Kianja MDRM, around the tall memorial south of the Zoma market. It is unlikely that you will miss your stop. Simply ask the driver where to get off; they are cordial and extremely helpful.

To leave 'Tana for other parts of Madagascar entails going to one of the busy gares routières for long-distance transport. There are three main ones in 'Tana. Smaller depots that accommodate taxis travelling to local areas are found on the outskirts of the city. For public transport going north to Antsiranana, north-west to Mahajanga or east to Toamasina, travel to the Taxi-brousse Station North, on Lalana Dokotera Raphael Raboto. Trying to walk there is a task in itself. The countless alleys, street markets and houses may confuse even veteran travellers. Rather take a taxi or bus from the city centre. The bus to take is the one to Ambodivona from Arabe Ampanjaka Toera.

Transport going to southern Madagascar, to Antsirabe, Fianarantsoa, Ihosy, Toliara and Tolanaro, leaves south of the city centre, at Taxi-brousse Station South on Lalana Pastora Rahajason. It is quite easy to walk to this large depot south of Lac Anosy. At Kianja Karl Marx, turn south-west into Lalana Dokotera Ravoahangy Andrianavalona Joseph. This street changes name after crossing the railroad tracks, becoming Lalana Pastora Rahajason. You will find the bus depot on the right in the Anosibe district.

Public transport to the western regions, such as Morondava and Maintirano, is found on Lalana Pasteur, north of the train station. Turn south-west at Kianja P Minault, cross the railway line and continue about 150 m to the depot.

Antananarivo is one of the easiest cities in which to get hopelessly lost. A maze of stairs, alleys, roads and dead ends will prove a puzzle to many who walk the city. The best reference point is the main thoroughfare known as Araben ny Fahaleovartena. This road, which starts at the train station (RNCFM Tananarive), and becomes Araben ny 26 Juin 1960, is often referred to as Avenue de l'Indépendance. This is the busiest part of 'Tana. Other good reference points, if you are in the southern, lower parts of the city, are the tall Hilton Hotel, Lac Anosy and the Rova palace on the hill to the south-east of town. The older parts of 'Tana are grouped together on a small hill that edges Lac Anosy, and up the sides of the hill to the east of the CBD, around which the newer, less visually pleasing parts cluster Many visitors may initially find a city street map useless. This only persists until you can get the relative suburbs in perspective to the map.

Access to the medieval suburbs on the eastern hill is made by walking up Lalana Ranavalona III from La Maison du Tourisme de Madagascar or by going up Lalana Razanakombana or Arabe Sadiavahy from Kianja 19 Mey 1929.

TOURIST INFORMATION

As well as being available at the reception counters of the Hilton and Radama hotels, tourist information can also be obtained from La Maison du Tourisme de Madagascar. Located along Lalana Ratsimilaho on Place de l'Indépendance, on top of the hill in the middle of 'Tana, this tourist office is worth a visit. The staff speak little English, but are fluent in French, Italian and have a working knowledge of German. Maps, guidebooks, brochures and several promotional pamphlets are available. You are expected to pay for most of the things, but the staff do provide free city maps and sometimes the informative *Madagascar: a practical guide*.

Both the Hilton and Radama hotels have staff who are experienced and efficient at helping foreigners. It is not necessary to be a guest to receive help. Just go to the reception counter and request tourist information or assistance. The managers at these hotels will go out of their way to provide you with detailed information about 'Tana and Madagascar.

Air Madagascar's promotional division, on Araben ny Fahaleovantena (Avenue de l'Indépendance) also has loads of useful tourist information. Publitours, next to Le Buffet du Jardin restaurant on Place de l'Indépendance, has a few informative brochures and can help tourists plan trips. Silver Wings Travel, a little further up Lalana Ranavalona III, has a wealth of experience in supplying visitors with tourist information.

Banks

Antananarivo is well supplied with financial institutions. From official banks, through hotel foreign exchange counters and down to the black market, 'Tana is where most of your currency transactions should take place.

On Rue Rabehivitra, you will find the BFV (Banque Nationale pour le Commerce), arguably the most efficient and pleasantly staffed bank for visitors. Further east, on the corner of Rue Rabehivitra and Place de l'Indépendance, is BTM (Bankin' ny Tantsaha Mpamokotra). Opposite La Maison du Tourisme de Madagascar, on Lalana Ratsimilaho, is a branch of BMOI (Banque Malagache de l'Océan Indien). Next to the Roxy Cinema, at the top end of Lalana Paul Dussac, is another BTM bank. Along Araben ny Fahaleovantena, on the corner of Lalana Refotaka, is a large branch of the BMOI. Other counters of BTM are located next to the Reve Dile Chinese restaurant on Araben ny Fahaleovantena and near La Bouffe restaurant on the same side of Fahaleovantena as the Hotel de France.

It is also possible to change traveller's cheques and hard currency at the city's top hotels; the Hilton, opposite Lac Anosy on the lower southwestern side of town, on Lalana Ranaivo Jules, and the Radama along Avenue Grandidier in the upper part of 'Tana.

Travel agencies

Antananarivo is well supplied with travel agents. As the tourism industry grows, so too does the number of agencies. Not all are recommended though. Some are fly-by-night one-man operations who could disappoint you. They are all able to reconfirm flights and provide you with domestic airline tickets and excursions. Spend time visiting a few reputable agencies before choosing one – often there are large differences in prices asked for the same tour. Top of the list is well-known Madagascar Airtours, followed closely by SETAM. Tourists can find most of the established travel agencies around Araben ny Fahalaovantena. In the narrow streets of the old town, you may find newer companies that are willing to negotiate better deals. The Ministry of Tourism has recommended the following:

Madagascar Airtours, Hilton Arcade, Hilton Hotel, west of Lac Anosy, tel. 241.92
Voyages Bourdon, 15 Rue Patrice Lumumba, tel. 296.96
Motofolies, 15 Rue Paul Dussac, tel. 200.63
Rova Travel, 35 Rue Refotaka, tel. 276.67
SETAM, 56 Avenue du 26 Juin, tel. 329.09
Visit Madagascar, 16 Rue Patrice Lumumba, tel. 249.62
Madagascar Discovery Agency, Espace Dera Route de l'Université, tel. 351.65
Madagascar Safari Tours, Immeuble Ramaroson, Rue Rainizanabololona, tel. 231.22

Post office

The post office that will be used by most visitors is on Araben ny 26 Juin (Jona) 1960. The ground floor is for general postage and poste restante collection. The upper floor has public telephones and facilities for telegrams, telexes and faxes. Up Lalana Paul Dussac is the rear entrance to the main post office. You may also access the telecommunications offices from here.

If you are spending considerable time at one hotel or will be returning to the same hotel, get the people sending you mail to address it to the hotel. The mail is delivered, saving you agonising hours of sifting through poste restante trays.

Bookshops

Outside of urban centres visitors will find a dearth of bookshops. Bookshops are usually located near tourist districts, and offer a good selection of books – mainly in French and Malagasy – plus stationery and advice for tourists. The bookshop with the widest choice of reading material is Librairie de Madagascar. This large book and stationery shop is along the west side of Araben ny Fahaleovantena in the arcade opposite the Jean Ralaimongo memorial park.

Tout pour l'École, on Rue de Nice, is geared mainly for the reader of educational books. It has a wide selection of non-fiction books, textbooks and a few copies of English classics. Librairie Mixte at the northern end of Araben ny 26 Juin has a supply of local and international newspapers and magazines. Its book selection is limited but intriguing. Another bookshop worth trying for current Malagasy literature and maps is Librairie Avotra on Avenue de l'Indépendance, next to Co-op Pêche. Opposite Kianja MDRM, readers will find several stalls selling magazines. All the magazines are long outdated, but there is an amazing variety to read on a long overland journey.

There are two libraries worth visiting. They are both called Bibliothèque Municipale. The one is next to the Patisserie Suisse on Lalana Rabahevitra, and the other is near the BNI (Banque Crédit Lyonnais) on Araben ny 26 Juin 1960.

Photo supplies

Rather bring all your own photo needs with you. The prices of equipment, repairs and film in Madagascar are high, with the film often having passed its expiry date. Specialised film such as ASA 50 or ASA 1 000 is unobtainable in the country. Should you be forced to purchase film, batteries or have a minor repair done to your camera, then the Kodak offices are best. There is one as you descend the stairs from Place de l'Indépendance to Araben ny 26 Juin 1960. Just past the Church of Jesus Christ in Madagascar is an opening to an arcade. Kodak Express Photo Supplies is located in here. It is able to carry out repairs to most makes of camera. Its biggest attraction must be the postcard counter in the middle of the centre. Nowhere else in Madagascar will you find such a selection of postcards. They include silk cards, hand-painted cards, ordinary picture cards and cards with old photos of early Madagascar. Just browsing through them is like going on a pictorial journey through the country and its history.

Opticam Photo Supplies on Lalana Ranavalona III is modern and expensive, with knowledgeable staff and a good supply of equipment. It caters almost exclusively to the affluent visitors who stay at the Hotel Colbert. Its technicians are qualified enough to carry out major repairs to Nikon, Minolta and Pentax cameras.

A few hotel boutiques stock film and batteries, but make sure you check the expiry date on the box before buying film.

Lab' Art Studio on Lalana Rabahevitra is a large and well-stocked shop that can carry out quick photo developing. Its speciality seems to be enlarging pictures. Its stocks are limited to a few well-known brand names. Its supply of print film is extensive, but less so for colour slide reversal film. The shop also carries a stock of various sized batteries suitable for most cameras and flash units.

Medical attention

The best place to go if in need of medical attention is your country's embassy. All embassies keep lists of doctors and dentists who are considered suitable for their staff. Should your country not have representation in Madagascar, then consult the American or British embassies. The staff of these missions are extremely helpful.

Top-class hotels also have a list of medical personnel and doctors on call. Ask at the reception desk of the Hilton or Radama for assistance in this regard.

On Araben ny 26 Juin 1960, next to the Select Hotel, is the well-stocked Pharmacie Hasina. The pharmacist can diagnose minor ailments and provide the necessary treatment. Another good pharmacy, for both medicine and consultation, is the Pharmacie de l'Océan Indien, next to the Royal Marche, on the western side of Araben ny Fahaleovantena. Pharmacie d'Isoraka, west on Avenue Grandidier, is small and traditional and has an old chemist who will peer intently into your eyes for a few moments, make a diagnosis and prepare a mixture for a few FMg.

North on Lalana Rainandriamampandry is a cabinet médical (surgery). You do not need an appointment for a visit.

Even if you have medical insurance, in Madagascar you will be expected to pay the bill and then settle with the insurance company.

Whatever else you do before leaving for Madagascar, get your teeth seen to. One thing you do not want to experience is a visit to a local dentist. The tribal art of dentistry is taken to its highest form in the backstreets of 'Tana. Just peering into their dingy interiors is enough to scare most visitors off. Carry your own basic dentistry kit; it should include oil of cloves, amalgam, mouthwash and vaseline. If you are unfortunate enough to develop tooth problems, contact the UK embassy for recommended Western-trained dentists in the city.

Airline offices

Air Madagascar has two offices. Both are on the eastern side of Araben ny Fahaleovantena. One is for domestic flights and the other, which also handles local flights, is mainly for international flights, sales and confirmations. Air France is located north of Air Madagascar, in the same arcade as Transam Rent-a-Car. Aeroflot has a small office on Lalana Ratsimilaho.

THINGS TO DO

Once the initial confusion about finding one's way around 'Tana is resolved, visitors should consider a walking tour of the city. There is no need for a guide. If, however, you'd feel more secure with a guide, then speak to the local tour operators for assistance; they often run guided, driving tours of the city. For those who prefer to walk alone about this town, I have detailed a brief self-guided tour.

Start from outside the Hilton Hotel on the corner of Lalana Ranaivo Jules and Rue Pierre Stibbe. Walk east from here, skirting the edge of Lac Anosy. Opposite Kianja Karl Marx is a causeway out into the middle of the little lake. This ends at the Monument aux Morts, which is a memorial to those who died in the defence of France during various wars. Continue around the lake onto Lalana Mohammed V, and then left into Lalana Titsy and the site of the presidential residence. Soldiers patrol the right side of the road, and no one is permitted to walk on that side. Taking photographs will, obviously, result in problems. The residence is in a park-like setting of trees, lawns and flowers. Visitors cannot enter unless a permit has first been obtained. This is fairly easy to arrange via a local travel agent or La Maison du Tourisme de Madagascar.

At the end of the presidential grounds turn right into Arabe Rain-itsarovy and take the first left which winds uphill on Lalana Rakoto-nirina. Taking the first right into Rue Docteur Theodore Villette, visitors will be plunged into a maze of cobbled streets. On the corner of Rue Docteur Theodore Villette and Lalana Réunion is the Museum of Art and Archaeology – look for the bare tree decorated with upside-down clay pots. Open every afternoon from 14h00-17h30, except Monday, this little museum has a wealth of information for interested visitors. There are fascinating displays of Zafimaniry and Sakalava crafts, plus tribal artefacts used for sorcery. A collection of old photographs, taken mostly at the turn of the century, provides evidence of how little the basic structure of Malagasy life has changed. The staff are informative and pleasant. For specific information, it is advisable to phone ahead and make an appointment, tel. 210.47.

Continue walking north-east. Less than 100 m from the museum is the Art Gallery Yerden, near the Japanese embassy. You will find a small but comprehensive display of local art here. Most of the works are for sale to the public. At the T-junction of Rue Docteur Theodore Villette and Avenue Grandidier turn left onto the avenue. The next road on the left is Rue de Russie. The Malagasy Art Centre is located a short way down this road, and is well worth the detour for visitors interested in buying Malagasy curios and the paintings of local artists. Avenue Grandidier then changes name to become Arabe Victoire Rasoamanarivo. Here the road commences to drop past the College de France to the mansion of Louise Berger with its high fence and manicured garden. Next to the mansion is the Souvenir Colonial Française to Alfred Grandidier, geographer, ethnographer, naturalist and explorer.

Following the bend of the road, walkers arrive at the entrance to the tomb of Prime Minister Rainiharo, opposite Coiffure Mahadiste. Neglected and crumbling, the top of the tomb allows spectacular views of the lower city. Turn left out of the gate and go downhill on Lalana Benyowski into Arabe Rainibetsimisaraka. You will now be on the fringes of the 'Tana market. There are mainly second-hand clothes and motor vehicle parts for sale at these stalls.

Then you arrive outside the train station, looking south-east down Araben ny Fahaleovantena. In front of you is the famous Zoma (Friday) market, the largest street market in the world. The sight is unbelievable. A sea of humanity washes around the islands of white umbrellas that cover each stall. Pirated music pulsates from countless speakers, while traffic clogs the roads. Every day is busy, but on Friday, country folk bring in their goods for sale and 'Tana becomes one enormous open-air market. The people are friendly and welcoming, but be careful of pickpockets and fake items. First walk the entire length of the market up to Kianja 19 Mey 1929. Having seen the main part of the market, swing left along Arabe Andrianampoinimerina, and stroll through the fresh produce stalls, all the way to Kianja Ambiky. Turn left and re-enter the main road outside the train station, and pass the stalls on the western side of the road.

At the small monument to the mysterious Jean Ralaimongo, 1884-1984, proceed into Araben ny 26 Juin 1960. At Kianja MDRM, where there is a tall column and two cannons, turn right up the hill on Lalana

Andriandahifotsy. Take the first left in Lalana Tsiombikibo. Follow this road up to the cathedral. Here, turn left again, and proceed up the steep cobbled road. At Tsena Maros take the right-hand road to where it overlooks south-western 'Tana, the stadium, Lac Anosy and the presidential mansion. Stay on this road past St Joseph's School to the impressive Roman Catholic cathedral on Lalana RP Venance Manifatra.

Numerous churches are grouped around the Fahafahana Memorial Park. This is where you are likely to encounter freelance guides. Mostly children, they will offer to take you on a conducted tour of the Rova Palace on the top of the hill. Go up the right side of the park alongside the old French school. At the top end of the park, where you turn right into Lalana Ravelojaona, is one of the old gates to the palace. Large, heavy, round stones, one on each side of the gate, were used to close the entrance. Follow this road as it winds past the South African Trade Promotions (SATPRO) office and up to the prime minister's former residence, constructed in 1872. The National Education Centre and a small post office sit on the hill between the residence and Tribunal building. To the right, down the slope, are the huts where the monarch's servants lived. These huts are still inhabited. The people who now use them are delighted to let foreigners take a peek inside.

At the Tribunal building turn left onto the open piece of land west of the ruins. There are magnificent views from here, across rice paddies, of the university and Catholic seminary and the forested slopes east of Antananarivo. Just before the road swings right to become Lalana Ramboatiana, is the entrance to the Rova. The palace was built for Queen Rasoherina, who ruled Madagascar from 1863-1868. There are actually five palaces on the grounds of the Rova. Closed on Monday, the palace is open to the public on all other days of the week from 9h00-12h00 and 14h00-17h00. An entrance fee must be paid. The most interesting parts of the palace are the pitch black, wooden, royal house of Madagascar's first king, Andrianamponimerina; the famed Silver Palace of Radama I; a stone church built by Ranavalona II and the centrepiece of the site, the Rova of Queen Rasoherina (also known as the Supreme Beauty). Other points of interest are the tombs of the Malagasy kings and queens who ruled the country before colonisation and Marxism imposed their own dictators.

Tourists are forbidden from taking photographs without prior approval. Permission is easily obtained by contacting the curator, at least 24 hours in advance, tel. 200.91.

Return the way you have come, as far as the cathedral on the corner of Lalana Andriandahifotsy and Lalana Ranavalona III. Continue along the latter road. This road will take walkers past La Maison du Tourisme de Madagascar and a small craft and fresh produce market to Place de l'Indépendance. Turn left into Avenue Rainilaiarivo, which ends at the main entrance to the presidential residence. Turn right at the mansion and walk past the Central Bank of the Malagasy Republic to Kianja Dahle. Proceed along Avenue Grandidier then turn left down Arabe Rainitsarovy, opposite the Radama Hotel. By continuing down this road you will exit next to the presidential grounds and Lac Anosy. The Hilton is on the western side of the lake.

No tour is complete without a visit to the zoological and botanical garden of Tsimbazaza. It is too far for most people to walk. Rather flag down a taxi and get it to drive you out. If you prefer, go to Kianja MDRM and take the Antafita bus, which passes the site. There is an interesting collection of plant and animal specimens at the Parc Botanique et Zoologique de Tsimbazaza. It is the best place to see the majority of Malagasy flora and fauna in one place. Several research projects are under way, and interested visitors may be allowed to see some of the results. There is a good selection of prehistoric artefacts on display: a reconstructed *Aepyornis* skeleton and egg, the once thought extinct coelacanth and a collection of dinosaur bones. In addition to items of historical significance, there is a well-stocked vivarium and an interesting display of Malagasy culture gathered by anthropologists.

The site is only open on Thursday, Sunday and public holidays. The opening times are 8h00-11h00 and 14h00-17h00.

At night there are discos, nightclubs and street cafés to occupy visitors. The veranda bar of the Hotel Glacier, on Araben ny Fahaleovantena, is a favourite with male tourists in search of a woman's company. The same is true for the terrace of La Buffet restaurant on Place de l'Indépendance. In front of the Hotel Colbert is a narrow street bistro that serves drinks and provides privacy for patrons late into the night.

Le Caveau nightclub, on Lalana Rabahevitra, is highly recommended on a Friday and Saturday evening from about 23h30. On the same road is the Kaleidoscope Bar and Nightclub. This, too, is recommended for those in search of loud music and a festive atmosphere. The Kaleidoscope really only gets going from around midnight. The entrance fee to a nightclub or disco entitles you to one free drink. The best

Malagasy nightclub in 'Tana is, without doubt, the Indra Nightclub, between Lalana Mahafaka and Lalana Karija.

On the corner of Lalana Paul Dussac and Lalana Jean Ralaimongo is the Rex Cinema. The latest American and European movies are shown here each night of the week, usually with French sub-titles.

THINGS TO BUY

Antananarivo is a curio-hunter's treasure trove. Excluding the international clothing boutiques, there are jewellers, artisan's markets, craft shops and, of course, the Zoma. At small jewellers and art galleries in the suburbs and side streets, visitors will find excellent work at high prices. In the Zoma, shoppers can delight in the traditional crafts on sale. Remember that buying in the market means hard bargaining, good humour and compassion. When buying gemstones, it is advisable to buy from a reputable dealer who can supply you with a validated certificate of authenticity from the Ministry of Industry and Mines. A dealer recommended is Haba Gem Stones near the Japanese Embassy on Rue Docteur Theodore Villette.

The Mboahangy Gallery and Souvenir Shop on Rue Rabahevitra has a good selection of traditional and modern Malagasy crafts and art works. Another place to try for authentic local art is the Malagasy Art Centre in Rue de Russie.

By far the most interesting and enjoyable place to do your shopping is the awesome Zoma street market. What you cannot find here is unavailable in Madagascar. Items seem to be grouped into specific areas – although clothing is on sale everywhere. The craft vendors tend to be around the Air Madagascar and Air France offices, with one or two stalls near the post office.

ACCOMMODATION

Accommodation in 'Tana is not a problem. Experienced budget travellers need not bother making prior reservations, unless they are planning to stay at top-class hotels in the city.

Madagascar Hilton (high tariff)

The Hilton is one of the largest buildings in the country, making it a useful landmark when trying to get orientated. It is Madagascar's top international hotel. The service is exceptional, the facilities extensive

and entertainment excellent. The hotel changes foreign currency and cashes traveller's cheques. The rate, which must be paid in foreign currency, is inclusive of breakfast. A restaurant, offering superb international cuisine, is also open for lunch and dinner. On Thursday evening a Malagasy buffet is laid out for dinner. There is a sparkling swimming pool outside the dining room and the hotel can arrange a variety of activities for clients. In the Hilton Arcade you will find Madagascar Airtours, duty-free boutiques, a newsagent and car hire representatives. At night a good disco raves with both locals and foreigners. Regular shows and competitions are held at the disco. Reservations for the hotel must be made at least 30 days in advance:
Madagascar Hilton International, BP 959, Antananarivo, tel. 260.60, fax 260.51.

Radama Hotel (medium-high tariff)

Situated along a cobbled lane in the heart of the city, the Radama Hotel is ideal for visitors. Foreign currency payment is expected. Traveller's cheques, credit cards and cash may all be used when paying. Additionally, there are facilities for cashing traveller's cheques or changing hard currency. Despite having fewer stars than the colonial Hotel Colbert or expensive Hotel de France, the Radama Hotel is comparable, in service and comfort, to the Hilton. It will only be a matter of time before the Radama is considered one of the best hotels in Madagascar. The capable management also provides airport transfers and storage of luggage.

The owners have created a luxurious hotel that stresses Malagasy culture. In the cosy Tatao restaurant, diners may choose from a menu that includes several typical Malagasy dishes. On Friday evening, there are Valiha musical performances at the hotel. You do not have to be a resident to see and enjoy these recitals and plays.

Business people have access to a functional business centre that includes secretarial services, translators, computers and fax machines. A small city map is provided on registration which includes sites of banks, cultural centres, ministries and points of interest.

The hotel has recently built an annexe. Despite being somewhat distant from the city centre, its rooms are ideal for long-term, self-catering guests. There are four self-contained apartments, all of which are serviced daily. A catering and laundry service is available. Transport can be arranged to and from the flats, and even grocery shopping is offered for those too busy to reach a supermarket. A new concept in Madagascar, these luxury suites, at reasonable prices, are worth considering if you need to spend longer than five days in 'Tana.

Reservations are strongly recommended about 30 days ahead: Radama Hotel, 22 Avenue Grandidier, Isoraka, Antananarivo, tel. 319.27, fax 353.23.

Other hotels

Other medium-high-tariff hotels in the city are:
Hotel Colbert, 23 Rue Printsy Ratsimamanga, tel. 202.02
Panorama, Route d'Andrainarivo, tel. 409.65
Hotel de France, 34 Araben ny Fahaleovantena, tel. 213.04
Solimotel, Lalana Doktera Ravoahangy Andrianavalona Joseph, tel. 250.40

Hotel Muraille de Chine (low-medium tariff)

Located across from the train station at the northern end of Araben ny Fahaleovantena, the Muraille de Chine is a long way behind the hotels described above. However, for travellers using the train or wanting quick access to the bus stop, it is ideal. Construction is presently underway to upgrade the hotel and restaurant. Rooms are spartan but adequate. All have their own showers and toilet facilities. This hotel is frequently used by travelling salesmen and foreign gem dealers. There is an air of conspiracy and intrigue hanging over the veranda bar, as dealers and sellers whisper over their beer and dark rum. Reservations are not necessary, but preferable:
Hotel Muraille de Chine, BP 1557, Antananarivo, tel. 230.13.

Low tariff

Finding low-tariff accommodation is simple, if you are prepared to endure the inevitable problems. The best "cheapies" are along Arabe Andrianampoinimerina, east of the Zoma. These are the hotels used by country folk on their infrequent visits to the capital. These hotels are suitable if you are only spending one night in 'Tana before an early bus, train or air trip. Between the medium and low-tariff category hotels are a number of guesthouses worth considering. *Le Jean Laborde* is on Rue de Russie, just off Avenue Grandidier. The *Hasina Chinese Hotel and Snack Bar* is south on Avenue Grandidier. No reservations are necessary for either of these basic, but clean, lodgings.

PLACES TO EAT

Your best bet for a reasonably priced meal in 'Tana is the *plat du jour* offered by many restaurants. This is usually a house speciality that includes such delights as paella, ravioli and grilled chicken. Do not expect international cuisine. In fact, rather choose local food to avoid disappointment. Visitors do, however, have a good selection of Chinese and Indian restaurants. On the streets of the Zoma, you will be able to choose from a wide variety of traditional snacks such as roasted corn on the cob, chicken or beef kebabs, thick vegetable and zebu stews or spicy chicken and rice.

At *Patisserie Suisse* on Rue Rabehivitra and *La Potiniere Patisserie* on Araben ny Fahaleovantena, delicious pastries and bread are baked daily. Near Patisserie Suisse is *La Hutte Canadienne,* where home-made pâté de foie gras and light meals are available. On Place de l'Indépendance is the well-patronised *Le Buffet du Jardin* snack bar and terrace. This is where most tourists take their lunches from a good menu of high quality food and reasonable prices.

Two restaurants worth trying for Malagasy and Continental meals are the *Restaurant Fiaremana* and *Restaurant Arnica* near the Hotel de France, on Araben ny Fahaleovantena. The Hotel Muraille de Chine has a splendid Chinese restaurant downstairs known as the *Reve Dile.* Other Indian and Chinese restaurants that are recommended include *Le Grand Orient,* 4 Kianja Ambiky; *Le Shanghai,* 4 Rue Rainitovo; *Restaurant de la Grand Île,* 8 Lalana Paul Dussac; *Restaurant Asiatique,* 17 Lalana Rabezavana; *Indra Restaurant,* Lalana Karija.

Light snacks and teas are available from salon de thé cafés open from early morning to late afternoon. The *Honey Salon de Thé* in the arcade east of Araben ny Fahaleovantena has the best reputation and ice creams in the city. *Tropique Snacks,* opposite Librairie Avotra on Araben ny 26 Juin 1960, does a good range of fast foods, both from an American and Malagasy menu.

Top of the range, excluding international-class hotels, is the *Acapulco Restaurant and Piano Bar* on Lalana Ratsimilaho, around the corner from the Hotel Colbert. It has a tasty but slightly expensive *plat du jour*, plus accommodating staff and great music. For a taste of traditional Malagasy food you can either try one of the dishes from the extensive menu of the Radama Hotel's *Tatao Restaurant,* or walk a little further to the *Rommy Snack Bar and Café* on Lalana Réunion, near the museum. Another place to try for local dishes is the *Amidyato Café* in Rue de Russie.

Both Italian and French restaurants have proliferated since the tourism boom. Now, you can order pizza, pasta, frogs or snails from a number of foreign eateries. For French cuisine try *La Rotonde*, 19 Rue Besarety; *Le Relais Normand*, 2 Arabe Rainibetsimisaraka Soarano; *Le Zebu Grill*, Hilton Hotel, Rue Pierre Stibbe.

Those keen on Italian food are advised to try *Lou Midjou Pizzeria*, Hotel de France, Araben ny Fahaleovantena.

Note that snack bars and bistros usually open for breakfast from about 6h30 and shut their doors at around 17h00. Restaurants are open for lunch, then close until dinner time, which starts at around 19h30. Bars open at about 9h00 and shut at 18h30. The numerous salons de thé are open for breakfast, closed from 12h00-14h00, and then work until 17h30.

90 *Madagascar*

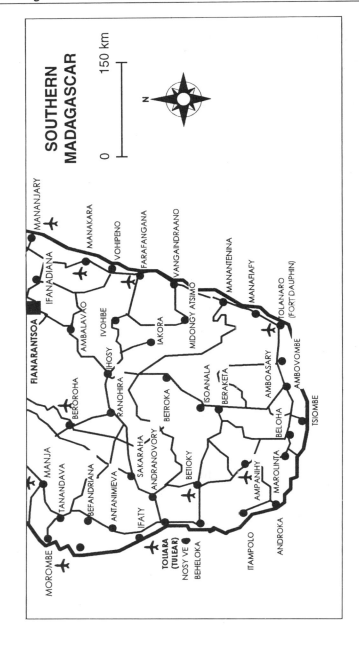

6 SOUTHERN MADAGASCAR

Straddling the Tropic of Capricorn, southern Madagascar is a veritable wonderland of contrasting wilderness, rare wildlife and traditional cultures. The highlight of any visit to this remote region of Madagascar is a tour through the Spiny Desert, south of the tropic line. Other points of particular tourist interest are the oldest European settlement on the island at Tolanaro (Fort Dauphin); the Vezo fishing villages on the coast between the Mahafaly Plateau and the Onilahy River, near Toliara (Tulear) and Massif de l'Isalo National Park, with its strange geological formations and runiform canyons.

Isalo is the only official national park in southern Madagascar, but there are several nominally protected areas that warrant a visit. These include the wilderness around Lac Tsimanampetsotsa, the nearby caves of Mitaho and a few kilometres further south-east, the caves of d'Andavaka. Another area for outdoor and wildlife enthusiasts is the vegetated region stretching from Italy village (south-west of Tolanaro) to the banks of the Mananara River, between the coastal settlement at Vangaindrano and the village of Iakora, on the Ionaivo River. This entire district is still home to numerous isolated forest and plain dwellers. Between Amboasary and Antanimora, on the RN13, is an area with varied floral species. Finally, in the convoluted hills of Rebobd Manambien, walkers can explore a semi-desert landscape whose desolate hills give rise to the Mangoky River.

The climate in southern Madagascar is generally hot and dry throughout the year, though it can get slightly cooler in the evenings on the south-eastern and south-western coasts during late June and July. Most of the rain that falls – very little in comparison to the eastern and northern areas of the island – does so over a six week period in December and January.

Most tourists to southern Madagascar combine flying and driving to see the region. The usual tourist route sees visitors flying to Tolanaro, then taking another flight to Toliara. From there, people usually drive to Isalo National Park, and then go further north to Fianarantsoa, Antsirabe and finally, Antananarivo.

There are regular flights between these locales on Tuesday, Wednesday, Thursday, Saturday and Sunday.

Visitors wanting to travel overland from 'Tana should take one of the daily buses that leave the capital from near the Taxi-Brousse Station South, in Anosibe. Instead of taking one long 24-36 hour ride, consider a series of hops that takes you from 'Tana to Antsirabe, to Fianarantsoa and from there either to Tolanaro or Toliara. One of the most exciting and arduous journeys you can take in Madagascar is to find a ride on a truck travelling between Tolanaro and Toliara, especially during the short rainy season at the end of the year.

The people who inhabit this harsh region are still predominantly tribal in their way of life. It is one of the few areas where tourists will see signs of malnutrition among the populace. The largest ethnic group in southern Madagascar is the Bara, but there are a number of lesser tribes whose customs and life styles should also be seen. Starting from the east coast, these include the Antanosy and Antaisaka. Moving west you will encounter Antandroy, then Mahafaly and finally, hugging the west coast, Antanosy and remnants of Sakalava. While these are the predominant cultures in the region, perceptive visitors will notice many other clans as well. Along the south-west coast are the Vezo; near Tolanaro the Antatsima; between Betroka and Beraketa live the Antaivondro people; north of Toliara are Antifirenana communities.

As can be expected of traditional cultures, taboos (fady) are very much a part of their lives. All visitors should be aware of as many of these fady as possible before venturing into southern Madagascar. A few of the more important Bara tribal beliefs are listed below. You must find out more about current restrictions from hotels, guides and wherever possible from the tribesmen themselves in the settlements.

- Access to graves, which are normally caves in the mountains, is forbidden to foreigners.
- If you enter a village where many of the people have shaved off their hair, be aware that there has recently been a death and show the proper respect for those in mourning.
- When referring to someone who has died in the tribe, always use the term, Rafanjava (Master Shining). This denotes respect.

The Bara are very strict when it comes to fady concerning pregnancy and birth.

- A pregnant woman must never sit in a doorway.
- Never, when staying in a Bara village, step across the sleeping mat of a woman with child.

TOLANARO (FORT DAUPHIN)

Located deep in Antanosy territory, in the south-east of Madagascar, lies the oldest European settlement on the island. Known in the tourism industry as Madagascar's answer to the Côte d'Azur, the region around Tolanaro is blessed with beaches, private nature reserves, an excellent selection of tourist accommodation and a relaxed atmosphere. It is a small town, whose original name, Taolankarana (Land of Dreams), is still used in folk tales of the Antanosy, Antatsino and Antaisaka clans.

Historians believe that it was here, in 1501, that a group of shipwrecked Portuguese seamen landed and built a rudimentary settlement. The now overgrown ruins of there efforts can be viewed on the banks of the Ambinanibe River. The Portuguese, however, had trouble being accepted by the tribesmen and frequently broke important fady, while also trying to exploit the locals. The situation reached a climax in February 1528, when Antanosy warriors attacked the sailors' village. Ill-equipped to resist the onslaught, the Portuguese fled into the forests around Pic St Louis. It was in those forests that they died from disease, lack of food and clashes with the veteran Antanosy soldiers.

Following in the wake of French empire building in the Indian Ocean, a group of French marines, sailors and adventurers made landfall near Manafiafy in 1642. Their initial settlement and attempts at claiming Madagascar for France were fraught with difficulties and they later abandoned the site and moved to where modern-day Tolanaro is located. The governor, Pronis, ordered the building of a fort and changed the name of the Malagasy village already existing there, Taolankarana, to Fort Dauphin, in deference to Louis XIV. The fort itself was named Flacourt, in honour of Baron de Flacourt, another Indian Ocean conquistador. It was Governor Sieur Pronis who sent 12 French sailors to live in exile on deserted Île Bourbon (Réunion), near present-day St-Paul.

As with the Portuguese, the lack of cultural sensitivity, attempts at exploitation and disregard for local customs brought the French into conflict with the Antanosy. A warlike tribe, the Antanosy were not easily going to be subjected to French authority. Numerous Antanosy attacks, failed French reprisals, untreated illness and a lack of assistance eventually forced the French to flee Fort Dauphin in about 1674. They did not, however, leave Madagascar. As the trade in human cargo grew, French sea captains occasionally landed off decaying Fort Dauphin to replenish their stocks of fresh water and wood for cooking fuel. The Antanosy could not escape, nor stop, the expansion of French claims in Madagascar. Faced by large numbers of highly trained, well-equipped French troops, they bowed their proud heads and accepted French control in 1897.

Getting there

Visitors can reach Tolanaro by air, road and occasionally, boat. Remember to book or confirm flights at least 38-72 hours before your intended departure. You will find the Air Madagascar office on the hill behind the BTM bank. Many of the hotels will gladly do your air ticket confirmation via telephone, or send one of their staff down to the Air Madagascar office.

Getting to Tolanaro by road is not for the timorous, squeamish or inexperienced. You could, of course, hire a private taxi or arrange with a tour operator to drive you down in a luxury 4x4 vehicle. This is expensive, albeit a lot more comfortable than the adventurous way of reaching Tolanaro. The best place to track down taxi drivers or tour operators willing to make the trip is in the bustling city of Fianarantsoa. There, speak to either *Frontiere Voyage*, near the Hotel de Madagascar, tel. 511.52, in Haute-ville, or get hold of *Angelo Rakotonirina* at Chez Papillon, opposite the train station. He speaks fluent English and French and is able to offer you the best prices for hiring a car and finding accommodation between Fianarantsoa and Tolanaro.

Visitors should use a taxi-brousse or bus to reach Tolanaro. There are two buses per week from Antananarivo doing the arduous trip to Tolanaro. If you want to go on a bus, make sure to book, and pay for your seat, at least two days before departure. Around the festive season and Easter a few taxi-brousses go from 'Tana's Taxi-brousse Station South to Tolanaro. The best place to find frequent buses or taxi-brousses going to Tolanaro is Fianarantsoa. There are at least three buses per week on the route, and almost daily taxi-brousses. The taxi-brousses leave at about 7h00, while buses depart at 9h00.

From Fianarantsoa the trip takes anything between 14 and 24 hours, depending on the road, weather and mechanical condition of the taxi-brousse, as well as the mechanical ability of the driver to repair the inevitable breakdown. The route takes you along the tarred road until reaching the Zomandao River. Then the road becomes good gravel as far as the sizeable settlement of Ihosy. From here, you swing south onto the RN13, a red sand road. Passing stark plains, barren hills and semi-desert, travellers cross the Tropic of Capricorn a few kilometres south of Betroka village and the Mangoky River. The dusty road edges the Rebobd Manambien hills near Isoanala and then veers south-east to Ambovombe. From Ambovombe the road is again tarred (well, sort of!) all the way to Tolanaro.

Trying to reach Tolanaro by boat is difficult. Despite being a coastal settlement, the port has long faded into obscurity and disuse, apart from a few local fishing boats and the infrequent supply ship. The best places at which to find a vessel going to Tolanaro are the east coast towns of Manakara and Mananjary, but these are so seldom that it hardly warrants investigation.

If arriving by aeroplane, visitors will be met at the airport, about 5 km west of Tolanaro, by several hotel touts, who are able to provide free transport to their particular establishment. A few taxi drivers also wait for fares and are the best people to ask about cheap accommodation. Do not immediately reject the offer from the hotel touts, especially if they are from the Motel Gina or Hotel Mahavoky. These two hotels are the best for budget-conscious travellers.

Tourist information

Tourist information may be obtained, free of charge, from Air Fort Services, on the corner of Avenue du Marechal Foch and Rue Blondlat. It offers tours of the area, and provides tourists with loads of pamphlets, maps and brochures on Tolanaro and its environs. Equally helpful are the information counters of the Hotel le Dauphin, Hotel Miramar and Hotel le Galion. All these hotels also arrange excursions to the countryside and have their own private nature reserves, Berenty and Bealoka. Other tourist information is available from Air Madagascar. Good local information about tribal villages and ceremonies can be had by speaking to the staff in the Village Petit Bonheur, not far from the market.

The post office is next to the Chambre de Commerce, on Place de France, above the port. The BTM bank is opposite Mahavoky Restaurant, on Avenue du Marechal Foch. Banque National pour la Commerce is near Delice on the corner of Avenue du Marechal Foch and Boulevard No. 1. BNI (Crédit Lyonnais) is opposite the church, next to the Navigation Trust on Avenue Galliéni.

Tolanaro is arguably the best urban centre in which to apply for a visa extension. There is none of the painful rigmarole that usually accompanies an application in other centres. In Tolanaro the visa is issued the same day if you apply before 9h00, or early the next morning. Tourists are only required to pay for the extension upon collection of their stamped passport. You are required to fill out just one form and give them one photograph of yourself. The office of the police commissioner, which will deal with your application, is situated along a sand road, south-west of Avenue du Marechal Foch. Once you pass Air Madagascar, take the sand road which leads past the sisal warehouses towards Baie des Galions. Speak to the Inspecteur de Police a la Brigade du Police, tel. 213.69.

Opposite the BNI bank is Librimad, where you will find daily Malagasy newspapers, a few outdated French newspapers, French magazines, stationery and a limited selection of books.

Medical treatment is obtainable from the hospital, which is on the seaward side of Tolanaro, at the end of Rue de la Corniche.

To visit the Andohahela nature reserve, see the Manangotry rainforest, or climb to the summit of Mont Trafonomby (1 972 m), you will need a permit from the WWF. It has an office in Tolanaro, north-east of the taxi-brousse station, just off the RN13.

Things to do

Tolanaro has something to interest the majority of tourists who stop here. The biggest attractions are trips to Berenty Private Nature Reserve, affiliated to the De Heaulme hotels, Le Dauphin, Miramar and Le Galion, or to one of the private reserves owned by other hotels, notably the Motel Gina and Hotel Kaleta.

Berenty is the best known of the nature reserves around Tolanaro, and is worthwhile for those who can afford the high prices demanded. It is, however, unique in what it has accomplished and has to show visitors. Get out to Berenty as early as possible in the morning. This is the time when visitors are most likely to see the amazing faunal species that populate this little reserve.

To reach Berenty, visitors can join one of the De Heaulme tours that leave his hotels each day, or take a taxi-brousse from Tolanaro to Amboasary. From there take another taxi-brousse and ask the driver to let you off at Berenty. It is about a 300 m walk to the entrance gate from the main road.

Located close to the main road, the RN13, where it crosses the Mandrare River – a dry riverbed through most of the year – the Berenty

Reserve was started in 1936. For many years the only people who visited Berenty were scientists and friends of the De Heaulme family. Finally, in 1980, it was opened to public visitation. Environmental organisations were so impressed by what had been done to conserve the wilderness of Berenty that they awarded the coveted Getty Award for Nature Conservation to Jean de Heaulme.

Today, over 30% of all the remaining tamarind trees on the "Great Red Island" are protected in Berenty. This alone is worth the tariff charged. People who visit Berenty are assured of seeing ringtailed lemurs, grey mouse lemurs, sifakas, red lemurs and, if you are there at night, sportive lemurs.

Birdwatchers too are in for a veritable feast. The Wildlife Preservation Trust has recorded over 85 species of bird in Berenty. Among the more impressive bird families are paradise flycatchers, shrikes and Madagascar buzzards.

Other creatures that you may see are tenrecs, 28 species of reptile, including the rare and highly threatened spider tortoise, fruit bats and civets (fossa).

Botanists have recorded 115 plant varieties in Berenty and they claim that there are many more still to be catalogued. An area of spiny desert encroaches onto the reserve in the south. This is a fascinating area of harsh beauty and stark images. Most intriguing of the plants are the carnivorous pitcher plants (*Nepenthes madagascariensis*) and *Adansonia* baobab trees. There are also banyan trees in the more vegetated areas of Berenty.

Accommodation is available in bungalows and the rate (high tariff) includes a light breakfast. You can buy lunch, dinner and snacks throughout the day. To arrange accommodation or to take part in an organised tour contact the SHTM (Société Hôtelière et Touristique de Madagascar), BP 54, Fort Dauphin (614), tel. 212.38, or BP 37, Fort Dauphin (614), tel. 210.48.

Another site of particular beauty around Tolanaro is the summit of Pic St Louis (529 m). Walking north from the Panorama Bar, along the beach road, continue through the fishing and sisal-growing villages that hug the coast. There is a small lake used by the locals for doing their laundry. Follow the road to the east of this lake that skirts the fuel tanks of Solima. On the deserted palm-lined beach is a water-pumping station and the last remnants of a forest. Proceed through the trees to the T-junction. Turn left and follow the sand road towards the red-roofed sisal factory (SIFOR).

About 100 m before the entrance to the factory a narrow path turns north, towards the hills. Take this path, which is well marked with white indicator arrows. About a third of the way up the hill is a band of exposed rock that numerous people have used for graffiti. You will usually encounter a few children here who offer to act as guides. Their offer should be accepted, as it is easy to get lost once into the forests on the slopes of Pic St Louis. Visitors will possibly see lemurs, pitcher plants and orchids, plus several specimens of reptiles ranging from chameleons to lizards. Butterflies are also a feature of this wilderness. In the dense vegetation near the summit, you can stand with your arms outstretched and have hundreds of butterflies settle on you in a glorious display of colour.

Tourists who enjoy lazing on a beach all day should visit the beach at Libanona, south of the CBD.

Visitors can also see the site where the first French claim to Madagascar was made, in 1581, at Paroisse Cathedral. There are several graves of immigrant clergymen in the grounds of the untidy garden.

Between the Chambre du Commerce and the Hotel Mahavoky is a lovely little stone church built in 1962. Its interior is cool and quiet, an ideal escape from the heat, dust and noise of Tolanaro. At various places around town, walkers will discover abandoned French mansions. No one lives in them now; their upkeep is just too expensive for the average Malagasy. Next to La Cotonnière – Poste Commercial de Tolagnaro, is the fresh produce market. Busy, colourful, loud and exciting, the market swells on Thursday and Friday with the arrival of people from the rural districts around Tolanaro.

There is an excellent reef off the beach for snorkelling over, but you should wear shoes if you are to avoid being injured by an urchin. The currents can become troublesome during the changing of tides, but apart from that, this large, flat reef is definitely worth seeing.

Tolanaro has a number of nightclubs and other evening pursuits for those so inclined. Travellers in search of loud music, friendly affectionate locals, cold beer and laughter should attend the nightly raves at the Panorama Disco, near the salon de thé of the same name.

Visitors wanting a quieter experience may want to consider going to the Cultural Centre, opposite the sports ground. It has a library, small art studio and frequently shows movies.

Things to buy

Tolanaro is not the ideal place to go curio hunting. It takes quite an effort to locate a curio that is specifically from this region, and when you do the vendors ask exorbitant prices. If you are travelling to the more remote parts of southern Madagascar, between Tolanaro and Toliara, then rather wait until you arrive at some of the isolated tribal villages on the edge of the Spiny Desert or around the Rebobd Manambien hills.

Should you not be travelling overland and would prefer to find something local as a memento, then the place worth browsing through is *Produits Artisanaux du Sud*. It has the largest selection of Malagasy curios. You will find it opposite the Mahavoky disco. Air Fort Services, tel. 212.24, can arrange a shopping trip to a few of the surrounding villages. It can be costly, but aided by a knowledgeable guide you should be able to make some really fine Antanosy, Antaisaka and Antatsima purchases.

Accommodation

Tolanaro has a number of hotels catering to the tourist trade. These range from top-class accommodation, through medium-tariff rooms to basic and cheap guesthouses. The most expensive hotel, but not necessarily the best, is Le Dauphin. In the medium-tariff category, and, in my opinion, the best hotel in Tolanaro, is Motel Gina. Finally, at the bottom end, but suitable for the majority of travellers, is the Hotel Mahavoky.

High tariff

Hotel Miramar, Hotel le Dauphin and *Hotel le Galion,* Tolanaro's three-star tourist hotels, all belong to Jean de Heaulme, have similar prices, well-trained and attentive staff and are pleasantly located around town. These hotels will transport guests from and to the airport, to their private nature reserve at Berenty, and arrange excursions into the surrounding countryside. Miramar possibly has the best location, on a promontory overlooking both Libanona Beach and the Baie des Galions. Visitors are advised to book ahead. Reservations can be directed to SHTM, BP 54, Tolanaro (614), tel. 212.38 or 210.48.

Medium tariff

Falling into this grading are the Motel Gina, Kaleta Hotel and the Hotel Libanona.

Motel Gina has a young energetic staff who seem to have figured out all the right things to do to make your visit a memorable experience. The motel is divided into the original buildings and a new annexe – Gina Village – across the road. There are different prices for different rooms. The cheapest are the basic palm-fond huts behind the kitchen. If you do decide to stay at the Motel Gina, opt to stay in the annexe. The splendid bungalows are clean, airy and have ablution facilities. Transport is provided to and from the airport for all guests.

Motel Gina has recently opened its own nature reserve. Its prices are excellent when compared to those asked by Berenty. A minibus transports tourists to the reserve. Lunch and a guided walk are included in the price. Nonresidents of the motel are also encouraged to take part in a visit to its little reserve: Motel Gina, BP 107, Tolanaro (614), tel. 212.66.

Kaleta Hotel, opposite the church where Avenue Galliéni meets Rue Marechal Joffre, also has a small private nature reserve for guests and tourists. Painted an austere white, the hotel commands panoramic views over the port and up the beaches of the north coast. Visitors have the choice of rooms with full washing facilities, or slightly cheaper rooms that only have a shower. Reservations are not required, and if you call from the airport, the hotel, tel. 212.87, will send a vehicle to fetch you, at no extra cost. The Kaleta Reserve is certainly worth a visit. Situated in rolling semi-desert plains, this reserve competes strongly with that of the Motel Gina. If you have brought a tent with you, then this is one place to make use of it. There is no additional fee for camping and the staff of the hotel are happy to pack you an overnight food hamper. Despite there being no facilities (whatever you do, take along your own water – enough to last the duration of your camping trip), the reserve is pleasant and has ringtailed lemurs, a wide variety of plants and numerous bird species.

Hotel Libanona is set on a hillside, surrounded by whispering *filaos* trees, directly above Libanona beach. Offering guests bungalows in a remote setting a little way out of the CBD, the Libanona is for those visitors in search of serenity and picturesque views of beaches and the sea. A number of incentive packages are available to guests staying longer than five days. Speak to the manager about the discounts offered if you intend staying. As at the other hotels in Tolanaro, prior reservations are not necessary. Simply phone from the airport and someone will be despatched to collect you, tel. 213.78.

Low tariff

In the low-tariff category, the places to try for cheap accommodation are Hotel Mahavoky, Age d'Or and Chez Jacqueline.

Hotel Mahavoky is the place to meet fellow travellers and exchange information about other parts of Madagascar. Located near the stone church, the hotel is in what was once a Lutheran mission school. The size of the ablution and latrine facilities is a clear indication of the age of the initial occupants – young school children. The school was built by a combined team of American and Norwegian missionaries in 1888. The site was abandoned in 1984.

The management is friendly and able to offer travellers a great deal of local information. Due to its popularity, this is one hotel where it may be advisable to make reservations: Hotel Mahavoky, BP 137, Tolanaro (614), tel. 213.32.

The cheapest place at which to stay in Tolanaro is the *Age d'Or*, near the market in town, at the south-western end of Rue Marechal Lyautey. This is a private home with a few attached rooms for hire. Conditions are primitive, but the family who own and manage the guesthouse will quickly make up for any lack of amenities. They are a happy family who frequently encourage solo travellers to have a meal with them and spend a few hours talking about what should be seen in and around Tolanaro. You may arrange to have meals cooked for you, or choose to use the family kitchen to prepare your own food. The meals that the family prepares are tasty and hard to beat for quality, quantity and price. If there is one dish you must try while staying at the Age d'Or, it is the crayfish. No tourist transport is provided and visitors will need to make their own way from the airport or taxi-brousse station to the guesthouse.

Between the Age d'Or and Hotel Mahavoky in price is the Chinese-owned and managed *Chez Jacqueline,* along the RN13. The six spartan rooms are seldom full and therefore no prior bookings are needed. All rooms have showers and are adequate for a short stay. There is an attached Chinese restaurant that does some good dishes with seafood and noodles.

Places to eat

Finding a place to eat in Tolanaro is more dependent on your budget than availability. The *Le Dauphin* has a good set menu and serves a *plat du jour* that, while being small, is always tasty. Prices are rather high, but the service and setting are excellent. The *Motel Gina* too, has a great restaurant that is always full, thanks to the marvellous cuisine. The Motel Gina has the largest menu in Tolanaro, prices are reasonable and the service is top notch. Nonresidents are advised to make a table reservation at least 12 hours in advance.

At the *Panorama Salon de Thé and Restaurant*, diners can choose from an adequate menu that includes seafood and an interesting assortment of snacks. Light meals can be bought from *Delice Patisserie*, opposite the entrance to Le Dauphin Hotel.

Vegetarians or those visitors doing self-catering should do their food shopping from the fresh produce market, near the Age d'Or. There is a staggering selection of fruit and vegetables for sale, and the vendors are a vocal bunch who will crowd around you and occasionally even assist you to bargain with other vendors. In many of the side streets you will find women selling a variety of snacks, boiled vegetables, grilled fish and rice. This is where most of the local Malagasy eat. The food is always freshly cooked, spicy, cheap and filling.

Clustered together near Air Fort Services are a number of traditional Malagasy hotelys. They offer the usual selection of pork or chicken with rice, but have additional delicacies in the form of fresh seafood and smoked eels.

The sleaziest-looking place to eat in Tolanaro is *Chez Henriette*. You will find this restaurant tucked away behind the market. Do not be put off when you first walk in. The staff are overjoyed when a *vazaha* arrives, and go out of their way to please. The servings of Malagasy food are huge and surprisingly delicious.

Overlooking the sea on Avenue du Marechal Foch is the *Mahavoky Restaurant*, which is just as popular as the Hotel Mahavoky itself. Two other restaurants that offer enormous meals and good prices are *Chez Perline*, south of the turn-off to the WWF offices and *Chez Anita*, on the southern side of the CBD along Rue General Brulard.

LAC ANONY

A mere 78 km south-west of Tolanaro lies Lac Anony. This lake, formed by seepage from the Mandrare delta, has a shoreline and nutrient-rich shallows full of seabirds. Many of these are migratory birds from northern climes, which winter in the warmth of southern Madagascar. Camping is permitted to the seaward side of the lake shore. Take along your own food and drinking water for the duration of your visit. A few basic foodstuffs and supplies can be bought from the small market in Amboasary. To get to the lake, you have the choice of an organised tour or public transport. Organised tours, through the Hotel Mahavoky and Motel Gina, include food and drink, and will take you right to the lake site. If using public transport, take a taxi-brousse from Tolanaro to Amboasary. Behind the taxi-brousse stop, turn south-east and take the gravel road another 6 km to Lac Anony.

BETANTY (FAUX CAP)

The biggest attraction to Betanty is the solitude and empty beaches that stretch west, all the way to Madagascar's southernmost point. Equally alluring is what you can see on the beach off Betanty. Lying shattered and scattered across the coarse-grained sands are thousands of fragments. At first they appear like broken pansy seashells, but on closer inspection they resemble ostrich eggs. They are, in fact, the remains of dinosaur-era eggs, from the *Aepyornis*.

A few enterprising Malagasy have gathered up many of these pieces and ingeniously "glued" them together to form a complete egg. Despite most of this coastline being full of eggshells, avoid the temptation to pocket a few pieces. This is a sacred place, the scene of traditional celebrations by the local Antandroy clans during April and October.

To reach this prehistoric site, 208 km from Tolanaro, first take a taxi-brousse to Ambovombe. There find a taxi-brousse to Tsiombe or further west to Beloha, 122 km away. It is about a two hour adventure along sand roads to Tsiombe. From Tsiombe you will have to walk the 26 km to Betanty, hitch a ride on an ox wagon or try to get one of the Tolanaro De Heaulme hotels' tour buses to stop for you. Don't expect too much assistance from the latter. Alternatively, arrange to go on one of the hotel's tours that depart from its Berenty private nature reserve, to Betanty and Tanjona Vohimena (Cap Ste Marie).

There is no tourist accommodation at Betanty. You will have to arrive with your own tent or befriend one of the locals.

TANJONA VOHIMENA (CAP STE MARIE)

This is the southernmost tip of Madagascar. It lies along the coast, about midway between Betanty and Lavanono. There is not a great deal to see or do at Tanjona Vohimena. It is a lonely place, buffeted by the

Indian Ocean and swept by constant breezes. The villagers in Lavanono and Marovato claim that the site once saw a battle between the various Zanahary (gods) who wanted to possess Madagascar. Many of them died and the Supreme Deity, Wakan, banished all the combatants who survived. Pregnant Antandroy women, and very old people from the smaller settlements near Tanjona Vohimena, are not permitted to walk on the beach during the full and new moor.. These are the times when it is believed a few of the Zanahary try to sneak back into Madagascar by way of the unborn child or through the last gasps of an old person.

To reach Tanjona Vohimena takes considerable endurance and desire. Take a taxi-brousse from either Tolanaro or Ambovombe to Tsiombe, or further to Beloha. From Tsiombe follow the route indicators south-west to Marovato. In the village turn south to Ankaratravitra on the coast. Tanjona Vohimena is 1 km west along the beach. If coming from Beloha proceed south to Lavanono. From this seaside settlement, walk south-east along the beach for about 2,5 km to Madagascar's southernmost point. The De Heaulme hotels also run a 4x4 tour to Tanjona Vohimena. They usually combine it with a trip to Betanty. Meals are provided, as are guides and comfortable vehicles. Contact the SHTM in Tolanaro, at Le Dauphin Hotel.

LOKARO PENINSULA

Turning north-east from Tolanaro, a gravel road goes about 15 km up the coast onto the Lokaro peninsula. This is a mystical area of lakes, channels, grassy plains, mountains and canals. It is still primarily rural, but a growing number of tourists are being brought to the area by Air Fort Services.

Exploring this part of south-eastern Madagascar warrants a few days of any vacation. Take a taxi-brousse going to Mahatalaky or Manantenina. Get off near Lac Lanirano. On the lake shore find a fisherman to sail, motor or paddle you across this estuary-like lake and over Lac Ambavarano to the settlement of Evatra. It is easy to find overnight accommodation with one of the fishing families in Evatra. Speak to the village headman for assistance. He speaks fluent French, a little English, and for some bizarre reason, a smattering of Spanish.

East of Evatra is a wonderful beach that is empty all day except early morning and midday, when the fishermen work. From Evatra visitors can arrange a dugout to get across the short strip of ocean to Île

Lokaro. In addition to seeing Île Lokaro, visit the old lighthouse on Pointe Itaperina. The view from the top of this 19th century structure is spectacular.

MANAFIAFY (STE LUCE)

This is where the French, under Sieur Pronis, first landed to try to establish a permanent colony on Madagascar. His settlers called the place Baie Ste Luce, but when they left in 1643, the local Malagasy changed the name to Manafiafy. Manafiafy is graced with beautiful stretches of deserted coastline, smiling villagers and a small private nature reserve. To visit this reserve, ask permission from the Miramar Hotel or Le Galion Hotel in Tolanaro. You may be required to pay a small fee, though a number of solo travellers have recently been allowed in without paying.

Cashing in on this obvious tourist attraction 55 km north of Tolanaro, the owner of Le Dauphin and the other two top-class hotels in the town has built a few bungalows (high tariff). You can reach the site on one of the SHTM tours that leave from the De Heaulme hotels in Tolanaro. Most tourists who make use of the tour book themselves overnight accommodation at the bungalows. However, it is possible to return with the tour minibus the same day.

Independent travellers will need to take a taxi-brousse going to Manafiafy or all the way to Manantenina. These are fairly infrequent and it is recommended that you make enquiries, and reserve a seat, at least three days before you intend going. Ask around the taxi-brousse station in Tolanaro, or speak to a manager of the Motel Gina, who will send someone to make the necessary arrangements for you. Take along your own tent, food and water. The best place to set your tent for the evening is beneath the trees on the edge of Baie de Mananivo.

TOLIARA (TULEAR)

Toliara lies north of the Onilahy River, and although primarily a Bara town, it has links to the Vezo, Antanosy and Antifirenana clans. Toliara is the newest of the provincial urban centres in Madagascar. Origins of the name range from the sublime to the ridiculous. One travel guidebook claims that the name was given by an English skipper who asked a local where he could moor his vessel. "Toly eroa" (make fast down there), was the reply, and when asked what the Malagasy had said, the captain answered, "the place is called Tulear." Another explanation is that the name comes from the ancient Vazimba people, to whom Toliara means "the town that was founded by those who fled from the Imerina waters (lakes?)".

Most tourists who visit southern Madagascar inevitably make a few days' stop in Toliara. Scene of the devastating anti-Indian riots in March 1987, Toliara has now settled into being a quiet, dusty town perched on the edge of vast, smelly mudflats. Despite there being relatively few points of specific tourist interest in Toliara, a few things are certainly worth doing. These include watching the arrival of the pirogue fishing fleet, taking a pousse-pousse ride along the wide tree-lined avenues, visiting the enthralling and highly informative museum, seeing the work and displays in the oceanographic museum and a night out at the legendary Zaza Club. For those who are interested, you can take a 14 km walk south to where the Tropic of Capricorn crosses Madagascar, near the settlement of Anartsogno.

The Vezo tribesmen are considered among the most hospitable in Madagascar. For example, should you find yourself on a beach at which Vezo fishermen are arriving, you will immediately be given some fresh fish as a gift. Travellers who venture into Vezo territory should be aware of the fady that prevail. The following are particularly noteworthy:

- Never ask the name of people still living, or the name of the settlement.
- Never leave the village on your own; you could mistakenly wander into a sacred area or stumble upon an ancient Vazimba tomb.
- Ask which trees, rocks, rivers and springs are considered sacred in the region, and keep well away from them.

Getting there

The easiest way of getting to Toliara from the capital or other urban centres is by aeroplane, while travelling there by bus or public transport is the most enticing.

Contact Air Madagascar or your local travel agent for the current schedule of flights to Toliara. Ticket purchases and reservations can be done at the Air Madagascar office on Rue du Lieutenant Chanaron in Toliara.

Reaching Toliara by road needs some planning and lots of endurance. While there are buses and daily taxi-brousses travelling the whole way from Antananarivo, doing this entire trip in one go is not only exhausting, but also means missing points of interest en route. Completing the journey in one long stint should take about 30 hours, depending on weather and road conditions, not to mention the condition of the bus.

This is the recommended way of making your way overland from 'Tana to Toliara. Take a taxi-brousse from the Taxi-brousse Station South in 'Tana, to Antsirabe. Spend a while exploring the fascinating area around this highland town. Then, take another taxi-brousse, from the taxi station next to the Hotel Manoro, to Fianarantsoa. Again, stop for a while to discover all the delights that the region around Fianarantsoa has to offer. From there take one of the long-distance buses or taxi-brousses to Ihosy or Ranohira. After visiting the Isalo National Park, wait along the main tarred road and flag down a bus or taxi going to Toliara.

Tourist information

Tourist information is available from the capable and helpful reception staff of Motel le Capricorn. There is a tour operator on the hotel grounds who has loads of brochures, maps and pamphlets for interested visitors. On Boulevard Philibert Tsiranana is Express Tours, opposite the Central Hotel, which offers prospective clients detailed information on what to see and do in and around Toliara. Its tours are excellent, well priced and fully inclusive of meals, accommodation and transport. If you can speak and read French, you may obtain information about the area from the French consulate on Boulevard Branley.

The post office is opposite Imprimad General Dealers on Boulevard Galliéni. There is also an entrance around the corner, on Avenue de France. There are three banks serving Toliara. BTM is opposite the city treasury on Rue Gouverneur Campistron, BFV is along Rue Flayelle, while BNI is on the corner of Rues Estebe and du Lieutenant Chanaron, not far from the market.

Visa extensions can be arranged through the local police commissioner. The offices are opposite Lion Star Coiffeur on Route Belemboka. Take along two photographs, your passport and money to pay for the extension. It is usually issued within two days. At Librairie Ny Fandro Soana, visitors can purchase stationery, newspapers and a few magazines and books, all in French or Malagasy.

Prescriptions and basic remedies are available from the Mozambique Pharmacy, near the bookshop. Emergency medical treatment is best sought directly from the hospital. Use the entrance on Boulevard Branley.

For a berth aboard a cargo vessel sailing to and from Toliara, speak to the lading clerk at Auximad Shipping, near the Port Captain's office.

Things to do

One of the most impressive buildings in Toliara is the cathedral next to Air Madagascar. The cool interior offers wonderful respite from walking the dusty, hot streets. The market is a must. Fresh produce, handicrafts, clothing and music recordings are offered for sale from numerous vendors around this crowded marketplace. There is a very relaxed atmosphere about this market, a marked difference to the Zoma in 'Tana.

There are two museums in Toliara: the Regional Museum (also known as the Musée Mahafaly-Sakalava), and the Musée Océanographique. The Regional Museum is on Rue Lucciardi. It is a must for tourists interested in the rich cultures and traditions that abound in this region of Madagascar. Although no entrance fee is charged, a small donation for the upkeep of the facility is suggested by the curator. Concentrating on Vezo and Sakalava tribal customs and artefacts, the museum is spread over two floors.

The Musée Océanographique is on Rue du Marche, near the head office of Solima and the huge fuel storage tanks, along the road from town to the harbour. You must be accompanied by a guide for a tour of the centre. There are several displays of submarine life, but the museum is directed more at research than public information. As at the historical museum, no fee is required, but as a consideration to future visitors, give the guide a few FMg.

Those visitors particularly interested in the arts and subtle nuances of the local tribes' culture should make a trip to the university research building, near the seafront. The staff are friendly and helpful.

Every visitor should see the arrival of the pirogue fishing fleet. Walk along Avenue de France to the entrance gates of the port. The guard will allow most tourists onto the pier and across to the mudflats. The sight of hundreds of small wooden pirogues sailing towards the beach, with sails up and the sunlight casting golden rays, is something not to be missed.

No self-respecting traveller who enjoys meeting the locals should miss at least one night at the Zaza Club, on Boulevard Lyautey. This disco and nightclub is known throughout Madagascar as the place for dancing, partying and a total "rave". If you only ever visit one nightclub on your trip to Madagascar, then make sure it is the Zaza Club.

Things to buy

Shopping in Toliara is enjoyable. Few of the shop owners are overly adamant about fixed prices. Nearly all insist on bargaining and the quality of local craftsmanship is exceptional. Tourists will find a good but costly range of curios for sale in the boutique of *Motel le Capricorn*. Numerous jewellers have tiny workshops around the central area of Toliara. Look for the bijouterie signs on the outside of their shops. As gold is fairly common in this region of Madagascar, the jewellers are especially proficient at working with the precious metal. You can draw them an item you would like, pay a small deposit and return within a day or two to collect the unique piece.

On Avenue de France is *L'Artisan Galerie d'Art*. This is a stop on the tourist trail and fixed prices indicate the fact. The selection is impressive. Visitors will be able to choose from the largest range of curios from south-western Madagascar. It has an intriguing selection of animist masks. These masks exhibit evidence of the African connection and are not only beautiful, but are also said to hold powers for those who believe.

Accommodation

Toliara has several hotels, bungalows and inns for tourists. Naturally, there are also numerous private homes which offer cheap accommodation to travellers.

Medium-high tariff

The best place to stay is the comfortable *Motel le Capricorn*. It is situated on quiet, tree-lined Avenue de Belemboka, a few kilometres out of the frenetic CBD. It is part of the SHTM organisation that owns much of Tolanaro, Berenty reserve and Le Dauphin, Le Galion and Miramar hotels. There are 32 rooms, a tour operator, a pleasant restaurant and a bar. The hotel expects payment in foreign currency from tourists.

However, if you can convince the congenial manager that you only have FMg, he will usually allow you to pay that way.

The front desk is able to make airline reservations and confirm air tickets. Tourists are also able to arrange for tours of the area and obtain transport to the swimming beaches of Ifaty and Manombo. Very occasionally, the staff are able to find transport for you all the way up the coast to Morombe and Morondava. Speak to them as soon as possible after arrival if you plan to travel overland to Morondava.

Meals are something not to be missed. The servings are enormous, the quality of food hard to beat. Prices are higher than in other hotels, but the attentive service and tranquil ambience are worth the rates.

Reservations are necessary. Make sure to book at least 60 days before arrival. Transport will be sent to fetch you at the airport: Motel le Capricorn, BP 158, Toliara, tel. 426.20, fax 413.20.

Another of the expensive hotels, though nowhere near as good in service or quality as the Capricorn, is *Hotel Plazza*, tel. 419.00, fax 419.03. This somewhat fading establishment is at the end of Boulevard Galliéni, on the seafront. It has good sea views and is well placed for excursions to experience the town and nightlife. The restaurant is good and offers a *plat du jour*, a set menu and an extensive à la carte menu. This hotel is seldom full and if you just turn up accommodation will usually be provided. If not, the front-office manager will transport you to the hotel annexe, *Hotel Sud*, in town opposite Glace des As. The Hotel Sud is actually cheaper and a lot friendlier than Hotel Plazza. The rooms may be smaller, but they are clean and adequate for a few days' visit. If you arrive by plane and telephone Hotel Sud for accommodation a vehicle will be sent to fetch you, tel. 415.98, fax (via Hotel Plazza) 419.03.

Medium tariff

Another place popular with package tourists and short-term visitors is *Chez Alain*, tel. 415.27. Situated down a narrow lane opposite the long-distance bus and taxi-brousse station, on Rue d'Interel General, this tourist-orientated hotel is surrounded by coconut palms, bamboo and sand. Accommodation is in spacious bungalows, all with washing facilities and a tropical character; noticeably in the variety and number of insects that share your room with you. The Chez Alain restaurant has an impressive selection of seafood dishes, and a few Malagasy ones, as well as an abundance of Continental food.

The *Longo Hotel* has basic bungalows and delicious meals. The turning to reach this hotel is at the stadium, near the Court of Justice building. There is a large billboard there indicating the way west. In the same price range, but better located, is the *Central Hotel*, in the CBD on Boulevard Philibert Tsiranana. This hotel is a favourite haunt of French expats. It prepares tasty meals from an à la carte menu, and if you ask, will supply you with a set menu as well. Reservations are not necessary.

For those visitors who have the time, consider taking a three hour boat ride to the beach bungalows of *Safari Vezo*. Located on a wild stretch of coastline, the Safari Vezo offers an ideal getaway from the crush of Toliara. Contact it a minimum of 90 days before arrival. For pre-booked guests it will arrange for someone to meet them at the airport and supply sea transport to its site: Safari Vezo, BP 427, Toliara.

Low tariff

A bit of walking is required to find the least expensive places to stay. You should ask around the market. Good places to try are the unnamed bars in the narrow lanes immediately north of the market.

Places to eat

The largest centre in this part of southern Madagascar, as well as a port and public transport junction, Toliara is well endowed with places to eat. The selection is amazing and offers something to suit most tastes and budgets.

As mentioned, the restaurant and dining room of *Motel le Capricorn* is the best place to try for Continental dishes, set menus and lavish buffets. *Hotel Plazza* does a good range of expensive meals that are usually inclusive for package tourists. *Chez Alain* also does an acceptable range of predominantly French cuisine.

Visitors should forego the insulated world of their hotels and venture out to eat at a few of the many restaurants, hotelys, salons de thé and snack bars. *Le Maharadjah* restaurant, opposite Hotel Sud on Boulevard Philibert Tsiranana, specialises in Indian, mostly Muslim-orientated, meals. They are a delight to the palate and can be ordered as sweet, mild or hot. Be warned that the "hot" is very hot. If you choose one of the "hot" curries be sure to also order some milk or yoghurt to ease the burning in your mouth. The restaurant is popular over weekends and you should get there quite early if you want a good table. Opposite the post office entrance on Boulevard Galliéni is the Malagasy *Du Carrefour*. Most meals are traditional here, accompanied by mountains of rice and spicy seafood. This cheap, yet clean restaurant is one of the places where travellers may be able to find accommodation.

At the *Étoile de Mer* restaurant, on Boulevard Lyautey and the seafront, visitors will find the best seafood dishes in Toliara. Each plate arrives piled high with fresh seafood, a gigantic bowl of rice and several sauces. The restaurant's fresh line fish with rice, piment sauce and vegetables should be tasted. It also does a number of dishes which include zebu, pork or chicken. An Oriental menu, that caters to those searching for Chinese and Vietnamese food, can be found at the *Restaurant Sud*. You will find this unobtrusive little place on Route d'Interel General, near the bus and taxi-brousse station and Chez Alain.

Visitors who want to try local Vezo and Sakalava food should walk the busy streets around the markets and public transport depots. The best place, though not the cleanest, is the hotely *Ravinala*, on the edge of the bus station on Route d'Interel General. Its meals are filling, cheap, tasty and made to traditional Sakalava recipes.

For snacks try eating at the *Maharadjah Salon de Thé*, in the restaurant of the same name. It does a fine range of pastries, samosas and hot snacks, plus delicious light lunches. *Le Gras Salon de Thé* is a miserable place whose inattention to hygiene deters most foreigners from eating there. This place is famous for its pastries, iced teas and frothy coffee, if you can brave the insect hoards. *Glace des As* and *Snack Mambo* do a limited range of takeaways, fresh bread and, if their machines are working, rich, fruit-filled ice creams.

Street vendors are another feature of Toliara. You will find them strung out along Boulevard Branley, around the bus and taxi station and near the market in the CBD. Provided that the food they are selling has been freshly fried or roasted, it is quite safe to digest a few roasted zebu brochettes, corn on the cob, roasted seafood or fried samosas. The squid and shark steaks are unique and thoroughly delicious.

To enjoy a drink or evening with some of the locals, go to the little *Bar Mahavita Azy*, down the alley immediately to the north-west of the market on Rue Estebe.

GROTTE DE SARONDRANO

These caves lie about 33 km south of Toliara, at the tiny settlement of Sarondrano. It is possible to do the trip in a day from Toliara. To reach Sarondrano catch one of the early morning taxis which make the journey to Anartsogno or Beheloka. They leave from the bus and taxi-brousse station on Route d'Interel General, usually departing at about 7h00 and taking an hour to reach Sarondrano. A few travellers have reported that hitchhiking this route is also easy. Bear in mind that trucks and supply vehicles going south always leave before 9h00. A pleasant alternative is to shoulder a pack and start walking. Chez Alain will provide transport to guests who wish to spend a night or a few days at its sister hotel, Les Mangroves. You can then hire a bicycle and pedal the 13 km to the caves.

Many travellers rather opt to spend the night at Les Mangroves bungalows, about 13 km north of Sarondrano. Make your bookings through Chez Alain in Toliara, tel. 415.27.

At the bottom of these sacred caves are deep clear pools of ice-cold water. Although there is no geological evidence to prove it, it would appear that the water in the caves is from the same water table that causes the nearby spring of Source Bina to bubble with crystal-clear water. There is a haunting beauty to the caves and in the hills are several Vezo and Vazimba graves. It is forbidden to wander about without a guide here and it is considered fady to swim in, or even splash your face with, the waters in the caves. A guide is easily found in Sarondrano, and for a few FMg will not only show you through the caves and to the source, but will also guide visitors to view some of the sacred tribal sites in the area. Take along a bottle of rum and some food if you go to burial grounds. You will need to make offerings to appease the ancestors for your intrusion.

ANARTSOGNO (ST AUGUSTIN)

Just 4 km south of Sarondrano is the wide sweep of Anartsogno bay. It was here, in the heady days of corsairs and pirates, that many French, English, Dutch and Danish ships dropped anchor to gather provisions before setting out on their hunting expeditions on the Indian Ocean trade routes. It was not uncommon at that time, during the late 16th and early 17th centuries, to find reeking slave ships also moored in the bay. Hearing of this isolated bay, a British empire builder, John Smart, took 100 settlers and sailed for the bay in 1645. Their idea of establishing an English colony was soon crushed. Unused to the weather, without immunity to local diseases and unable to reach peaceful terms with the Vezo tribesmen, many of the immigrants died or were killed. Desperate and terrified, John Smart commandeered the empty British slave ship of Jonas Winslow for the return to England. Of the 100 people who initially landed, a mere 12 arrived back in Britain in 1646.

To reach Anartsogno from Toliara, take either of the two daily taxis that make the one and a half hour trip from the taxi-brousse station on Route d'Interel General. The first usually leaves Toliara at about 7h00, the second departs at around midday. Military vehicles travelling south from Toliara to Beheloka or across the Mahafaly Plateau to Itampolo and Androka will usually give hitchhikers a lift. The best place to wait for a lift south from Toliara is along Route d'Interel General, or outside the airport gate.

There is no tourist accommodation in Anartsogno and unless you can arrange to sleep with locals, you must take along a tent, or return to Toliara. There are some delightful pitches around Anartsogno, but you should ask the local headman where you may set up your tent – a number of places here are fady to foreigners.

The Tropic of Capricorn crosses Madagascar where the Onilahy River flows into the sea. The river spills red lateric silt into the ocean at an amazing rate, most of it coming from the once fertile plains and hills south of the Massif de l'Isalo.

ANAKAO

Across the river, and 20 km down an assault-course sand road, is the fishing settlement of Anakao. The biggest attractions at Anakao, apart from the wonderful people, are the pirate graves and ruins along the coast and on the island of Nosy Ve. Fishermen will take you across to the island from Anakao. In the writings of pirates Olivier le Vasseur (Le Buse), John Avery and George Taylor, there are references to this island. Is there treasure buried here? No one has really searched yet!

Safari Vezo has the most exciting way of getting to Anakao; it sails you down the coast from Toliara in a pirogue. The trip takes about three hours depending on weather conditions. Book your trip through Safari Vezo, BP 427, Toliara, tel. 413.81.

Independent travellers should take a taxi-brousse from Toliara, south to Anartsogno. From there cross the Onilahy River and set off walking along the gravel road that turns towards the coast. Apart from getting a lift in the odd ox cart that may trundle past, you will have to walk the 20 km to Anakao. It can get really hot in this region and walkers are advised to take along water and a hat.

The only tourist accommodation in Anakao is at Safari Vezo. If you are not willing to pay the rather high price at the bungalows, you must make plans to spend a night in a local's hut.

TSIMANAMPETSOTSA NATURE RESERVE

It is possible to reach the remote Tsimanampetsotsa nature reserve from Anakao. Travellers who wish to make their own way to the reserve from Anakao will need fortitude though. You will not find public transport from Anakao to the reserve; therefore you need to trek the nearly 50 km south-east to Lac Tsimanampetsotsa. You need to carry all your own food and water if doing this arduous hike. From Anakao walk through plains, hills and coastal vegetation to the village of Ambilalialika, about 27 km south-east. You can find accommodation with the village headman here. He is a talkative fellow who has a surprisingly good command of English.

Turn west towards the coast from Ambilalialika and take the much improved road to the beach settlement of Beheloka. There are some fascinating Vezo and Vazimba tombs worth seeing around this village. Ask at the small school if someone will guide you to them. Remember to take along the offerings! From Beheloka, it is about a 17 km walk to Lac Tsimanampetsotsa and the 43 000 ha reserve. It is unlikely that you will encounter any park rangers while you walk about this isolated conservation area, but if you do they may ask whether you have a permit to visit here. I was unable to find out whether you did actually need a permit or not, and was allowed to continue my visit without having to pay anything, except share some of my food that night.

On the northern edge of the lake are the Grotte de Mitaho. These caves are said to have once been the home of a sorcerer. Many of the rocks have fossil imprints on them. This prehistoric area has yet to be explored by archaeologists and visitors are still permitted to wander at will anywhere within the reserve.

Lac Tsimanampetsotsa is odd. Due to the dolomitic limestone bedrock that lines the bottom of the lake, the water is milky white in colour. At sunset the reflected sunlight off the opaque waters creates weird shadows on the surrounding vegetation. At night, under a full moon, the white surface of the lake glitters and shimmers, tantalising the imagination and heightening your awareness of how lonely and remote this place really is.

Flamingoes sieve the water through their beaks in the shallows of the lake and add to the pristine and ethereal beauty of the site. There are endemic blind fish that live in the waters of the lake. You are not permitted to catch them, and it is fady to swim in the lake.

Further into the park, higher up the Mahafaly Plateau, are the Grotte d'Andavaka. These caves were obviously inhabited at some stage. Inscriptions on the walls, strange markings in the ground and scorch marks on the walls are all evidence of human visitation. Who were the early visitors? Villagers in both Beheloka and Itampolo insist that these caves were home to the original inhabitants of southern Madagascar, even before the Vazimba arrived. Many of the scratched and dyed markings are similar to those found in southern African caves in the Drakensberg and the sandstone mountains of Lesotho. There are no records of any academic studies being done here, and the archives in 'Tana (at least the one into which foreign visitors are allowed) has nothing on the Grotte d'Andavaka.

There are over 74 species of bird here. In the pockets of dense forest, visitors may see ringtail lemurs in the trees and glades. Those who are sharp eyed may notice the endangered radiated tortoise in the undergrowth or sitting contentedly in puddles.

Other ways to reach the park are on an organised tour with Safari Vezo, tel. 413.81, or hiring a vehicle through the Motel le Capricorn in Toliara and driving down. From Toliara drive north-east to Andranovory. There turn south-east until reaching the turn-off south for Betioky. Cross the Onilahy River at Tongobory, pass the hot springs and drive into Betioky. A few kilometres south of this village turn west towards the coast. From Beheloka it is a short drive to one of the many tracks that go into the park itself. Do not drive around inside the reserve. Rather leave your vehicle on the shores of Lac Tsimanampetsotsa, and walk through this beautiful area.

MIARY

This hamlet, which is about 12 km north-east of Toliara near the southern bank of the Fiherenana River, is renowned for its impressive groves of Indian banyan trees. The origins of these trees, here in this hot and dry region of south-western Madagascar, is something of a mystery to botanists. The trees are protected and it is considered fady for anyone to deface or damage them in any way.

There are frequent taxis running between the taxi-brousse station on Route de Manombo in Toliara and Miary. The journey takes about 20 minutes. The taxis which travel this route are always packed to bursting. The last taxi back to Toliara leaves from Miary at about 16h00.

IFATY

Just 24 km north of Toliara, Ifaty is one of Madagascar's best known tourist destinations. The biggest attractions are the water sports and beaches. The accommodation too is of a fairly good standard.

While the countryside around Ifaty is semi-desert, the beach is strikingly different. Offshore there is a fascinating coral reef which is home to multitudes of fish and numerous plant species. Most of the reefs have been charted by local scuba instructors and divers. To the seaward side of this reef, where the plunging sea walls disappear into the depths of the Mozambique Channel, experienced divers will encounter sharks, barracuda and sailfish. To further entice visitors to the town, many of the tourist resorts advertise whale watching from late June to the middle of September.

Getting there

Visitors have various options to get to Ifaty. The one most frequently used by tourists is a hotel courtesy bus. Should you be booked into one of the hotels at Ifaty, it will send a vehicle to collect you at the airport. You are required to pay for these transfers, but it is the easiest, most comfortable way of reaching Ifaty. By far the cheapest and most uncomfortable way of getting to Ifaty is in a taxi-brousse, from the taxi depot on Route de Manombo in Toliara. Taxis leave for the 45 minute trip to Ifaty throughout the day. The first departs at about 7h30, and the last returns to Toliara at about 16h30. You could arrange for one of the tour operators to drive you to Ifaty for the day, but expect to pay a high price for this. Express Tours runs daily excursions to Ifaty and back to the hotels in Toliara.

Things to do

All four luxury hotels have water sport and scuba diving facilities. The Ministry of Tourism has recently clamped down on poor safety standards at these hotels and now international diving instructors regularly visit the resorts for inspections of equipment and to observe the standards of training being offered. Be warned, however, that a few of them are still not suitable, particularly for novice divers.

Although the hotels offer diving courses, it is recommended that visitors arrive already scuba-qualified. Diving off the reefs here requires some experience in drift-diving and handling tidal streams. One place to avoid at all costs is the diving centre at the Mora Mora Hotel. No qualifications are asked of divers here and the lack of attention to maintaining equipment is worrying.

The best dive and water sports centre is at the professionally managed nautical centre of the Lakana Vezo Hotel. It is known as the Centre Nautique, and nonresidents can also take part in scuba-diving lessons and excursions. The staff are experienced in leading tourists through the underwater wonderland offshore. You may hire well-maintained scuba equipment from the centre and arrange for a dive boat to take you out to the reefs and shoals. While prices are high, the attention to detail makes it a good choice for divers who want safety, knowledgeable guides and reliable equipment. To book yourself onto a dive – if not a guest at the hotel – call the centre at least 24 hours before arrival, tel. 426.20. You can also write to them for details and suggestions of dive locations in and around Ifaty and Toliara: BP 158, Toliara.

The legendary Bamboo Club has the friendliest dive staff in Ifaty. Divers must present their qualifications before being allowed to hire scuba gear, and if there is any doubt the divemaster will insist that you take a short test in the nearby shallows.

All the hotels offer water sport equipment to their guests. While the Lakana Vezo and Bamboo Club encourage nonresidents to use their windsurfers, boogie boards, snorkelling equipment and fishing tackle, the other two hotels refuse to allow outsiders to use their equipment. Whether you are a guest or not, you are expected to pay for the use of all water sport equipment.

Visitors who do not want to get wet yet still want to see the marine life on the reef should ask about the glass-bottomed boat rides offered by the various hotels. Deep-sea fishing trips can be arranged through the Centre Nautique and the Bamboo Club. The high fee includes food, fishing tackle and bait, but excludes drinks and the fish landing fee.

Accommodation

Accommodation at Ifaty is predictably expensive. The two most reasonably priced places are the Lakana Vezo and the Bamboo Club. Lakana Vezo is along the beach at the southern end of Ifaty, while the Bamboo Club is at the northern end, just off the road going to Manombo.

The most expensive, but not the best, hotel at Ifaty is the *Dunes Hotel* (high tariff), built on a gentle headland to the north of Ifaty beach. Guests have the choice of single or double rooms or family bungalows. Prices are high and no meals are included in the rate. The Dunes Hotel does have a good excursion office though. Staff are able to arrange for sightseeing trips to see local flora and fauna.

Lakana Vezo (medium-high tariff) has quaint beach bungalows, good service and excellent food. This is arguably the most popular accommodation at Ifaty and visitors should book well in advance. Contact SHTM, BP 158, Toliara, tel. 426.20, fax 413.20. Sometimes the management insists that tourists pay in foreign currency, but usually backpackers are exempt from this and can settle their bills with FMg.

At the *Bamboo Club* (medium tariff), guests are provided with accommodation in bungalows near the beach. The mosquitoes in this area are monsters, and apart from using the provided nets, you should take along mosquito coils to burn. Excellent meals are offered. Every visitor must try at least one of the seafood dishes. Reservations are not necessary, and if you call from the airport or before arrival, someone from the club will be sent to collect you at the airport or public transport depot: BP 47, Ifaty-Toliara (601), tel. 427.17.

Finally, the dilapidated *Mora Mora Hotel* (low tariff) offers budget-conscious visitors accommodation in bungalows or rooms. This accommodation is suitable for those who don't mind rather basic facilities. The management is courteous if distant, but is able to arrange for a bewildering variety of excursions, not only to the immediate area but to as far away as the Isalo National Park, Fianarantsoa, or even all the way across the Spiny Desert to Tolanaro. Families should take advantage of the roomy family bungalow which can sleep five people, breakfast included. All other guests should note that the charge for accommodation excludes meals, water sport equipment and excursions. Prospective clients are approached by touts on their arrival at the airport; otherwise phone the manager, he will send a car to collect you, tel. 410.71.

IHOSY

Dozing on the southern edge of the central highland plateau, Ihosy is the traditional capital of the Bara people. Situated between the Spiny Desert wastes of southern Madagascar and the cool highlands of the interior, Ihosy acts as the gateway to the south. It is also the place where public transport stops before turning either south-east towards Tolanaro or south-west to Toliara.

A feature of Ihosy is the vast herds of zebu cattle (*Bos indicus*) that graze the fertile plains around the town. Cattle rustling is rife in this region and the feel of a Wild West town is enhanced by the arrival of shady looking characters wearing wide-brimmed hats pulled low over their eyes and driving cattle in front of them. A note of warning. Cattle rustlers are not to be taken lightly. If confronted while stealing they will fight back and if necessary, kill anyone who opposes or hinders them. The regions north of Ihosy, along the road to Fianarantsoa, are particularly notorious. Avoid travelling in this area of Madagascar alone or in a private taxi at night.

Getting there

Ihosy can be reached aboard propeller driven aircraft, bus, truck or taxi-brousse. Of course, it is also possible to get there by hitchhiking, but this will take a long time and you are likely to end up being asked to pay for the ride anyway.

There are Air Madagascar flights to Ihosy on a Monday and Wednesday from Toliara and Fianarantsoa and from Morondava on Saturday. Contact Air Madagascar for the current schedule.

There is daily public transport from 'Tana to Toliara via Ihosy. Rather take one of the daily buses or taxi-brousses going from Fianarantsoa to Ihosy or Toliara. There is also a daily bus and four taxi-brousses making the journey north-east from Toliara to Ihosy and on to Fianarantsoa. In both Fianarantsoa and Toliara the public transport departs fairly early and it is advisable to purchase your ticket the day before departure.

To find a trucker who may be willing to take you to Ihosy, speak to the staff at Motel le Capricorn in Toliara or visit the truck stop in Fianarantsoa. You will be expected to pay a fee that is close to that charged by a taxi-brousse. A truck has a slightly higher degree of comfort.

There is not a great deal to see or do in Ihosy, and few foreigners ever spend long here, preferring to speed on to either Isalo National Park, Tolanaro or Fianarantsoa.

Accommodation

Three hotels cater to the passing traveller trade through Ihosy. The best of the bunch is the *Zahamotel* (low tariff). This place offers rooms in clean bungalow accommodation with ablution facilities. The hotel itself is about 1 km from the local government administration buildings, close to the taxi-brousse and bus station. Meals are not included in the rate, but may be taken in the austere dining-room-cum-lounge. The *Hotel Ravaka* (low tariff) is on the national road through town and is popular with Malagasy tourists. It cooks delicious food that is presented in huge quantities. At the *Hotel Relais Bara* (low tariff), across from the post office, visitors can mix with locals, truckers and travellers in the noisy bar. Many of the guests at this hotel are long-distance truck drivers and travelling merchants.

RANOHIRA

This is the closest town to the spectacular and enthralling Massif de l'Isalo National Park. Most walkers depart from here with guides to explore the runiform canyons, cirques and hidden valleys of Isalo. If you have not arrived with a permit to visit the park, you can purchase one from the Hotel Berny or Hotel les Joyeux Lemuriens.

Getting to Ranohira from Toliara is straightforward. Take one of the daily buses or taxi-brousses that travel along the RN7 to Ihosy, and on to 'Tana and Fianarantsoa. From the north, take the bus going to Toliara and ask to be let off in Ranohira.

Leaving Ranohira is where the problems start. There is no public transport starting out from this village. You will just have to wait and ask each bus and taxi-brousse that stops in town. The best alternative, if coming from Toliara, and planning to go north, is to book your seat for a fixed date and pay half the fare in Toliara. The bus or taxi-brousse will then stop for you in Ranohira.

The *Hotel Berny* (low-medium tariff) is the only suitable tourist accommodation in Ranohira, though a new hotel is being planned closer to the national park at Isalo. This somewhat run-down hotel has capitalised on its position and prices are high for what you get. Meals are available from a limited menu that lacks flavour and is served by lackadaisical staff. The main attraction of this hotel is the festive bar that really gets going on weekend evenings. Hotel Berny is seldom full and reservations are not necessary. This hotel is also the favoured destination of lower-priced tour operators.

For hardier travellers, the Hotel les Joyeux Lemuriens and Rasolafo Guesthouse are better alternatives to the over-priced Berny. *Hotel les Joyeux Lemuriens* (low tariff) has a splendid staff and management who endeavour to accommodate guests as best they can in what they have available. You will need to wash from buckets, but they do heat the water up for you first. Despite the simplicity of the place, this is really the friendliest and cleanest place to stay if visiting Ranohira. Bookings are not necessary. If it is full, the management will scout around for a room with one of its friends for you, and even send someone to fetch you at dinner time.

The *Rasolafo Guesthouse* (low tariff) is rustic, clean, cheap and provides adequate comfort in five rooms. There is no hot water and bucket baths are the norm. Meals can be arranged by speaking to the owner at least three hours in advance. The dishes are creatively prepared, with lots of spices, rice and zebu meat. You will be able to arrange for a guide to Isalo through the owner. Ask him to negotiate the price for you, and arrange for all your food, water and equipment.

MASSIF DE L'ISALO (ISALO NATIONAL PARK)

A visit to Isalo National Park should be on the itinerary of all tourists to Madagascar. Fully inclusive tours are offered by all the large tour operators in Antananarivo, Antsirabe and Fianarantsoa. The most challenging, enlightening and pleasant way to experience the mysteries of this glorious park, however, is to find yourself a guide, hire a tent, buy food and set off into the wilderness on your own.

Established in late 1962, this 82 000 ha national reserve is a geological oddity. The only worthwhile comparison to Isalo is the canyon ranges of mesas and buttes in the USA. Isalo is a mystical place, full of Bara tombs and sacred sites. The cliffs, valleys, canyons and plains of the Isalo National Park are held sacred by surrounding villagers. Often, local guides will not take visitors to certain areas or seem hesitant about approaching cave tombs.

Guides are not really necessary while walking along the main routes of Isalo. The trails from the entrance gate to Piscine Naturelle, Canyon des Singes and Canyon du Rat are well marked and easy to follow. However, if you plan on trekking to the distant sites, such as the Zohin' i Tenika (Grotte des Portugais), the summit of Mitsinjoroy (1 268 m), or across the Keliambahatsy Plateau to Lac Sambalahitsara, you will need the services of a guide and possibly porters. Try to arrange your guide in Ranohira and get him to also obtain a tent and cooking equipment for the trek. You are expected to pay the guide and porter a daily fee and supply all their food for the duration of the excursion.

It seems rather a waste to visit this magical place for just one or two days. Travellers should do a comprehensive hike of the park. I have detailed a hike on a circuit that takes in the major places of interest. If, however, you are short of time, then consider walking to just a few of the sites; those close to the main RN7 are suitable for a one or two day visit.

Starting from the entrance to the park, walk along the trail to the south-west. After about an hour you will arrive at the Piscine Naturelle. This picturesque site is set below an overhang, at whose base there is a pool, shaded by graceful pandanus trees, where you can swim. Following the stream to the west, walkers arrive at a lovely little beach where you may wish to camp. If camping here look around for the shallow depressions in the flat rock slabs, carved over centuries by herdsmen who whiled away their time by playing a game similar to backgammon.

Leaving the Piscine Naturelle, walk north-west until reaching the Andranokove River. Turn north-east here and follow the river through canyons and over stark rocky hills into the Canyon des Singes. Camping is allowed in this eerie canyon, but the villagers in Ranohira request that you do not swim or wash anything in the river which flows through the canyon; it is their source of drinking water. If overnighting in the Canyon des Singes, look out for the numerous Verreaux sifakas that gambol about in the area.

From the Canyon des Singes cross the river and beat your way through the bush and into the Canyon du Rat. The Andranombilava River flows from the Kelyhorombe Plateau through this tree-covered canyon to where it joins the Menamaty River near Ranohira. Close to the village is a pleasant little camp site, known as Manguiers. It is well protected by an orchard of wild mango trees, but tends to get rather overcrowded with tour groups.

If you plan to proceed further into the park to the isolated and seldom visited spots, it is recommended that you employ a guide to take you further from Manguiers camp site. It is easy to get lost in the strange world in the northern reaches of Isalo.

From Ranohira take the trail which hugs the west bank of the Menamaty River. This well-defined route passes a remote settlement at Ianaboty and reaches the gravel road from Beroroha along the Andriamanero River. Turn north-west to follow this river up into the "badlands" and across to Zohin' i Tenika (Grotte des Portugais).

It was here, below the glowering summit of Bevato (783 m), in about 1528, that a band of shipwrecked Portuguese sailors sought refuge. Their ship had foundered on the wild west coast of Madagascar. Knowing that there was a Portuguese settlement at Tolanaro, they were attempting to cross southern Madagascar to reach their fellow countrymen. Whether they ever made it is cause for speculation. There are no records of this episode and the villagers in nearby Bekijoly insist that the cave was used by migrating Vazimba herdsmen. No one knows for sure. That there was human habitation in this large cave is undeniable. The scratchings on the walls and faint inscriptions will captivate the imagination. You may sleep in the cave, though guides seem a little reluctant to and rather choose to sleep outside.

Take the indicated trail east to Bekijoly and return south to Morarano. Turn directly west here and begin the difficult but rewarding ascent to the top of Mitsinjoroy mountain. The views from the summit of this mountain are breathtaking. It is the highest point in Isalo National Park and offers visitors uninterrupted views over canyons, forested valleys, dry river beds, rice paddies and plateaus. The top of this mountain must surely rate as one of the best tent pitches in the world.

From Mitsinjoroy walk south across the Bekoaky Plateau, where you are bound to see ringtailed lemurs and the endangered rockthrush. It is a demanding six-day walk up and down and through numerous valleys, canyons, streams and over high plateaus to the swamp lake of Sambalahitsara. You will not find package tourists or day-trippers along this route and will pitch tent at night in places where few foreigners have ever walked before. Brown lemurs will shyly poke their heads out of the trees to peer at you as you pass by. Birdsong fills the canyons and the scent of nature will be strong in your nostrils. On the sandy banks of the Andranomena River are *Pachypodium rosulatum*, which look like baby bottle baobab trees. In late spring and summer they grow exquisite clusters of bright yellow flowers, which brighten the otherwise drab blondes of this region. Camp on the edge of Lac Sambalahitsara, but make certain that you have something to keep the bloodthirsty mosquitoes away.

The next day follow the path east, across the Keliambahatsy Plateau to the new airstrip along the RN7 national road between Ihosy and Toliara. Walk along this road, past the overpriced Relais de la Reine Hat Soarano and visit La Reine (the Queen) rock formation, about 3 km from the hotel. This odd geological shape really does resemble a queen with her crown. North-west across the Mariany River is the spot called

L'Oasis. When you see it you will know straight away why it has been given this name. About 300 m from the RN7, L'Oasis consists of a number of deep water-filled pools. Camping here is enjoyable and you can spend hours drifting about the convoluted cliffs and the maze of rock passages.

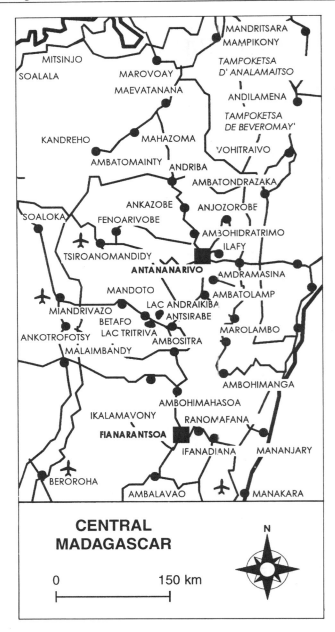

7 CENTRAL MADAGASCAR

Central Madagascar is the highland region of the country. It is also the area in which the two largest cities in Madagascar can be found: Antananarivo and Fianarantsoa. Most foreign visitors arrive in the central highlands and must make their way across the so-called hauts plateaux to reach the southern, northern, eastern and western parts of the country. Central Madagascar is home to the largest tribe in Madagascar, the Imerina. Also found in the central highlands are the Betsileo people, the third biggest tribal population on the island.

It was from central Madagascar that the Imerina kings started out on their campaigns to unite or conquer the other tribes and build a Malagasy empire under Imerina rule that is still evident today. The central districts of Madagascar are dotted with historical artefacts, memorials and graves in memory of the Imerina wars, first waged against rebellious tribesmen and then in defence against the powerful assaults and subsequent colonisation by the French. While the Imerina are known for their administrative, political and military abilities, the Betsileo are renowned agriculturists and herders.

Between June and August, the weather in central Madagascar is cold. At night, temperatures frequently drop to 0 °C and daily maximums seldom exceed 20 °C. April to October is the dry season, and while it is cool, this is the best time to explore and discover the many wondrous sites, cities and villages of central Madagascar.

Central Madagascar has an extensive network of roads, public transport, airports and tourist services. There are regular flights between the cities and larger urban centres and daily taxi-brousses and buses to all the towns. It is the easiest region for travellers to get about in, and has the highest standards of accommodation and tour services and the best restaurants in the country.

The two dominant tribes in central Madagascar are the Imerina and Betsileo. The region populated mostly by Imerina stretches from the Plateau de l'Anjafy in the north to the Mangoro River in the south. A mixture of Imerina and Betsileo then occurs around Antsirabe and south to the Mania River and the village of Fandriana. The territory populated mainly by Betsileo extends from the Mania River in the north, to Ivohibe and Ihosy in the south.

Although the Imerina and Betsileo have abandoned much of their traditional culture and beliefs, there are still a few fady that visitors need to be aware of. Blunders are, however, not viewed as seriously as they would be, for example, in an Antandroy area. Below are a few of the remaining fady that you should treat with the required sensitivity and respect:

Imerina
- During a funeral wake it is forbidden to speak or make any noise whatsoever at midnight, for it is believed by the Imerina that midnight is when the witches go out. These witches are not make-believe either, they are real old women who steal into the tombs at night and dance on the graves of the recently dead. If no noise is made, the mourners believe that the witches will not know that someone has recently died and may bypass the tomb and allow the dead person a peaceful journey to the ancestors.
- Between June and August the "Turning of the corpses" feast takes place in Imerina territory. Known in Malagasy as famadihana, this ritual may only be attended by foreigners who have been invited by a village chief or headman. It lasts for three days, during which the corpses are removed from the tomb, their clothes changed and the major events of the last two to three years are whispered to them before they are re-entombed and the villagers turn to celebration. And what a celebration it is. Should you be fortunate enough to get invited, the following rules apply: keep to the rear of the crowd, never take photographs, avoid speaking or making any undue noise during the actual turning ceremony, join the family in drinking and eating afterwards, but remember to make some sort of offering to the ancestors of that particular village.
- Pregnant women must never sit in an open doorway. This represents the birth canal and any intimation of blockage will lead to a difficult birth and bring shame on the family.

Betsileo
- Children are forbidden from mentioning the name of their father or the village chief.
- No one is permitted to start eating, or even lift the eating utensils, until the father or head of the household has first tasted the food.
- Hedgehogs or any other spiny creature, notably tenrecs, are taboo and may not be eaten, killed or kept as a pet. Even walking into a

village with a hedgehog motif on a T-shirt will result in annoyance and the request that you hide the item away.
- The Betsileo believe that once a person dies, the soul departs to the sacred heights of Mont Ambondrombe in southern Madagascar. For this reason, corpses are always placed with the head pointing south. It is fady to walk on the south side of a recently entombed person. You could prevent the flight south of the soul, meaning that it will become lost and forever wander in search of heaven.
- You may not enter or even touch a new tomb until the local chief has returned after about five days to smear ox fat onto the face of the recently deceased person.
- During the famadihana ceremony, the same rules as for the Imerina apply (see above).
- Never step across the bed or sleeping mat of a pregnant woman.

Whether you only have a week in Madagascar or longer, the following places are recommended as an introduction to the beauties, complexities and problems of Madagascar. They are all within a few hours of Antananarivo, public transport is frequent and several of them have suitable accommodation and splendid restaurants.

ILAFY

Ilafy is a small Imerina village about 12 km north-east of the capital, Antananarivo. Ilafy should be the first site visited by travellers to Madagascar. It is here that the Madagascar ethnographic museum is located, inside a wooden rova atop a hill overlooking the village and rice paddies.

To reach Ilafy, take one of the taxi-brousses going from the Taxi-brousse Station North in 'Tana to Ambohimanga or Ambohidrabiby. They leave every 30 minutes from 'Tana, from about 8h00-17h00. Ask the driver to let you off outside the Société Malagache de Couvertures factory along the RN3. The tar road turns east and winds its way past houses and farms to the base of a forested hill. There is a split in the road here, and visitors should take the right fork, which climbs the hill and ends at the steps leading to the double-storey wooden ethnographic museum, next to the École Primaire Publique.

First built in 1692 by the Imerina tribe's King Andrianasinavalona, the wooden rova (Rovan 'Ilafy) was later remodelled to its present style by Queen Ranavalona I, in 1836. From 1861 to 1863, this Malagasy palace was used by King Radama II as his weekend retreat and for entertaining foreign guests and dignitaries.

The museum is a must before venturing out to explore other areas of Madagascar. Around the outside of the rova are the so-called Royal Trees; fig trees, which were planted around most royal residences belonging to the Imerina rulers of Madagascar. An excellent collection – far better than in the museum in 'Tana – of tribal relics is presented in labelled displays that lead visitors through a maze of cultures, traditions and customs.

The palace and museum are open Monday-Saturday 9h00-12h00 and 14h00-17h00. On Sunday, it is open from 9h00-12h00. There is a caretaker-cum-guide who conducts independent visitors on a French-language tour of the various rooms and artefacts. The tour is free, but a small donation is always gladly accepted.

AMBOHIMANGA

The once forbidden village of Ambohimanga lies about 23 km north of 'Tana. This sacred site was once home to the Imerina royal family, and Malagasy people still travel to Ambohimanga to perform ritual sacrifices to seek the royal ancestors' blessing and protection. It is also considered auspicious to be buried in the revered area of Ambohimanga, hence the large number of tombs you will see in the vicinity. Allowing foreigners beyond its walls has quickly established Ambohimanga as the most visited settlement around Antananarivo.

Getting there

There are frequent taxi-brousses leaving the Taxi-brousse Station North in 'Tana throughout the day. These taxis usually depart every 30 minutes and take about an hour to reach the village. They go directly into the square of Ambohimanga and wait for passengers near the stone gateway. The easiest, most comfortable but restrictive way to visit Ambohimanga is with an organised tour group. There are expensive daily trips from 'Tana to the rova and back, excluding the price of lunch in the restaurant next to the palace. The following is a list of reasonably priced tour operators who may be able to assist you:

Agence de Voyages Mercure, Rue Refotaka, Antananarivo, tel. 229.61. fax 336.73

Aventour, 55 Route de Majunga, Antanimena 101, Antananarivo, tel. 317.61, fax 272.99

MDA Madagascar Discovery Agency, Espace DERA, Route de l'Université 101, Antananarivo, tel. 351.65, fax 351.67

Rova Travel Tours, Rue Refotaka 101, Antananarivo, tel. 276.67, fax 276.89

Things to do

A large stone gateway marks the entrance to Ambohimanga. The round stones which sealed the entrance in case of attack still stand silent sentry to the side of the open gateway. The gate is no longer used and a road has long since made its way around the support pillars and massive lintel.

The rova is located at the top of the hill above the village. Leading to the visitors' entrance, which is in the north wall of the palace, are steps on which sit blind musicians, playing their melodious instruments for pennies and warning the caretakers that tourists are arriving. The rova is open Monday to Saturday 9h00-11h00 and 14h00-17h00. A French-speaking guide, who is also the curator, takes visitors on a free tour of the grounds and palace.

Built by King Andrianampoinimerina (1788-1810), this magnificent Imerina rova offers a unique insight into the world of the monarchs who unified Madagascar. The king's tomb is located inside the grounds of the rova. King Andrianampoinimerina's living quarters – the Bevato – are, to say the least, spartan. The lofty room is made of dark wood, and like all other royal Imerina buildings, is painted black. Incorporated in the construction of this 10 m high by 7 m wide and 6 m long room, were several escape routes should the king's life be threatened. Malagasy royalty seemed to have a paranoia about getting killed and built intricate security measures to ensure their survival.

The king's living space had a sitting area, with logs for stools, and a fireplace to cook over and to provide warmth during the bitter winter nights. The bed on which the king slept was raised several metres off the floor. This offered some security should someone try to assassinate him. He had 12 wives who slept in a communal compound within the walls of the rova. As was the custom, he slept each night with a different wife. She was also responsible for that evening's meal, which was cooked while the king peered down from his raised bed.

Stout rosewood poles at either end of the room were notched and served as an escape route for the king if his room was attacked. The two prominent breasts in the top beam are symbols of fertility, motherhood and the role that the king played in supporting the nation. Arrayed on shelves around the walls are eating utensils, guests' plates and several weapons. The original cooking utensils, from about 1787, are still here, as are the five plates reserved exclusively for the king's use.

There is one ritual that visitors need to be aware of if they are not to upset any Malagasy visitors who may be present. Always enter any building on the rova grounds by placing your right foot forward, and leave by putting your left leg forward first.

Of interest in the grounds of the rova are the place where the king used to suntan, an 18th century form of solarium, secret passageways and escape routes, and the enclosure where the symbolic black bull was kept. A wooden guard tower juts over the king's entrance gate, and overlooks the courtyard where public speeches, gatherings and judicial sentencing were held. Although the king seldom left the security of his rova, the queens who followed him would venture out onto the platform at the northern end of the courtyard and address the populace. There are two sets of stairs to every building. The one set was for the exclusive use of the monarch, while the second was for queens, government officials and visitors.

The two outdoor baths were filled by seven virgins who carried amphoras of sacred water from the holy lake at Amparihy. The kings and queens who stayed here only bathed once a month. There are several sacrificial stones near the baths, and it was here that small religious sacrifices were made with ducks and geese. King Andrianampoinimerina, who died in 1810, was buried in the royal compound, but then in 1897 he was exhumed and taken for reburial in Antananarivo. A private chapel was constructed for the king inside the rova.

Queen Ranavalona I, who despised Christians, did not however destroy the chapel; her animist faith prevented her from doing anything that would upset the ancestors too much. She did not live in Ambohimanga, but did use the rova as a weekend retreat. In 1869, Queen Ranavalona III, who replaced Rasoherina as ruler of Madagascar, had Jean Laborde build her a house in the Ambohimanga palace. Visitors can still see the original furniture used by these queens. Much of the linen and other materials are purple, the colour of royalty. For some inexplicable reason, when Queen Ranavalona I died, the ornate clock in the bedroom stopped at that instant. It has been left untouched since then, blithely showing the hour as 5 o'clock.

Many of the items on display were gifts from foreign royalty and guests to the rova. Of particular beauty is the Italian marble-topped wash basin and original bedstead. From the conference room there are splendid views over the surrounding valleys. The sitting and dining rooms built by the queens are downstairs. Again, there are two sets of stairs leading down from the queen's chambers.

In the dining room is a long wooden table that could be folded out to accommodate whatever number of diners were being granted an audience at the time. There is also a secret doorway in the eastern wall of the dining room, behind the shelves. Mirrors were strategically placed around the room so that the queen could constantly see all her guests and what was going on around the entire room. The wall coverings were done by Spanish, Chinese and French workmen, who laboured beside English craftsmen tooling the crystal chandeliers that still grace the dining room.

On the cement walls of the rova are three cannons pointing to the north-west. In 1787, the king had the two smaller cannons delivered and placed near the main entrance. In 1860, the queen ordered a larger cannon added to the collection.

Once you have finished a tour of the rova, go outside the wall and walk east to the slab of granite that drops steeply into rice paddies. Clearly marked is the sacrificial slab. Take the narrow path to the north, into the trees. A small sacrificial shrine has been constructed here, and there are frequent pilgrims making their offerings. Beyond the shrine, where the path goes back towards the rova, is a hollow in the rock. This stagnant water-filled cavity is said to have some mysterious power that guarantees pregnancy. It is not uncommon to see Malagasy women tossing coins into this hollow and closing their eyes in fervent prayer that the spirit of the queens help them become fertile.

Accommodation

There is no accommodation in Ambohimanga, and with the numerous hotels of 'Tana so close, few visitors ever look for a place. The nearest lodgings are at the *Auberge de Soleil Levant* (low tariff), tel. 426.12, in Soavinimerina, 6 km south of Ambohimanga on the road to 'Tana. The low-tariff and delicious meals make up for the lack of washing facilities, the long-drop toilet and the frequent electrical failures. There are three categories of rooms. All are clean, with enormous soft beds and a place at which to stand while pouring buckets of hot water over yourself.

It is a pleasant walk from the auberge to Ambohimanga, though the final bit near the town does get quite steep. It is also easy hitchhiking from outside the auberge, either to Ambohimanga or 'Tana. Trying to catch a taxi-brousse going to Ambohimanga can be difficult as most of them are full on the way from 'Tana, but always have an empty space when returning.

Places to eat

The best place to eat in Ambohimanga is the *Restaurant d'Ambohimanga*, outside the rova. Perched on the edge of a hill, facing towards Antananarivo and the airport, this restaurant does a tasty selection of food in a beautiful garden. At *La Colline Bleue* restaurant, at the start of the steps leading up to the rova, you may choose from a Malagasy and Continental menu at good prices, with huge servings of food. As the majority of tourists eat at the Restaurant d'Ambohimanga, those that do stop at La Colline Bleue are received like long-lost children.

Things to buy

With the many tourists who visit the site, it is inevitable that a thriving curio industry exists. Outside the rova, you will find trestle tables with a bewildering array of exquisite wooden statues, table settings, toys and fabrics. Bargaining is expected and the prices are a far cry from those demanded in the Zoma of 'Tana. Before reaching the steps to the palace there are two art shops: *Batik Malagasy* and *La Capital Art*. In Batik Malagasy shoppers will find several beautiful works of batik art done by the shop owner himself. At La Capital Art, there is a wider selection of handicrafts, all of high quality, with negotiable prices. In the village, near the Malagasy hotelys, is *La Cabane Arts Malagasy*. It too has a variety of locally crafted goods for sale, and if you give them a few days, they will craft something specifically for you.

AMBOHIJANAKA

Meaning "the place of children", Ambohijanaka is a 17th century Imerina village, situated south-west of the capital. It is a rural settlement where men still work their rice paddies with oxen and animist customs are still prevalent. Few visitors ever come to this village, which has maintained traditional ways and has a wonderfully hospitable populace. Children often run away screaming at the approach of a *vazaha*, but the reception after the initial shock is one of gracious welcome.

Although you can reach Ambohijanaka by road, the recommended way is on the train which runs south from 'Tana to Antsirabe. The ride only takes about 30 minutes. The train leaves 'Tana every second day at 7h00. To take the taxi, go to the Taxi-brousse Station South, near the Hilton Hotel in 'Tana, and take any taxi-brousse heading south. You will be dropped about 8 km from the capital and then must hop on the taxi-brousse that travels the 3 km along a dirt road to Ambohijanaka.

From the train station, gravel paths lead into the medieval village and through the rice paddies to Malagasy tombs covered by wooden huts. These sacred sites must not be visited without a guide and permission from the chief in Ambohijanaka.

There is neither tourist accommodation nor tourist-class restaurants in Ambohijanaka, but there are numerous Malagasy hotelys in and around the village centre. If stuck for accommodation, approach the police or village chief for assistance. More often than not the chief will arrange a bed for you with one of the villagers and you will be expected to have an outdoor dinner with him and the villagers that night.

AMBATOLAMPY

Lying on the fringes of the Ankaratra mountains, Ambatolampy is 70 km south of Antananarivo. Straddling both the railroad and RN7, Ambatolampy is surrounded by rice paddies, exotic forest plantations and tribal settlements. There are incredible vistas from the hills around town.

Getting there

You can reach Ambatolampy by road or train. Take any of the taxi-brousses driving south from the Taxi-brousse Station South in 'Tana along Lalana Pastora Rahajason. At least four each day travel between 'Tana and Ambatolampy. The first leaves the capital at 7h00, the last at about midday. The trip takes two to three hours, along a good tarred road, through scenic countryside, across bridges over raging highland rivers and alongside ancient terraced rice paddies that are still worked in the same manner as in Southeast Asia.

The journey by train is made from the station in Antananarivo, at the northern end of Araben ny Fahaleovantena. The train travels south to Antsirabe, but makes a long stop at Ambatolampy. It departs 'Tana at about 7h00 every second day. The trip takes between two and four hours, depending on the number of passengers embarking and disembarking at each of the stops on the way down.

Tourist information
The post office is across the railway tracks along a gravel road near the market. Just look for the tall communications aerials behind the post office. Tourist information on the locale is available from the Maison du Syndicat d'Initiative, near the memorial gardens, on the main road south from Ambatolampy. Medical attention is available from the Cabinet Medical (surgery), up the cobbled road north of the railway crossing. Drug prescriptions may be filled at Pharmacie Havana, on the main road south of Au Rendezvous des Pêcheurs Hotel. There is also a large military encampment on the outskirts of Ambatolampy. The area around the camp is off limits and no photographs may be taken.

Things to do
Most tourists who come to Ambatolampy do so to reach the heights of the Ankaratra mountains, see the Réserve Forestière et Piscicole de Manjaktompo, take a dip in Lac Froid or clamber to the summit of Tsiafajavona (2 643 m). This leaves the rice paddies, hamlets and people open to the exploration of travellers looking for authentic Imerina culture.

Permits to enter the forest preserves must be obtained prior to arrival, by visiting the ANGAP offices on Lalana Dokotera Razafindratandra Randramazo in 'Tana. By taking a taxi-brousse bound for Ankeniheny, you can walk north from the hamlet to the reserve. Lac Froid and the top of Tsiafajavona are located within the confines of this soon to be proclaimed nature reserve.

Around Ambatolampy, there are several paths that will take walkers into the rural settlements, with their Imerina architecture and Polynesian customs. On many of the hills are stands of blue gum and conifers; part of a scheme started in 1926 to reintroduce trees to the district. To date it has not been very successful, and the organisations involved have finally decided to plant indigenous trees instead.

One of the best places from which to get an overall view of Ambatolampy and the majestic countryside is from the school on the top of the high hill south of town. Walk along the RN7 to the sign which advertises Manja Ranch. Beyond this sign is a sand road to the left. The school is about 100 m along here. Instead of returning to the main road, follow the sand road, which becomes a track through the suburbs and exits on the main road near the railway line. Along this walk, visitors will pass numerous, ornate family tombs.

Where the national road is split by a tranquil garden, there is a small memorial to Governor General Carbit, and to the many men from Ambatolampy who died in the Great War of 1914-18.

Accommodation

The *Manja Ranch* (medium-high tariff) is the preferred destination of tour groups and tourists. Meals can be eaten at the sprawling farm house. Accommodation is in adequate rooms with facilities. The Manja Ranch caters for several tourist activities. Horse riding, hiking and mountain-biking can all be done here. The prices of the excursions are high, but the sheer thrill of galloping across grasslands, or walking through the wind-blown hills of the Ankaratra is not to be missed. Tours into the Ankaratra mountains include a guide, all meals and must have a minimum of four participants.

The most popular place to stay, for foreigners visiting Ambatolampy independently, is the *Au Rendezvous des Pêcheurs* (low-medium tariff), along the main road south of the memorial garden. This hotel has a reputation for fine food and clean rooms.

Near the train station and along the main road is the clean *Chez Marseilles* (low tariff). The rooms are large, spotless and with incredibly soft beds. In the older part of the hotel are basic rooms that share a communal washing facility. Next door, the annexe has first floor rooms, with a veranda which looks out over Ambatolampy, and a shower and toilet en suite. This hotel seldom has foreign guests and the staff try hard to please those who do stay, even going so far as to bring you coffee in bed, at 5h30! The hotel is well placed for visitors arriving by train or catching a taxi early the next morning – taxis stop across the road and the train station is less than 200 m away. No one should miss eating in the hotel's restaurant. Checked tablecloths and fresh flowers create a country setting that goes well with the enormous set menus that feature spicy soup, fresh-water crayfish, rice and crisp salads.

The cheapest place to stay is the *Hotel Faneva* (low tariff) on Place du Marche. Conditions are a little basic here, with bucket showers and a few bedbugs. The Malagasy meals are tasty with large servings.

Places to eat

The recognised hotels all serve delicious meals. Locals, however, prefer to eat from the many small hotelys that huddle alongside the main road through town. The menu is changed daily, but always includes bowls of rice and that strange bowl of hot water filled with green leaves that is given with every Malagasy meal, and is meant to be ladled over your rice. The best hotelys for Imerina cuisine are clustered around the post office in the old suburbs, south of the Mangoro River.

Fresh bread and a few pastries are baked daily at *Boulangerie d'Ankaratra,* up the cobbled lane north-west of the railway crossing. *Boulangerie Mimosa* also does a range of pastries, snacks and has a daily supply of fresh baguettes.

ANTSIRABE

Antsirabe, about 132 km south of Antananarivo along the RN7, straddles a transition zone between the Imerina and Betsileo tribal regions. It is the industrial centre of Madagascar, but has somehow managed to avoid spiralling into a place of pollution and dirt. This enthralling city is also the pousse-pousse capital of Madagascar, and no one is safe from being hounded by these insistent, laughing rickshaw pullers. Antsirabe is one of the most attractive cities in Madagascar. Wide, tree-lined boulevards, thermal springs, colourful crowded market areas and a warm, friendly population make Antsirabe a popular stop. There is something tangibly sweet about the air in Antsirabe. Perhaps it is the 1 500 m altitude of the city, or the fragrance of the breezes that drift over the city from grasslands, forests and lakes.

Little has changed since independence, or even since the Norwegian Missionary Service first set up here in 1872. You can still see its original stone building on Boulevard Marechal Foch. When the French colonials arrived, part of their reason for settling here was to turn the thermal mineral springs into a health resort for members of the colonial office.

Getting there

Getting to Antsirabe is simple. Most travellers use the train which travels between 'Tana and Antsirabe. The train departs Antananarivo every second day at 7h00. There are first and second class carriages. Tourists using first class are sometimes required to pay in foreign currency; it depends on who is manning the ticket counter on the day you decide to travel. There is a substantial price difference between first and second class but little in the way of comfort differences.

There are several daily taxi-brousses from 'Tana and Fianarantsoa and at least two from the west coast town of Morondava. Taxi-brousses from 'Tana leave from the Taxi-brousse Station South, at Anosibe. The first taxi-brousse leaves 'Tana at about 7h00, the last as late as 16h00. There are also night taxi-brousses making the run to Fianarantsoa. They usually accept passengers only going as far as Antsirabe. The trip from the capital takes between two and four hours. From Fianarantsoa, about 238 km to the south, you may take any of the numerous daily taxi-brousses going north. Two taxi-brousses only go as far as Antsirabe, all the others continue to 'Tana. However, these will gladly take you as far as Antsirabe. The trip from Fianarantsoa to Antsirabe takes between five and eight hours. The 15 to 22 hour drive from Morondava is not for the inexperienced or those used to five-star comfort. It is one of the great journeys of Madagascar though, and those with sufficient time are advised to give this Camel Adventure-type trip a go.

Although there is an airfield at Antsirabe, Air Madagascar does not fly to the city, possibly because it is so close to 'Tana.

Tourist information

Tourist information on Antsirabe and the surrounding region is available from the Syndicat d'Initiative Tourism Office, opposite the post office. It has a good selection of mostly French literature and is able to advise on suitable local excursions. The reception desk at the grand old Hotel des Thermes has a few brochures on Madagascar in general and can arrange for tours of the town and into the countryside. At the Hotel Baobab, too, travellers will be helped with useful tourist information.

The post office is on Grande Avenue, which links Boulevard Marechal Foch to the Antsirabe train station. BTM bank has a branch opposite the Ritz Cinema, while the BFV is next to the Ritz Cinema on Avenue de l'Indépendance. BMOI bank has offices opposite the Nouvelles Galeries Antsirabeenes, on Boulevard Marechal Foch. BNI is near the corner of Avenue de l'Indépendance and Rue Labourdonnais.

The Pharmacie Tony, next to Hotel Lito, is a small, well-stocked chemist that can fill most prescriptions and suggest remedies for minor ailments. Bicycle hire can be arranged through your hotel or by going to the Restaurant Razafimamonjy, opposite the market stalls on the corner of Avenue de l'Indépendance and Rue Voltaire. Visitors wanting to try horse riding around Antsirabe or into the countryside will find docile mounts for hire in the small park south-east of the Hotel des Thermes. About 1 km east of the CBD, along Rue Benyiowsky, is the Parc de l'Est, where horses can also be hired directly from the stables.

For orientation purposes, Antsirabe, which means "the place where salt is found", can be grouped into three districts, each unique, each vibrant and each worthy of a few hours' visit. Tourists will find the area between Rue Labourdonnais and Route de Velodrome particularly pleasant. This is where the French built their gracious mansions, lined the boulevards with fragrant trees and filled their large gardens with flowers. It is a quiet area of clean streets, few people and tranquillity. Relatively few Malagasy now live in the mansions. These magnificent houses are almost solely owned and inhabited by Indian merchants. As recently as 1992-3, there were racially-directed attacks on Indian houses by Malagasy. The situation has since cooled down, but there is still a noticeable tension between wealthy Indian traders and Antsirabe's disturbingly large, poor Malagasy community.

The most interesting part of Antsirabe for travellers is the cobbled lanes, alleys and markets clustered around Lac Ranomafana, between Avenue de l'Indépendance, Rue le Myre de Villers and Rue d'Andon. This crowded, odorous area is full of street stalls, pousse-pousses, buses and taxis, the Asabotsy market and a small taxi-brousse station for vehicles travelling west.

In the little park, where Avenue de l'Indépendance meets Boulevard Marechal Foch, is a sculpted bust of one of the missionary founding fathers of Antsirabe, Misionera TG Rosaas (1841-1913). At the western end of Grande Avenue, where it crosses Boulevard Marechal Foch, near the post office, is a memorial to the locals who died in the 1947 Malagasy uprising, which was savagely crushed by French troops. It not only glorifies those who died from Antsirabe though, and there is an honour list to all the 18 tribes that defied the occupying French forces. At Easter, the area around this memorial and all the way to the train station is taken up by an enormous fête.

Things to do

The second busiest centre for precious and semiprecious stone trading (Fianarantsoa is the capital of the industry), Antsirabe has several lapidary workshops that deserve a visit. Look for the bijouterie signs outside the shops. Here you will be able to see skilled craftsmen cutting and polishing the beautiful stones. Their selections of aquamarine, amethyst and zircon semiprecious stones are well priced. Dealings in emeralds and other precious stones requires some knowledge of what you are doing and the ability to negotiate with wily Indian traders.

The Parc de l'Est and Arboretum d'Ivohitra are certainly worth an afternoon's visit, even if just to lie on your back in the long grass and watch the clouds passing by. The cathedral on Avenue de l'Indépendance is a massive church of intricate Gothic architecture. An impressive crucifixion statue – for the 1933 jubilee – is just outside the church.

Then, of course, there are the thermal spa baths. They must have been glorious during the colonial period, but have recently been allowed to slip into a somewhat shoddy state. Not many foreigners use the facility anymore, which is a pity as the resort relies heavily on tourist visits to maintain the site. A swimming pool, near the thermal baths, offers a cool dip after the hot soak in the mineral tubs. There is an entrance fee to the pool and you will need to bring your own towel. Prices at the spa are high, but well worth paying after a strenuous day cycling or hiking. Massages are also offered, though whether the staff are trained in the art is dubious. The spa also has a curative programme that is apparently beneficial for those who suffer from rheumatism. This treatment schedule takes a week and is monitored by qualified staff and a medical doctor.

Lac Ranomafana is an artificial lake that was constructed to allow the escape of thermal gases from the mineral springs. It is an unimpressive swamp that bubbles with smelly brown mud. When it rains, the lake gets a small amount of water that seeps into the ground and results in a riot of colourful flowers, which carefully hide the ugly, shrinking site. There are several unofficial thermal baths around the lake. Those on the south side managed by the Hotel Niavo Fitsangantsanganana are cheap and basic. You will be given a metal bucket full of the pungent-smelling water, and a big spoon.

The Bain Thermal et Piscine is open Monday and Tuesday 8h00-10h00 and 14h00-17h00, Wednesday to Friday 8h00-12h00 and Saturday 14h00-17h00. For some odd reason the swimming pool is closed on Saturday morning and all day Sunday.

Guided tours of the Star Brewery are conducted on Monday, Wednesday and Friday mornings. Prior reservations are necessary and should be made about five days in advance through the head office in Antananarivo: Star Madagascar (Brasserie), BP 3806, Rue du Dr Raseta, Andranomahery 101, Antananarivo, tel. 277.11, fax 346.92.

Antsirabe's nightlife is surprisingly placid. Club Sagittaire is on the corner of Grande Avenue, near the train station, and is a favourite of locals. Although it plays most nights of the week, it really gets going on Friday and Saturday evening from about 22h30. At the Diamant Hotel there is a modern nightclub, Club Tahiti. This is where most tourists go, and the atmosphere is definitely First World. Doors open at 21h30, but nothing happens until after midnight.

Things to buy

Shopping in Antsirabe usually includes visits to the many jewellers that can be found around town and to the handicraft centre of *Groupements des Artisans d'Art d'Antsirabe*, up a lane north on Boulevard Marechal Foch. The quality of workmanship is exceptional and the prices reasonable. One memento that every visitor who spends any length of time in Antsirabe should buy, is the little handmade pousse-pousse models. It may be difficult to find these little treasures, so if you are unable to locate them in the market, speak to the staff at the Manoro Hotel. Staff members will send someone to fetch the chap who makes them from wood, strips of fabric, wire and plastic.

Accommodation

Antsirabe offers suitable accommodation for all levels of travellers; from the elegant halls of the colonial Hotel des Thermes, to the military dormitory of the Cercle Mess Antsirabe.

At the top end of the market is the *Hotel des Thermes* (medium-high tariff). This elegant 18th century building lends a gracious and old-world charm to the Boulevard Marechal Foch, above Lac Ranomafana. Accommodation is provided in suites, standard rooms and the attic. Bathrooms en suite and tastefully furnished rooms offer comfortable beds and panoramic views. The hushed tones in the restaurant and personalised service add to the gentility of the Hotel des Thermes. Tennis courts and a sparkling swimming pool complete the establishment. Excursions, bicycles and horse riding can be organised for guests.

Near the corner of Boulevard Marechal Foch and Route d'Andranobe is the *Diamant Hotel* (medium-high tariff), tel. 488.40. Rooms have showers or baths, and a reputable restaurant serves food from a comprehensive menu that includes a few vegetarian dishes.

The best accommodation for travellers is the *Manoro Hotel* (medium tariff), tel. 480.47. Located next to the Taxi-brousse Station North and

South, the Manoro is popular with independent travellers. It has an excellent restaurant that serves tasty dishes from a large menu, at reasonable prices. The *plat du jour* is recommended if you are on a budget but hungry. Rooms are clean, with washing facilities and good views of Antsirabe. There are 13 rooms in two categories, but despite the difference in price the only actual difference is the size of the room.

Opposite the military mess on Boulevard Marechal Foch is the *Hotel Trianon* (medium tariff). Renowned for its excellent cuisine, the Trianon offers accommodation in large rooms that look out onto the central suburbs of Antsirabe. The French owner is fastidious about cleanliness. He sells local handicrafts made from rare wood, stone and natural fibres and will offer precious and semiprecious stones.

The *Hotel Soafytel* (medium tariff), tel. 480.55, opposite the BNI bank on Avenue de l'Indépendance, is another popular place for travellers. Rooms have either showers and communal toilets, or complete en suite bathrooms. The sedate Pierger Restaurant, in the hotel building, offers good meals, notably vegetarian cuisine, but is closed all day Sunday. Tours and excursions, bicycle hire and horse riding can be arranged by speaking to the manager. In a slightly lower price range is the *Hotel and Resto Baobab*, tel. 483.93, on the corner of Avenue de l'Indépendance and Rue Benyiowsky. This run-down hotel has a few permanent expats, and the veranda gets really noisy with visiting Malagasy salesmen most nights of the week.

The very basic but functional *Hotel Bon Voyage* (low tariff) is on Avenue de l'Indépendance. Some protection against visitors, of the insect variety, is recommended when staying here. Despite the lack of hygiene, the hotel serves delicious Malagasy meals and the attentive manageress goes out of her way to make your stay as enjoyable as possible.

Male travellers may find short-stay accommodation at the army's *Cercle Mess Antsirabe*, tel. 483.66, opposite SA Ranomanoro on Boulevard Marechal Foch. Prices are low, and as can be expected, conditions austere. There are rooms with showers or a communal shower near the dormitory quarters. No meals are offered to tourists, so you will need to dine at one of the other hotels or the many eateries scattered about Antsirabe.

Another "cheapy" is the *Hotel Rubis* (low tariff). There are communal washing facilities serving the homely rooms, and the location is suitable for walks around central Antsirabe. The tariff includes a Continental breakfast, but lunch and dinner are at extra cost from an à la carte menu. With a dedicated staff and committed management, the increasing popularity of the Hotel Rubis is not surprising. The hotel is on Boulevard Marechal Foch, but the entrance is at the back of the building.

By taking the lane west of the cathedral, you will find *Le Synchro Restaurant and Hotel* (low tariff). A few basic rooms are offered here, and the restaurant serves meals from a verbal menu that includes freshwater crayfish, zebu steak and fresh salads.

The *Hotel Niavo Fitsangantsanganana* (low tariff) is on the southeastern side of Lac Ranomafana. It has shabby rooms with wondrous views of the lake and flowers, offers thermal spring water from buckets and can arrange meals if you order at least two hours ahead.

Also in this price category is the *Villa Nirina,* tel. 485.97, at the northern end of Boulevard Marechal Foch. The biggest advantage to staying here is that the owner can speak English. She prides herself on her delicious cooking as well. Visitors should try her giant pizzas with all the trimmings. In the restaurant are dishes made to Malagasy, Continental and American recipes. Accommodation is in spotless rooms in a quiet area of Antsirabe.

The Malagasy hotel, *Hotel Antsirabe* (low-tariff), is near the junction of Rue le Myre de Villers. Next door is the equally reasonably priced *Tantely Hotel,* which is known more for its extensive, cheap, set menus than its accommodation. A word of warning if you do try the set menus: eat quickly. The dishes arrive every 10 minutes, so that by the time dessert arrives your table will be strewn with plates and possibly uneaten Malagasy delicacies. *Hotel Stop* (low tariff), is a Muslim hotel. The rooms are clean and comfortable, though the early morning call to prayer may upset visitors who enjoy sleeping later than 4h30.

Places to eat

While many visitors may be tempted to only dine at their hotel, you should consider a few meals in one of the numerous restaurants, salons de thé and hotelys of Antsirabe. *La Fleuve Parfum Restaurant* offers a large selection of Vietnamese and Malagasy dishes at good prices with abundant servings. Opposite the market, in the CBD, is *Restaurant Razafimamonjy.* It specialises in Malagasy cuisine and has a crowded bar that fills up quickly at lunch time and in the evening. It is a good place to meet locals while sampling Antsirabe home brew.

The most acclaimed restaurant in Antsirabe is *La Halte,* near the corner of Route d'Andranobe and Route de Velodrome. It has a comprehensive menu of Continental food, plus a few Malagasy and Chinese meals as well.

For breakfast, snacks and fresh pastries make sure to pay a visit to the marvellous salons de thé. The *Helena Salon de Thé and Bakery*, near Hotel Soafytel, bakes bread and cakes daily and does a delicious, filling breakfast of café au lait, croissants, home-made jam, fruit and a slice of cake. At the Muslim-run *Salon de Thé Moderne*, on Boulevard Marechal Foch, there is a wide selection of fresh pastries and a good range of snacks and enormous sandwiches.

Hotelys are grouped around the two taxi-brousse stations and along Rue le Myre de Villers. Those at the Taxi-brousse Station North and South are well known for their chicken and sauce dishes. In the alleys of the Asabotsy market you will find many street vendors selling hot snacks, fresh produce, local wine and Malagasy rum.

LAC ANDRAIKIBA

Lac Andraikiba is about 8 km west of Antsirabe, along the tarred RN34 to Betafo. To reach this small lake in the caldera of a long-since extinct volcano, you need to go to the Taxi-brousse Station West and take a Betafo taxi-brousse. They leave every hour and will drop you along the main road, at the hamlet of Talata, about 1 km north of Lac Andraikiba.

There is also a local bus that departs every two hours from outside the Asabotsy market. A few tourists hire a taxi-be for the trip. It is expensive and the drivers are often in a hurry to get back, leaving you precious little time to explore the countryside around the lake. One of the most pleasant ways of reaching Lac Andraikiba is to hire a bicycle in Antsirabe and spend a few hours pedalling about the lake and region. Many of the hotels will even pack you a cold lunch for your outing. A few hardy individuals walk the 8 km to the lake.

From where the taxi-brousse drops you off there is a well-used gravel track running down to the lake. This track circles the lake, and by following it along the banks of the Iandratsay River you will reach the main road again, at the rural settlement of Masinandraina, in the shadow of Mont Androhibe (1 639 m).

It was to Lac Andraikiba that Ranavalona II would come, during her 15 year reign, to escape the chaos and pace of Antananarivo. Surrounded by gentle hills, shallow valleys and a reserved populace, the lake was once the site of a French colonial retreat during their domination of Madagascar.

As expected, there is a legend associated with Lac Andraikiba. It seems that an Imerina nobleman made a local maiden pregnant in 1885, and was in two minds whether to marry her or another woman from a better lineage. Apparently both women were hopelessly in love with this fellow. To resolve the matter, he demanded that they take part in a swimming race across Lac Andraikiba. Handicapped by an advanced pregnancy, the one woman drowned and her body was never recovered from the depths of the lake. Local villagers say that on certain summer mornings, and at full moon in December, she can be seen sitting on the rocks that mark the southern rim of the lake.

LAC TRITRIVA

Also situated in the caldera of a volcano, Lac Tritriva is about 20 km south-west of Antsirabe. One of the great mysteries of Madagascar's environment remains unsolved at Lac Tritriva. For some inexplicable reason, though no lack of theories, the level of the water in the lake rises during the dry season and falls during the rainy season.

You can reach Lac Tritriva by taking a taxi-brousse or trekking west to Lac Andraikiba, and then walking south for 12 km. Alternatively, hire a bicycle or walk from Antsirabe directly to Lac Tritriva. It should not take longer than about four hours to reach the lake shore. The route from Antsirabe to Lac Tritriva immediately shows visitors the lives of the rural Malagasy.

Dwarfed by green, erosion-scarred hills, Lac Tritriva also has a sad legend associated with it. Local folklore tells of two young lovers, who, forbidden to marry, threw themselves from a steep cliff into the deep blue waters of the lake. When they were eventually pulled out of the lake, it is said that where their hearts had been was a space filled by a single Comet orchid. As a memorial to their tragic love, someone entwined two saplings together, which now grow as one. Locals say that the lake is cursed and the changing hues of the blue water are the souls of the lovers trying to escape their limbo. Geologists, however, have a more dull and soulless explanation for the changing colours – volcanic lava tubes suck and expel water as the magma deep in the earth shifts. Do not make the mistake of thinking that Lac Tritriva is extinct. As with the enormous volcanic crater on Grande Comore, this water-filled caldera is continuously monitored and regularly shows signs of subterranean activity.

There is no tourist accommodation at either of these lakes, but the villagers around the lakes are hospitable and quite likely to assist you if approached for shelter.

BETAFO

Meaning "many red roofs" in the Imerina dialect, Betafo is recommended for those who have limited time in Antsirabe. It is typical of the traditional villages in the central highlands and is well worth a few hours' walking tour.

Visitors can reach Betafo by taxi-brousse or bus from the Taxi-brousse Station West in Antsirabe. Taxis leave every hour between 8h30 and 17h00. There are also two buses that travel between Betafo and Antsirabe Monday to Saturday. It is also fairly easy to hitchhike from Antsirabe to Betafo, though you must get beyond the Star Brewery before sticking out your thumb.

The best way of experiencing this town is to wander about the streets alone. South of the taxi-brousse station is a magnificent Roman Catholic cathedral that deserves a visit and a few minutes' introspection in its cool blue, serene interior. The colourful stained lead-glass windows depicting Catholic saints are from the last century, and lend an ethereal air to the whispering cornices.

Scattered around the lanes and alleys of Betafo are numerous stone monoliths. These are dedicated to a long line of local chieftains who were active in their fight for independence from the oppressive rule of France. Known as vatolahy, these rock slabs, with their strange motifs and chiselled designs, can be seen near the market, down the road near the Solima fuel station and in the lanes both north of the hospital and behind the cathedral.

A memorial to those from Betafo who died in the 1914-18 war is surrounded by the stalls of the fresh produce market, east of the taxi-brousse station. The usual 1947 memorial to the Malagasy uprising can be viewed (again) near the Bar Volatiana.

Walking north into the hills for about 3 km, through the terraced rice paddies, you will come to the picturesque waterfall of Chute d'Antafofo, along the river that flows from Lac Andranobe. The pool at the base of this waterfall is deep and offers a lovely place to cool off with a swim after the walk from Betafo.

Although there is no tourist accommodation in Betafo — Antsirabe is so close anyway — there are several Malagasy hotelys serving good local food. Near the fresh produce market and covered meat market are the hotelys *Nirado* and *Miladial*. Their pork cutlets, stewed vegetables and rice are tasty and filling. The nearby *Hotely Malala* offers a similar menu, but also serves fresh river fish and crisp salads. Along the main road, diners will find the hotelys *Ny Antsika*, *Soa* and *Betafo*. If stuck for a place to sleep, you can arrange something with the staff in the hotely Betafo.

AMBOSITRA

Located at the northern end of the Betsileo tribal regions, Ambositra means "the place of eunuchs", after the humiliating actions exacted on the Betsileo warriors who were defeated by the powerful armies of the colonising Imerina from Antananarivo.

You can reach Ambositra, about 89 km south of Antsirabe along the RN7, by daily taxi-brousse. Although there are no taxi-brousses only going as far as Ambositra, all those that travel to Fianarantsoa will gladly take you along. You will find these taxis departing from about 7h00 at the Taxi-brousse Station North and South in Antsirabe. The trip takes about two hours and passes through some beautiful countryside, edging the misty heights of Col des Tapia and the lofty summit of Mont Ibinty (2 252 m), on the upper reaches of the Mania River.

The main reason for visiting Ambositra is to look for the remarkable Zafimaniry wooden carvings (sculpture marqueterie). The biggest and most reasonably priced selection of carvings is at the old monastery which is now a co-operative facility for sculptors from the Zafimaniry villages around Ambositra. The finest and most intricate of the wooden statues and furniture come from the remote villages in the forests along the Sakaleona River and the town of Analamarina. If you can spare the time, take a few days' hike from Ambositra across the hills and valleys and into the forests to Analamarina. If you have not found a carving by then, it is unlikely that you ever will. Particularly impressive are the steel knives hidden inside tooled wooden walking sticks.

An interesting museum is located on the hill of Ambositra Tompon' anarana. Not many tourists know of this place. You will be given a detailed guided tour, in French, of the fascinating exhibits that depict the history of the Betsileo, Zafimaniry and Tanala peoples. Entrance is free, but the curator does appreciate a small donation for upkeep.

There is a large market in Ambositra that swells to double its size on Thursday and Friday, when rural people flock into town with their livestock, fresh produce and handicrafts. A fascinating few hours can be spent wandering about the lanes, gazing at the delicate architecture and fine craftsmanship that goes into the building of Betsileo homes.

There are only two places worth considering for tourist accommodation: the Grand Hotel and Hotel Violette. The *Grand Hotel* (low-medium tariff) tel. 712.62, is near the taxi-brousse station in the centre of town. It offers a good restaurant and acceptable rooms. The *Hotel Violette* (low-medium tariff), tel. 711.75, is south of the CBD. Its local speciality meals are highly recommended and you will find numerous independent travellers staying here.

Hardened travellers might think about staying at the sweetly named *Hotel Baby* (low tariff), near the market. The management is overjoyed to have foreigners staying and, although you must share a communal washing facility, the visit is nearly always pleasant. The staff cook up wonderful meals and then sit down to watch you eat, jabbering away in French, Malagasy and colourful English.

FIANARANTSOA

Surrounded by shallow valleys, cliffs and wooded hills, Fianarantsoa is Madagascar's city par excellence. The name is derived from two Malagasy words: Fianar, which means "study" and Soa, which means "good". Therefore, the name means "the place where good is studied", and is thought to refer to the huge numbers of Christian missionaries who descended on the area and brought Biblical teachings to the Betsileo nation. Fianarantsoa is also renowned as the town of intellectuals. There are colleges, seminaries, schools and university faculties, and the town is crowded with students and academics. Fianarantsoa is a lovely, cool town with classical Betsileo architecture, cobbled lanes, preciousstone merchants and several sites worth visiting.

Founded by Queen Ranavalona I in the 19th century, Fianarantsoa was modelled on Antananarivo and served as a forward military garrison for Imerina soldiers exerting the queen's authority over the southern regions of her empire.

Fianarantsoa is actually divided into two parts: the original town or Haute Ville, and the lower town or Basse Ville. Haute Ville is an interesting maze of cobbled lanes and steep alleys which edge numerous churches and schools and offers panoramic views over the suburbs and agricultural fields that make up the magnificent medieval city. Basse Ville is where most of the inhabitants live, and is the area where travellers will find suitable accommodation.

Getting there

Visitors can reach Fianarantsoa by plane, road or rail. Air Madagascar flies to Fianarantsoa on Monday, Wednesday, Thursday and Saturday, from Toliara, 'Tana and Morondava, with various stops en route. Contact them or a travel agent for the current schedule and fares.

There are daily taxi-brousses running from Antananarivo and Antsirabe to Fianarantsoa. There is also a regular bus service between Toliara and 'Tana, which stops for passengers in Fianarantsoa. A train runs through the rainforests between Fianarantsoa and Manakara.

Most tourists to Fianarantsoa arrive by road from points north and south, though an increasing number of travellers have begun to come from the east coast towns of Mananjary and Manakara. From Antananarivo, taxi-brousses leave daily from the Taxi-brousse Station South. It is advisable to reserve your seat the day prior to departure. The first taxi-brousse leaves at about 7h00 and the last at around 14h00, depending on the number of passengers. This journey takes between eight and 10 hours, with frequent stops for meals, drinks and shopping. If you take one of the early morning taxi-brousses, an hour-long lunch stop is usually made in Antsirabe.

Buses also leave daily from Toliara and take the atrocious RN7 past the Massif de l'Isalo and Ihosy, and stop in Fianarantsoa, before pressing on to Antananarivo. The bus leaves Toliara at about 9h00 and gets into Fianarantsoa at 20h00 that same night.

The train trip between Fianarantsoa and Manakara is not to be missed. The train passes through some of the most beautiful forest regions of Madagascar. There are both first and second class carriages, and the train runs down to the coast one day and returns to Fianarantsoa the following day. It leaves at 7h00.

Tourist information

Tourist information is available from several places and people in Fianarantsoa. There is a Syndicat d'Initiative a block west of Chez Papillon, but it has limited literature and is not particularly keen on assisting independent or solo travellers. A better alternative is Sud Voyages, beneath the sports stadium in Basse Ville. It has a good selection of tours available and also gladly hands out small town maps and makes useful suggestions about what you can see and do while in Fianarantsoa. In Haute Ville, at the Hotel de Madagascar, is Transile and Frontiere Voyage. It runs excellent trips around Fianarantsoa and further afield, notably into the spiny deserts of southern Madagascar.

At the Sofia Hotel, on Nouvelle Route d'Antananarivo, at the northern side of town, you will find tourist information from the reception desk and the travel agents located in the shopping arcade. However, your best contact for tourist information on Fianarantsoa and its environs is Angelo Rakotonirina. He hangs about the Chez Papillon; just ask for him at the restaurant, or write to him a few weeks before arrival in Fianarantsoa: Angelo Rakotonirina, 114 Cité Antarandolo, 301 Fianarantsoa. He can also be contacted telephonically: 508.15. This chap has compiled a comprehensive list of things to see and do in and around Fianarantsoa, has excellent contacts for cheap hotels and can arrange car hire and tours to southern Madagascar. His fees for guiding are reasonable and his knowledge of local customs and culture will have you coming away with a profound understanding of the Betsileo, the highland environments and the problems facing this region of Madagascar.

The post office is across Rue MDRM, opposite the train station in Basse Ville. There is another, smaller post office in Haute Ville, on Rue Ichonard Smadia. All the banks, BNI, BTM and BFV, are grouped together along Rue Philibert Tsiranana, on the way to the summit suburbs of Haute Ville, in what is known as Nouvelle Ville. The Sofia Hotel is also able to change foreign currency and cash traveller's cheques. Traveller's cheques transactions are handled during official working hours, and thereafter hard currency only is changed at the reception desk.

Visa extensions can be arranged through the commissioner of police on Rue Ichonard Smadia. You need to fill in forms in triplicate, have two passport photos, FMg, and wait for two days while the visa is processed. Books, maps, newspapers and magazines are available from the Librairie Mamy on Rue Nouvelle Route d'Antananarivo. A smaller bookshop, Librairie du Sud, is near the Somacodis Building in Basse Ville. Permits to visit Ranomafana or any other nature reserve in central and southern Madagascar may be purchased from the Service Provincial des Eau et Forêts Fianarantsoa. To find the rather well-hidden office, take the narrow lane that goes uphill and west of the taxi-brousse station. The office is around the corner on the right.

Medical assistance is available from the sprawling hospital on the aptly named Rue Pasteur in Basse Ville, on the way to the suburb of Mazavatakona. There is a well-stocked dispensary that dispenses prescription drugs. Opposite the train station is Pharmacie Lam Seck Roland, where the chemist is able to diagnose minor illnesses and supply a variety of remedies for upset stomachs, flu, colds and aches.

In the grounds of the Sofia Hotel visitors will find a photo shop with a comprehensive supply of photographic goods. It has stocks of print film, a few colour reversal slide films and batteries, offers developing and can carry out basic repairs to camera equipment.

Things to do

The best way to appreciate what Fianarantsoa has to offer is to shoulder a day-pack and set off on a solo walking tour of the city. All the roads in Basse Ville are named after some or other Imerina or Betsileo prince.

In the CBD, there are many small cobbled and gravel alleys that deserve exploration. They lead walkers into the cluttered suburbs of Fianarantsoa's Basse Ville. Along Rue Xavier Thoyer is the clothing market. In a myriad wooden cubicles, colourful though poor quality clothing is sold at bargain prices. On Rue Frere Raphael Louis Rafiringa is a magnificent Roman Catholic cathedral, whose doors are always open and provide a tranquil haven after braving your way through the markets.

There are two mosques that allow visitors Monday to Thursday. The one is in Basse Ville and the other near the banks. High on the cliffs of Kianjasoa (1 370 m) is a statue of St Joseph holding baby Jesus. You can reach the statue either from Haute Ville or by way of Route de la Grande Corniche. The views from up here are spectacular and provide an excellent way of getting your bearings.

In Haute Ville several churches cluster together on the hilltop. The Christian edifice that steals the show is undoubtedly the sacrosanct chapel of Ste Camille, in the grounds of the hospital in Basse Ville. In an alley opposite the stadium is an old neglected mosque that must have once been a grandiose building. Now it is cared for by an ancient mullah who will regale interested visitors with the fascinating history of Islam in Madagascar.

On the way to the main market, on the top of the hill above the taxi-brousse station, is the Civilisation Museum (Anthropological) of the university. Visitors are welcome here from Monday to Friday 8h00-

12h00 and 14h00-17h00. The displays are somewhat disappointing, but the staff who work there have an amazing amount of information on anthropological history in Madagascar.

At the top of the hill, above the museum, is the large Fianarantsoa market. It is a chaotic, enjoyable place of fresh produce, meat, snacks and affable vendors. From the market it is a pleasant walk to Rue Philibert Tsiranana and then up Lalana Pasteur Alfred Ramasitera to the small circle on Place Monseigneur Oivelet, in Haute Ville. North of the circle, take the gravel road that goes on to become Route de la Grande Corniche, to the viewpoints and blue gum plantations on the cliffs of Kianjasoa.

Things to buy

Most visitors to Fianarantsoa would like to buy some curios of the locale. Remember that Fianarantsoa is the gemstone capital of Madagascar. It is recommended that you pay a visit to the bijouteries of the city. Probably the best of these, for selection, quality and price, is *Tsakou*, next to the Hotel Cotsoyannis on Rue Printsy Ramaharo. Its prices for Malagasy precious and semiprecious stones are negotiable, though for the gold and imported stones the owner insists on a fixed price.

A number of shops sell local curios and handicrafts in Fianarantsoa. At *Linda Garcia Arts*, in the grounds of the Sofia Hotel, there is a good selection of curios at high prices. A few hundred metres south of the Sofia Hotel, on Nouvelle Route d'Antananarivo, is the best curio shop in the city, *Vonea Bijoux*. It has a bewildering selection of traditional Betsileo crafts. All prices are negotiable and the helpful shop assistants make every effort to accommodate shoppers. You could easily spend an entire morning browsing through this shop, and unlike other curio vendors, the saleswomen do not pester you after their initial offer of assistance. Opposite the Somacodis Building, near the sports stadium, is the *Art-Mad Souvenir Boutique*. It has a collection of leather and art goods, plus a few wooden statues. Once again, bargaining is the norm for these high quality, exquisitely crafted products.

Accommodation

Fianarantsoa has many places offering accommodation. From the up-market tourist hotel, Sofia, through medium-tariff hotels such as the Cotsoyannis and down to the cheap wooden rooms of the Sakafo, there is something to suit all budgets and grades of visitor.

The top hotel in the city, though with poor service, is the *Sofia Hotel* (high tariff), tel. 503.53. Located along the Nouvelle Route d'Antananarivo, this bizarre-looking structure is owned by one of the wealthiest men in the country, a Chinaman. Do not be fooled by the impressive exterior; the room I stayed in was dark, dingy and hardly worth the high rate demanded. There is, however, an excellent restaurant that serves delicious food from either an à la carte menu or an extensive set menu that is changed daily. In the arcades you will find travel agents, boutiques and tour operators. In the grounds of the hotel are a pizzeria, ice-cream parlour, bistro and salon de thé. Guests and visitors may also make use of the swimming pool, bar and snooker table. All rooms have bathrooms en suite, and there is also a family room for those who prefer doing a little self-catering.

Presently being constructed in Nouvelle Ville is the hotel that will definitely become Fianarantsoa's best tourist accommodation, the *Radama Hotel*, on Araben ny Fahaleovantena. Obviously falling into the high-tariff category, this hotel, under the management and ownership of the same people who own the luxurious Radama Hotel in Antananarivo, will cater to exclusive tour groups and provide the highest standard of service available in Fianarantsoa. The environmentally-aware owners have also set about planting indigenous trees on Araben ny Fahaleovantena, to spruce up the locale and turn it into an attractive park-like setting. A mini-market will be located on the hotel's grounds and in the galleries will be travel agents and tour operators. It will have 18 well-appointed rooms with full bathroom en suite. Guests will be able to eat traditional Malagasy and Continental meals in the restaurant. This laudable hotel is due for completion and opening in June 1995. Reservations may be done and information obtained through the Radama Hotel in 'Tana: Radama Hotel, 22 Avenue Grandidier, Isoraka, Antananarivo, tel. 319.27, fax 353.23.

The favoured accommodation of package tours not staying at the expensive Sofia Hotel is the *Hotel Moderne* (medium-high tariff), tel. 508.15, opposite the train station. This hotel is well located, has a well-trained staff and clean, comfortable rooms. Downstairs is the legendary Chez Papillon restaurant, and the offices of Air Madagascar are around the corner.

On the way to Haute Ville, next to the old Rex Cinema on Rue Xavier Thoyer, where Rue Rondriantsilanizaka Joseph meets Araben ny Fahaleovantena, is the *Hotel de Madagascar* (medium tariff), tel. 511.52. Guests have the choice of large rooms, with grand views, either with or without en suite bathrooms. The faded grandeur of this hotel is obvious on entering. Without doubt, if the owners put in a little effort and finance this place could give the over-priced Sofia Hotel a run for its money. A small restaurant is located downstairs, and for some peculiar reason a large part of the menu consists of Italian pasta dishes!

The *Hotel Cotsoyannis* (medium tariff), tel. 514.86, is near the junction of Avenue du General Leclerc and Rue Rondriantsilanizaka Joseph. It is on the first floor and offers acceptable accommodation in spacious rooms with showers. There is a menu at the reception desk, but the quality of food is poor and hardly worth the price. The hotel is a favoured destination of low budget tour groups, but can be a little austere for travellers who want more than just a clean, comfortable place to sleep.

East of town, behind the taxi-brousse station on Rue MDRM, is the *Tsara Guesthouse* (low-medium tariff), tel. 502.06. It usually sends touts to meet taxi-brousses, so you are likely to be approached as soon as you step out of the vehicle if carrying a backpack. Accommodation at the Tsara Guesthouse is recommended for travellers. The rooms are spotless, the ablution facilities are scrubbed daily and the food served in the restaurant is among the best in central Madagascar.

One of the cheapest places to stay is *Hotel Escale* (low tariff), near where Nouvelle Route d'Antananarivo becomes Rue Printsy Ramaharo. Accommodation here is in wooden rooms, with or without showers. Meals may be taken in a small restaurant with a Malagasy menu.

If you are really desperate, or on a really tight budget, you cannot beat staying at the *Sakafo* (low tariff), opposite Domremy Liquor Store on Rue Michel Ranamana. This Malagasy dive is not for the meticulous or those used to luxury accommodation. Accommodation is in simple rooms, with rickety iron bedsteads and cold water bucket showers.

On Rue Pere Henri Dubois is *Hotel Ideal* (low tariff), suitable for budget travellers and backpackers. The rooms are well kept and the communal washing facilities are clean.

Along Boulevard Besson, close to the Ministry of the Interior, is the *Hotel Rova* (low tariff). The accommodation is agreeable, and the restaurant, where delicious Malagasy cuisine is served, is a must for all visitors who enjoy traditional food.

Places to eat

Most of the hotels have dining rooms and good menus. The one at the *Sofia Hotel* is especially recommended.

On Nouvelle Route d'Antananarivo is the *Lotus Rouge* Chinese restaurant. It has good set menus and a huge à la carte selection that caters for most tastes. On the corner of Nouvelle Route d'Antananarivo and Rue Marechal Lattre de Tassigny is the *Resto Rak Malagasy Restaurant*. It has a good selection of Malagasy dishes and a loud, high-stakes card game that continues until well after closing time at around midnight. In the row of shanty stalls that line Rue MDRM you will find another cheap Malagasy restaurant, *Gasikara Bazar and Bar de la Glace*. Its menu is changed daily, but there are no ice creams for sale. The servings of food here are large and the flavour is spicy, with lots of Malagasy rice, often cooked in coconut milk.

Then there is the tasty fare of *Chez Papillon*, opposite the train station on Rue MDRM. Some would claim the best meals in Madagascar are served here. The prices are high, but the quality of food and the standards of service are exceptional as well. It offers filling set menus and an exhaustive à la carte selection that includes pizzas, steaks, fish and huge sandwiches. The restaurant is always busy at lunch time and during the evenings and it is recommended that you reserve a table for dinner. *Le Panda* restaurant, opposite the Hotel Cotsoyannis on Rue Printsy Ramaharo, has an extensive menu that also offers vegetarian and scrumptious fish dishes. Its fresh-water crayfish and prawns vinaigrette are scrumptious and not to be missed. It even brews its own white rum, Rhum Spéciale – try some!

For fresh pastries, bread and light snacks you will be hard-pressed to find anything better than the *Salon de Thé Abou*, on Rue Printsy Ramaharo. It specialises in samosas and bakes sweet cakes each morning at sunrise. At the reasonably priced *Restaurant Maharajah*, on Rue Pasteur, diners may select from a large Indian menu that has lavish servings of curry. Make sure that you specify what "hotness" you want your food to be. It might also be prudent, if you insist on "hot" curry, that you order a tub of natural yoghurt with which to cool your mouth down.

SAHAMBAVY

This small town, whose name means "the camp of girls", is about 26 km north-west of Fianarantsoa and is known for its tea plantations and Lac Sahambavy. It makes for an interesting day trip from Fianarantsoa, and independent travellers will have a wonderful opportunity for meeting rural Betsileo in the hamlet.

You can reach Sahambavy either by road or rail. Unless on an organised tour, visitors arriving by taxi-brousse or train will need to walk about 2 km to the tea estate and lake. Travellers coming by train get off at Ampaidranovato station. Those arriving by taxi-brousse must walk south from Sahambavy to the sites.

Travellers opting for the train take the Fianarantsoa-Manakara train which leaves Fianarantsoa every second day at about 7h00. The journey from Fianarantsoa to Ampaidranovato takes one to two hours.

Taxi-brousses leave from the local taxi-brousse station across from Descours and Cabaud Store on Rue MDRM in Fianarantsoa. There are taxi-brousses going to and from Sahambavy four times per day. The first leaves at about 8h00 and the last returns from Sahambavy at 16h00.

Sahambavy is the only tea growing area in Madagascar and was established by British and Dutch planters who brought saplings from the tea estates in Ceylon and Indonesia. Located high in the cool, misty hills north-east of Fianarantsoa, Sahambavy is an area of trees, rolling plantations, rivers and rural Betsileo houses.

Today, the tea plantations are under the management of a Dutch company, Fofifa-Cendraderu, who have controlling shares in the enterprise. The factory is open to visitors and the factory manager will take you on a guided, French-language tour of the facility. Not quite as modern or sophisticated as factories in the Seychelles, the factory does however process enough tea to meet all the demands of Madagascar, plus several hundred tonnes for the European markets.

Malagasy tea, Thé de Sahambavy, is primarily a blending tea, of the "pekoe" variety. The "flowery pekoe" teas are flavoured with vanilla and make for a delicious cup of tea. At the end of the guided tour the manager hands out a few packets of pure Malagasy tea, of "clonal tip" quality. No payment is expected for his services, but a few FMg is appreciated.

Visitors are free to walk about the estate unaccompanied and should consider spending a few hours watching the pickers and wandering down to the nursery and Sahambavy lake.

Beautiful blue Sahambavy lake lies in a gentle hollow surrounded by forests and holiday cottages. This natural lake is used by the estate for irrigation purposes, and is also well stocked with fish. Over weekends the edges of the lake fill up with families and couples from Fianarantsoa. Fishing is allowed but for some unexplained reason – I could get no satisfactory answer – no one ever seems to swim in the cool, clean water of the lake.

Although there is no tourist accommodation in Sahambavy, campers are permitted to pitch their tents around the lake. Speak to the estate manager, whose gracious house you will pass while walking from the tea plantations to the nursery.

RANOMAFANA

Madagascar's most successful nature reserve, and one of the most visited, Parc National de Ranomafana, is located in the rainforests, hills and deep valleys west of the village of Ranomafana, about 88 km northeast of Fianarantsoa. Both the national park and village lie in the beautiful valley of the Namorona River. The area is full of contradictions. While the forestry personnel struggle to maintain the pristine primary rainforest conditions of the reserve, the destructive traditional tavy culture of the local Tanala clan infringes constantly on the remaining wilderness areas.

There are thermal springs at Ranomafana, hence the Malagasy name, Rano, which means water, and mafana, which translates as hot; "the place of hot water".

Getting there

The majority of visitors to Ranomafana arrive as part of a tour package group that includes transport, accommodation, park visit and food. Others must use public transport from Fianarantsoa or Antananarivo. The taxi-brousses from 'Tana go all the way to Manakara or Mananjary and it is not easy finding a lift with them only as far as Ranomafana. Fianarantsoa is a better place from which to start.

From Fianarantsoa, there are at least five taxi-brousses passing Ranomafana. Only one travels solely to Ranomafana village. The others continue to Ifanadiana, Irondo, Mananjary or Manakara. The first taxi-brousse departs from the main taxi-brousse station in Fianarantsoa at about 7h00, and takes two to three hours along the terrible road to Ranomafana. Leaving Ranomafana can prove difficult. Book an onward or return seat for a specific date with the taxi-brousse company you use getting there. Another option is to pay the taxi tout in Ranomafana a few FMg and let him approach each taxi-brousse that stops in the village.

Tourist information

The post office in Ranomafana is across from the 1960 Independence Memorial near the market. Look for the telecommunications aerials; the post office is beneath them. A small but well-staffed hospital caters for emergencies and the Pharmacie Communautaire is able to fill most unscheduled drug prescriptions. There is, as yet, no bank in Ranomafana and you must arrive with sufficient cash to last your visit. Credit cards and traveller's cheques are not accepted at any of the hotels or hotelys in the area.

Things to do

Although the thermal springs and baths are suitable for all visitors, especially after a few days of trekking through the rainforest, at the time of writing access was impossible for most tourists. Cyclone Cristal had just cut a swathe of destruction through eastern and south-central Madagascar that washed away the bridge connecting the village to the thermal centre. This, however, is not the only way to reach the springs. For those who do not mind the walk, take the road towards Ifanadiana. About 600 m from the school at the northern side of Ranomafana, turn right for the Namorona River. On the banks of the river you will find a ferryman with a small wooden boat, poling villagers from Sambivinany, Menarano and Ranovao across to Ranomafana. Once across the river, turn right (west) and follow it upstream to the thermal baths, swimming pool and spring. Take along your own towel and prepare yourself for a relaxing time soaking in the pungent waters.

The market in Ranomafana is also worth a walking tour. A colourful fresh produce market offers sweet wild pineapples, vegetables, huge bunches of bananas, mangoes and lychees. Fresh bread, baked by the bakery of the Sofia Hotel in Fianarantsoa, is brought to the little shops of Ranomafana daily. Take a stroll into the northern suburbs of the village, to the abandoned tavy plots and up into the hills, where there is the sickening site of burnt forest, and logged trees lie around like some grisly corpses after a battle. The people in these hills are not happy about having foreigners here. Repeated visits by environmental journalists and groups have caused them to become reserved and secretive about what they are doing. While "green" groups denounce them and put pressure on the government to stop the tavy, little is done to treat the problem in a holistic way – the one exception being Duke University, which is involved in the management and research at Parc National de Ranomafana.

Things to buy

There are a few curios, T-shirts and other memorabilia for sale at the Salle d'Exposition. Everyone who ventures into the rainforest should consider buying one of the small wooden pendants of the forest god Ezenia. The woman and man who carve and sell these pendants and buttons, with faces tooled on them, can be found in the village near the fresh produce market, or, more likely, they will find you at your hotel or as you walk around Ranomafana.

Accommodation

In Ranomafana tourists have two options, Hotel Ravinala and Hotel Thermal de Ranomafana. The *Hotel Thermal* (medium-high tariff), tel. 1, must have once been an elegant, sophisticated place. Today, the musty rooms and peeling walls make for an unpleasant stay, aided in no small way by the rude staff, who are unwilling to help, or even make the bed in your room. In spite of the name, there is no hot water, and the communal washing facilities are abysmal.

Rather choose to spend a few nights at the friendly, clean *Hotel Ravinala* (medium tariff). Situated along the main road near the Salle d'Exposition, the Ravinala is a popular hang-out for locals in the evening and the ideal place at which to find knowledgeable but unofficial forest guides.

Another hotel is going to be built shortly. Although the land has already been bought and plans have been passed by the provincial council, it will be a few more months before the project gets off the ground. Should you use this hotel once it is open, please write and give me details for updated editions of this guidebook.

Places to eat

There are many Tanala hotelys in Ranomafana village, all serving basically the same dishes, with a few house specialities. Avoid eating in the dirty dining room of the Hotel Thermal, though you may consider eating one of its enormous breakfasts on the veranda.

PARC NATIONAL DE RANOMAFANA

The biggest attraction around Ranomafana is undoubtedly Parc National de Ranomafana. This 40 000 ha rainforest reserve is one of Madagascar's most beautiful protected areas. Protected, that is, to a certain degree only. National parks in Madagascar are modelled on the concentric circle paradigm. The inner circle is off limits to everyone, the next circle is open to researchers and scientists, then there is a buffer area followed by those areas accessible to tourists, and finally the outer circle is the transition zone between the reserve and locals. This last area is increasingly under pressure from tavy agriculture, but the park staff are loath to offend tribal customs or anger the local chiefs.

All visitors to the park should first stop at the Musée Ranomafana and Salle d'Exposition. Here you will be able to get an excellent visual introduction to the work being done to protect the park, what you can see and do in the park and where to find reputable guides, each a specialist in a particular field and language.

In the exhibition hall are graphic displays of projects being carried out in the park, plus live snakes and tenrecs, which may be handled. Remember that none of the 12 species of snake found in the park is poisonous. The botanical inventory list is interesting, while the climate graphs include information on daily rainfall, humidity and temperatures.

Duke University, with assistance from the WWF, has since 1987 had three main areas of involvement:

- Rural development: This aids Tanala forest dwellers start up beekeeping and aquaculture practices, helps them find alternative methods of transport, rather than hacking down more trees for rafts, carts and dugouts, and encourages the locals to become active in the preservation of the forest.
- Research: Under the expert guidance of Dr Patricia Wright, education programmes have been started, and the tribespeople are actively included in research projects, that involve almost 40 researchers, in the study, location and identification of lemurs, birds, reptiles and the spectacular floral specimens of the park.
- Health: Medical doctors, nurses and medical advisers have been brought in to assist the locals with medical consultations, treatment, family planning, hygiene, nutrition, child health and even the building of hygienic latrines.

The best guides are the official guides sanctioned and trained by Duke University and the WWF. That is not to say that the unofficial guides who approach you at the hotels in town are not suitable. Official guides are expensive, but obviously have a lot more detailed information on the flora and fauna than unofficial guides. A comprehensive list of registered guides is pinned on the wall inside the Salle d'Exposition.

You can contact these guides by speaking to the women who work in the exhibition hall.

From the Salle d'Exposition, walk about another 5 km west to the official park entrance along the main road from Fianarantsoa. You are required to purchase a permit to visit the park.

Leave for the park by 6h00 so that you are able to hitch a ride with park workers up to the entrance. Otherwise it is a sweaty, wet walk up the steep tarred road, through the village of Ambatolahy, across the steel bridge and up to the Talatakely section of the park. Wear long trousers, socks and long-sleeved shirt; there are many brown leeches in the rainforest, especially during the wet summer months. It is also advisable to take along some water, something to eat and wet weather gear. The staff at the Salle d'Exposition suggest that the best time to visit Ranomafana is between August and October, when the least amount of rain falls – you can still, however, expect rain daily.

Once across the raging Namorona River, you immediately enter the rainforest proper. Among the 14 species of lemurs found here, the broad-nosed gentle bamboo lemur is considered the rarest primate on earth, while another, the golden bamboo lemur, was only discovered in 1986. There are also other diurnal lemurs such as brown lemurs, red-bellied lemurs and grey gentle lemurs. Of the nocturnal families, visitors on guided night walks may be fortunate enough to see the greater fat-tailed dwarf lemur, red mouse lemur and both sportive and woolly lemurs. If you are specially lucky, you may catch a glimpse of the *Propithecus diadema* and Milne-Edwards diademed sifakas.

There are 12 species of snake in the forest reserve, plus numerous other reptiles that include 32 species of chameleon and lizard, and several species of rare tree frogs, notably the golden mantilla frog. High in the canopy, the phenomenon of "crown shyness" can be seen quite clearly: the flat-topped trees are closely spaced but their crowns do not touch. Birds are among the glories of Ranomafana. You may notice paradise flycatchers, galidia, 14 species of Vangidae and ground rollers.

Birds, mammals and reptiles may be the main reason that visitors come to Parc National de Ranomafana, but the sheer majesty of the forest itself is what makes the visit so exciting and memorable. Look for the epiphytes that grow as rosettes of leaves on tree trunks and even other leaves. Deep in the interior of the forest you will come across wrist-thick liana, scented and brightly coloured orchids and some giant ferns. Climbing plants too are a feature of the rainforest here and the low herb layer creates aromatic compost for the emergent trees and the canopy. Unexpectedly you may come across palm trees and dense stands of creaking bamboo. Equally captivating are the colours, shapes and scents of the moss, fungi and lichen that are found on fallen logs and the prop roots of trees.

The best way to end a tour of the park is a walk to the awesome Cascade del Riana and the ferocious Namorona River as it thunders eastward to the sea. The ground trembles near the waterfall and during the heavy summer rains the sheer force and inspiring natural beauty should be enough to convince many visitors that they need to get involved with the protection and preservation of this fragile, threatened and beautiful region. Those who are interested in helping should contact the World Wide Fund for Nature (WWF): Département de l'Information et de l'Education, Avenue de Mont Blanc, CH-1196 Gland, Switzerland; South African chapter: WWF, Southern Africa Nature Foundation, PO Box 456, Stellenbosch 7599, South Africa. If you are keen to help both the tribal people and preserve the park, contact Survival International, Freepost PAM 5410, 11-15 Emerald Street, London WC1N 3BR, United Kingdom; South African contact: Marco Turco, PO Box 508, Ifafi 0260, South Africa.

There is no tourist accommodation within the park, though there are plans afoot to construct wooden bungalows for guests. However, if you have a tent, you are welcome to pitch it at the Belle Vue camp site, near the start of the Ankerana River, deep in the forested hills of Ranomafana.

AMBALAVAO

Meaning "the new village", Ambalavao is the centre for the production of the famous Papier Antaimoro Soierie and the weaving of checkered Betsileo lamba oanies.

Getting there

Travellers may get to Ambalavao by taxi-brousse from Fianarantsoa, though hitchhiking between the two centres is also easy. Tour operators in Fianarantsoa offer day trips to Ambalavao and the vineyards north of the village, fully inclusive of transport, entrance fees and lunch. Taxi-brousses, or auto cars, leave the main taxi-brousse station on Rue MDRM every hour, starting from about 7h30. It takes about an hour to do the

54 km between Fianarantsoa and Ambalavao. The last taxi-brousse returns from the village at 17h00. There are no taxis after this, as there has been a growing incidence of highway robbery.

Things to do

The wine estate of Soavita, which means "well done", is about 3 km north of Ambalavao. Taxis will drop you off at the entrance to the farm. Walk about 500 m along the wide gravel road to the wine factory and cellars. The Swiss were the first to introduce and grow wine in the region, but have since left and the viticulture is now in the hands of French and Chinese who are nationalised Madagascar citizens. The French growers concentrate on export quality wines, while the Chinese produce for the Madagascar market.

The vines themselves originated in France, and now are the only cultivars of that variety left in the world, the French having since found new, improved cultivars. In the open-sided factory visitors will be able to see the fermentation and production and taste the red, white, rosé and orange wines produced by the estate. It also produces a range of white, red and brown vinegars. Outside, you will find women washing bottles, imported from France, into which the wines will be decanted. The large concrete vats are grouped together and the glass of wine you are given will be taken directly from the vat. A few visitors are given a glass of the fine apéritif to sample as well. You cannot buy the produce here and will need to shop for it in Fianarantsoa and Antananarivo.

From the wine estate it is a short pleasant stroll into Ambalavao. Opposite the taxi-brousse station is the entrance to the busy workshop of Papier Antaimoro Soierie. There are always loads of tour groups here and independent travellers may prefer visiting the site before 9h00 or after 15h30, when they will have the site to themselves.

The paper making is all done by hand. The bark from the avoha tree comes from the east coast. These strips of yellow bark are boiled for three hours in cauldrons, until they are nothing more than a soggy mass of pulp. Then the pulp is washed three times in cool water, before being passed to a wizened old woman who sits pounding the pulp with a wooden mallet. The soft pulp is then rolled into fibrous balls which are immersed in water. After an hour of soaking the balls are pulled to pieces and packed into thin layers in shallow pans of water. Once the water is drained from the pans, the layers of paper are separated into sizeable strips. Deft, nimble women place wild flower petals onto these strips in colourful creative designs. The flowers are grown locally, specifically for the factory's use. After the pattern is complete, a thin watery layer of fibres is poured over the picture and set on filters to dry in natural sunlight. There are no fixed designs; each person is allowed full freedom of artistic expression. In the curio shop, visitors will be given a free pamphlet, printed on Antaimoro paper, explaining the history of the factory and the processing of the unique paper and motifs.

The craft originated with the Antaimoro clan from the south-central forests of Madagascar, who used the paper for recording their history, religion and tribal legends in, oddly enough, the Persian Farsi alphabet. Their traditional methods were introduced to the Ambalavao region by a French colonial farmer, who brought several Antaimoro with him when he moved from Manakara.

Once you have seen the factory and vineyards, spend a few hours wandering about the lanes and alleys of this quaint southern Betsileo village. The distinctive architecture is apparent in the filigreed balconies, tooled windows and doors and the style of building double-storey mud and wood houses. From Wednesday to Friday the market area swells to three times its normal size for the weekly livestock auction. Ambalavao is transformed from a sleepy hollow into a vibrant, colourful festival of traditional tribespeople, long-horned zebu and bleating goats.

Accommodation

Few visitors ever want to overnight in Ambalavao. The best hotel, for accommodation, cleanliness and tasty meals, is the *Hotel Verger* (low tariff) near the centre of town. The cheapest place is the Malagasy hotel, *Tsikivy* (low tariff). Its meals are a must, though the bucket wash can be uncomfortable in the depths of a highland winter.

Places to eat

There are several excellent hotelys located around the taxi-brousse station, near the Roman Catholic church. Their lunch menus are recommended, as is their ice cold beer and local rum. You may find it difficult getting a table in these hotelys during the livestock market.

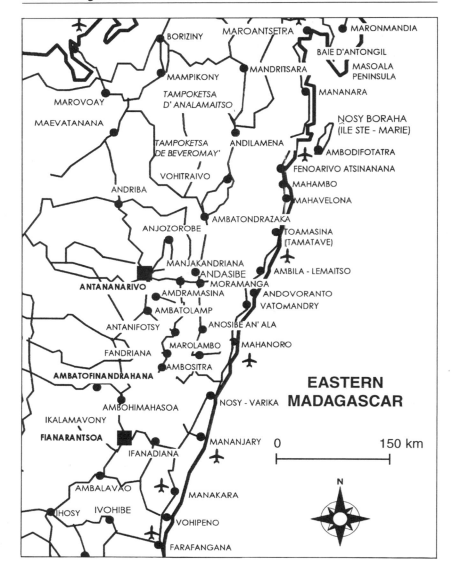

8 EASTERN MADAGASCAR

Edged by the blue waters of the south-western Indian Ocean and shrouded with rainforests and tall hills, mainland eastern Madagascar is the preferred destination of adventure travellers. Offshore, Nosy Boraha (Île Ste Marie) offers tourists luxury hotels, sparkling beaches, palm trees and entertainment.

Between the wild reaches of the Masoala Peninsula, colonial buildings of Toamasina (Tamatave) and remote Farafangana, visitors will discover a region of Madagascar that has defied proper exploration for centuries. The coast from Mahavelona to Navana, and the island of Nosy Boraha, was once the haunt of Indian Ocean pirates and corsairs of the calibre of Olivier le Vasseur and John Avery. Their brazen raids from these forested shores on richly laden merchantmen returning from the East resulted in the area becoming known, in the 17th and 18th century, as the Pirate Coast. Between the awesome Gorges du Mangoro in the north and Mananara River in the south lies some of the most beautiful and inspiring landscape in Madagascar.

Once the pirates had been routed, planters moved in and turned the east coast into one of the country's richest agricultural regions, on what they called the Vanilla Coast. Vanilla, cloves, coffee, tropical and subtropical fruit are grown and together with an increasing number of sugar estates, provide high quality produce that is the mainstay of Madagascar's agricultural export programme.

The desire to reach First World standing has, sadly, led to exploitation of many primary forest areas. This has been aided in no small way by the traditional slash and burn (tavy) agriculture of east coast tribes. In the Maroantsetra region, massive logging vehicles and the scream of chain saws can be heard through most of the daylight hours. Between Mananjary and Manakara entire hillsides have been eroded away to stain the rivers and streams a blood red. Forest-dwelling clans, flora and fauna are now threatened, and scientists estimate that at least 22 species of life are rendered extinct each day in this ancient coastal region. Forest cultures are disappearing under the combined onslaught of progress and habitat destruction. Visitors to eastern Madagascar should do whatever they can to preserve this unique location.

Cyclones are regular visitors to eastern Madagascar. Although each year at least one violent storm rages down the coast, occasionally a monster cyclone comes tearing down from the equatorial zones to smash into the hills, valleys, villages, towns and forests of eastern Madagascar. The last such attack occurred in 1995, when Cyclone Cristal wreaked extensive damage by flattening buildings, uprooting trees and crops and injuring hundreds of people. In a week of havoc – witnessed by this author – that cut a path of destruction from the Masoala Peninsula to Farafangana, and as far inland as Fianarantsoa, millions of francs' worth of agricultural, industrial and development projects were devastated.

Eastern Madagascar experiences rain throughout the year. The heaviest falls occur between late November and March. During this time the humidity is high, as are temperatures and insect attacks. From April to mid-November visitors can expect frequent light drizzle. If you plan to tour the east coast make sure to take along wet weather gear and insect repellent.

Getting around eastern Madagascar is a pleasure. From aircraft to bus, and boat to hitchhiking, eastern Madagascar provides all the possibilities, plus a few you probably hadn't even thought of, like riding in an ox wagon or mountain-biking.

There is a regular air service by Air Madagascar to the larger urban centres on the east coast, and several weekly flights to smaller district towns. Taxi-brousses and buses travel daily between the capital, Antananarivo, and Toamasina. From Toamasina, numerous taxi-brousses and 4x4 taxis journey up the awful north-east coast roads to Maroantsetra. It needs a little more effort getting from 'Tana to the south-east coast. If you can spare the time, take a series of taxi-brousse hops that should have you in Farafangana within a week.

Boats ply the Pangalanes Canal all the way from Toamasina to Farafangana. This is a splendid voyage and every visitor to the area should spend a few days floating along the sluggish canal and sleeping in villages overnight. Hitchhiking is uncommon in Madagascar, and as a result can be time consuming. However, from Ambila-Lemaitso to Maroantsetra and between Anosibe (An'Ala) to Mananjary hitchhiking is easy. Virtually every vehicle that passes will stop and seldom will you have to wait longer than 30 minutes for a suitable lift. Sometimes travellers may be expected to pay, while at other times, especially on trucks, the ride is free.

Eastern Madagascar is home to three major Malagasy tribes and eight clans. By far the most prevalent tribe is the Betsimisaraka along the north-east coast. In the forested hills between Nosivarika and Vondrozo are the Tanala, an offshoot of the mighty Betsileo nation further inland. Around Farafangana live the Antaisaka people. The eight clans, starting in the south, near Farafangana, are: Antaifasy, Sahafatra, Antaimoro, Antambahoaka, Antatsimo, Bezanozano, Sihanaka and the Bavaratra north of the Soamiamina River.

As with other tribal areas in Madagascar, foreign visitors should acquaint themselves with and respect the various fady (taboos) which are in effect. The following require particular attention:

- In the evening do not expect a formal invitation to sit down and eat. The wife simply calls out to the four cardinal points a summons to come and eat. Never offer to pay should you eat at one of these meals, it is considered an insult.
- Never start to eat before the father, or head of the household, has had at least one mouthful of food.
- The great autumn celebration is called kinahandro by these tribes, and means "the preparing of food out in the open". Once again never refuse an invitation to attend this festival.
- When offered a new bottle of rum to taste, make certain that before you drink you first offer the headmen some and sprinkle a little around the traditional sacrificial stone found in most rural villages.
- During the harvest the villagers may seem reserved and quiet while working the fields. They often refuse to talk to strangers or even acknowledge them. They wish to keep any foul weather away and believe that by remaining silent they hide the fact that they are harvesting, and can then be sure of pleasant weather.
- Peanuts are considered a taboo food. Villagers say that peanuts lie on the exposed earth, and it reminds them of recalcitrant hens that will not lay in proper nests. The way in which a peanut plant stem curves along the ground symbolises cowering and grovelling to French colonial authority, an affront to tribal pride.
- It is believed that the aye-aye lemur has supernatural powers. In view of this it is taboo to hunt, eat or laugh at the aye-aye.
- The bustard quail too is a taboo creature. No one is permitted to kill or eat this bird.
- It is fady to clear a path to an ancestral tomb. It equates to clearing the way for death to arrive.

- Never use the door on the eastern side of a house. It is only for carrying out the dead.
- You must ask permission from the local chief to attend the annual sacrificial festival. This occurs in April and is the so-called Ny mahalala isan taona (the fady transgression sacrifice).

TOAMASINA (TAMATAVE)

When the Imerina king, Radama I, first arrived at the sea, in 1817, he apparently tasted the water and said, "Toa masina" (it's salty). The town where he visited, whose original appellation no one seems to remember, was promptly named Toamasina. Prior to its development into a colonial centre, Toamasina was under the authority of the Brotherhood of the Coast – a loose confederation of pirates and corsairs who had their bases up and down the east coast, but met four times per year in Toamasina to discuss piratical protocol.

The pirates had unanimously agreed that no one person would control the settlement. It was left to the French, under empire-building Napoleon, to first claim ownership. In 1809 a Frenchman, Sylvain Roux, arrived to commence trading ventures in Madagascar. His translator, Jean-René Ranitrarivo, was later to crown himself paramount chief of eastern Madagascar once the colonisers had left.

Noticing French interests growing in Madagascar, particularly in slave trading, the British, who had abolished slavery in 1807, sent battleships and Royal Marines to land on the beaches of Baie d'Ivondro. From then, until the signing of the Treaty of Paris in 1814, eastern Madagascar fell under the administration of the British governor on Mauritius, Robert Farquhar. The British brought in navvies, builders and members of the colonial service to establish a centre for the east coast. The harbour facilities in Toamasina were enlarged, warehouses erected and beautiful colonial mansions constructed. Wide, tree-lined boulevards transformed the dull little settlement and it became a thriving port and market community.

Things were going well for the people of Toamasina, both colonials and Malagasy, until Queen Ranavalona I embarked on her plans to purge Madagascar of the European "loto" (dirt) in May 1845. Initially she tried to get them to leave by insisting on heavy tax burdens for all trading activities. When this failed, the queen sent troops against the British soldiers and French merchants in Toamasina. Surprisingly, there was little resistance and the Europeans simply sailed away. It was a ploy. Within months they returned and launched an attack, but the soldiers of Queen Ranavalona were old campaigners and the unified British and French assault was repulsed. Unable to make landfall, the navies returned to their bases on Mauritius and Réunion.

For the next 38 years, the only Europeans in Toamasina were German, Portuguese and Dutch advisers to the royal house. Then, on a wet January morning in 1884, the inhabitants of Toamasina awoke to find a French armada off their town. After three days of naval bombardment that destroyed many of the fine English buildings and killed thousands of Malagasy civilians, the French stormed ashore at Rade de Toamasina. Unexpectedly, they ran into a wall of fire from entrenched Malagasy fighters. The French were forced to fall back and return to their ships. Despite the defeat of the French, the generals of the Malagasy army realised that they could not withstand these attacks. In a ceremony whose documentation can be seen in the public archives in Antananarivo, General Ramarline accepted French authority over Toamasina.

Today, Toamasina is a relaxed, quiet town with the largest and busiest harbour in Madagascar. The shady boulevards lend a gracious ambience to the town, which is frequently veiled by the alluring scent of cloves from the warehouses on Boulevard de la Libération and along Boulevard Ratsimilaho. The populace of Toamasina is used to seeing foreigners walking about their streets, yet remain friendly and interested in those who want to stop and talk to them.

Getting there

Getting to Toamasina is possible either by air, road, rail or water.

Air Madagascar flies jets and turboprop Twin Otters to Toamasina every day of the week. Contact it or a local travel agent for the current schedule and latest fares.

Road travel to Toamasina is well organised and pleasant, although the vehicles can get a little crowded. There are daily taxi-brousses and buses from Antananarivo to Toamasina. Taxi-brousses also make an arduous daily journey from Mananara to Toamasina. Three times per week two taxi-brousses make the trip from Mahanoro, via Ambila-Lemaitso, to Toamasina.

In 'Tana, public transport for Toamasina leaves from the Taxi-brousse Station North, on Lalana Dokotera Raphael Raboto, in Ambodivona suburb. The first taxi departs at about 7h00. Expect the journey to take eight or nine hours, with stops for breakfast, lunch and the occasional relief stop. From Mananara to Toamasina can take up to 12 hours, depending on road and weather conditions. During the wet season, wear sandals and shorts; you will have to get out and push through mud at some stage before reaching the tarred road at Fenoarivo. If coming up from Mahanoro, make certain to book your seat at least two days ahead, as competition for space is fierce. The journey from Mahanoro to Toamasina can take anything between six and 16 hours, depending on the amount of rainfall, the mechanical reliability of the vehicle and road conditions.

There is a train which travels from 'Tana to Toamasina through verdant forests, across shaking bridges and past isolated villages. It usually leaves at about 7h00 from the RNCFM Tananarive train station, at the northern end of Araben ny Fahaleovantena. The swaying journey comes to an end 10 hours later. This same train leaves Toamasina at 7h00 the next day and chugs into 'Tana at around 18h00. There is no need to take along food and drink; at all 36 stations at which you stop, locals will rush up to the window offering freshly cooked food, tea and coffee.

Reaching Toamasina on water-borne transport is a real thrill, whether coming up the Pangalanes Canal or crossing from Nosy Boraha. Should you have time constraints, but still want to try a trip on the canal, consider taking a ride from Ambila-Lemaitso to Toamasina. The 65 km jaunt takes just over a day, and offers a night at one of the villages that edge the canal. There are no fixed time schedules and travellers must just ask around the canal area in Ambila-Lemaitso. You must take along your own food and drink, and wet weather gear is recommended.

To arrange cruises on the Pangalanes Canal, contact the Soft Line Co. on Boulevard Joffre in Toamasina. It runs several tour packages and has schedules to suit most budgets and time considerations.

If coming from or going to Nosy Boraha, you have the option of a ro-ro ferry or getting a local fisherman to take you across. The ferry only makes the crossing and return once a week. It departs Toamasina on Wednesday morning at 6h00, and reaches Nosy Boraha at about 17h00. This dilapidated and rusty ferry leaves Ambodifotatra on Friday at 6h00 for the return trip to Toamasina.

Even though the ferry may be quicker than a fishing boat, it is always filthy and overcrowded. Many of the passengers get horribly seasick, and the entire episode is rather unpleasant.

If you do not mind getting a little wet, and have the time, then seriously consider arranging for a local fisherman to take you either to or from Nosy Boraha. The best place to look for assistance is along the beach, north of Boulevard Ratsimilaho and the hospital, in Toamasina. Negotiate the price and be there by 5h30 the next morning.

Tourist information

Tourist information in Toamasina is available from Air Madagascar, on Araben ny Fahaleovantena, next to the Provincial Youth and Sports Office. Airline tickets must be confirmed here 38-72 hours before departure. The staff are helpful and offer literature that is useful to both tourists and independent travellers. Equally helpful, if you can find its offices open, is the Ministry of Transport, Meteorology and Tourism, south on Boulevard Ratsimilaho. Visitors who read and speak French can get substantial information on what to see and do in the locale from both the French consulate, along Boulevard Labourdonnais, and the Alliance Française, on the corner of Boulevard de Livondro and Rue Blevec.

The post office is at the western end of Araben ny Fahaleovantena, opposite the Hôtel de Ville (town hall), near where Rue de la Convention crosses from north to south. Banque Nationale pour le Commerce (BNPC) is on the corner of Araben ny Fahaleovantena and Boulevard Joffre. Crédit Lyonnais bank (BNI), is on Boulevard Joffre, and also has a small branch on Boulevard Augagneur. Banque Malagache de l'Océan Indien is at the southern end of Boulevard Joffre, opposite the sleazy Eden Hotel. Banky Fampandrosoana ny Varotra (BFV) is on Rue Marechal de Lattre de Tassigny, close to the Auto-Stop Shop. BTM is along Boulevard Augagneur opposite the Chamber of Commerce, Industry and Agriculture.

The most experienced travel agent and operator in Toamasina is Voyages Bourdo, on Boulevard Joffre. It is able to arrange several local tours that include trips on the canal, down the Ivondro River, to Zahamena Nature Reserve and Mananara National Park, plus short boat voyages to Île aux Prunes. Also on Boulevard Joffre is Hotel Pangalanes Travel Agent, which specialises in 14 day boat trips down the Pangalanes Canal. It offers the most comfortable way of seeing life along the canal and the chance to encounter villagers en route. Shakti Voyages, opposite LCR Car Hire on Boulevard Joffre, has a similar programme of tours and travels, but tends to be somewhat more expensive than the other agents. Sagatrans Travel Agents, in Rue Lubert, cater primarily to those in search of sea voyages up and down the coast and to Nosy Boraha.

Maps for travellers and those planning to hike into the interior to discover the rainforests, hills and secluded settlements are obtainable from the Topographical Service, next to the kindergarten, Les Poussins, on Araben ny Fahaleovantena.

Several shipping companies are represented in Toamasina, and visitors interested in finding passage to other ports in Madagascar or in sailing from Madagascar to another country are advised to speak to their shipping clerks about seven days before intended departure. On Boulevard Ratsimilaho you will find Auximad Shipping. It arranges trips to Nosy Boraha and further afield to Antsiranana, Mahajanga and Toliara, with occasional crossings to the Comoros and East Africa. Transni Shipping, near the long-distance taxi-brousse and bus station, can arrange a berth aboard a coastal trader operating between Tolanaro in the south and Maroantsetra in the north, with stops on Nosy Boraha as well.

Visa extensions can be done in Toamasina, but it's frustrating and takes over three days to process. The offices of the police and immigration service are on Araben ny Fahaleovantena, near the old Tribunal building and the Tamatave Provincial Administration building. You will need four passport photographs and these, together with film, batteries and basic camera repairs, are available from Photo Star, next to the Chinese restaurant on Boulevard Joffre.

The only bookshop of any substance in Toamasina is the Librairie GM Fakra, close to the fresh produce market in Rue Bertho. Medical attention is available from a number of places in Toamasina. Obviously, the cheapest and most desperate option is the big hospital to the north of the Pangalanes canal between Boulevard Joffre and Boulevard Ratsimilaho. There are long lines of ill people waiting for treatment here, few medical staff and many crying, hollow-eyed children milling about. Private doctors are a better alternative if you are ill. There is a Cabinet Medical (surgery) next to the Hotel Étoile Rouge, Rue Marechal de Lattre de Tassigny. At Pharmacie du Bazarbe in Rue Bertho prescription drugs are available. A Centre Medical is located close to the Catholic church on Rue Amiral Billard. A dentist is opposite Coiffeur Minnie, near the Generation Hotel on Rue du Petite Thouars.

Things to do

At night Toamasina really comes into its own, as discos, nightclubs, restaurants, drug peddlers, prostitutes, snack vendors and taxis vie for custom. All the tranquillity of the day is discarded as the streets, hotels and cafés brim with talking, laughing, partying people.

A walk should be taken along Boulevard Ratsimilaho (Araben d'Ratsimilaho), where it passes the seafront from the Pangalanes Canal to the harbour. Swimming is not advisable off this beach. Spend a while looking out to sea and you are bound to see a few shark fins patrolling the polluted waters offshore. Boulevard Joffre also offers a pleasant stroll down wide tree-lined streets into the CBD. Start a walk from Hotel la Plage all the way south to where the road ends in a pot-holed gravel track to the Baie d'Ivondro. Araben ny Fahaleovantena, palm-lined and running west from the Rade de Toamasina to the Hôtel de Ville, is a wide boulevard edged by gracious old mansions, government buildings and manicured lawns.

West of Boulevard Joffre, between Rue Amiral Billard and Rue Bertho, is the covered market. The strong scent of cloves, pepper, coffee and spices that can be smelt everywhere comes from cavernous warehouses scattered about town. You can enter these warehouses and watch the workers grading, sorting and packing the products for export. The main clove depot is Société Produits de Madagascar on Boulevard Augagneur. The manager here is an amicable fellow who gladly takes visitors on a tour of the facility, explaining – in French – the fascinating process of clove production. He is also able to arrange for you to visit a clove, pepper and vanilla estate.

On the corner of Rue de la Réunion and Rue Sylvain Roux is the municipal Parque Zoologique et Botanique. There are cages holding animals here, including a few despondent lemurs. The main attraction is to see the beautiful floral displays and relax under the hanging roots of old banyan trees.

Tourists may visit the Jardin d'Essai by taking a taxi-brousse going to Fenoarivo Atsinanana. About 12 km north of Toamasina, this park is suitable for a day trip. For those with limited time, this is the place to head for to see the startling flora and fauna of north-eastern Madagascar. Although the park was established way back in 1898, it has only recently opened an environmental centre. Aided by the Jersey Wildlife Preservation Trust and scientists from Duke University (who also monitor the rainforest reserve of Ranomafana, in central-eastern Madagascar), a clean, open-system zoo has been started here. Part of their work is to quarantine and carry out final studies of endangered species that have been bred in captivity and are about to be let free into their natural habitats again. The staff at Jardin d'Essai are amiable and willing to answer any number of questions visitors may ask. The site is open for visits Monday to Friday from 12h00-17h00 and Saturday and Sunday 9h00-17h00. The best time to enjoy the serenity, animals, plants and scenery of this garden is during the week. Over weekends, families and groups from Toamasina descend in droves and the Jardin d'Essai becomes a riotous playground and ballpark.

Offshore, north-east of Rue Gourbeyre, is minuscule Nosy Alanana. There are no ferries to the island and travellers will have to arrange with a local boat owner for the crossing. A thriving reef extends off this island, but the presence of roaming sharks prevents snorkelling or scuba diving. Look out for the immense fruit bats that fly about, even during the day time. There are also a few lizards and geckoes on the island and one lonely tortoise that enjoys having its leathery neck scratched – if you can find it in the thick undergrowth!

Things to buy

Spices, particularly cloves, pepper and vanilla, can be bought in sachets, or loose, from the market and street stalls scattered around Toamasina. *Bijouterie Kalidas*, east on Rue Aviateur Goulette, has a wide array of well-crafted jewellery in gold, silver and several natural products that look suspiciously like ivory and tortoise shell, though the owner denies this. An impressive collection of precious and semiprecious gemstones is sold at *Bijouterie Liladhar* on Rue Marechal de Lattre de Tassigny. There are many clothing shops, owned mainly by Indian traders. Most stock a few souvenir T-shirts and lamba oanys.

Shoppers will find the biggest collection of local curios for sale at *Maison de l'Artisant*. Prices are high, but the counter assistant is prepared to bargain on certain items. The selection is good, workmanship of an exceptional standard and the pieces unique to the north-east coast of Madagascar.

Accommodation

Being a harbour and holiday town, Toamasina caters well for visitors in search of accommodation and restaurants. From the luxury of the expensive Neptune Hotel to the iron bedstead and bucket of water in the Hotel Venance, and everything in between, there is suitable lodgings for all budgets and preferences. Restaurants range from colonial dining rooms, through Vietnamese eateries and French bistros to Malagasy hotelys.

The *Hotel Neptune* (high tariff), tel. 322.26, is located on the beachfront promenade of Boulevard Ratsimilaho. Each room has ablution facilities and an air-conditioner. Tours are available and there is a fine restaurant, noisy casino and enjoyable nightclub. To make up for not being able to swim in the sea, the Neptune's owner has built a sparkling swimming pool for guests.

The most famous hotel in Toamasina is the delightful old colonial *Hotel Joffre* (medium-high tariff), tel. 323.90, on Boulevard Joffre. It has comfortable rooms with bathrooms en suite, fans or air-conditioners and includes breakfast in the rate.

One of those rare places that pull out all stops to make your visit as pleasant as possible is the *Eden Hotel* (medium tariff), opposite Banque Malagache de l'Océan Indien at the southern end of Boulevard Joffre. No meals are included in the rate, but the rooms are adequate.

Along Avenue de l'Indépendance are two hotels. *Hotel la Plage* (medium tariff), tel. 320.90, is to the seaward side of Boulevard Joffre and is a favourite with expats. It has rooms with bathrooms en suite and cheaper, dingy chambers that share a disgusting communal shower and toilet. There is not that much difference in price and visitors should rather take one of the studio rooms, which look out to sea instead of into a filthy courtyard. A big veranda fronts the hotel and a bar is always full at night. The biggest drawback is the many prostitutes who lounge about waiting for clients. They tend to be insistent and the best defence is to pretend that you cannot speak French. *Hotel les Flamboyants* (medium tariff), tel. 323.50, is further west along Avenue de l'Indépendance, on the corner of Rue de la Fraternité. It has a good restaurant and arranges excursions to Jardin d'Essai and out to Nosy Alanana. The rooms are basic but suitable and the service is excellent.

A popular travellers' hotel is the *Étoile Rouge Hotel, Restaurant and Snack Bar* (medium tariff), tel. 322.90, near the corner of Boulevard Marechal de Lattre de Tassigny and Rue Lubert. Rooms have showers, toilets and either fans or air-conditioners. This hotel is always busy, but guests are still given personal attention. It will even go so far as to send someone to collect you if you call from the taxi-brousse station.

Frequently recommended by travel guides is the *Pax Hotel* (low-medium tariff) south-west on Rue de la Poudriere. Rooms are clean and comfortable, with hot showers. The location is good, but security could be a problem, especially if winding your way back through the dark alleys after a night out. The staff are cordial and can arrange for fishing trips or a day tour to Jardin d'Essai and to the village of Vohitsara. Lunch is included in the rate. Another hotel worth trying is the *Jupiter Hotel and Restaurant* (low-medium tariff), on Boulevard Augagneur.

L'Escale Hotel (low tariff), north of the railway station on Boulevard Marechal Foch, is a hotel from which several reports of theft have recently been received. The management is, however, pleasant and will lock up belongings while you are out. The staff do cook meals for residents, but you should tell them at least four hours ahead that you plan to eat there. Often they request that a guest accompany them to the market to purchase the ingredients for the meal. Near the taxi-brousse station, and a good place to stay if you are only passing through Toamasina, is the family-run *Beryl Hotel* (low tariff), just past the Fisa Tanambo building.

Hardy travellers, on a shoestring budget and armed with insect repellent, should walk around the lanes west of the train station. Here you will find several cheap inns that offer light meals and cold showers. The best choice here is the *Hotel Venance*, followed by *Hotel Niavo*.

Places to eat

There are numerous restaurants, snack bars, cafés, bakeries and hotels in town, with a good selection of cooking styles, prices and standard available. Many tourists make the mistake of only eating from the Continental menus offered in tourist-class hotels. Take the plunge and venture out to discover the restaurants of Toamasina, with their array of dishes.

For reasonably priced seafood dishes, the best place to eat is *Chez Jo*, on Boulevard Joffre. The servings are large, the waitresses friendly and the variety of seafood amazing. Opposite Pangalanes Canal Cruises (Soft Line Co.) on Boulevard Joffre is the *Restaurant Chinoise*. Diners may select from an extensive Oriental menu that includes meals specifically for vegetarians.

On the corner of Boulevard Joffre and Rue Nationale is the *Adam and Eve Buvette Restaurant and Salon de Thé*. It serves breakfasts of fresh croissants, pastries and coffee. From about 11h30 it starts baking pizzas and preparing light Malagasy meals.

At *Restaurant and Bar le Loreol*, off Rue de la Réunion, you will find numerous locals at lunch time. It gets full from about 11h00. Its menu is small but the quality, quantity and price of food is agreeable. Try the Malagasy fish dishes with rice, spicy sauce and a quart of Three Horse beer.

Restaurant le Pousse-Pousse, near the end of Rue de la Réunion, is another haunt of Toamasina citizens. This is always a good recommendation for a restaurant and this place is no exception. All meals include rice and you have the choice of fish, beef, pork or vegetables as additions. *Dragon des Mers* Chinese restaurant, towards the beachfront and among the warehouses, is a marvellous place at which to eat. This family-run restaurant has smiling, talkative staff who serve steaming plates of delicious Chinese food. The *Lotus Rouge* restaurant also falls into this category.

At the markets, visitors may purchase fresh produce and freshly cooked samosas and brochettes. A good selection of snacks is sold at the *Salon de Thé Au Plaisir*, on Boulevard Joffre. Just as good for its range of cakes and snacks is the *Croissant d'Or Patisserie*, near the market on Rue Bertho.

Opposite the BNI bank is *Le Gourmet Restaurant*. This restaurant seldom seems busy, which is strange considering its low prices, extensive menu and attentive service. The seafood dishes are tasty, filling and prepared to recipes that are distinctly Indonesian in flavour. At the *Paradis du Peuple*, and the *Tsarafandray Bar Restaurant*, visitors will find a local crowd enjoying the appetising meals from a small but select menu. Along Rue Aviateur Goulette is one of Toamasina's best kept secrets, *Restaurant Vietnamien*. A lot of the menu is written in Vietnamese and Malagasy, so you may have to get someone to do some translating for you. Its dishes are highly recommended, and no matter what you finally choose, rest assured that it will be memorable.

For a taste of authentic Malagasy cuisine, eat at least one meal at *Restaurant la Romance*, near the bus stop and Transni Shipping offices. Behind the taxi-brousse station, where the long-distance trucks park, are a number of Malagasy hotelys serving traditional dishes.

MAROANTSETRA

Perched on the coast at the mouth of the Antainambalana River, Maroantsetra is becoming the tourist centre on the Baie d'Antongil. It is from here that many of the long hikes into the rainforests of the Presqu'île de Masoala start. One of the favourite trekking routes is between Maroantsetra and Maronmandia and thence to Antalaha (see section on northern Madagascar: Antalaha).

Getting there

The majority of tourists to the area arrive on board an Air Madagascar flight. There are flights to Maroantsetra on Monday, Thursday, Friday and Saturday. Contact Air Madagascar or a travel agent for the current schedule, routes and fares.

Getting to Maroantsetra by taxi-brousse means getting to Mananara first. There are daily taxis to Mananara from Toamasina. From Mananara, it is another 112 km of gravel road, hugging the coastline and travelling through some splendid regions of rainforest, to Maroantsetra. The first taxi-brousse or 4x4 taxi leaves Mananara at about 7h30, arriving in Maroantsetra five to eight hours later. Book your front seat, inside the cab, the day before, or else make sure to take along something to wrap yourself up in as protection from the dust or rain that usually accompanies these taxi rides.

Things to do

There is not a great deal of interest to tourists in Maroantsetra. The major area of interest is the enormous primary forests that lie north and east of the Antainambalana River, and the secondary forest growth south of the river and up onto the Plateau de Makira. The Presqu'île de Masoala has been gazetted to be a national forest reserve, but before the act becomes official, Malaysian, Korean and Taiwanese timber consortiums are rushing to harvest the rare trees, in deals that would anger most environmental organisations – if they knew what was happening in this remote place.

Rain is a feature of Maroantsetra, with virtually daily downpours. Visitors are advised to arrive with wet weather gear and mosquito repellent. Nearly 3 000 mm of rain falls annually in Maroantsetra; enough to keep the surroundings constantly green, humid and muddy.

Travellers are able to arrange for boat trips up the calmer reaches of the Antainambalana River, to where it enters the rainforest. From the village of Ambinanitelo, you can find guides for the adventurous 70 km hike through the dense forests to Andapa. This hike is not for the unfit. There are lots of insects, rain and jungle through which you must cut your way. Come prepared with a machete, hiking boots, gaiters and rain poncho. Remember to check for leeches at the end of each day's trekking. You will also need to carry all your own food for the 10 day trek, and something with which to purify water is also recommended.

South of Maroantsetra, about 5 km offshore, is the island of Nosy Mangabe. It is another reason why a growing number of tourists are coming to Maroantsetra. Transport to the island is fairly easy to arrange. Speak to the management of the Hotel Antongil or Hotel Coco Beach, or wander down to the port and ask the local fishermen and trading skippers for assistance. Note that a permit from ANGAP or the WWF is required to visit Nosy Mangabe.

The weird-looking aye-ayes are prominent on Nosy Mangabe. They are not endemic to the island, but were introduced in 1966 as part of a successful breeding programme. Another attraction is the chance of seeing *Pseudoxyrohopus heterurus*, a non-venomous snake that is found nowhere else in the world. Reptiles are prolific and visitors have the opportunity of seeing lizards, chameleons, leaf-tailed geckoes and noisy frogs. Families of brown lemur, black-and-white ruffed lemur and dwarf lemur also live on Nosy Mangabe. Flowers are abundant, and the dense forest of the island makes it a wonderful place for exploring.

Guides are not necessary on this little island, but do make the night walks a lot more interesting. You may have to arrange for a guide through one of the hotels; bear in mind that visitors must provide the guide's camping equipment and food. Despite there being no tourist accommodation on Nosy Mangabe, campers are provided for with a clean, level site and basic ablution facilities.

Accommodation

As Maroantsetra grows as a tourist destination, there is bound to be a burgeoning of accommodation. At the moment, however, suitable tourist lodgings are limited to the *Hotel Antongil* (low-medium tariff) and *Hotel Coco Beach* (medium-high tariff). A newer, friendly and recommended place is the *Hotel Tropical* (medium tariff). All three of these hotels are a far cry from anything available on other Indian Ocean islands, but are more than adequate for a few days' visit. The staff are helpful, especially at the Hotel Tropical. Staff members will even provide a hamper if you are spending the day on Nosy Mangabe. At all the recognised hotels, accommodation is in clean, basic rooms with ablution facilities. Meals are available, as are forest guides.

NAVANA

Following the eastward curve of the beach as it rounds the northern edge of Baie d'Antongil, visitors will arrive at the hamlet of Navana. The village is a relaxed place, quite used to seeing tourists and catering to the trade by offering a few curios, hiking guides and basic Malagasy accommodation and cuisine.

It was off Navana, in 1730, that the last and most infamous Indian Ocean pirate, Olivier le Vasseur (La Buse), was recognised by a French naval officer and forced to flee. Dragging his ship, *Victorieux*, from the dense vegetation, he cleared Vinanivao and sailed around northern Madagascar, making for the Comoros. By then, French naval vessels had been notified and a three month hunt ensued, which ended with La Buse caught in the Mozambique Channel, off Nosy Bé. His ship was sunk, the crew executed and he was taken to Île Bourbon (Réunion), where he was publicly hanged in June 1730. Even today, in the villages of Navana and Anjanavana, there are legends about La Buse. Apparently he married a chief's daughter from Anjanavana, and the unusual double-storey house that hugs the eastern part of the Bight of Antongil belonged to the family. Whatever the truth of the stories, the area between Navana and Anjanavana is rich with pirate history and not a little attractive to those in search of treasure and adventure.

MANANARA

Those few tourists who stop in Mananara invariably come to visit the wilderness around this relaxed village. Mananara National Park, the Biosphere Reserve, Aye-aye Island and the marine reserve around it are all soon to be part of massive promotional campaigns that are bound to make them popular destinations of tour groups and Malagasy tour operators.

Getting there

Travellers can reach Mananara by plane, road or boat. Air Madagascar flies to Mananara on Monday, Wednesday, Thursday and Friday from several towns. Contact it or a travel agent for the current schedule, routes and fares.

There are daily taxi-brousses from Toamasina and Fenoarivo Atsinanana (Fenerive-Est). The first of these leaves Toamasina at about 7h00 and Fenoarivo Atsinanana at 7h30. From Toamasina the 213 km trip should take between six and 10 hours. From Fenoarivo Atsinanana it takes four to eight hours to travel the 130 km. The road is tarred as far as Soanierana-Ivongo, after which it becomes a horrible gravel road all the way to Maroantsetra.

Once a week a coastal trading vessel sails from Toamasina and visits the larger settlements up the north-east coast. Contact Auximad Shipping about its few passenger berths. There are several sailing dhows that voyage between Nosy Boraha and either Manompana or Mananara. There is no fixed schedule, and days and times of departure depend on the cargo being moved. Go to the docks in Ambodifotatra on Nosy Boraha and speak to the dhow captains for assistance.

Things to do

Mananara is surrounded by almost 23 000 ha of national wilderness reserve. This stretches from the numerous islets off the coast westward into the rainforest and includes the lower reaches of the Mananara River, which flows off the hills of Tampoketsa d'Antsiatsia. Covering 137 000 ha around the Mananara National Park is the UNESCO International Biosphere Reserve, which encompasses 73 km of reefed coastal areas.

Offshore, visitors will be able to see hundreds of colourful reef fish, marine plants, deep-water predators and, occasionally, comical sea cows (dugongs) and their equally humorous calves. Onshore, within the confines of the forest, walkers may discover ruffed lemurs, sifakas and aye-ayes. Those who venture far enough off the tourist trail into the jungle may be fortunate enough to see the rare hairy-eared dwarf lemur, which is found nowhere else on earth. Look out too for the peculiar indri. Its spine-chilling call will notify you of its presence long before you actually see one. The best place from which to hire guides into the forest is the hamlet of Sandrakatsy, on the western side of the reserve between the Mananara and Anove rivers.

In the hilly interior of the park there is a staggering array of floral displays that will leave one bewitched. The wild orchids, blossoming trees and dense vegetation lend a graceful beauty to the Mananara National Park.

In the Mananara River is Aye-Aye Island, home to endemic aye-ayes and diademed sifakas. There are 83 bird species known to visit Aye-Aye Island during the year, and it is seldom that a trip around the island is not punctuated by birdsong and the sight of a lone Malagasy kestrel or crested drongo. The island is under the management of Chez Rogers in Mananara, and is known locally as Rogers' Reserve. Independent visitors are not welcome, and you must arrange a tour through Chez Rogers at least two days in advance. There seems to be some disagreement as to whether ANGAP permits are needed or not. I was told that so long as I visited Aye-Aye Island with the Chez Rogers' tour then no permit was needed. An Italian traveller, who had trekked from Andilamena through the forests to Mananara for the express purpose of visiting Aye-Aye Island, was refused entry because he did not have an ANGAP permit. If you do find out the facts, please write and tell me for the next edition of this book.

Accommodation

Tourist accommodation in Mananara is at Hotel Aye-Aye or Chez Rogers. The owners of *Chez Rogers* (medium tariff) seem to own Mananara, and both prices and service reflect the monopoly they seem to think they have. The accommodation is clean and in pleasant bungalows, with washing facilities. Meals can be selected from a good menu, and packed lunches ordered if you are going walking into the forest for the day. Forest guides and boats to the islets can be arranged at the reception desk.

Recommended however, especially for travellers, is the *Hotel Aye-Aye* (medium tariff). The German owner is a fascinating chap, with loads of useful tourist information on the area. He is able to organise forest and ocean trips, at reasonable prices, that include lunch and soft drinks. You may eat at the Hotel Aye-Aye, choosing from a comprehensive menu that features both traditional and Continental dishes. Accommodation is in comfortable bungalows with ablution amenities.

MANOMPANA

You can reach Manompana from either Toamasina or Mananara. There are daily taxi-brousses from both these places. From Toamasina, the taxi departs at about 7h30, and with stops in Mahavelona, Mahambo, Fenoarivo Atsinanana and Soanierana-Ivongo, gets to Manompana at around 14h30. The drive itself is marvellous, as the tarred road hugs the scenic coastline, and travels through forests to Soanierana-Ivongo. From there, a gravel track winds its way across the Marovoalavo Peninsula to Manompana.

There is nothing of particular tourist interest in Manompana, unless you find a guide to take you up into the forests west of the village. There are still stands of primary rainforest here, but the tavy agriculture has already started to denude the fringes of the forest region. Trekkers are advised to talk to the manager of the Hotel Antsiraka or Hotel Manompana. The former hotel is more helpful and will even pack lunch for a day trip into the jungle. Those visitors who enjoy hiking should consider the 60 km walk that crosses the Anove River and traverses the Mananara National Park to the village of Sandrakatsy and then goes on to Mananara. The walk takes about four days and will have trekkers exploring regions and villages that seldom see foreigners and are steeped in traditional customs of hospitality and generosity. You must carry your own camping equipment, emergency food and drinking water.

Most people who stop in Manompana do so to catch the boats which ply the straits to Nosy Boraha. At the hotels, and in many of the shops, sailing schedules have been put up for reference. Note that these are changed monthly, and you should check the date when ascertaining a departure time. The boats normally leave Manompana on Monday and Thursday, at about 7h00. Returning from Ambodifotatra, departure is at 7h00 on Tuesday and Friday.

Accommodation in Manompana is not for the tourist used to five-star resorts. You have the choice of staying in the clean but basic *Hotel Antsiraka* (low tariff), or, if desperate, the low-hygiene *Hotel Manompana* (low tariff). The Hotel Antsiraka is recommended, and while it has not yet got any electricity or showers, visitors are given two candles, mosquito coils and attended to by a joyous, affectionate young staff.

No visit to Manompana is complete without at least one trip to the Palace Bar. This quaint bar is renowned among travellers, and I have heard it mentioned in Kathmandu, Marrakesh and Istanbul. The sign outside reads, "The Best Place for You. You may Watch the Sea while Sitting in the Palace."

MAHAVELONA (FOULPOINTE)

Mahavelona's popularity as a tourist destination is growing. An increasing number of tour operators are now bringing their clients to the white beaches, reefs and sand dunes of Mahavelona.

You can reach Mahavelona by taxi-brousse from Toamasina, 60 km to the south. There are at least three taxi-brousses daily. The first taxi-brousse leaves Toamasina each morning at about 6h30, taking one to two hours to reach Mahavelona.

The town itself is typical of the Betsimisaraka tribe and well worth a short walking tour. On the northern outskirts of Mahavelona are the ruins of an Imerina rova, built some time in the 19th century as a military garrison for the empire-building troops of Radama I. The towering sand dunes on the beach east of Mahavelona are known as the

"Singing Dunes" by the villagers. When the south-east winds blow off the sea, the sand slides over itself, creating an eerie wail that overcomes the sound of the sea as it washes up the canted beach. Swimming here is not recommended, though a growing number of scuba divers have started exploring the pristine reef offshore. Sharks are a feature off the reefs, as are deep-water cruisers such as marlin, barracuda and sailfish. If you arrive with your own scuba gear, the Manda Beach Hotel can arrange to fill tanks and for a boat to take divers out to the reefs. Deep-sea fishing excursions are organised by the Au Gentil Pêcheur, while hand-line fishing can be had by talking to the people at the signless Hotel Foulpointe.

Visitors to Mahavelona have three accommodation options. The luxurious – by Malagasy standards – *Manda Beach Hotel* (medium-high tariff), tel. 322.43, has bungalows and rooms with washing facilities. Meals are not included in the rate, but can be taken from a good menu in the hotel's dining room. There are also tennis courts, a rudimentary golf course and a swimming pool. Nonresidents may also make use of the facilities by speaking to the general manager and paying a small fee.

The delectable *Au Gentil Pêcheur* (medium tariff) has bungalows that are clean, comfortable and adequate for a few days' visit. Breakfast and dinner can be ordered from a delicious set menu that concentrates on fresh seafood. The worst, and cheapest, place to stay in Mahavelona is the *Hotel Foulpointe* (low tariff). The restaurant is worth a visit, but the bungalows and pool are in need of a good clean. The washing facilities are atrocious and you must be hard-pressed to stay here for anything longer than one night.

ANDASIBE (PÉRINET)

About 252 km south-west of Toamasina, on the RN2 to Antananarivo, is the famed Analamazaotra Nature Reserve, commonly referred to as Périnet. It is Madagascar's most visited nature reserve and is a must for visitors. A little over 800 ha in size, Périnet will give walkers a glimpse of the recherché black and white indri lemur. The reserve itself is mostly secondary forest growth with secluded valleys of primary vegetation. The area edging the reserve is extensively eroded.

You can get to Périnet by taxi-brousse, train or with a tour operator. Train is the cheapest, taxi-brousse the most reliable and a tour operator the most expensive but comfortable. From the Taxi-brousse Station

North, in 'Tana, there are several daily taxis going to Toamasina. They leave 'Tana at 6h00. Occasionally, the taxi-brousse company clerks are unwilling to help if you are only going to Andasibe, but with a little firm persuasion and an extra FMg 500 you will get a seat. The longer, but guaranteed, way of reaching Andasibe is to take the Moramanga taxi from the Taxi-brousse Station East in 'Tana. There are only two daily taxis going to Moramanga from the capital and it's a case of first come first served. The first one leaves at about 8h00 and the second at 10h00. From Moramanga you will have to walk or flag down a taxi-brousse for the 18 km trip to Andasibe and the entrance to Périnet.

A scenic trip can be taken by train from Antananarivo to Andasibe on the 'Tana to Toamasina railroad. The train's schedule is hardly reliable and it tends to be an on-off thing throughout the week, depending on weather conditions and whether rebels have blown the line up or not. Under normal circumstances – you will need to make enquiries at the station in 'Tana – the train goes to Toamasina one day and returns the next. It leaves Antananarivo at 7h00, reaching Andasibe at about 11h00. The journey itself is wonderful as you rattle through silent forests, deep valleys, across swaying iron bridges over raging rivers, and make stops at isolated jungle settlements where vendors offer traditional Malagasy food.

All visitors to Périnet must have a valid permit from ANGAP. These may be purchased at the reserve entrance kiosk, Hotel de la Gare or through the ANGAP office in 'Tana. The hotel is able to arrange for specialist guides who can speak English, German or Italian. Remember that prices for guided excursions are set by ANGAP and you should be aware of these prices before starting to negotiate with a guide. Day walks are cheaper than night walks, but the reasons will become abundantly clear if you try both day and night tours.

It is not easy to find the indri lemurs, or any other lemurs for that matter, without the assistance of a guide. Under the expert tracking abilities of these guides you will be able to spot red-bellied lemurs, aye-ayes, bamboo lemurs, woolly lemurs and, hopefully, indri.

Some of the most beautiful birds of Madagascar are found in the forests of Périnet. From the rare brown mesite to the mysterious Madagascar red owl, there is a plethora of birdlife that also includes such wonders as ground rollers, flufftails and sunbirds, not to mention kingfishers and the solitary Madagascar buzzard.

Perhaps the most famous of reptiles in Périnet is the big Parson's chameleon. It is not easy to find and the services of a guide are highly recommended. Another six species of chameleon crawl slowly about on the foliage, and the ability to camouflage themselves makes locating them difficult. Look too for any number of the 12 species of tenrec found scurrying about in the undergrowth. At night, on the edges of the blue lakes and the dripping forest, over 24 species of frog croak out songs to one another. The elusive, delicate golden mantilla frog is one of Madagascar's most celebrated frogs, that appears on numerous postage stamps and postcards. The best place to look for these frogs is at Étang Nympea, west of the disco along the RN2.

During the wet season, walkers should wear hiking boots, socks and gaiters, plus a poncho. After the tour check carefully for any brown leeches that may have decided to attach themselves to you for a quick meal. Mosquitoes and other nasties, typical of forests, can make the visit unpleasant and you must take along insect repellent and mosquito coils if you are to enjoy Périnet and its environs.

Colourful orchids, multi-hued creepers and bowing ferns make Périnet an Eden for those tourists interested in the reserve's flora.

South-east of the visitors' centre is picturesque Étang de la Presqu'île lake, and beyond the Analamazaotra River the successful and fascinating fish farm (Bassin de Pisciculture). Continue walking east from the aquaculture project until reaching the shores of beautiful Lac Vert. East of Lac Vert the indigenous forest rolls away in a green haze to the Ancien Chemin Muletier (the Old Mule-skinners Road), which links the Sahatandra River in the north and the road to Toamasina in the south.

Accommodation in and around Andasibe has flourished. The most popular hotel is the *Hotel de la Gare* (medium-high tariff). It is the oldest tourist accommodation in Andasibe and has slacked a little on its standards. Still, its Swiss-like architecture is charming and the rooms comfortable, if somewhat musty. Recently, bungalows have been added to the hotel in an annexe, and they are a better choice. Meals are not included in the rate, but may be taken from a comprehensive menu in the hotel's dining room.

Hotel de la Gare also caters for campers, and there is a shady glade near the Anlamazaotra River available. You must walk the 1 km to the hotel to wash and for meals, but if you befriend the staff, someone will bring you breakfast at the camp site for a small fee.

In the new *Hotel les Orchidées* (medium tariff), tourists can find roomy lodgings with communal ablution facilities. The staff and management of Hotel les Orchidées try hard to please, and are able to arrange for knowledgeable guides to lead you through Périnet. They pack cold lunches for the outing.

The cheapest accommodation in Andasibe is at *Hotel Rakotozanany* (low tariff). This is more of a Malagasy restaurant than a hotel, but it does rent out a few spartan rooms to travellers. There is a communal hole-in-the-ground toilet and guests are provided with a bucket of hot water for washing. Whether you stay at the Hotel Rakotozanany or not, you should try at least one Malagasy meal in its noisy restaurant.

Those visitors who arrive with their own tents are permitted to camp in the reserve, but need to get clearance from the senior warden. You can usually find him in the offices at the visitors' centre. Campers may set their tents around Étang de la Presqu'île, but it is a little near the national road and you may prefer the solitude of Lac Vert. Make certain to take along a torch for night tours.

Closer to Moramanga are the bungalows of *Ambarikadera* (medium-high tariff). The accommodation is pleasant and the attached restaurant has a wide range of dishes that feature both European and Malagasy dishes, all at reasonable prices.

MANANJARY

On the Ampasary River, the old colonial town of Mananjary is divided into two parts by the Pangalanes Canal. The CBD and points of interest to visitors are on the eastern side of the canal, adjacent to the seashore. The town itself is laid-back, with a colourful market that fills to bursting on Friday mornings.

Getting there

The usual way of getting to Mananjary is by air from Fianarantsoa. Reaching the town from the east coast is not for the faint-hearted or inexperienced, but is recommended for those in search of adventure.

Air Madagascar flies to Mananjary on Tuesday, Thursday and Saturday. Contact it or a travel agent for the current schedule, routes and fares.

The quickest and easiest way by road is to take one of the four daily taxi-brousses from Fianarantsoa. The first of these leaves from the long-distance taxi-brousse station at about 7h00. The journey is through wonderful scenic countryside and includes a stop in the rainforest village of Ranomafana, on the fringe of the glorious Parc Nationale de Ranomafana. The road is tarred most of the way; well, tarred and potholed at least, and the journey should not take longer than about seven hours. There is also a stop for a snack in the junction hamlet of Irondo. Expect to be accosted by suspicious-looking characters selling emeralds here. The quality of the stones is excellent, but beware, minute cracks cannot be seen with the naked eye. Prices for precious stones are low in Irondo, and if you are planning to buy, ask to use an eyepiece before starting to negotiate. There is also one daily taxi-brousse from Antananarivo, that leaves from the Taxi-brousse Station South on Lalana Pastora Rahajason at about 18h00. It travels virtually all the way to Fianarantsoa before turning east for Mananjary at Ambohimahasoa. The trip from 'Tana takes between 12 and 16 hours.

Travelling overland from Toamasina to Mananjary is exciting, exhausting and unforgettable. Take a taxi-brousse from Toamasina to Ambila-Lemaitso. Here you must wait for the twice weekly taxi-brousse via Vatomandry to Mahanoro, or catch a canal boat on the Pangalanes Canal. There is an atrocious 76 km road from Mahanoro to Nosy-Varika. One taxi-brousse per week goes from Mahanoro via Nosy-Varika to Mananjary. Frequent supply trucks travel between Mahanoro and Mananjary. If you can convince a driver to let you ride in the back, you could reach Mananjary within four days. From Nosy-Varika it is another 119 km south, across the Sakaleona River and to Mananjary.

From Moramanga, take the thrice weekly taxi-brousse going south to Anosibe (An'Ala). From there you must trek or flag down a transport truck going the 95 km to Marolambo. From Marolambo there is a once weekly taxi-brousse going east to Mahanoro, from where you must find other transport south to Mananjary, via Nosy-Varika. The boat ride down the canal to Mananjary is the most relaxed and enjoyable way of getting there. It is however painfully slow, so perhaps you should rather try hitchhiking south.

Tourist information

The post office is beneath the tall communications aerials, in the old colonial part of Mananjary. Basic tourist information can be obtained from the Alliance Française, next to the defunct Les Paradis swimming pool and amusement park, near the beach. Tours, excursions and guides are best arranged by speaking to the staff at Jardin de la Mer hotel. Air Madagascar has an informative supply of literature. Its staff have a good knowledge of the locale and what could be of interest to tourists. Its office, where air tickets can be confirmed, is next to Auximad Shipping, opposite the Solimotel.

There are two banks in Mananjary, BFV and BTM. BFV does not change traveller's cheques and will only deal in hard foreign currency. BTM, on the other hand, not only changes foreign currency, but also cashes traveller's cheques and allows you to draw up to US $250 against a MasterCard credit card.

Things to do

There is not a great deal to see in Mananjary, though the beach, village itself and surrounding settlements make for enjoyable outings. All visitors should pay a visit to the spice warehouses, in the colonial part of town. The aroma from roasting coffee, cloves and pepper wafts over the town and lures visitors into the cavernous storerooms where the products are processed, graded, sorted and packed for export. Around Mananjary, look for the gracious, decaying French colonial mansions. A few of these have now been turned into government and municipal offices, while others are home to squatter families.

You can also take cruises on the Pangalanes Canal. The wooden boats seldom go far, transporting goods to villages on the edge of the canal. It makes for an interesting day trip and allows wonderful photo opportunities. The focal point of Mananjary is the market. There is both a covered market and an open-air market, which really come alive on Friday. The covered market is near the palm and *filaos*-filled park, west of the beach. There is a good selection of fresh produce, clothing and a few locally made curios for sale.

The police in Mananjary are strangely suspicious of foreigners, especially if you have more than one camera slung around your neck and seem to be snapping at people and buildings. Make sure to carry your passport with you at all times – many foreigners will be asked to produce it at least once on a visit here.

Accommodation

Tourists to Mananjary have the choice of two hotels: the Solimotel, which is popular with package tours, and the delightful Dutch-owned Jardin de la Mer. The *Solimotel* (medium-high tariff) is opposite Air Madagascar, along Boulevard Maritime, on the edge of the beach. Rooms have air-conditioners, and the restaurant offers expensive meals from a somewhat limited menu.

Recommended are the spacious and comfortable bungalows or rooms at *Jardin de la Mer* (medium-high tariff), tel. 940.80. The hotel is a little way out of town, at the southern end of Boulevard Maritime, where the Ampasary River and Pangalanes Canal spill into the sea. There are different prices for bungalows and rooms, depending on occupancy, number of beds and ablution facilities. All the bungalows have cold water en suite washing amenities. A flower-filled garden is fringed by palm and conifer trees. At night the scent from the tropical flowers and thousands of fireflies make walking about the garden a wonderful, romantic experience. The restaurant is renowned, and the meals cooked in coconut milk are a must.

A favourite haunt of expats and tourists is the *Hotel Nathalie* (medium tariff), tel. 940.41, across the Pangalanes Canal bridge, a few kilometres west of town. This clean hotel has showers, a good restaurant and an ambience that could only ever be found in the tropics.

Accommodation, without meals, is available at *Hotel Bons Amis* (low-medium tariff). This clean, Chinese-owned hotel is near the police station, and offers cold showers and can arrange excursions around Mananjary. North of the CBD, among the palm frond huts near the beach, is the *Hotel Stenny* and restaurant (low-medium tariff). There seems to be a resident group of French expats here who have raucous parties on Friday and Saturday evenings.

Places to eat

There are numerous Malagasy hotelys that are worth a visit. *Au Coin du Plaisir Bar and Restaurant*, north of the CBD near the village of Tanambao, has a festive atmosphere and cooks up enormous plates of fresh seafood, spiced with chili and accompanied by mounds of white rice. *Chez Hibiscus* offers a small menu of Malagasy food at good prices.

Super Sice is a small supermarket that keeps a few tinned goods and groceries that might be useful to visitors camping or self-catering. At both the covered and street markets visitors will be able to find freshly fried snacks that include samosas, beef brochettes and seafood.

MANAKARA

Surrounded by coffee estates, palm plantations and some of the worst erosion in Madagascar, Manakara is a busy town with dusty roads, amiable people and a seemingly endless ochre-coloured beach. Split by the Manakara River, the old part of town, along the seafront, has wide boulevards, colonial houses, parks and a serenity that is wonderful after the chaos of the new part of town. West of the river are the estuary and docks, rice paddies, markets and traditional settlements. Perceptive visitors may notice that many of the locals have decidedly Arabic features. They are descended from the early Arab immigrants to Madagascar, who over the years moved down from the north-east coast to settle around Manakara and Mananjary.

Getting there

Getting to Manakara is one of the pleasures of visiting this seaside town. You can travel by air, road and train. I recommend that you take the train ride through the rainforests from Fianarantsoa to Manakara. It is undoubtedly one of the great train journeys of the world.

Air Madagascar flies to Manakara on Tuesday, Thursday and Saturday, serving various towns en route. Contact it or a travel agent for the current schedule.

There are at least three daily taxi-brousses leaving from Fianarantsoa for the five to eight hour drive to Manakara, and one daily taxi-brousse making the 177 km trip from Mananjary. The best place to wait for lifts to Manakara is in the village of Irondo, where you can get taxis from Fianarantsoa, Mananjary, Antananarivo and Ranomafana. Two taxi-brousses leave 'Tana each evening at 17h00 for the long journey to Manakara. These taxis are frequently booked out well in advance and travellers should make their reservations at least two days before departure.

The train departs from Fianarantsoa every second day at 7h00. You will need to check with the enquiries counter in the station in Fianarantsoa for the next day of departure. The trip takes about seven or eight hours, along what is known as the Railroad of Orchids (Chemin de Fer des Orchidées). Through dripping rainforest and past forest villages, rice paddies and vineyards, travellers will be taken into a fairyland of trees, waterfalls, hills and 56 tunnels on the way down to the coast. The train station in Manakara, Fianarantsoa A la Côte Est, is about 2 km from town along the RN12.

Boats and ships from Manakara to other ports in Madagascar and further abroad can be found by speaking to the clerks of the Mediterranean Shipping Company (MSC), west of the taxi-brousse station, or Auximad Shipping, near the post office.

Tourist information

The post office is located beneath the exceptionally tall telecommunications aerials, along the road from the CBD towards the steel bridge over the Manakara River. The BFV and BTM banks have branches near the Hotel de Manakara, east of the river. BNI is west of the river, near the sports stadium. Tourist information is available from the Syndicat d'Initiative de Manakara.

Medical prescriptions can be filled, and minor ailments diagnosed, at Pharmacie Finaritra in town, or at Pharmacie du Levant on the way to the train station. Print film, batteries and developing facilities are obtainable at Photo Lumiere, close to Magasin Patrick.

Things to do

The best way of discovering what Manakara has to offer is to set off on a walking tour of town. There are wide sandy roads linking the various suburbs. A large informal sector spreads itself out around Manakara and you will be able to find the most amazing things being sold from the little wooden counters. The market is a must. Go inside, into the narrow alleys and between the covered stalls to where food, gemstones, drugs, cloth and anything you may desire are sold.

West of Manakara is one of the largest oil-palm plantations in the world. Established by the French, it is now losing its value as the world demand for palm oil decreases in favour of cheaper, synthetic products. The enormous plantation does, however, make for an interesting tour that can quite easily take up an entire day. The Hotel Sidi can arrange visits, as you are not allowed to just turn up unannounced. A tour includes the entire gamut of oil-palm production, from harvesting the kernels to pressing and storage.

East of the CBD, near the bridge, is the old stone building of the original Norwegian mission to Manakara. Across the bridge, before the beach, are wide tree-lined boulevards laid out by the French and refined by the British. The causarina-fringed beach is popular with locals, although swimming in the dirty sea is not advised.

Near the BFV bank is what appears to be a church. It is in fact a prison, built in the style of a church to fool Allied warplanes during their Second World War attacks against the Vichy French in Manakara.

Entertainment in Manakara is in the form of video shows, the Sidi Hotel nightclub and beach parties. Video shows start at about 10h00 each morning in the Video Club Mahatama, across from La Gourmandise Salon de Thé. The nightclub is open from about 21h30 on Friday and Saturday nights. It is small, smoke filled, always crowded and thoroughly enjoyable. Beach parties seem spontaneous, and if you have made a few friends you are almost certain to get invited to at least one.

Accommodation

The most expensive place to stay in Manakara is the *Parthenay Club Bungalows* (high tariff), on the beach east of town. Don't make the mistake of equating price with facilities though. The bungalows are run down, the salt-water swimming pool dirty.

A better option is the grand old *Hotel de Manakara* (high tariff), tel. 211.41. It, too, is east of the steel bridge and is well situated in a quiet boulevard near the BFV and BTM banks. Its restaurant is well known and the cheap fish dishes delicious. Rooms have bathrooms and the creaking floorboards and antique furniture make every stay here a trip into colonial history.

Along the coast, 12 km from Manakara, are the *Eden Sidi* bungalows (high tariff), tel. 212.04. Affiliated to the Sidi Hotel, the resort bungalows are suitable for tourists in search of comfort and tranquillity. The biggest drawback to staying at the Eden Sidi is its distance from town, though the management provides a daily courtesy bus that leaves at about 8h30 and returns from Manakara at 16h00.

The favoured tourist hotel in Manakara is the *Sidi Hotel* (medium tariff), tel. 212.04. This renowned hotel has pleasant Chinese management and rather dour Malagasy staff. There are several categories of rooms, most with ablution facilities. The management will gladly confirm air tickets for you, arrange tours of the locale and change money. The restaurant offers a good menu at fairly high prices, with large servings. On Saturday afternoon, boxing and karate competitions are held in the atrium behind the hotel. A lively nightclub gets going on Friday and Saturday evenings. Sidi Hotel regularly plays host to dance and DJ competitions; look for the current activity written on a banner and strung across the entrance to the hotel.

The cheapest places to stay are in the suburbs of Manakara. Near the Pharmacie Central is the Malagasy *Hotel Mamy* (the sweet hotel!), which is low tariff. You are unlikely to meet tourists staying in these basic wooden rooms or eating from the Malagasy menu. West of the market is another cheap Malagasy hotel, the *Hotel Morabe* (low tariff), tel. 210.70. Take along plastic sandals to wear while washing here, and insect repellent may also be a good idea. The restaurant offers a selection of tasty meals from a menu of Malagasy, Chinese and French dishes.

Highly recommended for budget travellers are the hotels *Fenosoa* and *Mifankatiavatsara* (low tariff). Both these cheap Malagasy hotels are south of the taxi-brousse station in the CBD. Accommodation is primitive, but the attention lavished on foreign guests by the families who run these hotels is not to be missed. Traditional Malagasy meals are available and buckets of hot water make washing bearable. They may even ask you to accompany them on food shopping expeditions to the market, where you are encouraged to select what ingredients you want for the evening meals.

Places to eat

Aside from the hotels at which meals can be taken, consider eating at a few of the restaurants and hotelys scattered about Manakara. The *Lotus Rouge Chinese Restaurant*, around the corner from the Sidi Hotel, offers a good selection of meals – if you can find it open. It seems to open whenever the owner feels like doing so. To find out when it will be open next, go down the left side of the restaurant to the house at the back, and ask any of the people there – they work in the restaurant.

Around Manakara are many hotelys that serve up the usual Malagasy cuisine at low prices. At *La Gourmandise Salon de Thé*, near the market and taxi-brousse station, you may select from a good menu that has mainly Chinese and Malagasy dishes. It also bakes cakes and pastries daily and has a few brands of foreign beer available. Tucked in beneath palm trees near the train station is the *Resto Tsarafandray*, where you can get plates of steaming, spiced Malagasy food. The *Salon de Thé Riminy*, near the market, serves up light Malagasy meals and strong coffee all day. At *Boulangerie Patisserie de l'Est*, hungry visitors have the choice of fresh cakes, pastries and bread each day. Delectable Malagasy and French dishes can be tasted at the *Restaurant Chez Lilie*, east of the market on the edge of rice paddies. Amiable staff make this little place a delight for late lunches or mid-morning snacks.

VOHIPENO

Hugging a small piece of land between the Pangalanes Canal and the mouth of the Matitanana River, Vohipeno is the destination for visitors looking to encounter traditional Antaimoro clan culture. There are several interesting tombs in the area and the villages in the countryside remain steeped in ancient rituals that are strikingly similar to practices on the Comoros, in Somalia and in Yemen. The Antaimoro consider their ancestry linked to the Muslim world, and though observing certain Christian ceremonies, refer to their beliefs as Silamo, an ancient religion that combines elements of both Christian and Islamic teachings, with a strong emphasis on the faith of Abraham.

You can easily reach Vohipeno from Manakara on the daily taxi-brousse that leaves at about 7h30. The 45 km long road is tarred all the way, and the trip should take less than an hour. You could also hunt around the canal in Manakara and try to find a boat that is cruising down to Vohipeno.

A visit to Vohipeno must include a tour to the sacred tombs of the kings at Evato, about 6 km from Vohipeno. On the walk to Evato, visitors will pass through villages where the women wear an odd looking four-cornered hat called a *satruka harefo*, which they claim originated in north-east Africa. It is not unlike the four-cornered hats worn by women in Somalia and the highlands of Ethiopia. Many of the men dress in kandous and the women tend to use their lamba oanys as a chador or chiromani. If you happen to pass a school en route to Evato, stop and ask if you can see the archaic form of Arabic script which is not only used in these villages, but still taught in many of the schools in the locale.

You cannot simply go wandering about the sacred burial sites around Vohipeno. First, you need to obtain permission from the village headman associated with the particular tombs. Already word has reached them of the desecration of Sakalava tombs on the west coast by tourists, and you may find it difficult to gain access. It helps if you have a letter of introduction, in French or Malagasy, from the Madagascar Tourist Board or the museum in 'Tana. To get a letter from the museum, speak to the curator. You will find his office on the first floor of the Musée de l'Art et Archéologie in 'Tana.

When visiting the tombs, take off your shoes and show the appropriate respect by bringing along a bottle of local rum and some fruit as offerings to appease the ancestors for your intrusion.

There is no tourist accommodation in Vohipeno and unless you find lodgings with a local family, or arrive with your own tent, you will have to travel back to Manakara for the night.

There are a few hotelys around Vohipeno. Pork is considered fady and no one should arrive with any pork products at all. The hotelys serve Malagasy cuisine, snacks and cold drinks. In the little market you can buy fresh produce, meat, fish and cassava.

FARAFANGANA

At the extreme southern end of the 736 km long Pangalanes Canal is Farafangana. Few visitors get to this town, and unless you want to see the forests west of Vondrozo or waterfalls on the upper reaches of the Mananara River, there is actually little reason to come here.

Visitors may reach Farafangana either by road or air. Air Madagascar flies to Farafangana on Tuesday, Wednesday, Thursday and Saturday from various towns. Contact it or a travel agent for the current schedule and routes.

There are two taxi-brousses per day running between Manakara and Farafangana. The first of these leaves from Manakara at 6h00, the second only when it is full, which could be as late as 14h00. The 109 km drive from Manakara is on a passable tar road, and includes a meal stop in Vohipeno. The trip should not take longer than three or four hours.

From Farafangana an exciting journey can be made over a terrible gravel road, through secondary forests and along the Andringitra mountains, to Ihosy. There are two taxi-brousses per month that undertake this odyssey. At least two trucks per week trundle their way between Ihosy and Farafangana. Speak to the police chief in Farafangana; he is sometimes able to find you a lift with one of these trucks. The 279 km drive along the RN27 takes almost 10 hours during the dry season, and anything up to 22 hours when the rains come. Take along your own water, wet weather gear and a strong determination to get through. Most trucks stop for a meal in Ivohibe, within sight of towering Pic Boby (2 658 m), the highest mountain in the Andringitra range.

Visitors will find suitable accommodation at two hotels. The *Tulipes Rouges* (medium tariff), tel. 911.86, is popular with tourists, and the restaurant does delicious meals from a comprehensive menu that features Malagasy, Continental and Chinese dishes. The *Rose Rouge* (low-medium tariff), tel. 911.54, is used by Malagasy holiday-makers and travelling salesmen – always a good source of information about the region. The Rose Rouge also dishes up large meals of good food at reasonable prices.

For authentic Malagasy food, visit the hotelys in Farafangana. Their dishes of fresh fish, rice and a piquant sauce are appetising. Their drinks are always ice cold.

NOSY BORAHA (Île STE MARIE)

Lying off the north-east coast of Madagascar, about 10 km east of Pointe Laree, is the 57 km long island of Nosy Boraha; Madagascar's tourist destination par excellence. While Nosy Bé, off the north-west coast, led the campaign to promote Madagascar as a sun, sea and sand destination, it is Nosy Boraha that has snatched the burgeoning tourist trade.

Despite severe erosion and overpopulation, Nosy Boraha somehow manages to retain an air of history, relaxation and a tropical island atmosphere that will continue to attract many visitors. The palm-fringed white beaches, excellent snorkelling and enchanting pirate history make Nosy Boraha a must on a visit to Madagascar's east coast.

Rain occurs through most of the year, and wet weather gear should always be included in your luggage. The lightest rains fall between September and early December. You can expect some rainfall during this time, but not so that it will drastically affect your visit. Cyclones are common to eastern Madagascar, and Nosy Boraha is no exception. Between late December and March, storms, often of cyclone intensity, come roaring down on Nosy Boraha in a sustained assault that could see tourists confined to their rooms or the hotel building for days at a time. When warnings of a particularly vicious cyclone are first heard, pack your bags and cross to the mainland. From there head west, inland, to where the weather is more stable and pleasant.

The largest settlement is Ambodifotatra, on the south-west of the island. This is where most visitors arrive, either on one of the ferry boats that sail between the mainland and Ambodifotatra on Monday, Wednesday and Thursday, or on Air Madagascar's aircraft every day of the week. Essential tourist business, such as visa extensions, banking, mailing and ticket confirmations can be done here and a few interesting sites can also be found in Ambodifotatra.

It has been deduced that Arabs were the first to establish a settlement on Nosy Boraha. Some artefacts have been found in the south-east of the island, at Ankarena Cave; both in the Ampanihy forest and north of Ambodiatafana are what appear to be ruins that match those of the Arab seamen who landed on Mauritius some time in the 10th century. But it was tribesmen of the Betsimisaraka nation who really settled Nosy Boraha. The strong similarity, in appearance, culture and customs, between mainland Betsimisaraka and the modern Ste Marians contradicts the islanders' claims that they are a separate tribe. The Ste Marians live mostly from fishing and subsistence agriculture, though a growing number are now being employed in the far more profitable tourism industry. When visiting villages independently, adhere to the Betsimisaraka tribe's fady laws and customs.

The fascinating history of Nosy Boraha is worth investigation. Meaning the "Island of Abraham" in Farsi (ancient Persian), the name is attributed to those early Arab seafarers who first made landfall on the island. Local Betsimisaraka folklore ascribes the name to "Those of the light skin" whom the first tribesmen encountered when they reached the island.

The first records of Europeans settling on Nosy Boraha were written by French navigator Pascal Pluchard in 1693. He encountered what he describes as a functioning pirate republic. Pirates such as George Taylor, John England and Olivier le Vasseur all used Nosy Boraha as their base at some time during their reign of terror in the Indian Ocean. There was considerable intermarriage between this carefree band of adventurers and the beautiful Malagasy women. Their children, known as *zana malata,* formed a cohesive clan that supported Princess Bety, who was given the island as a wedding gift by her Betsimisaraka father, King Ratsimilaho.

Malagasy rule came to an abrupt and unpleasant end when lovestruck Bety agreed to the suggestion of her French husband, Jean-Onésime Filet, that she cede Nosy Boraha to the French colonial government in 1750. The French gave administration of the island over to the expanding French East India Company. It requisitioned troops and battleships to entrench its authority on the island, and stripped the island's clan chieftains of all power.

Two years later, there was a ferocious revolt. French soldiers were given orders to crush the rebellion, which they duly did, with the death of over 70 islanders and three Frenchmen. Then, totally out of keeping with past practices, the French handed over control to the Betsimisaraka king again and promptly exiled his daughter, Princess Bety, to Mauritius, where she died.

In 1818, the French government had a change of heart and decided that they wanted Nosy Boraha back. They despatched warships and marines to wrest the island from the Betsimisaraka. The tribesmen, however, by now knew of the military power of the Europeans and offered no resistance to the soldiers. The French encouraged planters from Réunion to settle on Nosy Boraha and introduced vanilla, coffee and cloves. By 1825, estates proliferated on Nosy Boraha, while the rainforests were hacked further and further back to allow agricultural crops to be planted. As the planters intruded on the highly leached, shallow soils of the forests, they discovered that after a few years crop harvests were exceedingly poor. Instead of seeing the obvious, they abandoned old fields in a practice of shifting cultivation not unlike that of the islanders. By 1930 most of the original families had left their defunct, exhausted estates, and the French administration on Madagascar decided that the island would make a suitable penal colony for anti-French activists, which it remained until Madagascar's independence.

Getting there

Most tourists reach Nosy Boraha by aeroplane, either from Antananarivo or Toamasina, though an ever-increasing number of travellers are using the ferry, cargo and fishing boats that voyage between the mainland and Nosy Boraha.

Air Madagascar flies daily to Nosy Boraha from 'Tana or Toamasina. Contact it or a travel agent for the current schedule and fares.

Reaching Nosy Boraha by boat is exciting, frustrating, memorable and often sickening (seasick I mean!) Manompana is the closest ferry port to Ambodifotatra. From here, a ferry leaves on Monday and Thursday morning. The same boat then returns from Nosy Boraha on Tuesday and Friday. Occasionally, during August and September, when demand is highest, this ferry also sails to Nosy Boraha on Saturday and returns Sunday. The voyage takes about four hours. From Toamasina, a ferry leaves on Wednesday morning for Ambodifotatra. This rust bucket of a boat sails back to Toamasina on Friday morning. From Toamasina, the journey takes between eight and 14 hours, depending on sea and weather conditions.

The cheapest and probably most exciting way of getting to Nosy Boraha is to arrange for one of the coastal fishermen to sail you across on his wooden boat, complete with outrigger and tattered sail. The most helpful can be found at Soanierana-Ivongo and around Pointe Laree, though many of those at Pointe Laree are now demanding fees that come close to that asked by the ferry in Manompana. If you do decide on using a fishing boat to sail across, take along something with which to keep your pack dry, water to drink, a hat and strong sunscreen.

Tourist information

Tourist information is available from the reception desks of all the top-class hotels on Nosy Boraha. In Ambodifotatra, travellers will find loads of useful information about the island by contacting Sodextour on Lalana Firinga. The Alliance Française, along Arabe la Bigorne, has tourist information in French and a handy little map of the island. Air Madagascar is also on Arabe la Bigorne. You can confirm and buy air tickets here, and it is also a useful source for tourist information. Emergency medical treatment is available from the hospital, east of Arabe Ratsimilaho. The tourist hotels change foreign currency and cash traveller's cheques. Credit cards are useless on Nosy Boraha, though there is talk that the bank in Ambodifotatra is negotiating for the use of internationally recognised credit cards such as MasterCard, Visa, American Express and Diners Club.

Things to do

There are several sites around Ambodifotatra that deserve a visit. Foremost among these are the oldest Christian church in Madagascar and the pirate cemetery. The church, built in 1837, is on the edge of Baie des Forbans, south-west of Lalana St Joseph. It was given as a gift to the colonists on Nosy Boraha by Empress Eugénie.

The pirate cemetery is south-east of Ambodifotatra, towards the village of St-Joseph on the Baie des Forbans. Most of the inscriptions on the grey rock headstones are illegible with age and none of the names that can be deciphered are noteworthy. Still, the cemetery is a frequent destination of tour groups and visitors and does add to the mysterious ambience of Nosy Boraha.

Other points of interest include the market and fort. The market is a must for visitors. It reaches its zenith on Thursday, although Tuesday also sees an enlarged market area. Throughout the rest of the week, the usual array of stalls can be browsed through.

There is a forbidding fort, constructed in 1753, east of Lalana Sylvain Roux. It is, however, off limits to tourists and is now used as a crumbling military garrison. You may take photos of the outside of the fort. To be certain though, check with the guards at the gate what you may take pictures of. This also applies to the harbour area. A number of visitors have reported that the police harassed them after they had taken photographs of the docks.

Venturing out from Ambodifotatra, travellers have a number of sites and islands that should be visited. To reach the regions north of town, travellers can walk, take part in an organised tour, or hire some means of transport. Sodextour rents out vehicles and motorcycles, while most hotels keep a few bicycles for hire.

In the Baie des Forbans is the tiny island of Île aux Forbans (the island of pirates). Any number of small boats on the northern edge of Baie des Forbans will ferry you across for a few FMg. The fascination of Île aux Forbans is the ruins which crown the island. No one is certain by whom or why this structure was built. A few local guides claim that it was once a watchtower for the pirates, but why they would need a watchtower in the bay is a little baffling. Others claim that it's a gateway, but to what?

North-east of the Fanilo Albrand lighthouse, in the far north of Nosy Boraha, are several wide, deep holes which have been eroded into the granite. They are known as the Ambodiatafana piscine naturelle. When the tide comes in, these holes are filled and offer delightful paddling in the surge and rush of the foaming waves. To get there visitors first travel up the west coast road to Ambatoroa. Turn north-east here. Continue past the lighthouse and you will find the pools east of Ambodiatafana village.

Taking the road that swings east from the west coast settlement of Ankirihiry, visitors will reach the end of the driveable road at a region of swampland filled with birdlife. It is inadvisable to go walking in these swamps alone; there is apparently quicksand here. Get yourself a guide from the hamlet where the road from the west coast swings south-east to Sahasifotra. Off the beach, east of Sahasifotra, you can see the skeletal remains of HMS *Gladstone*, which foundered here in 1872. What became of the crew is a puzzle, though according to records in the public archives in 'Tana, it must have taken considerable time and effort to empty the ship's food larder and armoury, and the cargo she was carrying from the Orient was never recovered.

The highest point on Nosy Boraha is the top of Davolo Hill (112 m). There are several tracks to the summit. The one most used by tourists leads up from the west coast village of Maronmandia. It takes about two hours of easy walking to reach the top of the hill.

Across a narrow strait of water and hemmed in on three sides by magnificent coral reefs, south of Nosy Boraha, is the small island of Île aux Nattes (Nosy Nato). The only way of getting to Île aux Nattes is by boat. Fleets of them wait on the beach south of the airport. Prepare yourself for a stiff bout of bargaining, and make sure that the final fee includes your luggage. There is nothing of particular tourist interest on Île aux Nattes, and most visitors simply come to taste the food and experience the legendary hospitality at Chez Napoleon. The reefs offshore offer wonderful snorkelling and scuba diving, provided you stay inside the reef and resist the temptation to slip over the plunging sea walls, where you will encounter predatory sharks and barracuda.

Accommodation

Accommodation on Île aux Nattes is either in the Hotel Nautilus or Chez Napoleon, occasionally referred to by its official name, Hotel Orchidée.

The *Hotel Nautilus* (medium tariff) has bungalows on the beach and a restaurant that specialises in reasonably priced seafood dishes. The *Chez Napoleon* (low tariff) is known for its excellent service and fabulous meals. It offers guests basic bungalows with shared ablution facilities, or slightly more expensive lodgings that have showers. You must eat in its restaurant. The recommended dishes are the fresh fish or chicken in coconut milk with Malagasy rice, washed down with a glass or two of Chez Napoleon's home-brewed palm wine.

There is no shortage of accommodation on Nosy Boraha. From luxury hotels, through beach bungalows to a hut in some village, no visitor will go without a place to sleep for the night.

At the high-tariff end of the market are the resort hotels, many owned and managed by foreigners. The best hotel on Nosy Boraha is the three-star *Saonambo* (high tariff), midway between Mahavelo and Vohilava on the south-west coast. This hotel offers guests accommodation in thatched bungalows, and provides a nautical centre that gives scuba diving lessons that commence in a sparkling swimming pool. It also rents out snorkelling gear. There is a picturesque restaurant and a comprehensive à la carte menu. Reservations are advised well in advance: Soanambo Hotel, PO Box 20, Île Ste Marie, tel. 40.

The one-star *La Cocoteraie* (high tariff) is in the far north-west of Nosy Boraha at Lohatanjona Antsiraikiraiky. It is about 30 km from Ambodifotatra and about 43 km from the airport. It does however provide a courtesy bus to the airport for arriving and departing guests. This huge resort has over 50 beach bungalows and possibly the best stretch of swimming beach on Nosy Boraha. The restaurant is one of the finest in Madagascar and no visitor should miss the opportunity of dining here. Excursions on Nosy Boraha and to some of the outlying islets are organised by La Cocoteraie. Write to Hotel la Cocoteraie, Antsiraikiraiky, Île Ste Marie.

The *Betty Plage* (medium-high tariff), 5 km north of Ambodifotatra, is popular with tour groups. It has bungalows, with or without washing facilities. *La Cirque* (medium tariff) is about 20 km north of Ambodifotatra on Baie Lonkitsy. There are lodgings in 10 palm-frond bungalows and a good restaurant. Make your reservations about 30 days ahead: La Cirque, PO Box 1, Île Ste Marie.

At *Orchidées Bungalows* (medium-high tariff), south of Belle-Vue, tourists stay in either spacious rooms or charming bungalows. This is fast becoming the most popular hotel on the island, and one visit there is enough to convince visitors why. The service is superb, the location ideal and the personal attention lavished on each guest exemplary. In addition, it offers non-motorised water sport equipment and tailored excursions on Nosy Boraha.

The Malagasy three-star *Lakana* (medium tariff) offers visitors wooden bungalows and meals. It is about 5 km north of the airport on the same beach as the Soanambo. Meals can be taken in a clean dining room, served by smiling staff who bring enormous plates of food. Also graded Malagasy three-stars is *Chez Vavate* (medium tariff), north of Ankarena Cave, about 500 m north-east of the airport. The food is delicious and the close proximity of the beach is an added attraction.

For travellers wanting spotless bungalows, at low prices and within a few metres of the sea, there is little to beat the *Hotel Atafana* (low-medium tariff), on the west coast, about 12 km north of Ambodifotatra. Malagasy and Continental meals are available in the restaurant from an à la carte menu, set course menu or *plat du jour*.

One of the cheapest places to stay is *Stany's* (low tariff). Just 2 km north of the airport, outside the settlement of Ravoraha, the bungalows here offer splendid views of the ocean and along the west coast of the island. There are clean, communal washing amenities and a highly recommended restaurant. About 6 km north of Ambodifotatra is *Le*

Bambou (low tariff). It is more of a restaurant than a hotel, but it does have a few basic, comfortable rooms for rent.

There are two cheap hotels available to budget travellers where the last stands of forest touch the west coast at Maronmandia. The *Hotel Voanio* (low tariff) has bungalow accommodation and can arrange for boat trips to the mainland at Pointe Laree. Food is decidedly Malagasy, but is cheap, filling and tasty. More bungalow accommodation can be found at the *Hotel Orange* (low tariff). A *plat du jour* is offered in the dining room and is a good way for budget travellers to stretch their finances.

For an experience of true Malagasy holiday accommodation, consider sleeping at the *Tsimialonjafy Hotel* (low tariff) in Ambodifotatra. The toilet is your typical Malagasy long-drop; just that this one drops directly into the sea. Idyllic, if somewhat rustic, bungalows are available at *La Baleine* (low tariff) south of Mahavelo. Prices for accommodation are negotiable from December to July, and the rate usually includes a breakfast of fresh fruit, bread, jam and coffee.

Places to eat

Eating is one of the joys of visiting Nosy Boraha. Top prize undoubtedly goes to *Chez Napoleon*, on Île aux Nattes. No visit to Nosy Boraha can be complete without crossing for at least one meal to this quaint restaurant.

At the *Ratinola* restaurant, in Mahavelo, there are tasty Malagasy meals, cold beers and lots of locals – always a good indicator of the quality, price and quantity of food dished up. The *Restaurant au Bon Coin*, near central Ambodifotatra, has received good reports, though prices are surprisingly high and the staff's attitude is "mora mora" (easy-going, slow).

For breakfast, snacks and fresh pastries, cakes and bread, try *La Barachois Salon de Thé*, in Ambodifotatra. A few snacks are also sold at the market. The grilled fish, rice with coconut milk and chili sauce is especially delicious. Also sold are freshly fried samosas, and in the evening, beef and chicken brochettes grilled with tomatoes and onions over an open flame.

9 NORTHERN MADAGASCAR

Northern Madagascar is a region of rainforests, plateaus with caves, remote islands and savanna. This is where the majority of package tourists are brought to enjoy the hotels, beaches and balmy climate that grace this part of Madagascar. The weather in northern Madagascar is divided into two vaguely defined seasons. The "wet" season occurs during the summer months, from September to the end of March, and is accompanied by cyclones. The so-called "dry" season lasts a mere four weeks from late June to early July, except immediately around Antsiranana, where the weather is dry from May through to December. On either side of the winter months, visitors can expect light rainfall at least three times per week.

Getting around northern Madagascar is best done by aeroplane. There are frequent flights from Antananarivo to several urban centres north and daily flights from 'Tana to Nosy Bé and Antsiranana. On Monday, Wednesday, Thursday, Friday and Saturday, there is a plane from 'Tana to Sambava. Travelling by road is only recommended for experienced and truly adventurous travellers who do not mind discomfort and dust. However, touring this region by taxi-brousse is certain to catapult you into the lives of the local people.

The principal settlement in the district, at the northern tip of Madagascar, is the once-fabled pirate town of Antsiranana, also known as Diego Suarez, and once capital of the pirate republic of Libertalia. In the east there are rainforests and vanilla estates around Sambava, while to the west are the enchanting islands on the edge of the Mozambique Channel. The biggest of these islands is Nosy Bé, with the most developed tourism infrastructure in Madagascar. South of Antsiranana is the alluring Montagne d'Ambre forest reserve, Tsaratanana Massif and Antanavo sacred lake.

The dominant tribe in northern Madagascar is the Antakarana. There have, however, been influxes of other tribes, such as the powerful Sakalava. Other tribes that have moved into the territory of the Antakarana include Makoa, Tsimihety and Betsimisaraka. Being the major tribe, it is the traditions and rules of the Antakarana that visitors must observe.

208 *Madagascar*

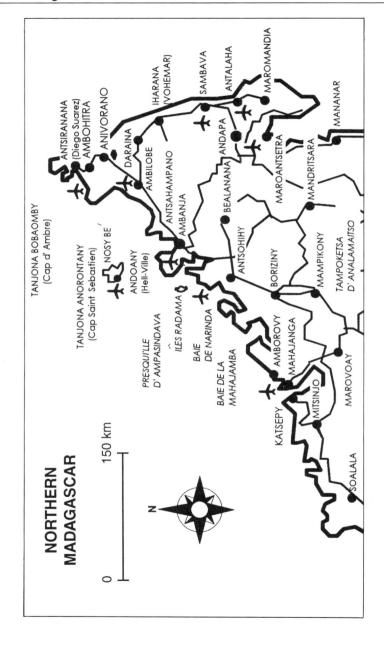

Founded by the offspring of the Sakalava king, Andriandahifotsy, in the late 17th century, the Antakarana nation is known as "the Children of Silver". This is because their lineage is from the non-royal wives and concubines of King Andriandahifotsy. There are several taboos which are practised by the Antakarana, and visitors would be wise to follow them. Below is a short list of important fady that travellers may encounter while visiting Antakarana villages in northern Madagascar:
- The legs of chickens are always reserved for the head of the family. Similarly, the rump of an animal is always reserved for the children.
- An unmarried girl is not permitted to wash the trousers, shorts or underwear of a single male.

When entering a village, locate the headman or chief and ask about fady that apply to that particular settlement.

Three items of cultural significance that all visitors should see are: the honouring of the ancestors ceremony (the Tsakafara), feeding the reincarnated spirits, in the form of crocodiles (Fitsanganan'ny Maty), and the royal post raising, which symbolises the union of the Antakarana with Great Mother Earth (the Tsangantsainy). The Tsakafara usually takes place along the north-east coast during the few short weeks of winter. Fitsanganan'ny Maty takes place on a weekly basis at lakes in north-west Madagascar.

The most frequented of these is Lac Antanavo, near Anivorano Avaratra village, about 75 km south of Antsiranana. The raising of the royal post, the Tsangantsainy, is done every five years at the capital of the Antakarana people at Ambatoharanana.

Nature reserves worth visiting in northern Madagascar include the Ankarana Reserve (18 000 ha), with its fascinating tsingy formations, Marojezy Reserve (60 000 ha), filled with primary rainforest, and Analamera Reserve (35 000 ha), in the remote Andrafiamena region.

ANTSIRANANA (DIEGO SUAREZ)

Under orders from the Portuguese Viceroy of India to settle and claim Madagascar for Portugal, the navigator and explorer Diego Suarez threaded his three wooden caravels past present-day Cap Mine and sailed into the great bay in 1543. The site where he landed and started establishing a settlement was named in his honour. To the local Malagasy tribesmen, the village became known as Antsiranana (where white salt is found). Since independence, there has been a concerted move to discourage using the name Diego Suarez in favour of the Malagasy Antsiranana. Despite the government's efforts, most people continue to refer to the town as Diego Suarez.

The Portuguese did not remain long and soon sailed away to establish more lucrative and accessible settlements on the African mainland. Into this vacuum, some time in the mid-17th century, supposedly sailed the French buccaneer, Mission. Together with a defrocked Italian monk, Father Carraccioli, he set about creating a utopian state known as Libertalia. The settlement flourished. With slaves from friendly Comorian and African sultans, the village was expanded to include schools, houses, a church and administrative buildings on the bay between Diego Suarez and Ankarikakely. The community prospered for almost 40 years. The only trouble, it seemed, came from the local tribes of Antakarana who for some inexplicable reason did not want the foreigners around. In 1695, without warning, while Mission was away raiding in the Indian Ocean, a war party of tribesmen attacked Libertalia. They slaughtered every inhabitant and set fire to the buildings. What became of Mission is an unsolved mystery. Today, nothing remains of the pirate republic, and sceptics say that it was all in the vivid imagination of Daniel Defoe, who first brought it to the attention of the world in 1726. Yet, spend a while exploring the area east of Diego Suarez and you will come upon ruined buildings and the remains of structures in the shallow waters across from Nosy Lonja. No one, not even the guides in the area, is certain who built these structures or what purpose they served.

The recorded history of Diego Suarez shows that the colonising French sailed into the sheltered bay and landed on Anse de la Dordogne in 1885. In 1901, Colonel Joffre arrived and set about building fortifications in the area and developing the French garrison. Diego Suarez remained a quiet colonial backwater until World War II, when France fell to German forces of occupation. Hitler allowed the pro-Nazi Vichy French government, under Marshal Pétain, to stay in token control of the country and all her colonies. Many of the French in Madagascar remained loyal to Marshal Pétain. The British were furious, especially as so many French had declared themselves "Free French" and joined the British forces abroad.

In the now-famous Operation Ironclad, the powerful British navy trapped remnants of the Vichy fleet in the bay off Diego Suarez in 1942. The French were too weak and only offered token resistance, which the British quickly crushed. After a lacklustre defence by French colonials ashore, Diego Suarez fell within a few hours and British troops occupied the town. The biggest surprise for the pro-Nazi settlers was that many of their French neighbours and local Malagasy tribesmen sided with the British forces, attacking the Vichy from the south, east and west, while the Allies poured heavily armed and highly motivated soldiers onto the beaches from the north. The wilderness area known as Montagne des Libre Française is named in honour of the men who died fighting on the side of the Allies.

Diego Suarez, and Madagascar, stayed under Allied, notably British, jurisdiction until the end of the war. Then the town was returned to the French and slid into relative obscurity, from which it has not emerged, despite having the safest and most beautiful natural harbour in the entire Indian Ocean region.

Getting there

Tourists wanting to get to Antsiranana are advised to take an aeroplane. The Air Madagascar office in Antsiranana is on Avenue Sourcouf, opposite Hotel la Rascasse. Consult them or your local travel agent for the current schedule and fares. Remember to re-confirm your tickets timeously.

Hardened travellers can reach Antsiranana overland from Antananarivo. Until recently, it was almost impossible to reach Antsiranana other than between May and early November, the so-called dry season. Now, however, there have been radical improvements to the roads, and you can reach Antsiranana throughout the year. Taxi-brousses leave 'Tana daily for the long journey. The trip from 'Tana takes about four days, provided nothing goes wrong. The first night is spent at Maevatanana, the second at Antsohihy, the third in Ambanja and finally on the evening of the fourth night you arrive in Antsiranana. There are frequent stops for food and drink along the way, but you are advised to take along some extra bottled water and something soft to sit on.

Reaching Antsiranana from Nosy Bé – other than by aeroplane – involves a ferry ride from Hell-Ville to Antsahampano on the mainland. From there it is fairly easy to find a taxi-brousse going north to Antsiranana, via Ambilobe. The road trip takes about eight hours, including a 30 minute break for lunch. Getting to Antsiranana from the east coast is difficult. During the rainy season it is impossible, and travellers will be forced to take a flight from Sambava or Antalaha. From April to November a taxi-brousse leaves Sambava for Antsiranana on Tuesday, Thursday and Saturday mornings. Depending on road conditions, the journey takes about 14 hours and passes through the coastal town of Iharana (Vohemar) en route.

There are two taxi-brousse stations in Antsiranana. The one serving all destinations south of Antsiranana is located in an open square at the southern end of Rue de l'Ankarana, on the road to the airport. A much smaller taxi depot, for transport north and immediately east and west of town, is on the corner of Route de la Polytechnique and Route d'Anamakia.

There are numerous taxi-be dashing about the town streets. To attract their attention, simply clap your hands once or twice. There is a set price for trips around Antsiranana, so make certain you ask a local before deciding to ride about in a taxi. Buses serving local villages gather near Place Foch. Ask the drivers their destinations.

Tourist information

Tourist information about the town and its surroundings is available from two locations in Antsiranana. The most helpful and useful for independent travellers is the WWF (World Wide Fund for Nature) office on Avenue Sourcouf. It has several informative brochures and English-speaking staff. This is also where visitors may obtain their permits to visit the montane rainforest reserve known as Montagne D'Ambre, near Joffreville. For those wishing to take part in an organised tour of the locale, contact Quatro Evasion, on Avenue Lally Tollendal. It has several tours that take in most of the local sights from the comfort of a 4X4 vehicle. If you have your international driving permit you can also hire an off-road vehicle or motorcycle from this tour operator. Mad Airtours, near Hotel la Rascasse on Avenue Sourcouf, is able to provide limited information about Antsiranana and arrange tours of the area.

Several other tour operators offer tours of the area, and although not as big as the abovementioned, are a lot cheaper and make a great deal more effort to please their few customers. Budget travellers are advised to contact these operators first: Somacram, on Rue Lafayette; Valiha, on Rue Colbert; Voyages Colbert, along Rue Colbert and the one I used, and found thoroughly suitable and well-priced, Circuit Touristique, next to CEMM Maritime Experts.

There is an efficient post office on the corner of Rue Colbert and Place Foch, near the local government administration offices. The Banque Malagache de l'Océan Indien (BMOI) is on the corner of Rue Colbert and Rue Flacourt. It does not change traveller's cheques, but will exchange foreign currency. BNI (Crédit Lyonnaise) is on the corner of Rue Colbert and Avenue de France. This bank accepts traveller's cheques, foreign currency and the French Carte Bleu. At the T-junction, at the northern end of Rue Colbert, is the BTM bank, across from the old Tribunal building. This bank accepts all traveller's cheques in major currencies. BFV bank is in the same area, next to a magnificent old abandoned French colonial mansion on Rue Richelieu.

The Librairie Ekena has a good selection of stationery and a few French and Malagasy books. Basic photo supplies, passport photographs and batteries are available from Quotbi Photo, next to La Taverne. Emergency medical attention is obtainable from the clinic on Boulevard Sylvian Roux near the Seventh Day Adventist church, at the hospital (hopital) near to the WWF office, or privately from Docteur Irene Rajerison, next to the Hotel l'Orchidée. Pharmacie Nora, west of Voyages Colbert, is able to fill most prescriptions.

Occasionally sea-going transport from Antsiranana can be arranged by contacting one of the shipping offices. It has become more difficult finding passage as crew, but if you are willing to pay a fee, a berth can sometimes be found. Compagnie Balinere de Madagascar, near the oil storage tanks, has a good reputation for finding travellers a cabin, while SCAC shipping and SCTT tour agents, both located between Hotel de la Poste and the monument to Joffre, Marechal de France, are the most helpful. Saga Océan Indien, east of Hotel de la Poste, seems to have the most contacts with shipping, and although it asks a commission, is usually able to secure a passage to Africa or other Indian Ocean islands within a few days. The Mediterranean Shipping Company (MSC) is the largest shipping company serving this part of the island. It tends to ignore requests from travellers for cabins, but if you can speak directly to the captain, you could be fortunate. Its vessels are easily identified by the huge MSC lettering emblazoned on the funnel.

Any application for a visa extension or other business affecting tourists should be directed to the commissioner of police. His office, and the visa office, are located at the Commissariat de Police along Boulevard Sylvian Roux. If you want detailed historical, geographical or cultural information – and you can read French – then visit the big library of the Alliance Française, at the southern end of Rue Colbert, near Place Foch. The staff are cordial and will assist you with texts concerning your interest or query.

Things to do

Both in and around Antsiranana there are several points worth visiting. On the circle known as Place du 14 Octobre, near Hotel l'Orchidée, is a commemorative memorial. It is similar to others all over Madagascar, and celebrates independence, the uprisings against the French and the unity of the Malagasy people. Leading off and along Rue J Bezara, west of the Rex cinema, are narrow dusty streets edged with stalls and markets.

Along Rue Richelieu, walkers will find abandoned yet still gracious French colonial mansions. Sadly, many of these are now starting to decay and crumble. What must once have been a beautiful little park is tucked away between the BFV bank and an empty house. From here there is a good view across the bay and down to the narrow strip of land known as Anse de la Dordogne. A pleasant walk west will take visitors along above the ocean and down to the lighthouse and busy harbour. Above the port, at the north-western end of town, along Rue Joffre, is a memorial to General Joseph Joffre (1852-1931), Marechal de France, a truly amazing man. The statue bears the following inscription: Tombouctou 1894, Diego Suarez 1903, La Marine 1914. A detailed account of his adventurous life can be read from French manuscripts housed in the Alliance Française library on Rue Colbert. The sleepy village of Joffreville, on the edge of Montagne d'Ambre national park, has been named in his honour.

No visit to Antsiranana is complete without two trips into the surrounding countryside. The first must be out to Ramena Beach, the other to Montagne d'Ambre National Park.

Ramena Beach is edged by Baie des Française, about 17 km east of Antsiranana. Most tourists get there by hiring a taxi for the day. However, you can also reach the palm-lined beach by taking a bus going to Anoronjia via Ankorikakely. The beach itself is quite narrow, with a gentle shelf into the sea. A short walk north-east along the beach will bring you to Cap Mine and the lighthouse at the entrance to the bay. By continuing around the headland, walkers will find themselves among the softly sighing dunes of Baie des Dunes. Few foreigners ever visit this windswept beach, and you will be quite alone here, with time to slowly walk through the vegetation further west and clamber about the weird rock sculptures created by aeons of wind, water, salt erosion and the cyclones that scream down onto north-eastern Madagascar.

By following the beach further south visitors will arrive on the quiet Baie des Sakalava. Many historians believe that it was here that the first arrivals landed from Indonesia. Whatever the reality, the bay is a strange place full of whispers and mystery. Leaving the riddles of Baie des Sakalava, turn west and follow the gravel path back to the settlement of Ankorikakely, from where there is public transport back to Antsiranana.

Other sites within the vicinity of Antsiranana that tourists should consider visiting are the islands of Nosy Antaly Bé, Nosy Suarez and Nosy Diego. It is fairly easy to get a local fisherman from Anoronjia, or along the beach opposite Nosy Antaly Bé, to ferry you across for the right price. There is not a great deal to see on the islands, but they are deserted and make for a wonderful castaway experience for a few hours.

Being a harbour town, Antsiranana has a busy nightlife. La Taverne Disco, near Nouvel Hotel on Rue Colbert, is a favourite haunt of expat patrons, while the unnamed dance hall near the Royal Hotel is the place to go for an authentic Malagasy boogie, on Friday and Saturday night. Hotel de la Poste occasionally puts on a disco for its clients and the more affluent locals. It finishes early though and lacks atmosphere. La Vahinee Nightclub, however, on Avenue de France, is a vibrant meeting place for all classes of Malagasy and foreigners. It starts at around 23h00 and continues through to 5h00.

Things to buy

Visitors interested in shopping for curios have a fine selection from which to choose. A small but good collection of Malagasy crafts is available at *Marthe Ravaozanany,* on Rue Colbert. *Bijouterie M Kalidas,* the jeweller, has used rich red Malagasy gold to create wonderful designs, pendants and rings. He is willing to craft something special for you and will work through the design with a client. Give him about three days to finish the work. Another jeweller popular with tourists is *Alankar Malagasy Jewel Work,* on Rue Colbert. For the biggest selection of handicrafts, visit *Maison de l'Artisanat,* along Avenue Lally Tollendal. It has a staggering assortment of goods, and while many are local, you will also find curios from all over Madagascar being sold here. *Chez Babou,* also on Rue Colbert, has a limited selection of local handicrafts. Traditional grass baskets and other grass items, typical of this region of the country, are sold via the *Blaise and Christine* outlet.

Accommodation

Antsiranana is certainly not short on either tourist accommodation or places to eat. The biggest drawback is that even those establishments considered "budget" are high priced by Malagasy standards. Unless you arrive with pre-booked accommodation, you will need to make a few enquiries before choosing a hotel. The local taxi drivers are your best bet in this regard. Give them an idea of how much you are prepared to pay and leave the rest to them.

The most expensive hotel in town is the dilapidated *Hotel de la Poste* (high tariff), tel. 220.44. Exactly why its prices are so ludicrously high is a mystery. Service is poor, the rooms are musty and dirty and the bistro is always full of rather forceful prostitutes, drunken sailors and package tourists. It has a restaurant and puts on a disco when the mood takes the management.

One of the most interesting places to stay is the *Nouvel Hotel* (medium-high tariff), tel. 222.62, on Rue Colbert. It has a restaurant, plus a disco that is popular with tourists. Two hotels that were once highly recommended, but have now certainly gone to seed, are *Hotel la Rascasse* (medium tariff), tel. 223.64, and next door, *Hotel l'Orchidée* (medium tariff), tel. 210.65, on Avenue Sourcouf. Their rooms are clean, they are close to Air Madagascar and Mad Airtours, but apart from that there is little to recommend them. One of the best and most reasonably priced places to stay in town is the *Valiha Hotel* (low-medium tariff), tel. 221.97, also on Rue Colbert. It has a range of tariffs and rooms, plus an exceptional restaurant. The rooms are clean and the staff friendly. It is well located and close to restaurants, bars, banks and nightclubs.

The cheapest accommodation, and a guarantee of getting to mix with Malagasy people, is located in the southern parts of Antsiranana. The *Royal Hotel* (low tariff) is a Malagasy hotel near the fresh produce and medicinal plant market on Rue J Bezara. Nearby, along Avenue Jillaret Joyeuse, is the slightly cleaner hotel, but just as character-filled, *Le Paradis du Nord* (low tariff), tel. 214.05. On Rue de l'Ankarana, budget travellers will find the basic yet adequate *Ma Constance* (low tariff) chambre and hotely. Conditions are primitive, but adequate for experienced Third-World budget travellers. The meals are heaped with rice and liberally spiced.

Along Boulevard Etienne is the popular *Fian-Tsilaka* (low tariff), tel. 223.48. It has rooms with or without showers, is well placed, yet off the main thoroughfare and has one of the best value for money restaurants in Antsiranana.

Places to eat

Antsiranana is filled with restaurants, hotelys and street stalls selling food. Vegetarians may find a whole host of fresh produce to buy around town and in the market. Apart from the market, *Chez Fazileabasse Hamid*, on Rue Colbert, has a particularly good selection of produce. Antsiranana's snack shops and bakeries are certainly worth trying, especially for their fresh bread and pastries. Highly recommended are: *Amicale Boulangerie*, behind Hotel l'Orchidée; *Buvette l'Été Indien*, opposite Maison Moustafa on Avenue Philibert Tsiranana; *La Vahinee Snack Bar*, on the corner of Avenue de France and Rue Colbert and *Nina Glace Salon de Thé*, along Rue de Suffren.

Tourist hotels are usually a good choice for a "splash-out" dinner, but are also a lot more expensive than Malagasy hotelys. If you do decide to eat at one of the hotel dining rooms, choose one that has a set menu rather than an entirely à la carte menu. The *Valiha Hotel* has a renowned restaurant, with an à la carte menu and a *plat du jour*. *Libertalia* restaurant, on Place de Foch, is the place to go for seafood specialities. A good Chinese restaurant, *l'Extreme Orient*, next to Solima fuel station, has a large menu of tasty food at good prices. It too, has a daily set menu of five dishes. Opposite Madagascar Automobil, on Avenue Sourcouf, is *Le Vanilla Restaurant and Bar*. It caters primarily to tourists and although a little costly, has a select menu of lavishly prepared meals, including a few local dishes. *La Rascasse Hotel* has a small, dingy dining room offering mediocre meals and lots of flies. A good eatery offering traditional Muslim food is *Restaurant Abou*, on Rue Jein Bezara. For a taste of real Malagasy food, you must visit the *Diego Restaurant* down Rue Jein Bezara. *Hotel de la Poste* provides meals, but the service is poor and the prices prohibitive. By far and away the most popular restaurant for travellers is the *Yachy*, on Avenue Lally Tollendal.

MONTAGNE D'AMBRE NATIONAL PARK

Montagne d'Ambre National Park is about 38 km south of Antsiranana. This 18 700 ha montane rainforest reserve, whose lowest point is 832 m, is the site of the highest peak in northern Madagascar, Pic d'Ambre (1 475 m). It is off this mountain's slopes that the tributaries which feed the large rivers in the area flow.

The most common ways of reaching the park are by private taxi, taxi-brousse or with a tour operator. Going with a tour operator is the easiest but costliest method. Hiring a private taxi to drive you out and then collect you a few hours later is reasonable, provided you are able to negotiate a good price. The cheapest way is to take one of the frequent taxi-brousses going to Joffreville (Ambohitra), and then walk the 5 km to the park entrance.

Assuming you have taken the taxi-brousse, you will be dropped in the main road of Joffreville. Walk up the hill and turn left to pass the enormous, abandoned white school building. Follow the road through several stands of trees, past a few local houses and then onto a small open valley that edges the magnificent trees of the montane rainforest. Unless you have already purchased a permit from the WWF office in Antsiranana (on Avenue Sourcouf), or the ANGAP office in Antananarivo, you will be required to buy a permit from the office at the entrance boom to the park. Camping permits are issued free of charge. It is actually a better idea to get your permits from the WWF office in town, because it also provides you with a comprehensive visitor's pack that includes maps and brochures on the Montagne d'Ambre region's history, geography, flora and fauna, details of the WWF involvement in the Montagne d'Ambre Project, principal sites of interest and a fascinating introduction to Antakarana history, traditions and customs. The detailed map, "In a Naturalist's Footsteps", includes directions for one day, two to three day and extended walks in the rainforest reserve.

Most visitors only undertake the one day walking tour of the northern parts of the forest. This is an easy and thoroughly enjoyable stroll that can be done with or without a guide. You may be approached both in Antsiranana and Joffreville by would-be guides. If you feel you do need a guide, it is recommended that you arrange for a recognised guide, and pay the slightly higher fee, through the WWF office the day before. The trails in the forest are all clearly marked, and it is far more interesting and exciting to do the tour on your own with the map provided. Take along a small day-pack, some drinking water, food, wet weather gear, good shoes or hiking boots and a hat. If visiting in summer, wear long trousers, a long-sleeved shirt and socks. Be prepared for clouds of mosquitoes and make certain to check for brown leeches when you get back to the hotel. Those visitors wanting to camp in the park should take along a guide. He will know the best camp sites and where to go on evening walks. You will be required to take food for yourself and the guide, a good tent, light sleeping bag and sufficient drinking water.

The Montagne d'Ambre has two definite climatic zones, which naturally affect the types of flora found within the park. On the western slopes of the mountain seasonal monsoon rains fall, while on the eastern side tropical trade wind-carried rain falls. However, on the summit itself there is no wet and dry season, and rain is experienced throughout the year. The majority of typical montane rainforest floral species are therefore located on the eastern side of the park. Visitors to this region will discover orchids, fungi, moss and epiphytes. Among the creatures that populate the park are seven species of lemur, including the unique Sanford's lemur, which is only found here. There are two diurnal species and five nocturnal species of lemur in Montagne d'Ambre. Aside from the entertaining lemurs, there are mongooses and the country's largest carnivore, the fossa. As recently as 1992, the most elusive and secretive carnivore in the world, the falanouc, was identified here.

There are also tenrecs and the giant fruit bat. Over 75 bird species have been sighted in the reserve. The most conspicuous is the crested ibis, and without doubt the most beautiful is the ground roller (*Atelornis pittoides*). Other birds include rails, magpie robins and impressive Madagascar buzzards. A staggering 49 species of reptile and 24 species of amphibian live in the confines of Montagne d'Ambre National Park. Butterflies are one of the most beautiful features of this rainforest. Over 3 000 species have been identified, made up of 36 genuses, including one of the most dazzling found anywhere, the swallow-tailed butterfly (*Papilio delalandei*).

The "Short Tour", which takes in waterfalls, flora and fauna, begins at the park entrance. After 1,5 km take the gravel road to the right. All along this road are majestic *Canarium madagascariense* (Burseraceae), used for treating pain and fever, and *Eugenia rotra* (Myrtaceae) trees with their edible fruit. This will take you to a point above the spectacular Grande Cascade, which plunges 80 m into a lake formed by an extinct volcano. Less than 500 m back along the path you previously walked, turn right onto a narrow track that leads you along the Botanical Trail. Visitors will find themselves in primary rainforest here. The fragrance of scented wood, flowers and dense vegetation fills the air. Among the more notable trees are *Cedrelopsis grevei* (Ptaeroxylaceae), much prized by traditional healers of the Antakarana people, *Dalbergia* spp. (Leguminosae), the sought after and highly threatened rosewood tree, and the *Dracaena* spp. (Agavaceae), also called the bliss tree due to the hallucinogenic effect of chewing its leaves.

Back on the main road, walk another 200 m and turn right, along the track which takes you to the Antakarana waterfall. The pool at the bottom of this waterfall is regarded as sacred by local tribes and swimming by foreigners is forbidden. Only chiefs are allowed to take ritual baths in the deep pool. It is a purification act and is followed by a procession to the Petite Cascade, where they perform obeisance to the ancestors with offerings of food, money, honey and alcohol. Retrace your steps and then turn right, to cross a small bridge to the Roussettes Forestry Station. There are several gardens around the forestry station, and visitors should spend a while walking in them. For some totally inexplicable reason part of the garden nursery has been prepared for the introduction of exotics. Several of these are already well established and have been planted within the indigenous forest. These include species such as the fragrant eucalyptus and strange Peruvian bark tree. Fruit trees are also presently being cultivated, as are a number of vegetables that could be suitable for local production.

Campers are provided with a camp site here, and the idyllic setting makes for a delightful place to spend your first night. Facilities are basic but adequate for those visitors used to camping in the wilds. A short distance west of the camp site is the small waterfall mentioned earlier. This too is a sacred site and it is highly insensitive to swim there.

Return to the main gravel road and turn right. Climbing gently, the road takes walkers to a lookout above Lac de la Coupe Verte, a thickly treed caldera filled with green water. There is a small beach around the water's edge with a path leading down through the dense forest to the lake. Adventurous day-trippers should walk further south into the forest. After a few hundred metres you arrive at a boom across the road. No vehicles are permitted beyond this point, but hikers are allowed free access. Trudge for a while along the path that enters the very depths of the forest and commence the 6 km climb to Pic d'Ambre at 1 475 m. Hikers who reach the summit are richly rewarded with amazing views of the region. To the north, one of the largest bays in the world, Baie du Diego Suarez, lies protected behind a rim of volcanic hills, with only four small inlets allowing the passage of sea traffic. Fern Pass is a good place to stop and rest before returning to the entrance of the park.

LAC ANTANAVO

This sacred lake, 4 km from the village of Anivorano Avaratra, and 78 km south of Antsiranana, has a most peculiar legend surrounding it. It is believed that the site on which the lake lies was once a village. Apparently the locals were not well known for their hospitality to strangers. One day a man of the Zafitsimahito people stopped and asked for a drink of precious water. Out of the entire populace, only one woman would aid him. In return he warned her of impending danger in the form of severe rains and flooding; she and her family should leave immediately. Within days of their departure, floods had destroyed the countryside, including the village which is now at the bottom of Lac Antanavo. Locals are adamant that the numerous crocodiles which lounge around the lake edges are actually the reincarnated villagers from that time. Frequent rituals are held around the lake, with zebus being sacrificed to the crocodiles in return for a continuation of peace and benevolence from the powerful spirits that inhabit the lake.

To reach Lac Antanavo, take one of the early morning taxis from Antsiranana to Anivorano Avaratra. The first leaves at about 7h00. The trip takes about two hours and you must then walk for about another hour along the gravel road to the lake. There is no accommodation in the village, and unless you have a tent or befriend one of the locals, you will need to catch a taxi back to Antsiranana. The last taxi-brousse leaves from outside the school at around 16h00.

ANKARANA RESERVE

This 18 185 ha reserve is one of the world's most mystical wilderness destinations. You will need either an ANGAP or WWF permit to visit Ankarana. It is also recommended that you employ a guide for your tour. With its convoluted formations, blind passages and hundreds of cave entrances, it is a simple matter to get yourself lost. Ask the WWF in Antsiranana to recommend someone for you. The actual price must be negotiated between guide and client, though the WWF provides guidelines for prices of guides. Meaning "Crocodile Caves", the Réserve Spéciale d'Ankarana is famous for its tsingy limestone formations. These have been eroded into the strangest of shapes, most tapering to sharp pointed peaks. Beneath these rocks are countless streams and subterranean rivers, plunging through uncharted caves and exploding out into the waterways of northern and north-western Madagascar. Other streams have formed deep pools that are home to fresh-water shrimp and crocodiles. On the steep, dry sides of the limestone walls, visitors will notice succulents clinging precariously to narrow perches. Down in the ravines miniature baobabs, wild figs and acacias grow. Spend enough time exploring the reserve and you are bound to encounter lemurs, sometimes sifakas, and if very fortunate, aye-ayes. If searching for birdlife, be prepared for some spectacular finds, such as the Madagascar fish eagle, banded kestrel and bright orange and white kingfisher.

These caves and protected recesses offered refuge to Chief Tsimiharo in the early 1800s, when the powerful Imerina were rampaging through Madagascar on empire-building wars. Realising that he could be trapped within the Ankarana tsingy, the king moved his people at night, loaded them on rafts and crossed to the island of Nosy Mitsio. In remembrance and honour of the king and his tribesmen, their descendants, the modern-day Antakarana, hold a ceremony every five years. Known as the Tsangantsainy celebration, it symbolises the union of the Zafimbolafotsy people and the soil of the Antakarana region. A flagpole, made from entwined hazoambo trees, is raised to indicate the king and masculinity. Planting it in the Antakarana earth, the fertile Mother, symbolises the marriage between the two. This ritual occurs in the settlement of Ambatoharanana, and foreigners who insist on taking photographs are not welcome. For an official invitation, arrange an appointment with the prince through his secretary at his residence in Ambilobe. If possible, try to get a letter in French explaining your reasons for wanting to attend the Tsangantsainy ceremony.

Due to its remoteness, it is almost impossible to get to Ankarana and back to Antsiranana in one day, unless you have arranged with a tour operator that provides 4x4 transport. Instead, consider taking along a tent or some form of shelter and spend a few days camped at Campement des Anglais, where the scientists also stay. Take all your own food and drink. You can reach one of the entrances to Ankarana by taking a taxi 20 km south from Anivorano Avaratra to the village of Matsaborimanga, along the road towards Ambilobe. From Matsaborimanga you must walk about 12 km to reach the camp sites in Canyon Grand. It must be stressed that you should employ the services of a reputable guide. Usually one either travels from Antsiranana with you, or one will arrange to meet you in Matsaborimanga.

AMBANJA

This is the closest town to the ferry port at Antsahampano for those travellers planning to cross to Nosy Bé. Ambanja is both an agricultural centre and taxi junction. Whether coming from the north or south, all taxis make a protracted stop in this bustling town.

There are branches of both BTM and BMOI banks in Ambanja. Only BTM will change traveller's cheques though. BMOI deals exclusively with hard currency.

Most people who arrive in Ambanja are required to spend at least one night there, awaiting the ferry or taxi. Up-market visitors are advised to catch a private taxi to the *Au Rikiki Club* (medium-high tariff), near Ambolokazo, where they can find more expensive, but a slightly better standard, of accommodation than in the low-tariff places. The best tourist accommodation in the area is *Ankify Marina* (medium-high tariff), 5 km from the ferry terminal at Antsahampano. It has luxury bungalows along a fine stretch of swimming beach and a restaurant that consistently produces delicious food.

The best place to stay, for price and location, is the *Hotel Patricia* (low tariff). This establishment has both bamboo bungalows and concrete rooms. There is a clean communal shower with cold water. The rooms are comfortable and well priced. A pleasant Chinese restaurant belonging to the hotel is across the road, next to the bar. Other hotels worth consideration by budget travellers are the *Roxy*, *Paradis* and the *Tsara* (all low tariff).

NOSY BÉ AND SURROUNDINGS

Nosy Bé means the big island. Nosy Bé is the country's main tourist destination; prices are higher than anywhere else, tourists crowd the streets and beaches, and the expensive resort hotels are little self-contained communities on their own.

What little natural vegetation remains on Nosy Bé is among the most threatened in Madagascar. Despite warnings about ecological disasters, and attempts to halt the decline of forests, wildlife and reefs, still they fall to the advancing production of ylang-ylang, sugar cane, pepper, coffee, to tourism and commercial fishing. The WWF predicts that in less than seven years Nosy Bé will have no more indigenous forest and few species of wildlife left, including marine life.

Although Nosy Bé and the surrounding islands fall under Malagasy rule, their history is closer to that of the nearby Comoros than the Madagascar mainland. In the forests of the north and west are the remains of Arab graves, similar to those constructed by 10th century Arab traders on other Indian Ocean islands. Less than 2 km east of the Sarondravay Research Station is the historical village of Marodoka. Historians believe that a small community of Arabs thrived here for about 15 years before succumbing to tropical disease. In the colouring and many traditions of the islanders are definite African, notably Swahili, traces.

Despite the Arab influences, it is the distinctly negroid, warlike Sakalava tribe that dominates Nosy Bé and most of western Madagascar.

As the mighty Imerina king Radama pushed his way steadily across Madagascar, the Sakalava chiefs approached their queen and requested her help in keeping away the advancing Imerina. She turned first to the Sultan of Zanzibar, who was virtually powerless to stop the infantry of the Imerina. Fearing for her life, the Sakalava queen Tsiomeko, together with her entourage and some hundred soldiers, crossed from the mainland to Nosy Bé. But still the troops of Radama sought out the Sakalava royalty. Desperate, she turned to France for help in 1841. France was only too quick to exploit the situation. In return for protection by the French military on Réunion, the queen had to cede Nosy Bé and all the surrounding islands to the French crown. And that is how they remained until France finally relinquished her iron grip on Madagascar and gave her independence.

Bear in mind the Sakalava fady when visiting the more isolated Nosy Bé communities:

- Men always eat to the north or east of the wife and other women of the house.
- The Sakalava give their ancestors posthumous names, but are very loath to mention them to outsiders. It is considered fady to talk openly of the names given to the dead. Visitors will have to get used to hearing family history discussed or explained in a very neutral way, without reference to anyone who has died. Mention of the earthly name brings up sad memories for those still living. By giving a posthumous name, they virtually nullify any earthly memories. They believe that the new name is also a way of keeping the power of death at bay. The Sakalava usually burn down the hut of someone who has died.

Andoany (Hell-Ville)

Named after Admiral de Hell, governor of Île Bourbon (Réunion), this quaint town has the feel of a colonial backwater. French cannons still glower from the battery walls overlooking the harbour and bay. Wide boulevards, parks and colonial buildings add to the atmosphere. Mora mora (slowly slowly), synonymous with Madagascar, reaches its zenith in Hell-Ville. It is recommended that you spend at least one morning exploring and discovering all the hidden sides to this fascinating little town.

Getting there

Most tourists reach Hell-Ville on a flight from 'Tana, Mahajanga or Antsiranana. Contact Air Madagascar or your local travel agent for the current schedule, routes and fares. The airport is north-east of Hell-Ville, about 12 km from town. There will be taxis to meet you on arrival. Remember that they do have an official tariff card for distances – ask to see it after the driver has quoted you an initial price. Some of the more luxurious hotels have airport transfer vehicles waiting for guests with reservations.

Reaching Nosy Bé by boat is the most exciting and adventurous way to get to the island. Old World War II landing craft are used for the daily crossing from Antsahampano on the mainland to Hell-Ville. The voyage across takes about three hours, depending on weather and tidal conditions.

The sailing schedule is kept by most hotels in Ambanja. On Nosy Bé you will find the ferries' times of departure posted on the board of AM Hassanaly et Fils, on Avenue de l'Indépendance.

It is also possible to get a trip aboard one of the fishing pirogues that go out daily to fish in the sound between Antsahampano and Nosy Bé. Take a trip out to the fishing village of Antsahampano from about 14h00. There, speak to any of the fishermen who are unloading or working on their boats. For a small fee someone is usually willing to take you across the next day.

Tourist information

Tourist information is available from most hotels on the island. For a broader view, contact Voyages Bourdon, on Avenue de l'Indépendance. Its staff are able to provide information in French, English, Italian and German. Another helpful tour operator is Mermix and Co., along Rue Galliéni. For details pertaining to the forested wilderness areas, speak to the people in the Forestry Office, opposite the police station on Cours de Hell.

The main post office is located on the corner of Cours de Hell and Rue RP Dalmont. Nosy Bé is served by two banks, both able to change traveller's cheques and currency and allowing you to draw up to US $270 from credit cards. BFV has a branch in Rue Passot. BNI is on the Cours de Hell.

Photographic film, batteries and film developing are available, at ridiculously high prices, from Ynayat Photo and Postcards, down Avenue de l'Indépendance. A cheaper option is the Kodak office, in Rue Passot. There is a clinic and dispensary on Rue Lamy. Nonresidents are required to pay for treatment and then submit the receipt to their travel health insurance. A well-stocked pharmacy, Pharmacie Tsarajoro, is situated on Boulevard R Poincare. For emergency dental treatment, contact the dentist on Rue Georges V. Most of the tourist-class hotels have a list of suitable doctors and dentists available to their guests.

For a limited selection of books and stationery, visit Librairie Naima, along Avenue François Joseph. Car and motorcycle hire can be arranged through Nosauto, opposite the tiny Transtop Hotel, at the northern end of Boulevard General de Gaulle. Visa extensions are best done directly with the police commissioner at his headquarters on Cours de Hell. The new visa is issued and stamped in your passport within two days.

Things to do

The bustling, colourful old market (Hell-Ville Marche), at the northern end of Avenue de l'Indépendance, is certainly worth a visit. Visitors will find huge selections of fresh spices and fruit on sale here. Bargaining is accepted. The stalls that edge the main road are geared mainly to the more affluent Malagasy and the tourist trade. To discover the people's market, turn down Boulevard Raymond Poincare. Here is where most of the locals do their daily food shopping.

A pleasant stroll may be taken along the seafront by following Rue Camille Valentin, which loops behind the government buildings. Opposite Bon Bazar Store, in a small memorial garden, is a tribute to those who died for France in various military campaigns.

By walking north from the CBD, along Boulevard Raymond Poincare, visitors arrive at a crossroads outside the fuel station. Take the road to the right, signposted to the airport. Once past the filthy and noisy diesel power generators supplying electricity to Hell-Ville, you will find yourself among pepper and coffee groves, or lingering in the fragrance of ylang-ylang plantations. These perfumed flowers grow on severely pruned, gnarled trees. The distilled oil is bought by top international fashion and perfume houses, and used as the base in the most expensive perfumes. To the west of the plantation, on the hills, are unpruned ylang-ylang trees in their natural state. They grow to staggering heights and their yellow and green flowers cast a scented shawl over the region. The major ylang-ylang distillery is about 4 km north-east of Hell-Ville.

Take the road going towards the Sarondravay Research Station. Less than 2 km out of Hell-Ville take the road to the left. This will take you directly to the distillery. There are no entrance fees or fixed tour times, and a worker who can speak your language is normally despatched to take you around.

While in the area of the flower distillery, consider walking down to see the aquatic research station at Sarondravay on the coast. Known officially as the Centre National de Recherches Océanographiques de Sarondravay, the facility is manned by Malagasy and several contract foreigners working under the auspices of UNESCO. That part open to the general public needs attention, but still provides a glance into the fish species that swim about these islands.

The nightclub to attend while you are in Hell-Ville, or anywhere else on Nosy Bé, is Le Vieux Port Dance-Hall, down Rue Fardiux, near the commercial harbour. There is live music here. Do not miss a Friday night out at Le Vieux Port. On Saturday evening a smaller, yet just as vibrant disco, the No. 1 Night Club, with recorded music, is put on in what seems to be the basement of Hotel de la Mer. A recently opened nightspot is the New Harlem Nightclub, on Rue Georges V, popular with the island's younger people.

Things to buy

Tourists keen to buy local handicrafts, spices or some of the precious ylang-ylang perfume are well catered for in Hell-Ville. *Arts Madagascar*, on Avenue de l'Indépendance, has a fine selection of local crafts. The *Qui Qui Clothing* shop, next to Voyages Bourdon, does silkscreening and has a choice of locally sewn garments. At *Nosy Boutique* and *Ylang-Ylang Boutique*, there are curios and clothing for sale, plus a range of imported perfumes, but in spite of the name, you cannot buy ylang-ylang oil at the latter boutique. For a bottle of either the refined ylang-ylang perfume or the essence, shoppers need to visit *Chez Abud*. It also stocks souvenirs, cloth, spices and T-shirts.

Le Muriens Boutique specialises in clothing emblazoned with scenes from Malagasy life. *Artisanat* offers several handcrafted items. There is, however, a disturbing amount of turtle shell products being sold as well. Sensitive tourists should consider the effect of supporting a shop that aids the destruction of a threatened species.

Accommodation

Hell-Ville and the rest of the island have an abundance of accommodation. This ranges from four-star luxury at the Marlin Club to a basic room and bucket wash in the Sambatra Hotel. There is some form of tourist accommodation to suit every need and every budget.

The majority of tourists visiting Nosy Bé arrive as part of a tour group. For these people, the accommodation is pre-booked and usually expensive. For those travellers arriving alone, simply ask the taxi driver for a recommendation, or at least have some idea of where you plan to stay.

The closest place to the ferry pier is *Hotel de la Mer* (medium tariff), tel. 613.53, on Rue du Docteur Mauclair. Although the rooms fall into different categories, and there have been conflicting reports from travellers, the overall price can be termed medium tariff. The hotel is well situated for excursions around town, has clean rooms with shower and toilet and a restaurant whose menu and view are hard to beat.

A definite step down, both in price, service and standards of hygiene, is the *Venus Hotel and Restaurant* (low tariff) on Boulevard Raymond Poincare. Rooms are cheap, and seem to be used on an hourly basis. There is a small restaurant, but few people ever eat here, referring to the place as a bar and social hall.

Next to Ylang-Ylang Marine tour operators, on Boulevard Raymond Poincare, is the small and friendly *Chez Cloclo* (low tariff). This is a cheap hotel with a limited number of rooms, that while not being the cleanest around, will prove quite adequate for budget travellers. It also puts on enormous dishes of Malagasy food at excellent prices.

The best traveller's hotel in Hell-Ville is the *Sambatra Hotel* (low tariff). For some odd reason named after the circumcision ceremony that takes place every five years in Mananjary on the south-east coast, this hotel, located at the northern end of Boulevard Raymond Poincare, is a proper Malagasy hotel.

If desperate, and you don't mind the mind-numbing sound of diesel engines roaring, then try the *Chez Mme L'Aurence* (low tariff), where the airport road joins Boulevard Raymond Poincare. There are two small rooms here, and plans for two more. If you make a request at least four hours in advance, meals will be prepared for you.

Places to eat

Hell-Ville is full of restaurants, bars and eateries. Here too, there is a huge price range, depending on where you eat and what you choose. If you want to enjoy a plate of good Malagasy food, order up a lunch of rice (vary), fish (hazandrano) and cassava leaves at the *Tsimiavona* hotely, on Boulevard Raymond Poincare. *Restaurant Chez Nana* has a great ambience, and is popular with travellers. Its seafood dishes are tasty and well priced, although service can be tardy.

For a filling breakfast or snack, try eating at *Restaurant Classic Salon de Thé*, also on Boulevard Raymond Poincare. *L'Oasis Salon de Thé* does a good breakfast that includes fresh pastries and freshly ground coffee. Opposite the Roxy Cinema Hall is *Restaurant Degustation*. The food is excellent and the prices reasonable. Near the Venus Hotel, north on the boulevard, is the *Marotia Restaurant and Bar*, a favourite hangout for Hell-Ville youths. It does a few light snacks and serves ice-cold beers.

The small *Nintsika* hotely dishes up large helpings of food at lunch time, and is nearly always full from 12h00-13h30. Its spicy fish and chicken meals are a delight. On Rue Pierre 1e is the *Cafeteria Al Bon Gout*, which offers a small menu that concentrates on fresh seafood, coconut juice and fried rice.

The top restaurant in Hell-Ville is undoubtedly *Le Papillon*. Owned and managed by Italians, the menu is extensive, mouthwatering and budget destroying. If you have one "treat" dinner on Nosy Bé, or would like to take someone special for a meal, then Le Papillon is a must. Once you have finished your dessert and coffee the owners send over a few bottles of flavoured local rum, from which you may choose a glass. Down Avenue de l'Indépendance is the *Saloon*. Throughout the day its tables seem occupied by tourists munching on totally un-Malagasy food like pizza or sandwiches.

Two bars that should be visited after sunset are on Avenue Victor Augagneur: *Nosy Bar*, in the lower, port end of town, and *Bar Fleurs*. You can mingle with more islanders at *Bar Niandipo* on Cours de Hell. It keeps, stashed behind the counter, a few bottles of the local hooch, brewed from coconuts. If you dare, try a glass or two of the bubbly spirit. Its effect is dramatic to say the least.

Excursions around Nosy Bé

Once you tire of Hell-Ville, consider a number of day excursions out around Nosy Bé.

Perhaps one of the most interesting historical sights on Nosy Bé is the ruins of a 17th century settlement known as **Marodoka**. The site is about 5 km east of Hell-Ville along the same road that passes the Sarondravay

Research Station. Exact details pertaining to this ruined village are scarce. There is a disagreement between museum personnel from 'Tana and local Sakalava chiefs on Nosy Bé about the origins of the buildings. The view held by islanders is that shipwrecked Indian sailors built the settlement and then later all died from disease and malnutrition. Scholars claim otherwise, saying that the style of buildings reveals a distinct Arabic origin. Whatever the correct answer, the place is full of atmosphere and provides ample attraction to those with historically inclined imaginations.

By continuing south along this road visitors will arrive at the hamlet of Ampasindava and entrance to the 750 ha **Réserve Spéciale d'Lokobe**. As in other recognised nature reserves, all visitors are required to have a permit from either the WWF or ANGAP. There are no representatives of these organisations on Nosy Bé, and you should obtain your entry permit from 'Tana or the WWF office in Antsiranana.

The reserve itself is rarely visited by tourists. It seems abandoned and no one is likely to ask you for your permit – if you actually see anyone at all. Take any of the paths that lead east from the village and you will soon be in the wilds of this little park. The highlight of any visit is to see the black lemurs which gad about in the late afternoon and early morning. There are no visitor facilities at Lokobe and you should take along your own water and food for the day.

Taking the road that turns north-east of Marodoka, travellers will end up on the vegetated shores around the traditional Sakalava settlement of Ambatozavavy. East of you is the wide sweep of Baie d'Ambatozavavy, while even further away, in the same direction, are the misty heights of the Madagascar mainland.

One of the most remote and fascinating places to visit on Nosy Bé, provided you are prepared to make the considerable effort, is the tiny cluster of houses at **Tafondro**. The villagers will be surprised to see a foreigner arriving here. The people are hospitable and friendly. For a taste of arguably the last vestiges of true Nosy Bé Sakalava tradition, make certain that you somehow get to Tafondro for a few hours.

Returning to Hell-Ville and then proceeding west takes tourists towards the biggest attraction of Nosy Bé, the tropical beaches.

At the road sign indicating the way to Port du Cratere, Andampy and Ambatoloaka, turn left (south). This road takes visitors to one of the best beaches on Nosy Bé, **Ambatoloaka**. Between Ambatoloaka and Ambondro are long stretches of magnificent beaches as well. It is also here that you will find the most luxurious hotels and tourist accommodation.

South of Ambatoloaka village is **Port du Cratere**. This shattered caldera offers visitors an intriguing view of the mighty forces that nature loosens in the creation of volcanic islands. Follow the road to where it ends at the crater. The walk from the village is pleasant and takes you through agricultural lands.

Just 7 km from Hell-Ville, near Madirokely, is the most sumptuous holiday resort on Nosy Bé, *L'Hotel Marlin Club* (high tariff).

Situated on the edge of a beautiful white beach, this hotel has 15 rooms in delightful bungalows near the shoreline. A restaurant, bar and clubhouse are all available to residents.

The most reputable dive facility, Madagascar Dive School, is located at this hotel. It also offers guided and fully-inclusive outings to Nosy Bé and the surrounding isles of Nosy Komba, Nosy Tanikely, Nosy Sakatia, Baie des Russes, Nosy Iranja and Nosy Mitsio. The dive school also caters for guests wanting to visit Lokobe nature reserve or the summit of Mont Passot.

Airport transfers to the hotel are included in the service. Make certain to book your accommodation well in advance. This is one hotel where you cannot just arrive on the doorstep with a backpack: L'Hotel Marlin Club, Siege Social, 18 Cité Gallois-Ouest, tel. 206.50, Andrefanambohijanahary, 101 Antananarivo.

Apart from the lavish L'Hotel Marlin Club, there is also top-class accommodation at *Residence d'Ambatoloaka* (high tariff). This well-managed, 18 bungalow, scrupulously clean place specialises in Italian cuisine and top-flight service. Contact them well prior to arrival: Residence d'Ambatoloaka, Ambatoloaka, Nosy Bé, tel. 613.68, fax 268.92.

Visitors looking for slightly cheaper accommodation are well catered for. One of the finest places to stay is the *Soleil et Découverte* (medium tariff). The accommodation is right on the beach, isolated and highly recommended for those in search of solitude and relaxation.

For a taste of Malagasy hospitality and accommodation you will be hard-pressed to find a more suitable place than *Motel Coco Plage* (medium tariff), tel. 613.53. Another site well worth considering is the small but friendly *Chez Gerard et Francine* (medium tariff), tel. 612.70. This old French mansion is close to the beach and placed in a truly spectacular setting. A cheaper alternative is the wonderful bungalows of *Madame Chan Fah* (low-medium tariff). The spacious bungalows cater for up to six people, and if you can get a group together, this is the cheapest way of staying on otherwise expensive Nosy Bé.

For more sumptuous tourist accommodation, travel further north-west to the wide, palm-lined beach of **Ambondro**. Here visitors will find several reputable and busy hotels. With 25 bungalows, guided excursions, a site right on the beach and an excellent restaurant, *Les Cocotiers* (high tariff), a few hundred metres south of Ampasy village, is the most expensive hotel in the area. Reservations are necessary throughout the year at the resort-style accommodation: Les Cocotiers, BP 191, Nosy Bé, tel. 613.14. The most popular establishment is the 24-bungalow *Hotel Restaurant Villa Blanche* (medium-high tariff), BP 79, Nosy Bé, tel. 228.54. At the *Palm Beach Hotel* (medium-high tariff), tel. 612.84, visitors may be a little perturbed by the overworked and subsequently irate staff.

No one will go hungry while visiting this area. Most of the hotels have their own restaurants. Nonresidents are welcome, though reservations are preferred for evening meals. Eating at hotels tends to be rather costly. Instead try one of the number of small restaurants in the vicinity. For a taste of local rum and delicious Planter's Punch, plus good food and reasonable prices, eat at least one meal at *Chez Zou*. The best seafood dishes at Ambatoloaka can be found at the tranquil *Mora Mora* restaurant. The favourite haunt of up-market island visitors is *Chez Angeline*. An exhaustive menu is offered. In addition there are daily specials and an extensive wine list. As a treat this is certainly one restaurant to visit.

At Ambondro, the hotels have dining rooms open to both residents and nonresidents. Your choice of restaurants here, however, is limited, unless you enjoy traditional Malagasy food. The *Perroquet* appears to be popular, while three hotelys, serving tasty, filling meals, can be found near the taxi-brousse stop in the settlement.

Proceeding north from the tourist beaches, travellers arrive at **Dzamandzary**, Nosy Bé's centre for rum distillation. The Sirama Rum Distillery is situated in the sugar cane fields, a little way out of the village. An entrance fee must be paid, with different charges for foreigners and Madagascar residents. The site is open Monday-Friday 6h30-11h30 and 14h00-15h30 and on Saturday from 6h30-11h30. There are guided tours for an additional fee. You can buy bottles of rum from the curio shop near the entrance gate to the factory. This shop also sells packets of vanilla quills.

A new hotel, which has not yet capitalised on the Nosy Bé tourist mania, is the *Villa Fleuri Hotel* (medium tariff), near Dzamandzary. It is, however, currently being marketed overseas and it will not be long before it is as busy and brash as the other up-market hotels on the island. Hidden on the beach near the railroad are the magical *Au Coin de la Plage* (low-medium tariff) bungalows. You will seldom find them full, and this is the ideal place to lose yourself for a while from the tiresome impact of mass tourism. The restaurant makes enormous plates of seafood à la Malagache.

North-east of Dzamandzary is a volcanic area of several lakes that warrant further exploration. The centre of this pockmarked region is the highest point on Nosy Bé, Mont Passot (320 m). Reaching the water-filled craters and the base of the mountain can be difficult, unless you go with an organised tour and vehicles that use the main road running south from Andrahibo. Visitors walking to Mont Passot and the lakes from the west coast should follow the road to Anoronjia. These lakes are considered sacred by the Nosy Bé islanders and appropriate respect should be shown. Refrain from wearing a hat while at the lakes. Smoking is forbidden and fishing is unacceptable.

From **Anoronjia**, turn east until encountering the largest lake, Lac Amparihibe. South-east of this lake is Lac Antsidihy, at the base of Mont Passot. It is possible to reach the summit from here. From Mont Passot walk down to the smaller lakes of Bemapaza or Antsahamanavaka. North and west of these are the scattered craters of the split Lac Amparihimirahavavy. Lac Anjavibe and Lac Maintimaso are to the north-west and south-west respectively.

On the north-western peninsula of Nosy Bé is **Andilana beach**. You need to be a pretty wealthy tourist to stay and visit this isolated spot. The beach itself is wide, shelving and fairly well protected. Swimming is safe, provided you stay within the bay. The hotel here is the *Andilana Beach Hotel* (high tariff), tel. 611.76. This five-star, 110-room hotel has a sparkling swimming pool, tennis courts, casino and a pleasant disco. It also has scuba diving facilities and is able to arrange excursions around Nosy Bé and the offshore islands. The only other place at Andilana worth considering for accommodation is *Chez Loulou* (medium-high tariff). Its bungalows are clean and magnificently situated, but expensive in relation to what is received.

ISLANDS AROUND NOSY BÉ

Nosy Komba

In the calm channel between Nosy Bé and the Madagascar mainland is picturesque Nosy Komba. Known as the Island of Lemurs, this volcanic island is a mere 60 minute boat ride from Hell-Ville.

The majority of day-trippers to Nosy Komba arrive aboard a chartered launch with guides. The cheapest way of reaching the island is to arrange for a local fisherman to paddle or sail you across from Hell-Ville. He will drop you off at the landing pier at the village of Ampangorina, at the island's northern point. Arrange to leave in the early evening, when onshore winds make it possible to hoist sail, and often reduce the length of time taken to cross by as much as 20 minutes.

For something in between the expensive and cheap, opt to hop aboard one of the Nosy Komba hotels' motorboats that leave Hell-Ville for Nosy Komba at about 10h00 daily.

The main settlement on Nosy Komba is **Ampangorina**. Be prepared for a tussle on arrival. The village curio sellers are well versed in the art of separating tourists from their money. Bargain hard for items, but try not to get too ludicrous. Most visitors to Nosy Komba are interested in seeing the friendly black lemurs which are kept in a special compound on the edge of a few hectares of indigenous forest. While the males are indeed black, the females are a rust brown with white markings on their ears.

For a spectacular sight of Nosy Komba, Nosy Bé and the distant mainland, take the approximately six hour return walk to the top of the extinct volcano, Antaninaomby (620 m). Although there is no clearly marked route to the summit, village children in Ampangorina will be delighted to show you the way in exchange for some small gift.

Tourist accommodation is limited to three places, all in Ampangorina. The best accommodation is offered at *Madame Madio's* (medium tariff) bungalows. Conditions may be considered somewhat spartan by Nosy Bé standards, but are more than adequate for a few days' visit. *Hotel les Lemuriens* (medium tariff) is near the pier in Ampangorina. There are rooms and one bungalow, all with excellent views of the surrounding area. The cheapest is *Hotel Maki* (low tariff). The hotel is suitable for experienced budget travellers.

If you have a tent or can converse in even a little Malagasy, head into the forested interior of the little island. At any of the villages you will be helped.

Nosy Tanikely

Both the island and waters around it are a protected marine reserve. As such, this is the best island to visit for scuba and snorkelling adventures. Divers unanimously agree that the scuba diving and snorkelling around

Nosy Tanikely are the best in Madagascar. The island itself is uninhabited, apart from the lighthouse keeper and his family. Many of the tourist hotels on Nosy Bé arrange a day trip to Nosy Komba that usually includes a stop at Nosy Tanikely. One of the attractions of these organised tours is the lavish lunch that is served on the beach, complete with chilled wine, tropical fruit and fresh rolls.

A much more exciting way of getting to Nosy Tanikely is to arrange with a fisherman in the village of Mahatsinjo, on Nosy Bé, to sail you across. This trip is bound to get you wet and have you paddling for at least a part of the crossing. Returning may be a problem, particularly if you plan to overnight on Nosy Tanikely. However, if you speak discreetly to a skipper of one of the chartered tourist boats that arrive, he will usually arrange to take you back to Nosy Bé for a small fee.

Nosy Mitsio archipelago

Lying about 64 km north-east of Nosy Bé, these 14 islands are prime scuba diving and snorkelling destinations. Only Grand Mitsio has any habitation. A few scattered hamlets dot this island. Previously privately owned, the recently sold island is rapidly being converted by tavy agriculture and a rash of tourist attractions.

Snorkellers should get a boat ride to the volcanic outcrops off Grand Mitsio. There, the nutrient-rich waters offer a fairyland of submarine treasures. A profusion of sea life ensures that you will see parrotfish, angelfish, several species of colourful coral and the occasional white-tipped reef shark. Many of the waters around the really small islands have seldom been dived, let alone charted. So, for a peek into pristine dive sites, a trip to the islands of Mitsio is a must for all underwater enthusiasts. Of particular note as a snorkelling site is Nosy Tsarabanjina, the southernmost island in the archipelago.

Ashore, the real prize is being able to spot the nesting sites and observe the graceful flights of the beautiful *paille en queue* birds, with their long white tails and whisper-like calls. At the rock formation known as Les Cannes d'Orgue, visitors can gaze in wonder at the peculiar conglomerates forming what really does resemble organ pipes in some majestic open-air cathedral.

The only accommodation on the Mitsios is on Nosy Tsarabanjina, at the *RAP Madagascar* (medium tariff). It offers basic rooms and a small restaurant with an impressive menu of fresh seafood.

Nosy Iranja

About 40 km south of Nosy Bé, Nosy Iranja is covered by coconut palms, *filaos* trees and tropical flowers. There are two islands making up Nosy Iranja. At high tide they are separated from one another, but at low tide it is a pleasant 2 km stroll across a white sandbar to the uninhabited island. You can camp on this deserted island, and it is the best place to observe sea turtles coming ashore to lay their eggs in the soft coralline sand.

Finding transport out to Nosy Iranja can be a problem. It is unlikely that a fisherman will be prepared to make the long trip in his dugout or pirogue. Your only real chance of making a trip to the island is to contact the excursion desk at one of the tourist resorts on Nosy Bé, but be prepared for a high price.

Nosy Sakatia

This is one of the closest islands to Nosy Bé. It is still relatively untouched by tourism standards, and a great place to be lost for a few glorious days. The three main villages are Ampasindava, Ampasimena and Antanambe.

The fastest way of reaching Nosy Sakatia is by fishing boat from Ampasimoronjia. Of course, tourist hotels and tour operators run daily trips from Nosy Bé across to Nosy Sakatia, including a seafood lunch and loads of time to go exploring in the forested interior of the island.

Exploring the forest on Nosy Sakatia is one of the great attractions. Wild orchids proliferate in the steamy jungle, as do perfumed plants, giant ferns and towering pallisandra trees. Reptiles and insects are another feature of the primeval forests. As evening creeps up, fruit bats, as big as those found on the Comoros, leave their tree perches to scour the island for fruit delicacies.

You may camp anywhere on Nosy Sakatia, stay at the bungalows belonging to the *Sakatia Dive Lodge* (medium-high tariff), or try to find accommodation with a Malagasy family in any of the villages. This last option is the most enjoyable and recommended for budget travellers. Ask around in the hotelys, or request assistance from the police.

SAMBAVA

Sambava is one of the most isolated urban centres in Madagascar. It is also one of the most beautiful. Perched on the edge of the Indian Ocean, and warmed by equatorial breezes, Sambava is rapidly gaining popularity as a holiday destination, particularly for the Malagasy. The fragrance from tropical flowers and the alluring scent of vanilla are unmistakable as you drift about this little town. Sambava is, however, primarily an agricultural settlement. Most of the inhabitants are in some way or other involved in the production of agricultural products, mainly vanilla. Walk out along any of the roads from Sambava and you will encounter vanilla estates.

Vanilla belongs to the orchid family, and is one of the most expensive spices available. Recently, the production of an artificial flavouring, known as vanillin, has competed strongly against natural vanilla. This has caused a sharp drop in returns for the planters, and it is not uncommon to see abandoned vanilla estates around Sambava. Many of the plantations are owned by Chinese immigrants. The remainder are in the hands of a few Malagasy families. Madagascar's vanilla originated on the nearby islands of the Comoros, though scientists have also identified strains that could only have come from the Seychelles. Today, the vanilla market is depressed and many of the farmers are looking around for a substitute crop such as fruit.

There is nothing of any real tourist interest in Sambava, and unless you are using it as a base for exploring the region or enjoy lazing on the empty beach, there is not much to keep travellers here for long.

Getting there

There are three possible ways of reaching Sambava. The quickest, most frequently used and logical, is by aeroplane. There are flights on Monday, Wednesday, Thursday, Friday and Saturday. Contact Air Madagascar or a travel agent for the current schedule. The Air Madagascar office in Sambava is in the southern suburbs.

The most exciting way of reaching Sambava is by taxi-brousse. Although the trip from the west coast is done often, some periods are easier than others. The best months to attempt to reach Sambava by public transport are from the end of July to early October. The route to take is from Antananarivo to Ambanja. From Ambanja make your way to the busy taxi-brousse junction town of Ambilobe. In Ambilobe you will find taxis and trucks (camions) crossing to Vohemar (Iharana), about 150 km north of Sambava. The drive from Ambilobe to Vohemar should, in theory, take about 12 hours. Experienced travellers will realise that the trip is likely to take closer to 16 hours to complete. A walkman and good music will be a life saver on this daunting journey. Add a lamba oany to your kit. The dusty road throws up clouds of fine red sand that gets everywhere.

A much more demanding journey can be made by taxi-brousse from Antsiranana. This trip south-east is only attempted during August and September by the more daring and reckless of the Antsiranana taxi-brousse drivers. The vehicle leaves Antsiranana at about 7h30 and goes to the little village of Sadjoavato, on the edge of the Saharerana River. There is usually a break to eat here, before proceeding on to Anivorano Avaratra. Near this settlement is the small Lac Antanavo, where ritual crocodile feeding ceremonies are frequently held. From here the taxi-brousse swings south-west until reaching Isesy. Most drivers stop for a late lunch here and then commence the afternoon and night journey eastward. Sometime the next morning the taxi-brousse will come to a thankful stop at the small depot in Sambava.

The third and least used way of getting to Sambava is by sea. Most travellers using sea transport to Sambava do so from another port in Madagascar, aboard a coastal steamer. Speak to Auximad, MSC or Compagnie Balinere de Madagascar in Toamasina, Antsiranana, Mahajanga, Manakara or Toliara.

Things to do

For organised excursions into the surrounding countryside, the only reputable tour operator is Sambava Voyages. Its offices are located near the Air Madagascar building. This tour operator is able to arrange for guides and porters to lead hikers into the wilderness forests and mountains of the Marojezy Reserve, between Sambava and Andapa. Recently it has explored sections of the Mananarabe and Bemarivo rivers in the hope of exploiting some of the white water parts by offering rafting trips. Most of the tours include meals, transport and accommodation, either with locals or in tents. All alcoholic drinks must be paid for separately.

Accommodation

At the top end of the market is the busy *Hotel Carrefour* (medium-high tariff), tel. 60. This is a comfortable, well-run establishment that caters for the more demanding foreign guests. Telephonic bookings are recommended.

Providing substantial competition to the Hotel Carrefour is *Hotel Orchidea* (medium-high tariff), tel. 128. Visitors will find bungalows and a good restaurant. The accommodation is adequate. It is raised on short stilts and offers spectacular sunrise views over the Indian Ocean. This place should be a honeymooner's ideal getaway.

The friendliest place to stay in Sambava is at *Las Palmas* (medium tariff). This accommodation, in the form of quaint bungalows, has a splendid restaurant. The food is excellent, service outstanding and prices very reasonable. The cheapest accommodation available is at *Hotel Calypso* (low tariff). This is a Malagasy hotel of indefinite age and sagging a bit at the edges. The management are however cordial and make every effort to please.

All the tourist accommodation serves meals from good menus that cater to most tastes and pockets. As can be expected, seafood is a feature of Sambava dishes. A few of the places, notably Hotel Orchidea, also offer a daily set menu at reasonable prices. In the town itself, visitors may try meals from any of the numerous Malagasy hotelys that are characteristic of all urban centres. Their dishes of highly spiced fish or chicken, with mountains of rice and boiled cassava leaves, are recommended for all foreign visitors.

VOHEMAR (IHARANA)

This is the first north-east coast settlement that overland travellers using taxi-brousse transport arrive at. Vohemar is an agricultural village, concentrating on vanilla production and a few spices. Since the crash of the vanilla market, one planter has already started experimenting with ylang-ylang trees, while some have planted subtropical and tropical fruit trees in the hope of reviving their finances. Quite a number of foreigners have also moved into farming in this region and it is not uncommon to hear English, Afrikaans, Chinese and French being spoken around Vohemar.

Local legend claims that it was here, some time in the 10th century, that the first Muslim settlers arrived. No anthropological or archaeological finds to verify this have been discovered, but there is a definite Islamic attitude and tradition in Vohemar. Of greater historical interest is the recent excavation of ancient Oriental sites. These locations south and north of Vohemar are difficult to locate without a guide. Ask at the Sol et Mar Hotel for assistance in this regard. The exact origins of the pieces found at the digs are uncertain, yet their distinctive Asian characteristics have led a number of prominent scholars to claim that it was Chinese emissaries and sailors from the great Kublai Khan who were shipwrecked here who left the artefacts. In his writings, Marco Polo mentions having heard stories of a great island, Madagascar, far to the south in the furthest reaches of the Indian Ocean – where did this information come from?

About 5 km south of Vohemar, near the Fanambana River, is the holy lake of Lac Andranotsara. The local Betsimisaraka and Tsimihety tribes have a folk tale about how this natural lake was formed, not unlike that told by the Antakarana clans about their numerous crater lakes. Some time in the distant past, when the Vazimba walked the wilds of Madagascar, a giant sea dragon wandered ashore and lay down around a small village. Due to its enormous size, it formed a deep depression that caused the village to subside. The villagers were furious and, using spears and fire, drove the creature back into the sea. In retaliation, the sea dragon called on the spirits of rain to drown the village. This was duly done and the supposed settlement now rests beneath the green waters of the lake. There are crocodiles here, which people in the area believe are the reincarnated villagers, still living in their houses below the water. Fishing is forbidden, as is swimming. Not that you'd want to swim, after seeing just how many crocodiles there are. The eating of certain foods around the lake is also considered taboo.

The only place worth staying at is in one of the rustic bungalows of the *Sol et Mar Hotel* (low-medium tariff). Meal prices can be high though, and travellers should rather consider eating at the *Poisson d'Or* restaurant, which also has a few rooms (low tariff) for those who do not mind basic conditions.

ANDAPA

This is the place to visit if you want to see vast tracts of lowland, sections of montane rainforest and traditional rice-growing techniques. According to the Ministry of Agricultre in Sambava, Andapa is the biggest producer of rice in northern Madagascar.

The village is about 92 km west of Sambava. There are frequent taxi-brousses serving the locale.

There is only one designated tourist hotel in Andapa, the *Hotel Tam Yock* (low-medium tariff). Its accommodation, while adequate, is somewhat dilapidated. Instead, ask for a bungalow at the annexe, situated on the slightly cooler slopes outside Andapa. The view from these recently completed bungalows is breathtaking. Lavish meals are served for guests at the hotel. Several hotelys serve delicious midday meals near the small market in the village.

The major attraction in the area is the primary rainforest reserve of Marojezy. Encompassing almost 60 000 ha of wilderness, Marojezy includes the lofty summit of Mont Marojezy (2 137 m). Deep in the steaming lowland forest walkers will encounter shy lemurs, tree frogs, huge chameleons, boa constrictor snakes and at least 57 species of bird. Once up on the massif, in the montane forest, visitors may find the weather decidedly cooler, with occasional mist and frequent rain.

Located far off the tourist track, Marojezy offers minimal facilities for visitors. You do need a permit, which may be obtained either in 'Tana or at the village of Manantenina, on the slopes of Mont Marojezy. Take along your own food and water, and if planning to overnight in the woods, your own tent. A guide is advisable, as it is easy to get lost on the small paths that crisscross the dense forest and lichen-covered summit. Walkers can ask around Manantenina or Andapa for a guide, or make prior arrangements via the Hotel Tam Yock in Andapa or Hotel Carrefour in Sambava.

ANTALAHA

Surrounded by vanilla groves and tropical vegetation, Antalaha is the southernmost sizeable settlement before the rainforests of the Masoala Peninsula. It is a quiet coastal village, a few kilometres south of the Ankavia River. There is little to see or do in the village, and most foreigners use Antalaha as the start or end of the strenuous hike through the rainforests and rice paddies to or from Mahalevona on the Bight d'Antongil.

Getting to Antalaha is a relatively painless 90 km taxi-brousse ride from Sambava. Taxis travel this road throughout the day, and well into the night on Friday and Saturday. The journey takes between two and four hours. A few of the taxis make a detour en route, to the hamlet of Ambinanifaho.

Aware that this is a popular stop for hiking tourists, several locals provide accommodation, usually on a bed and breakfast basis in a private home. Lunch and dinner can be arranged by speaking to the wife or daughters at least three hours ahead. Ask around the taxi-brousse depot for directions to one of these places.

Should you prefer proper tourist accommodation, try the *Hotel Océan Plage* (medium tariff), tel. 812.05, which has bungalows and rooms for rent, or the *Hotel du Centre* (low-medium tariff), tel. 811.67. This hotel is the cheaper of the two, but has the best menu in Antalaha.

It is possible to hike to Mahalevona from Antalaha. The distance is about 116 km and should take most hikers between five and seven days to cover. Arrange a guide for the trip. Although the trail is clearly marked, a guide could prove useful in a number of ways. The guides always know someone in the many villages you will walk through, a boon when it comes to finding a bed for the night. Most of the guides arranged through the Hotel Océan Plage are knowledgeable about the flora and fauna of the Masoala Peninsula. Although you will usually end up eating at villages on the way, it is still advisable to take along a few emergency goods, vitamins and at least two water bottles.

Remember that you are expected to also provide the guide with food, and when necessary, a tent. Take along suitable wet weather gear and good hiking boots. At the end of each day's walk, check your entire body for the nasty brown leeches that wait for unsuspecting trekkers to pass their way.

To reach the start of the trail, take a taxi-brousse 25 km south-west to Maromandia, on the banks of the Ankavia River. The well-defined trail immediately swings south and follows the eastern bank of the Sakafihitra River to the slopes of Mont Beanjada (1 310 m). Leaving the river to scale the heights of the Beanjada plateau, trekkers then walk across wilderness and rural regions to Mahalevona. It is a mere 20 km further west to Maroantsetra. Taxi-brousses are frequent between Mahalevona and Maroantsetra.

10 WESTERN MADAGASCAR

Western Madagascar has the least developed tourism infrastructure on the island, making it undesirable to package tours but a must for adventure travellers. Travelling the wide plains, uninhabited beaches, rolling hills and magnificent nature reserves of western Madagascar requires planning and a sense of commitment.

Western Madagascar is hot, with sparse vegetation, huge agricultural estates and little rain. From late March through to late December barely a drop of rain falls in this region. It does get a little cooler during June and July, but not so that you'll notice. Morning temperatures range from "lows" of 17 °C to a staggering 46 °C. Around the town of Morondava, the thermometer regularly climbs to a blistering 50 °C during November and December. From January to mid-March light rain falls.

Getting around western Madagascar requires fortitude and lots of time, unless you are doing all your travel by aeroplane. For visitors who have limited time, then, going by air is advisable. However, if you are visiting on a budget and can afford the delays, then by all means use public transport. After using the taxi-brousses that service western Madagascar, no traveller will ever worry about using local transport anywhere in the world again. During the rainy season, tar roads are washed away, gravel roads become passages of deep mud and you can add another six hours to any time given for a trip that involves driving through rural areas, where puddles often hide holes deep enough to swallow a vehicle without trace!

Western Madagascar is home to the proud warrior tribe known as the Sakalava. Numerous sub-clans make the region a fascinating destination for visitors who want to learn about cultures that have been influenced by East Africa, Arabia and the Malayo-Polynesian influx. The clans that are of particular importance and interest in western Madagascar include the Vezo, Antimena, Antimahilaka, Antimaraha, Antimilanja and Antiboina, from whom the Sakalava royalty originate.

In addition to the fady detailed in the section on northern Madagascar, the following are most important to western Madagascar:

- Women are not allowed to eat together with men.

244 *Madagascar*

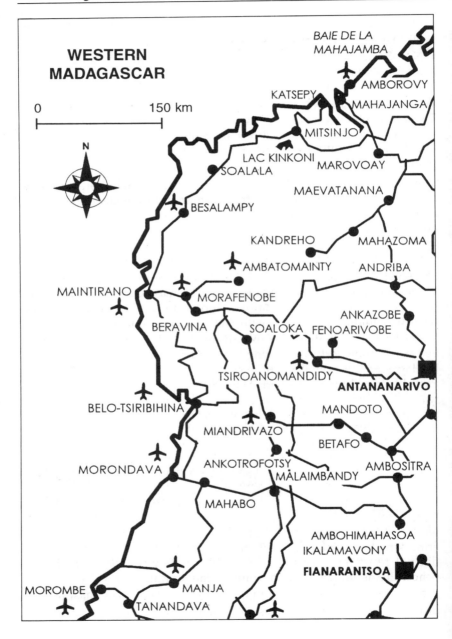

- Everyone is expected to take part in the autumn harvest celebration known as "The First Flower" festival.
- Non-Sakalava visitors to the area are not permitted to touch or visit tombs without first getting permission and a guide from the nearest village headman.
- Never touch anything that is wrapped in red cloth or a red box. This colour cloth or receptacle is used to keep mementos of the ancestors, and usually includes a lock of hair, nails, teeth, the first joint of the little finger on the left hand and weapons.
- Although it is not considered fady for people to engage in sexual intercourse, irrespective of whether they are married or not, it is severe fady (olo faly) to have sex with a woman during menstruation, or if she is pregnant and during the time when the rice is being threshed.

MORONDAVA

Morondava lies on the west coast, at the mouth of the Morondava River, and is the ancestral home of the Menabe clan of the Sakalava tribe. Seat of King Andrianahifotsy during the 1600s, Morondava and its surroundings were filled with soldiers, encampments and military defences. Bartering firearms and explosives from French and Arab merchants, Andrianahifotsy set about creating a Sakalava empire. He died after successfully conquering most of the west coast, leaving the kingdom in the hands of his quarrelsome sons. They could not agree on how their kingdom should be governed or who should have what part. As a result, they split, the one son staying around Morondava, while the other took his followers and went north to the banks of the Betsiboka River. This split resulted in the creation of the two main clans within the Sakalava, the Menabe in the south and Boina in the north.

This lack of cohesion was exactly what the Imerina king Radama I needed to sweep into western Madagascar with his experienced and well-equipped troops. In many instances Radama I used British and Dutch military officers to plan the campaigns, and it was not long before western Madagascar was placed under the imperial banner of the Imerina kingdom. Unlike their Boina cousins further north, the Menabe did not resist the occupation and within a few years they had been peacefully assimilated into a unified Madagascar.

From March to December Morondava is a dry, dusty, sleepy town of wide streets, empty beaches and mudflats. But when the rains come in January and February, everything and everyone is suddenly imbued with vitality. Trees turn green, the roads are regularly swept, the majority of weddings take place, the beaches are washed clean, and nine months later most babies are born in Morondava!

Getting there

Getting to Morondava can be as exciting or sedate as you choose it to be. The quickest but most boring way to reach this coastal city is by air. For those in search of adventure, with time to spare and wanting to encounter Sakalava culture firsthand, take a taxi-brousse to Morondava.

There are flights to Morondava from various towns in Madagascar each day. Contact Air Madagascar or your local travel agent for the current schedule, routes and fares.

For travellers, the most exciting, uncomfortable and adventurous way of reaching Morondava is by taxi-brousse. The only viable route is from Antsirabe, though a few hardy souls have reported making the journey up from Toliara. The English-speaking tourist guide at Chez Papillon in Fianarantsoa, Angelo Rakotonirina, did this trip by taxi truck. Those travellers considering this fascinating journey up the south-west coast, by way of Morombe, are strongly advised to contact him before setting off: 114 Cité Antarandolo, 301 Fianarantsoa, Madagascar, tel. 508.15.

Most travellers make the 17-20 hour overland journey to Morondava from Antsirabe. Even if you catch a Morondava-bound taxi-brousse from 'Tana, it will go via Antsirabe. Taxi-brousses leave daily for Morondava from the taxi-brousse station next to the Hotel Manoro in Antsirabe. Make certain to book your seat the day before departure and try to get a front seat, especially if going by bacchee.

The taxi-brousses leave Antsirabe at about 7h00. Take along something to sit on, something to wrap yourself up in against the thick red dust (a lamba oany is ideal for this) and something to drink. If doing this route during the January to February rainy season (as I idiotically did), wear shorts, a T-shirt and sandals. You will have to get out and push the vehicle through the mud, you will get filthy, wet and exhausted, but it will be a memorable adventure once it's over.

The taxi-brousses travel west along the tarred RN34 to Miandrivazo, where a stop is usually made for something to eat and drink. Then it's south through the spectacular Gorges de la Tsiribihina to the settlement of Malaimbandy. Here, the tarred road was washed away a few years ago and has never been repaired. The taxi-brousse will turn west and make its way along a rutted gravel road for about 15 km to where the tarred road commences again. It is this off-road stretch that offers the most challenge during the wet season. Once back on the tar the road hugs the edge of the Morondava River for 176 km to Morondava.

You could try to find a boat to bring you either up from Toliara or down from Mahajanga. The voyage is time consuming from both ports and conditions aboard are thoroughly basic. The price of this trip is high when compared to the taxi-brousse, but it is a unique way of reaching Morondava. In Toliara, just go down to the harbour and ask the skippers of the schooners berthed along the concrete pier, or ask at Auximad Shipping, near the Port Captain's office. In Mahajanga, you can walk around the schooner docks, behind the container yards in front of Le Rainala Nightclub, or speak to the shipping clerks at Auximad on Avenue de France.

Tourist information

The best places to get tourist information are from the tour operators and a few of the more reputable hotels. The area around Morondava is rich in Sakalava culture, traditions and customs and you should have a good idea of local fady and what is expected of you and what can be seen. At Shop Daya Location Voiture, tel. 523.25, visitors can arrange for vehicle hire, an excursion or information. The office is on the main road in Morondava, in front of the Hotel Continental. The staff at Artilux Location de Voiture, tel. 522.42, are helpful and accommodating. Staff members arrange for local tours, vehicle hire and can provide visitors with loads of information. It is along the main road, near the Brigade de la Police Urbaine. The young manager at La Sirene is a mine of tourist information. She speaks French, German, Arabic, a little English and of course Malagasy. For the most detailed information on the area, she is probably the best person to consult.

The post office is west along the main road, near the seafront. There is an efficient poste restante service. The BTM bank is down a dusty road, one block off the main road and near the Hotel Continental. BFV is close to the school, also in a side road one block off the main road.

The Librairie Chez Shabir on the main road near the Hotel Menabe sells daily Madagascar newspapers and monthly magazines and gets overseas newspapers the week following publication. Its selection of postcards is good and there are a few English magazines and books for sale.

Basic medical diagnosis and remedies are available from Pharmacie de l'Espoir.

Visa extensions must be done through the government offices near La Sirene Bar and Restaurant. You will need to take along four passport photographs, fill in forms in triplicate and then return in two days to collect your passport with its stamped visa. Remember that you cannot change money without your passport. Keep a photocopy of the front pages and get the commissioner to give you a letter in Malagasy stating that he has your passport, to allow you to draw cash from a bank.

The taxi-brousse station is in the big open sand square behind the covered fresh produce market. Here travellers will find long-distance transport leaving for Antsirabe, Antananarivo and Fianarantsoa. Taxi-brousses serving the area around Morondava park on the western side of this square.

Things to do

The main attraction is the magnificent funerary art of the Sakalava tribe, on view to the north-east and south of the town. Visitors are strongly advised to use a guide when visiting the sacred burial sites (fasambezo). It is easy to break fady, or misinterpret certain signs that could transgress local clan customs. Daya and Artilux tour operators run expensive, informative trips to certain Sakalava tombs, but many of the sites have been desecrated by insensitive visitors. For a trip to the most beautiful and well-preserved tombs, arrange through one of the hotels in Morondava for a local guide to take you to the remote settlements north of the Kirindy reserve or south-east of Mahabo.

Take along a bottle of local rum and some fresh fruit. To visit the sites will first involve a meeting with village headmen (fokonolona). The guides know the procedure necessary to secure permission for a visit and visitors should leave it to them to negotiate a price.

The tombs and funerary art of the Sakalava are unparalleled. The amount of attention given to the burial of people is a sure sign that animism is the dominant belief, irrespective of what the local Christians claim. Many of the totem-like carvings depict scenes from everyday life. Around many of the tombs are small wooden fences which are sometimes decorated with intricate carvings of men hunting, zebu cattle with large humps and dewlaps, birds, boats and waves. Frequently the skulls and horns of zebu are used to decorate tall poles as an indication of the wealth of the person buried there. On and around these tombs are massive wooden human figures with conspicuous sexual organs and huge breasts. While the scenes are to honour and remember the people buried there, there are deeper meanings that touch on spiritual allies, the pantheon of animist gods, fertility, rebirth and transient existence.

There are a few sights worth seeing in Morondava itself, but nothing quite as captivating as the Sakalava tombs and carvings. Tourists should pay a visit to the delicately crafted Mosque Khoja Chid, along the main road near Artilux tour operator and car hire.

The Grande Marche, most of it covered, must be visited. It is also along the main road in front of the taxi-brousse station. There is a staggering amount of fresh produce on sale, and solo travellers may be approached by people selling rongony (cannabis). It is illegal in Madagascar. Vegetarians and visitors doing self-catering are advised to stock up on fruit and vegetables at this busy market.

Mangroves and tidal mudflats are characteristics of the estuary and delta east of Morondava. Take a short walk east on the main road where the CBD gives way to a bridge and palm-thatched huts. Around here there are expanses of salt-water mangroves, swamps and mudflats. Morondava's nightlife can be enjoyable or disappointing depending on who you meet. The best place to visit on a Friday and Saturday evening is the Discothèque Soavadia, just off the main road, down a lane opposite the Hotel Menabe. The most popular disco with tourists is Discothèque Harry's, near the burnt-out shell of La Voila Rouge Bar Restaurant Hotel, on the main road.

Things to buy

Morondava is not the place for Malagasy curios. Travellers should be aware that the tribal artefacts that are surreptitiously offered in alleys have invariably been stolen from sacred burial sites.

Something certainly worth buying, however, especially if you are travelling through Madagascar by taxi-brousses, is a lamba oany. On the main road, near the Central Hotel, is the *Palais de Lambahoany*. Women sit on the veranda sewing and preparing these beautiful lengths of colourful cloth. Every traveller should have a lamba oany. They serve a multitude of useful purposes and will become an indispensable part of your travel gear.

Chez Dépêche Mode trading store also keeps a good selection of lamba oanys, groceries, T-shirts, European-style clothing and a few small Sakalava trinkets. The owner can arrange for local curios to be brought in to his shop if you can give him a day or two to arrange it, but I have a strong suspicion that a lot of the stuff he does offer has traditional significance, and has not been taken with the consent of the tribesmen.

Accommodation

Finding a place to stay in Morondava is easy. Popular with tourists, especially British and Italian, Morondava has a good selection of hotels at reasonable rates.

Worth considering is *Les Bougainvilliers* (high tariff), tel. 521.63. This hotel offers accommodation in bungalows, with either paddle fans or air-conditioners. It is close to the beach, but a little way from the CBD. On the main road, the *Hotel Menabe* (medium-high tariff) is highly recommended. It is used by tour groups and is a favourite of backpackers. The upstairs rooms with air-conditioners are more expensive than the downstairs rooms which have fans. This is the hotel at which to find guides to the Sakalava tombs. The staff at the reception desk are able to arrange transport, packed lunches and will even go and book your seat on the taxi-brousse the day before you leave.

Seaside accommodation worth trying is the bungalows of the *Chez Cuccu Restaurant* (medium-high tariff), tel. 523.19, 2 km away at Nosy Kely. The bungalows are well situated, spotless, airy and well worth the tariff asked. Transport into Morondava may be a problem but you should just walk along the sand road into town. Delicious seafood meals can be eaten in the restaurant, which also has a good selection of à la carte meals.

The *Hotel Riviera* (medium tariff), tel. 520.14, is used mostly by English-speaking tour groups, and has the best range of local excursions in Morondava. If you arrive by air, call the hotel from the airport and someone will come and collect you.

One of the best places to stay is the *Hotel Continental* (medium tariff). It has 27 rooms spread over three floors. Breakfast can be eaten from a small, twin-tabled kitchen on the first floor – provided you tell the cook the evening before. All rooms have showers, toilets and fans, while the higher-priced rooms have air-conditioners. Visitors may have their laundry done here and arrange for guides and, if necessary, vehicle hire. No reservations are necessary, but it might be a good idea to call, tel. 521.52, to reserve a room during March, July and August.

On the main road is the *Central Hotel* (medium tariff), tel. 523.78. All rooms have ablution facilities. The hotel is a quiet, serene place under the management of a Sunni Muslim family. You can organise tour excursions at this hotel. Among the cheaper accommodation worth considering, the *Rova-soa Bar-Épicerie* (low-medium tariff), tel. 522.16, has a few clean rooms that would suit experienced Third World travellers. It can arrange for meals and will locate a guide for trips to the surrounding countryside. Take along some insect repellent and wear plastic sandals in the showers.

Equally cheap and recommended is *Kismat Chambres* (low-medium tariff), tel. 522.06, on the same gravel road as the big school building. Travellers will find basic but clean accommodation in neat little rooms. Meals can be prepared if you give enough advance warning. *Hotel de la Plage* (low-medium tariff), tel. 521.30, near the beach, offers accommodation in spartan rooms. The rate excludes meals, although the management says that it will soon be opening a restaurant at the hotel.

Places to eat

Eating in Morondava is an experience not to be missed. Every visitor to Morondava must sample the fresh seafood that is bought daily by restaurant chefs. Prawns, calamari, shrimps, line fish and game fish are all prepared in a variety of interesting ways.

La Cantonaise Restaurant Chinoise on the main road has an extensive menu at reasonable prices. Although the food takes a bit of time to arrive – each dish is individually prepared – the taste and quantity are unsurpassed in Morondava. You will need to get there at the latest by 19h30 for a good table. During the high season you should reserve a table the day before. At the *Rova-Soa*, further along the main road, diners will be able to try authentic Sakalava dishes that include zebu steak, rice and vegetables. This small eatery is cheap and clean. At night, the mosquitoes tend to make things a little unpleasant.

Near the fresh produce market is the well-known *Restaurant Maharani and Salon de Thé*. Apart from the delicious pastries and strong coffee you can get here for breakfast, its light seafood lunches and lavish dinners are a must. The recipes lean heavily towards Indian and West Asian cooking, with lots of spices, rice and sauces.

For breakfasts, fresh bread and delicious pastries, the place to visit is the *Boulangerie Patisserie Bougheril-Charcuterie*, along the main road near Palais de Lambahoany.

Extending onto the sand of the beach is a delightful little wooden restaurant that as yet has no name. Take the sand road that passes the entrance to the Hotel Continental and goes all the way to the beach. The restaurant is at the end of this road. Prices are a little high, but the enormous servings of food and magnificent view make this an ideal place.

La Sirene Bar and Restaurant is undoubtedly the best restaurant in Morondava. You will find it one block down from the seafront, around the corner from the post office. The service is excellent, the servings huge, the ambience idyllic and the menu extensive. Prices are also reasonable. The house speciality is Crab Farsi. La Sirene is popular with both tourists and locals, a sure indication of quality.

Away at *Chez Cuccu* on Nosy Kely beach, guests at the bungalows can choose from a Continental menu that is made up mainly of fish, sauces and small helpings of rice. Be warned, eating here will put a serious dent in your wallet. Despite this, the food is tasty and the setting pleasant. The management suggests that you reserve a table at least the day before, tel. 523.19.

Authentic Malagasy meals are available from the *Ebony and Ivory Restaurant and Bar,* east of the main road where it crosses the causeway over the tidal flats. Around the taxi-brousse station you will find numerous hotelys offering cheap, filling Malagasy meals. Each plate arrives accompanied by a mountain of fluffy white rice, a bowl of hot water with a few greens (this is to be poured over your rice) and a little meat.

KIRINDY NATURE RESERVE

Known colloquially as the Swiss Forest, due to the Corporation Suisse management, the Kirindy Nature Reserve is run on a permaculture principle whereby sustainable harvests of the forest are carried out. This pocket of forest is just 48 km north of Morondava. It is under the auspices of the CFPF (Centre de Formation Professionnelle Forestière). The thinking behind the sustained felling of trees in Kirindy is that only certain trees – usually the oldest – are logged. Immediately after removal, a seedling of the same species is planted. In this way, it is hoped, a continual harvest of forest products will be possible without the usual accompanying environmental damage. The forest is divided into blocs separated by gravel roadways. Each of these sections is then logged in a systematic way that sees a flow of lumber products leaving the reserve for distant markets throughout most of the year.

Visitors can get to Kirindy Nature Reserve by taxi-brousse or bus from Morondava. Take the public transport that travels between Morondava and Belo-Tsiribihina. The first taxi leaves from the depot in Morondava at about 7h30. The last departs at 15h00. Ask the driver to put you out on the eastern side of the forest station. From there it is a short walk to the reserve. No permits are as yet needed at Kirindy, as the reserve is directed at experimental projects rather than eco-tourism.

Although there is a great deal of noise from machinery and humans in Kirindy, there is still enough wildlife to make a visit exciting. One of the rarest tortoises on earth, the flat-tailed tortoise, is found in the Kirindy nature reserve. Another oddity worth investigating is the queer fresh-water turtle known as the side-necked turtle! Over seven species of lemur dance about in the foliage, and the foresters are careful to cause as little habitat disturbance as possible. In comparison to other nature reserves in Madagascar, Kirindy is somewhat short on birds, and only about 42 species are found here.

ANALABE NATURE RESERVE

This reserve is part of the De Heaulme organisation and is one of the places from which flora and fauna are gathered for translocation to the much-visited Berenty Nature Reserve near Tolanaro.

The quickest and easiest way of reaching Analabe Nature Reserve is as part of a De Heaulme tour group. A tour can be booked via any of the De Heaulme hotels in either Tolanaro or Toliara. Be warned though, the trip will not be cheap, especially if there are less than six people taking part in the tour. Alternatively, budget travellers should take a taxi-brousse from Morondava and get out at Analabe, about 58 km to the north, beyond Kirindy.

There have been a few reports that independent travellers have been refused permission to enter the reserve, but these have not been confirmed. To avert any possible problems, check with tour operators in Morondava or the SHTM in Toliara, tel. 426.20.

Accommodation at Analabe Nature Reserve (medium-high tariff) is in 12 bungalows. Guides can be arranged via the reserve staff and basic meals are available if you give them enough warning. Consider taking along your own food instead. The employees will usually permit solo travellers to use the cooking facilities and normally help with the preparation.

Spread over 4 000 ha of alluvial land between Morondava and Belo-Tsiribihina, Analabe consists of mangrove swamps, deciduous trees and bayous. By far the major attraction is the nearly 115 bird species that fill the foliage of the reserve. On guided night walks into the denser parts of the vegetation, visitors may notice the secretive nocturnal sportive lemurs. As silent as ghosts, sifakas and brown lemurs sit in the trees during the day.

Unlike Berenty Nature Reserve, the lemurs at Analabe have not been corrupted with bananas and mangoes to make them tame. Here, the six species of lemur remain distant, wraith-like as they perform their acrobatic manoeuvres high in the trees. Analabe remains off the tourist trail, but it will not be long before tourists are making regular visits to the reserve and pressure mounts on the flora and fauna. An entrance fee must be paid, but no ticket is issued. For visitors in search of tranquillity, beauty and wilderness, Analabe is hard to beat – if they will allow you in on your own that is!

BELO-TSIRIBIHINA

Belo-Tsiribihina is renowned among travellers, and is situated where the mighty Tsiribihina River spills into a wide bird's-foot delta. 18 km south of this coastal village is the famous Avenue of Baobabs. A short walk in any direction from the village centre will have visitors among mangroves and swamps. The area around Belo-Tsiribihina is rich in Sakalava funerary art and tombs. Further east, walkers will discover Sakalava tombs and mausoleums.

Getting to Belo-Tsiribihina from Morondava is relatively simple. There are frequent taxi-brousses and buses leaving Morondava throughout the day. The rather tiring journey takes about five hours. (For details, see section on Kirindy Nature Reserve.) Recently, a number of hikers have followed the coast from Morondava north to Belo-Tsiribihina. The walk takes two to three days and trekkers sleep at remote fishing villages.

The Avenue of Baobabs must be seen. These towering *Adansonia grandidieri* baobabs are alluring and mysterious. Almost every brochure promoting Madagascar features at least one photograph of this amazing sight; grey-barked, ancient baobabs lining the main road between Morondava and Belo-Tsiribihina.

East of Belo-Tsiribihina are a series of oxbow lakes that have formed from the geomorphology of the Tsiribihina River. Hikers should consider walking further east, following the river to where it squeezes through the spectacular Gorges de la Tsiribihina, between Ankotrofotsy and the Plateau du Bemaraha. From Ankotrofotsy hitchhike to Miandrivazo, from where you will find taxis to Antsirabe.

At Miandrivazo tourists will be able to arrange for a descent of the Tsiribihina River to Belo-Tsiribihina. Numerous tour operators are starting to exploit the world-wide attraction of river rafting. Most are located in Antananarivo, and can be contacted via the Hilton or Radama hotels. Their prices are high for a 10-day trip, although all transport, camping gear and food is provided. The most experienced and popular operator doing this trip is Madagascar Airtours. Contact it about 30 days before arrival: Madagascar Airtours, PO Box 3874, Antananarivo, tel. 241.92.

Instead of spending all that money, get yourself to Miandrivazo from Antsirabe or Morondava, and negotiate your own trip with one of the local rivermen. In this way, the trip will be as much as 60% cheaper than through a registered tour operator. You must arrange for food and take along your own camping gear. Most of the boatmen know the river settlements well and you are likely to spend a few nights sleeping with villagers en route.

There is about 160 km of riverway to the coast. It takes between four and eight days to run the river, depending on water conditions. No previous experience is needed. White water is not a big feature of the river, yet for a Malagasy river it is exciting. After summer rains fill the river, boaters are in for some adrenalin-filled moments as they bounce their way over rapids and small falls. Get yourself fit before taking this river trip in the dryness of winter, as you will be doing a considerable amount of portage. Most of the trip is a float on a sluggish brown river that invites hopping overboard and drifting alongside the boat for a while. Remember, though, that in some places there are crocodiles. The boatmen will advise of these well before reaching the site.

Tourist accommodation in Belo-Tsiribihina is limited to the Hotel du Menabe (low-medium tariff). Meals can also be taken there, but visitors should rather eat at the many small hotelys that are found in the village.

You may have to stay overnight if starting a river trip from Miandrivazo. Independent travellers should chat to their boat guide for assistance in locating suitable accommodation. Tourists may, however, prefer to stay at one of the recognised hotels. There are three medium-priced hotels in Miandrivazo: *Relais de Miandrivaz, Hotel Bemaraha* and *Chez Rasalimo*. They all offer basically the same standard, but the Chez Rasalimo has by far the best menu. Guests at Hotel Bemaraha must inform the management at least four hours in advance if they want dinner, and the evening before if they want breakfast. The Relais de Miandrivaz prepares packed food for tourists taking part in the river journey.

TSINGY DE BEMARAHA

Accredited by UNESCO as a World Heritage Site, Tsingy de Bemaraha is an almost mythical place. Encompassing 152 000 ha of pristine wilderness, this reserve has six species of lemur, including the rare Decken's sifaka. Flora and fauna are still relatively undocumented in this remote reserve and new species are being discovered annualy. While the flora and fauna of Tsingy de Bemaraha are enthralling, it is the karst formations that are the main lure to tourists.

All visitors must have a permit from ANGAP, in Antananarivo, on arrival at the reserve.

Twice a day taxi-brousses leave Belo-Tsiribihina for the arduous 82 km drive north to Bekopaka. In this lonely hamlet on the banks of the Manambolo River, you can arrange for a local guide to take you across the river and into the southern reaches of Tsingy de Bemaraha.

Tour operators visit Tsingy de Bemaraha from late March to early November. These tours normally include a few days' boating on the Manambolo River, a short cultural tour of Bekopaka and two days in the reserve itself. The tour guides are excellent and speak several languages including English, Italian, German and French. Many of these tours start in Morondava and are spread over a few days to take in the sights between Morondava and Bekopaka. Contact Madagascar Airtours, tel. 241.92, for details of its latest itinerary to Tsingy de Bemaraha. It offers an all-inclusive tour from Morondava, with stops at burial sites, Belo-Tsiribihina and the mangroves north of town. Transport is provided in comfortable 4x4 vehicles and all camping equipment is provided.

There is no tourist accommodation either in the reserve or Bekopaka. Independent visitors must bring their own tents, and a few packets of dehydrated food is also recommended. Speak to the villagers in Bekopaka about suitable places to set your tent, or choose a site within Tsingy de Bemaraha. If you use a local guide you will be required to pay for his food and provide shelter during the visit to the reserve.

The Tsingy de Bemaraha is the largest tract of protected reserve in Madagascar. Despite this it is still difficult reaching the site on your own, and there are no marked hiking trails or information kiosks. Tsingy de Bemaraha has 55 species of bird, six species of reptile including ringed tortoises and boas and 11 species of frog. Everyone wants to explore the karst areas of the tsingy. Guides are recommended as it is easy to get lost in the caves and narrow passages that make a baffling maze of the reserve. No serious archaeological work has taken place in these ancient caves, and it is not unusual for a visitor to stumble upon some strange inscription or shards from some distant age.

MOROMBE

The biggest drawback to Morombe is getting there. It is almost 350 km south-west of Morondava. It is well situated for excursions to the waterbird-filled lakes of Ihotry and Namonta. There is a pleasant beach west of town and already plans have been lodged with local government for the construction of tourist accommodation.

Getting there

Most tourists to Morombe arrive by air. Air Madagascar Twin Otter aircraft fly to Morombe on Monday, Friday, Saturday and Sunday. Contact Air Madagascar or your travel agent for the current schedule and fares.

Travelling to Morombe by road means taking one of the three daily taxi-brousses that travel from Toliara to Morombe, a distance of some 287 km. The taxis leave from Toliara at about 7h00 and get to Morombe at 17h00. Getting to Morombe from Morondava is not for the timid. The unfrequented track south of the Morondava River is untravelled from November to April. In the parched months from May to October, a taxi-brousse, in the form of a Mercedes truck, departs from Morondava on Monday and Thursday for the 17 hour trip to Morombe. There are two routes that the truck follows, depending on the whim of the driver. The first hugs the coastline to the village of Belo, before swinging south-east to Manja. Around Manja are numerous Sakalava sacred burial sites and intricately carved funerary art works. It is another 81 km south to the tarred road near Tanandava and a further 89 km along the RN55 to Morombe. The second, and far more challenging, but equally interesting route, first goes east from Morondava. About 48 km from Morondava the truck fords the Morondava River and struggles along a rock-strewn track to Mandabe. Delicious traditional Sakalava meals are sold from two hotelys in Mandabe and foreigners are certain of a joyous reception. From Mandabe, the road traverses a midland region between the verdant coastal plains and the distant fringes of the Massif du Makay. After another 90 km the truck enters Manja for the passengers to enjoy a meal and refreshing drink. It is another 170 km south-west to Morombe.

Most people come to Morombe to see the amazing birdlife in the nearby lakes. There are no organised tours as yet, apart from a rather expensive and rushed visit offered by the Hotel Baobab in Morombe. By taking a taxi-brousse, hitchhiking and walking you will be able to reach the nearest lake, Lac Ihotry, within a day. Camping is allowed on the shores of the lake. There are 112 bird species to be seen at the lake and in the immediate environs. Further into the bush, walkers can track down a variety of lemurs that include sifakas, brown lemurs and ringtailed lemurs. Should you go wandering about at night, look out for the striped civet as it prowls the water's edge in search of prey.

Both Lac Ihotry and Lac Namonta are designated hunting districts, open to local hunters at certain times of the year. The ethics of hunting are still being debated by the government, environmental groups and local villagers. Whatever you do, do not enter the region around these lakes during the hunting season – which incidentally is moved each year. There are traps, snares, guns and dogs and a crazed mentality possesses the hunters. You may be mistaken for some animal or bird. Much of the hunting is done at night, using powerful torches to blind the animals so that they can be shot.

Between Lac Ihotry and Lac Namonta is an area rich in fossils. Already some people have shattered the rocks in search of these beautiful fossils. There is no need to cause more destruction; turn over rocks and pebbles on the paths and there you will see the intricate patterns of creatures that possibly existed when Madagascar was still a part of the supercontinent Gondwanaland.

The best hotel in Morombe is the *Hotel Baobab* (medium tariff). All the bungalows have panoramic sea views and the small dining room offers fresh seafood daily. At the *Hotel Datier* (medium tariff), guests will find communal ablution facilities and an unfriendly atmosphere that detracts from one of the best locations in Morombe. For the best meal and passable short-term accommodation, travellers should consider staying at the *Hotel Croix du Sud* (medium tariff). This hotel has an extensive menu of reasonably priced tasty meals that all arrive with stacks of fluffy white rice and tomato, onion or chili sambals.

The cheapest place to stay is the *Brillant* (low tariff). Rooms are basic but clean and sizeable meals are offered in the adjacent restaurant.

MAHAJANGA (MAJUNGA)

On the eastern fringe of the Mozambique Channel, Mahajanga lazes on reclaimed land at the northern edge of the Baie de Bombetoka. Established in 1745 by the Sakalava king, Andriamandisoarivo, Mahajanga is a centre for trade and shipping. Meaning "Town of Flowers" in Swahili, Mahajanga is a dusty, relaxed town of wide boulevards, secluded piazzas, wily Indian merchants, attractive Comorians and smiling Malagasy. The oldest baobab on Madagascar is in the town.

Mahajanga is the second largest, but by no means second busiest, harbour in Madagascar. Situated where the red silt-laden Betsiboka River spills into the sea, Mahajanga lacks many of the Christian influences found in other Malagasy cities. Followers of Islam and devotees of Hinduism have had the biggest effect on the development and style of Mahajanga. There are mosques galore and a beautiful Vishnu temple. Located on a protected bay, and within striking distance of Africa and the Middle East, it was inevitable that sailors, traders, adventurers and preachers would eventually find their way to these hot, wind-blown streets.

The French set up a naval and military garrison here in 1895, from where they launched campaigns against the tribes of western and central Madagascar. It was mainly due to the deadly successes of these marauding French troops that the Malagasy were forcibly brought to their knees in 1897 and had to accept French colonisation.

Mahajanga has had its share of ethnic violence too. In 1977, fed up with exploitation, unemployment and rising costs, the Sakalava tribesmen went on the rampage. Their primary targets were the tight clique of illegal Comorians who had infiltrated their way into business, smuggling and gun running, and the Indian population of storemen, moneylenders and gem dealers. In a few days of mass hysteria over 1 000 people died and thousands more were wounded in bloody street battles. The military was called in and started evacuating the Comorian community.

Almost 20 000 Comorians were airlifted by the Belgian airline, Sabena, and taken back to Grand Comore. To this day, those Comorians who came from Mahajanga are referred to as Sabenas by the islanders of the Comoros.

Racial tension is still a feature of Mahajanga and there is little mixing between the various groups in the town. In the suburbs, nationalities live apart, and it is seldom that any cross-cultural marriages occur. A large military and police presence keeps the delicate situation under control.

Despite the problems and overt nuances that plague Mahajanga, it remains a pleasant town to visit and makes an ideal place from which to set out on excursions to the seldom-visited regions of north-western Madagascar. There are several sites worth seeing in and around Mahajanga, including such beauties as the Jardin d' Amour, Ankarafantsika Reserve, the Cirque Rouge, Grottes d'Anjohibe and the first Boina clan capital at Marovoay.

Getting there

You can get to Mahajanga by air, overland or, for those with enough time, by sea. The quickest way of reaching Mahajanga is on one of the regular Air Madagascar flights. The most adventurous and demanding method is by taxi-brousse or bus and the slowest, most relaxed way is aboard either a cargo ship or island trading vessel.

Air Madagascar flies jets and Twin Otters to Mahajanga every day of the week. Contact it or a travel agent for the current schedule, routes and fares.

An increasing number of travellers are making their way from either Antananarivo or Ambanja overland to Mahajanga. There are daily taxi-brousses and buses from both Ambanja and 'Tana to Mahajanga. During the wet season, huge Mercedes, Bedford and GMC trucks augment the public transport network between Mahajanga and Ambanja.

Travelling south from Ambanja, the taxi-brousses leave from near the market at about 7h00 each morning. The first 193 km of the trip is over an atrocious gravel track that will frequently have you pushing and pulling the vehicle, or stopping to change punctured tyres. From Antsohihy, along a reasonable tarred road, it is about another 430 km south-west to Mahajanga. The journey from Ambanja to Antsohihy is the most difficult and all travellers are advised to take along food and drink and something to cover themselves with against the fine dust clouds that invade the taxi-brousse. From Antsohihy south through Port-Berge (Boriziny) and all the way to Marovoay, the road edges the natural reserve of Bongolava, with its isolated tribal settlements and forests of the Ankarafantsika. During the dry season the trip should take about 16 hours, but when the rains come, count on at least 22 hours of hell.

From Antananarivo, there are several daily taxi-brousses and buses to Mahajanga. The road is tarred the entire 553 km to Mahajanga. Don't be misled though, it is not a tarred motorway, but rather a thin layer of blacktop which has not been maintained since the French left in the 1960s. The public transport leaves at about 13h00 from the Taxi-brousse Station North in 'Tana. Book your front seat the day before if possible, or at least try to get a window seat for the night drive. It takes about 15 hours to reach Mahajanga. While it is cold in the highlands, you should take along a change of clothes for when you reach the searing heat of the coastal regions. There are stops for dinner and late night coffee at small villages where a hotely will stay open waiting for travellers.

Travelling to Mahajanga by boat is only advised for those with time to spare. Just finding a passage can be problematic. The best places to try are Hell-Ville on Nosy Bé, the shipping agents in Antsiranana and Auximad Shipping in Toliara.

For a real adventure, get a trip aboard one of the Arab sailing dhows that run up and down the coast and occasionally cross to Africa. Speak directly to the skipper of the dhow and be prepared to haggle. You must take along all your own food and wet weather gear is advisable.

Tourist information

Limited tourist information in French is available from the Alliance Française on the corner of Boulevard Marcoz and Avenue Gillon. English, German, Italian and French tourist information is best sought from the offices of Air Madagascar or one of the travel agents.

Air Madagascar has its office opposite the Sirama Agency on Avenue Gillon. Trans Tour, on Avenue de France, has several informative brochures for foreign visitors and is the most helpful to independent travellers. Its tours around the area are excellent value for money and are recommended for all visitors with time constraints. Detailed maps of the area and geographical information are obtainable from Service Topographique, also on Avenue Gillon. However, for the most comprehensive tourist information about Mahajanga and its environs, approach the management of the Sofia Satrana Hotel, which is down an alley east of the stadium on Avenue Philibert Tsiranana. While the staff do not have many brochures, their intimate knowledge of the town and surrounding area will prove useful to all travellers who are exploring Madagascar independently. You may also contact the hotel prior to arrival in Madagascar: Sofia Satrana Hotel, BV Marcoz, Mahajanga, tel. 229.69 and 236.32.

The post office is on Rue du Colonel Barre, opposite the Catholic church. Mahajanga is well supplied with banks able to cash traveller's cheques, change foreign currency and issue money against credit cards. Banque Nationale pour le Commerce is on Avenue de France. BNI (Crédit Lyonnais) is near the University of Mahajanga and Hotel de France, on Rue du Marechal Joffre. BTM is opposite Cultures Industrielles Malgaches on the corner of Rue Nicolas and Rue Georges.

The preferred method of getting around Mahajanga is either in a pousse-pousse or taxi-be. These usually crowd along either side of Avenue Philibert Tsiranana, near the long-distance taxi-brousse and bus depot. The Maha Bus Company and several privately owned taxi-brousses provide transport into the districts around Mahajanga.

Medical attention is available from Dr Andiranasy, next to the Safari Bar and Restaurant. The Pharmacie de l'Hôtel de Ville is on Avenue de Mahabibo and is able to fill most scheduled drug prescriptions. Only a script fee is payable if referred there by Dr Andiranasy. There is also the famous Institute of Tropical Diseases (Madagascar), along Rue du Marechal Joffre. If you have any strange symptoms or signs of a fever, approach this institute for a free medical checkup. No prior appointments are necessary; simply arrive and wait to be helped.

Librairie de Madagascar is a large bookshop on Avenue de France. Visitors may browse through a good selection of mainly French literature. It also stocks maps of Madagascar and one of the area around Mahajanga. It is however a little difficult to figure out whether this map is for land orientation or ocean navigation! By turning left opposite the BNPC, on Avenue de France, visitors will arrive at the Majunga Press, which also stocks books, magazines and newspapers. If you are staying for longer than three weeks it will put aside the Sunday national newspapers from France for you to collect.

Permits to visit the Ampijoroa Forest Station, Ankarafantsika Reserve and Tsingy de Namoroka Reserve may be obtained from the Direction des Eaux et Forêts, on the road to Pointe de Sable to the west of the harbour. Travellers wanting to travel from Mahajanga by boat should contact Auximad, on Avenue de France. SCTT, opposite SA Maxime Company, is also able to arrange for an ocean passage if you give them enough warning. There is an office of the French consulate on Avenue Jules Aubuorg. All EU passport holders are able to make use of this consulate in times of difficulty.

Photographic film and camera batteries may be bought at Assik Photo, west on Avenue de France. They also undertake minor equipment repairs. Tourists who must try game fishing or hunting should contact the strangely named Croisières, Pêche aux Gros and Hunting, opposite the Tribunal building on Avenue de France.

Things to do

At the western end of Avenue de France, where it meets Boulevard Marcoz, is the renowned 700-year-old baobab tree. This immense, convoluted *Adansonia digitata* baobab has been thoughtfully protected by the municipality. Exactly why a wide white strip is painted round its base is something of a mystery though. Almost 15 m in diameter, this is surely one of the most photographed things in Mahajanga.

There are many mosques and churches scattered around the town. While most of the Christian churches keep their doors locked for most of the week, the mosques are open to visitors daily, except Thursday afternoon and all day Friday. Wash your feet, face and hands, and remove your shoes before entering a mosque. Women are advised to cover their heads with something. On Rue Alberti is a 1902 French memorial to soldiers who died in the conquest and sustained colonisation of Madagascar. Between the customs office and the ferry pier for boats to Katsepy are a number of large sheds in which rope-making in the traditional manner is still done. Women sit on the concrete floor of these cavernous sheds and patiently and expertly wind the fibres into lengths of strong rope, which are then wound onto bobbins and packed for export.

The Grande Marche de Mahajanga is worth a visit. Located beneath an enormous roof on Avenue de la République, there is a staggering amount of goods for sale. Vegetarians and campers should seriously consider buying their supplies from the huge mountains of fresh produce that are sold here.

Mahajanga's organised nightlife is limited to restaurants and two nightclubs. Opposite the container yard in the harbour is Le Rainala Nightclub, adjacent to Hotel Rainala. It is open from Wednesday to Saturday nights. Saturday night is really the night to attend. The locals' nightclub is Discothèque le Toukan. Le Toukan is not easy to find. Look for the large Tranombarotra Liquor Store sign and turn south towards the port. The disco is on the left side. Dancing competitions are a regular feature and usually start from about 2h30.

Things to buy

Seldom do tourists visit Mahajanga with the sole intention of shopping. To avoid encouraging the sale of historical Sakalava art from sacred sites, sensitive visitors should do their Sakalava curio-shopping from the craft workshops in Mahajanga.

A bewildering selection of local handcrafted curios are available from *Chez Renée (Arts Malagasy)*, on Avenue de France. Prices are high but then so is the quality of workmanship. The shop assistants are helpful and will even arrange to have something special crafted for you from wood. If you do decide on something, avoid buying artefacts made from pallisandra or rosewood. These trees are endangered and their continual exploitation for curios may soon see them joining the long list of extinct flora and fauna in Madagascar.

The best place to purchase a locally made lamba oany is *La Cotonniere d'Antsirabe*. At *Arc-en-Ciel*, opposite the taxi-brousse and bus station on Avenue Philibert Tsiranana, shoppers can select paintings by Sakalava artists. The selection is enormous. An employee will carefully roll and pack the work for you in a protective cylinder.

Outside the Grande Marche de Majunga several curio vendors have set up small stalls full of interesting local crafts. The fascinating animist masks are a great buy, as are the figurines of tribesmen, people in dugout canoes and etchings. Jewellery is not plentiful, but the pieces on offer are unique to this region of Madagascar.

Accommodation

Mahajanga is well endowed with accommodation. It may not all be luxury standard but there is something to suit most budgets.

The recognised tourist hotels are the *Hotel de France* (high tariff), tel. 237.81, opposite BNI bank, and *Nouvel Hotel* (high tariff), tel. 221.11, on Rue Henri Palu. Service and quality are sadly lacking at both these hotels, the favourites of tour groups. They are well located however and immediately throw visitors into the centre of Mahajanga. Tours to the surrounding area and car hire can be arranged via the reception desk of the Hotel de France. Both hotels confirm air tickets for guests and cash traveller's cheques, but at exorbitant commission rates. Rooms are comfortable and adequate in both these hotels and all have en suite bathrooms. Most rooms have air-conditioners, which make a terrible noise all night long.

One of the best places to stay is the *Sofia Satrana Hotel* (medium tariff). All rooms have ablution facilities, mosquito nets and either air-conditioners or fans. The hotel is a little way out of the CBD, but close enough for most visitors to walk back. The rooms are clean and airy and the location of the hotel ensures a quiet, peaceful visit. Go north along Avenue Philibert Tsiranana, and at Chez Thilan Restaurant turn right. Behind the restaurant take the lane which goes downhill for about 100 m to the hotel. It is popular with Malagasy holiday-makers and visitors should book accommodation about 30 days prior to arrival: Sofia Satrana Hotel, BV Marcoz, Mahajanga, tel. 229.69 or 236.32.

The *Hotel Chinois* (medium tariff) is on Rue Rigault. The rooms are stuffy but have fans, toilets and cold showers. You may leave valuables with the manager, who can organise trips up and down the coast from Mahajanga. Next to the Grande Marche de Mahajanga is the *Hotel Islamque* (medium tariff). Strict rules and clean accommodation make this hotel a favourite of holidaying Muslim families. It can get a little noisy, what with children dashing about yelling and crying. No alcohol is allowed on the premises and respectful silence is expected during the daily calls to prayer.

At the northern end of Rue Marius Barriquand, on Boulevard la Corniche, is the *Hotel les Roches Rouges* (medium tariff), tel. 238.71. This grand old place has loads of atmosphere and comfortable accommodation. Bungalows have electric fans and bathroom facilities. Rooms have air-conditioners, bathrooms en suite and soft beds that continually try to swallow you during the night. Les Roches Rouges is a pleasant hotel out of the CBD. The employees are used to dealing with foreigners and have put together a comprehensive tour package of the region for those interested.

The colonial haunt of *Chez Karon* (medium tariff), tel. 234.98, is about 1,5 km from Mahajanga north of the peninsula off Boulevard Marcoz. Accommodation is in rustic rooms fitted with fans, showers and western-style toilets. On Avenue de la République is the *Hotel Continental* (medium tariff), tel. 234.98. This unobtrusive hotel is seldom full but its rooms, with showers, toilets and fans are recommended for a short sojourn.

On Rue Flacourt is the Malagasy hotel *Tropic* (low-medium tariff). Its rooms may be basic, but they are clean and the sheets are changed regularly. It is well situated for excursions around Mahajanga and is popular with travelling salesmen, who are often willing to give you a lift to wherever they are going next.

The cheapest and possibly dirtiest place to stay in Mahajanga is the sinister-looking *Hotel Boina* (low tariff), tel. 224.69, on Rue Flacourt. This is your typical "dive", with lots of insects in the beds and rooms and shady characters lounging about outside offering precious stones, drugs, women and black market rates on dollars and pounds sterling. The *Hotel Rainala* (low tariff), tel. 229.68, at the southern end of Rue Nicolas, opposite the port, is attractive and clean. Meals can be arranged at the hotel and you have the choice of rooms with air-conditioning or electric fan. The rooms have washing facilities and the hotel has what seems to be the cheapest laundry service in Mahajanga. The management can arrange guides for trips to the interior and will even provide a private car. Not as grandiose nor as costly as the tours put on by tour operators, a trip to Katsepy or the Cirque Rouge from the Hotel Rainala is fun, informative and memorable.

In the maze of narrow lanes that edge the national road to Antananarivo is the *Hotel Chez Chabaud* (low tariff). A favourite destination of backpackers, it is the best place at which to gather information about other parts of Madagascar. Accommodation is suitable for travellers, though some form of mosquito or insect repellent is recommended.

Places to eat

Eating in Mahajanga is a wonderful experience. With recipes influenced by Africa, the Middle East, Europe and the Orient, Mahajanga offers diners interesting meals, provided you are willing to ignore the sometimes poor hygiene standards and concentrate on the delicious meals instead.

Opposite St Gabriel College on Avenue Philibert Tsiranana is *Chez Thilan Restaurant*. It has an excellent menu at reasonable prices, and also offers an enormous *plat du jour*. To reach the *Satrana Vietnamese Restaurant*, turn left off Avenue de Mahabibo at Chez Tran. Its highly spiced dishes are tasty and are always accompanied by plates of steaming Malagasy rice.

The *Kalizy Bar and Café*, on Avenue Gillon, offers meals during the day from a limited menu that tends heavily towards traditional Malagasy food. The fresh fish is scrumptious and the beers always ice-cold. The run-down *Restaurant Boina*, on Rue Flacourt, has an extensive menu but far fewer items actually available. The prices are low, the servings – of what is available – large but the service is mediocre in what could be a wonderful tourist restaurant. At the *Sampan d'Or*, Rue Rigauld, diners may select from an interesting Chinese menu that includes such delicacies as shark steak, squid and glass noodles. You must get there early for a table on either Friday or Saturday evening.

Along narrow Rue Gam Etta is the *Aigle D'Or* restaurant. Most of its dishes are Malagasy style, but all are flavoured with herbs and spices that recall food eaten in the bazaars of Morocco or Egypt. *Restaurant Chabaud*, opposite École Normale Niveaui east of Avenue Philibert Tsiranana, is supposed to have the best food in Mahajanga. It is riding the wave of promotion from guidebooks and its prices are high and the staff surly and rude.

For authentic Eastern cuisine, pay a visit to *Kismet Restaurant* on Rue Rigauld. The curry dishes are breathtaking. For a milder taste, try the saffron rice meals. Prices are good, the management hospitable and the ambience relaxing.

The cheapest, biggest meals available in Mahajanga are from the numerous wooden hotelys which have sprung up around the taxi-brousse and bus depot on Avenue Philibert Tsiranana. They open from about 6h30 and keep pots of delicious food going until about 21h00. Rice is the staple, usually with the addition of chicken, beef or seafood. Especially good are their side dishes of tomato, chili and onion, or crushed and boiled cassava leaves. Cassava leaves are a mild form of relaxant and induce a peaceful sleep, ideal for that long night drive.

Mahajanga is full of places to buy snacks during the day. Opposite the cathedral on Avenue de Mahabibo is the *Zam Zam* snack bar, where bread, coffee and a few cakes are available. Undeniably the best place to have breakfast is the *Salon de Thé Patisserie Saify*. Near the municipal playground, this shop bakes fresh bread, samosas and pastries each morning. Its hot croissants with butter and homemade jam, washed down with strong filter coffee, is a perfect way to start the day. Across from the Institute of Tropical Diseases on Rue du Marechal Joffre is *Top Ten Confection*. The vast array of cakes, sweets and pastries is a temptation to everyone who wanders by. Near the end of Rue Nicolas is the small snack bar *De Mahajanga Lada*. It sells Indian sweetmeats, masala-flavoured tea and fresh bread.

KATSEPY

The best beaches around Mahajanga, apart from the crowded sands of Amborovy to the north, are found south-west of the village of Katsepy, across the wide, red Betsiboka River. Another reason for taking the ferry crossing is to eat at one of the most famous restaurants in Madagascar, *Madame Chabaud's*.

There are two daily ferry crossings each way from Mahajanga to Katsepy. The boat leaves Mahajanga from the quay at the southern end of Avenue de la République at about 7h30 and again at around midday. Return trips leave the beach at Katsepy at 9h30 and 15h00. Depending on weather and tidal conditions, the trip usually takes about 60 minutes. During the wet season, with a high spring tide and the river in flood, the trip can take anything up to three hours.

There is not much to see or do in Katsepy village, but the area around it is certainly worth further exploration. There are deserted beaches west of Katsepy all the way round the point to the fragmented delta of the Mahavavy River. Between this river and Katsepy is a small protected bay. On the edges of the bay inquisitive visitors may find fossils among the rocks and semiprecious stones buried in the soft sand. In this remote area campers will find pleasant pitches on the edge of the sea. The only excitement comes when Sakalava fishermen launch their dugouts at sunrise or return with hundreds of little fish at noon.

Back in Katsepy visitors who want to stay the night and enjoy the extensive seafood menu at the renowned restaurant should approach Madame Chabaud and ask for accommodation in one of the low-priced bungalows she rents out.

MITSINJO

The village of Mitsinjo is 84 km south-west of Katsepy, near Lac Kinkony. Not yet gazetted as a national nature reserve, this isolated lake sees the annual migration of thousands of birds from East Africa and southern Europe. Hunting occurs frequently and walkers should be on the lookout for snares and traps. A few lemur species, notably the sifaka and ubiquitous brown lemur, can sometimes be spotted in the sparse foliage which hugs the edges of Lac Kinkony. No public transport runs directly to the lake, nor anywhere south of Mitsinjo during the wet season. In the dry months one lonely taxi-brousse per day travels over an unbelievable track from Mitsinjo to Soalala. Ask the driver to drop you off where the excuse for a road briefly touches the south-western edge of the lake.

To reach Mitsinjo, you need to take the thrice daily taxi-brousse. The first departs Katsepy at about 7h00, the second at 10h00 and the third at 12h00. The dusty trip takes just over an hour. All three taxis return to Katsepy late the same afternoon. If you wish to sleep in Mitsinjo, speak to the women who work in the hotelys around the village and arrange with them to find a place to stay.

TSINGY DE NAMOROKA

Trekkers with adequate time should consider the 40 km trek from Soalala to one of the most remote wilderness areas in Madagascar, the Tsingy de Namoroka. There are wondrous caves to be explored in this reserve, and as few tourists ever get this far out, the locals get incredibly excited at those who do arrive. You do need to carry all your own food and water. A topographical map and compass are also necessary additions to your gear. Take the road south-east from Soalala, and where it swings back towards the coast keep walking directly south. The first sight of the tsingy, across parched plains with stunted trees, is inspiring. The Tsingy de Namoroka is a place that could have been created from God's dreams. A guide to the maze of caves, tunnels and formations may be found at the village of Silampiky. It is easy to find yourself spending several days exploring the region. Permits from ANGAP are supposedly needed, but there is no one to ask you for it and it is unlikely that you will encounter any official person during your visit.

MAROVOAY

It was here that King Andriamandisoarivo first settled in 1742 with his Boina clan after splitting from the Menabe communities. Located 70 km south-east of Mahajanga on the northern side of the Betsiboka River, the village itself is rather drab, but the surrounding area has some fine exhibits of funerary art. To see these you will need to ask the village chief, who will assign you a guide and request that you buy a bottle of rum and take some gift of food along. At the burial sites, rum is poured over the tomb and art works, then the food is laid out around the mausoleum. It is a sensitive, solemn occasion and visitors are expected to show proper respect and avoid intruding on local fady.

The only suitable accommodation for tourists in Marovoay is the Malagasy hotel *Tiana* (low tariff). Visitors may arrange an enchanting and reasonably priced trip on the Betsiboka River back to Mahajanga through the hotel. The sedate float takes about a day from Marovoay. You launch onto the river at about 7h30 and drift into the Baie de Bombetoka in the early afternoon, before threading your way through the delta to Mahajanga, arriving there at sunset. Meals are included in the fee, but drinks must be taken by yourself.

The same river trip can be done through Hotel les Roches Rouge and Hotel de France in Mahajanga. Both charge ludicrous prices, but do manage to squeeze in a hasty visit to the Ampijoroa Forestry Station. A packed cold lunch is included, as are soft drinks; clients are expected to pay for everything else. Both hotels only run these tours if there are more than four people taking part.

ANKARAFANTSIKA NATURE RESERVE (INCLUDING AMPIJOROA FORESTRY STATION)

Lying about 95 km south-east of Mahajanga, this 62 000 ha nature reserve is famous for its reptiles, birds, threatened pockets of tropical forest and galleries of deciduous trees.

This much-vaunted nature reserve is a popular destination with Malagasy tour operators. Spread out between the banks of the Mahajamba River in the north and the RN4 in the south, much of Ankarafantsika is inaccessible to tourism. It is the Ampijoroa Forestry Station adjacent to the national road that most people visit.

The reserve can be reached either with a Malagasy tour operator or independently from Mahajanga. If you make the trip alone remember that a permit must be obtained from the Direction des Eaux et Forêts in Mahajanga, or ANGAP in 'Tana. Taxi-brousses and buses travel the road south from Mahajanga throughout the day and night and finding a lift is hardly a problem. The problem may be in persuading a long-distance taxi-brousse or bus to allow you to pay to go only as far as Ampijoroa. Instead, take one of the morning taxi-brousses going to Ambato-Boeny or Andranofasika. The first of these leaves Mahajanga at about 7h00 each day. The trip to Andranofasika takes around two hours, with a breakfast stop en route. The last taxi back to Mahajanga leaves from Ambato-Boeny at 16h00 and arrives outside the Ampijoroa Forestry Station about 45 minutes later.

To see the best of what this extensive nature reserve has to offer, visitors are advised to tour the park from mid-May to early November. During the rest of the year it can get unpleasantly wet. Keen lemur spotters should brave the rain, mud and occasional leech to venture into the reserve from December to April, when the mongoose lemur is most active and likely to be seen.

Flora and fauna are abundant in the reserve, with the main attractions being the rare ploughshare tortoise and flat-tailed tortoise. Seven species of lemur can be spotted on walks through the reserve, the most beguiling being the aerial performances of Coquerel's sifaka. At night, on guided walks, visitors may see the dwarf and sportive lemurs as they search for food. Brown lemurs and grey mouse lemurs are also to be found in Ankarafantsika. For a real treat, hire a guide to help you track down the elusive and endangered mongoose lemur, endemic to the Ankarafantsika region. Another creature endemic to Ankarafantsika is the secretive long-tailed grey mouse. Consider yourself privileged should you actually see one of these. Shrews, tenrecs and solitary fossas are among the other animals that inhabit this silent place.

The most threatened creatures of Ankarafantsika are its estimated 33 reptile species. This is one of the reserves which is open to licensed reptile dealers. At night, logging trucks and saloon cars crowd the RN4 road outside Ampijoroa Forestry Station, and the reserve personnel wage a hopeless war against poachers. The reptile most sought by collectors and tourists alike is the rhinoceros chameleon, with the prominent bulge on the end of its nose. It is not easy to spot against the foliage, but when seen, is unforgettable. Around the lakeside trees, look out for dwarf iguanas, geckoes, boas and striped lizards.

In the tall trees of Ankarafantsika ornithologists have recorded 103 species of bird, including such beauties as the vocal vanga, colourful kingfishers and the majestic fish eagle.

Deep in the pockets of forest, visitors will encounter flowers and blossoms galore. From stark, grey-barked *Pachypodium*, with their bulbous yellow blossoms, to the red stem and petals of the *Bauthenia madagascariensis* flower, the flora of Ankarafantsika will delight everyone.

There is no tourist accommodation at the Ampijoroa Forestry Station, so you must arrive with your tent and food – unless you are willing to walk the 5 km to Andranofasika village. The *Blue Moon* hotely, near the produce vendors in Andranofasika, does wonders with chicken, fiery-hot sauce and rice.

A camp site has been set aside, but there are no amenities and visitors will need to get their water from the tiny lake. Don't drink this water unboiled and avoid washing in it with soap. There is drinking water at the forestry station, but to be on the safe side boil it first.

Well-marked trails crisscross Ampijoroa and there is no need for a guide unless you plan to venture into the remote parts of Ankarafantsika. Should you want to explore the isolated valleys and bush of the reserve, enquire about hiring a guide from the forestry station. The guide will arrange all the food that needs to be taken along and will expect to share your tent for the duration of the trip. With the assistance of the Jersey Wildlife Preservation Trust, ANGAP has recently started giving many of their registered guides language courses, though of course they can all already speak French. The guides enjoy taking visitors into the nether regions of the Ankarafantsika and will spend hours explaining about the flora and fauna. They encourage night walks and have an intimate knowledge of animal tracks, night-flowering plants and birdsong.

CIRQUE ROUGE

Just 14 km from Mahajanga is one of the greatest geological wonders and erosion catastrophes in Madagascar, the Cirque Rouge. The rocks, cliffs and soils here are splashed a multitude of colours that range from blood red to steel grey.

The cirque is an eerie place of whispering winds and fantastic rock shapes. The best time to visit is at sunrise or sunset, when the long golden rays of the sun paint the ancient landscape with a bewildering array of changing colours, shadows and images. There is little shade in the cirque at midday, and many visitors escape to laze beneath the ravinala trees (traveller's tree – Madagascar's national floral emblem). Near these stands of trees is a small spring that gushes sweet water into a pond. It is quite safe to drink this water and the bubbles give it an almost soda-like texture.

The Cirque Rouge is usually on the itinerary of tour operators to Mahajanga. Using a registered tour operator, visitors are driven in air-conditioned 4x4 luxury vehicles from Mahajanga to the site for the day. The fee includes a meal, guide and cold drinks; alcohol is at your own expense. The Sofia Satrana Hotel, Hotel de France and Hotel les Roches Rouges also run day trips to the cirque for guests, provided that there are at least four of you. The Sofia Satrana Hotel can, however, arrange a tour for one or two people with a local guide who will arrange a private car for the day. If you choose this option make sure to set the price before setting off, and confirm what it includes. The tourist usually has to pay for food, drinks and petrol, plus the guide. It still works out cheaper, albeit a little more uncomfortable, than using a tour operator.

Guides are not necessary. It is impossible to get lost in the Cirque Rouge anyway. Travellers have the choice of taking a taxi-brousse, taxi or bus to reach the cirque. The problem is that few taxi-brousse drivers are willing to take you the short distance, while a taxi driver inevitably asks laughably high rates. The simplest and most enjoyable way is to take a bus from Avenue Gillon in Mahajanga to Amborovy. From this village visitors walk another 5 km to the cirque. It is a hot, demanding walk and visitors should carry along some water, wear a wide-brimmed hat and coat their exposed skin with block-out cream.

There is no accommodation at the Cirque Rouge. With the hotels of Mahajanga less than 30 minutes away, most tourists return there. Campers are permitted to set up their tents anywhere in the cirque area.

GROTTES D'ANJOHIBE (ZOHIN ANDRANOBOKA)

The Grottes d'Anjohibe lie on the Baie de la Mahajamba, at the end of an 82 km long sand track, north of Mahajanga. Visiting these caves is a rare experience not to be missed.

The peninsula on which both the village and caves of Anjohibe (Big Caves) lie is inaccessible during the wet season from November to May.

You could sign on for a day trip with one of the tour operators or hotels in Mahajanga, but it is far more exciting doing it on your own. From April to October a solitary taxi-brousse leaves daily, at about 7h00, from Mahajanga for Androhibe. Very occasionally – if there are sufficient passengers – the driver will continue the extra 12 km to Anjohibe village.

To explore these enormous caverns, arrange a guide in Anjohibe. Ask your guide to show you parts of the caves off the recognised paths. At times you will be wiggling on your tummy through narrow passages, at others listening to your echo as it bounces off huge ancient rock domes. In the chambers closer to the surface the calcite formations have been vandalised, but those further in are filled with beautiful white carbonate stalactites and glittering stalagmites which are as pristine as they have always been. French surveyors first visited these caves in 1934, but local tribesmen had been using them as cool storerooms for as long as anyone can remember.

The nearest hotels are back in Mahajanga, and unless you are with a tour group, it is unlikely that you will be able to get there and back in one day. Take along a tent or speak to the headman in Anjohibe, who will be able to arrange a place for the night.

INDEX

Acapulco Restaurant and Piano Bar 52, 88
Accommodation 48, 85, 97, 99, 109, 118, 120, 133, 137, 142, 153, 160, 165, 176, 181, 184, 191, 195, 204, 216, 228, 234, 238, 250, 254, 255, 264
Adam and Eve Buvette Restaurant and Salon de Thé 178
Admiral de Hell 224
Aeroflot 61, 81
Age d'Or 101
Aigle d'Or 267
Air Austral 61
Air Fort Services 95
Air France 81
Air Madagascar 31, 32, 33, 49, 55, 61, 62, 64, 77, 81, 94, 95, 106, 120, 150, 154, 168, 171, 173, 179, 189, 182, 190, 193, 198, 199, 201, 202, 211, 225, 237, 246, 257, 260, 261
Air Route Services 68
Air transport 61
Airlines 61, 62, 81, 106, 120, 168, 173
Airports 127
Alankar Malagasy Jewel Work 215
Alcohol 53
Alliance Française 173, 190, 261
AM Hassanaly et Fils 225
Ambalavao 56, 163-5
Ambanja 43, 67, 211, 222-3, 237, 260
Ambarikadera 189
Ambato-Boeny 270
Ambatoharanana 209, 222
Ambatolahy 162
Ambatolampy 135-8
Ambatoloaka 230, 232
Ambatondrazaka (Lac Alaotra) 67
Ambatozavavy 230
Ambila-Lemaitso 168, 171, 172, 190
Ambilalialika 115
Ambilobe 211, 222, 237
Ambinanibe River 93
Ambinanifaho 241
Ambinanitelo 180
Amboasary 91, 96
Ambodiatafana 200, 203

Ambodiatafana piscine naturelle 203
Ambodifotatra 172, 183, 199, 201, 203, 206
Amboditsiry 57
Ambodivona 76, 171
Ambohidrabiby 129
Ambohijanaka 134-5
Ambohimahasoa 190
Ambohimanga 7, 8, 129, 130-34
Ambolokazo 223
Ambondro 230, 232
Amborovy 268, 273
Ambositra 148-9
Ambositra Tompon' anarana 148
Ambovombe 95, 103, 104
American Express 31, 47
Amicale Boulangerie 217
Amidyato Café 88
Ampaidranovato 157
Ampangorina 234
Ampanihy 132, 199
Ampasary River 189
Ampasimena 236
Ampasimoronjia 236
Ampasindava 230, 236
Ampasy 232
Ampijoroa Forest Station 262, 270
Anakao 58, 114
Analabe 253
Analabe Nature Reserve 253-4
Analamarina 148
Analamazaotra Nature Reserve 186
Analamazaotra River 188
Analamera Reserve 209
Anartsogno (St Augustin) 106, 113
Ancien Chemin Muletier (Old Mule-skinners Road) 188
Andampy 230
Andapa 59, 180, 238, 240-41
Andasibe (Périnet) Nature Reserve 49, 186-9
Andasibe 70, 71
Andilana Beach 233
Andilana Beach Hotel 233
Andoany (Hell-Ville) 224-9
Andohahela 96

Andrafiamena 209
Andrahibo 233
Andranofasika 270, 272
Andranokove River 123
Andranombilava River 123
Andranomena River 124
Andranovory 116
Andriamandisoarivo 259, 269
Andriamanero River 123
Andrianahifotsy 245
Andrianampoinimerina 7, 73, 83, 131
Andrianasinavalona 129
Andriandahifotsy 209
Andringitra 198
Androhibe 273
Androka 114
ANGAP (Agence Nationale pour la Gestion des Aires Protégées) 19, 136, 180, 187, 218, 221, 230, 256, 269, 270, 272
Animism 18, 109, 134, 248, 264
Anivorano Avaratra 209, 220, 221, 222, 238
Anjanavana 182
Anjohibe 273, 274
Ankarafantsika Nature Reserve 260, 261, 262, 270–72
Ankarana 59
Ankarana Reserve 71, 209, 221–2
Ankaratra mountains 135, 136, 137
Ankaratravitra 104
Ankarena Cave 199, 205
Ankarikakely 210
Ankavia River 241, 242
Ankeniheny 136
Ankerana River 163
Ankify Marina 223
Ankirihiry 203
Ankorikakely 214, 215
Ankotrofotsy 255
Anoronjia 214, 233
Anosibe (An'Ala) 168, 190
Anosibe 92
Anove River 183, 184
Anse de la Dordogne 210, 214
Antafita 84
Antaifasy 13, 169
Antaimoro 13, 18, 165, 169, 197
Antainambalana River 179, 180
Antaisaka 13, 92, 93, 99, 169
Antaivondro 92
Antakarana 218, 207, 209, 210, 219, 222, 240
Antalaha 179, 211, 241–2

Antambahoaka 13, 18, 169
Antanambe 236
Antananarivo ('Tana) 4, 7, 8, 19, 20, 26, 31, 33, 43, 55, 65, 67, 70, 71, 73–9, 91, 92, 127, 129, 138, 150, 158, 164, 168, 171, 186, 190, 193, 197, 201, 211, 225, 237, 241, 248, 255, 260, 261
Antanavo 207
Antandroy 13, 14, 92, 103, 104, 128
Antanimora 91
Antaninaomby 234
Antankarana 13
Antanosy 13, 92, 93, 99, 105
Antatsima 92, 99, 169
Antatsino 93
Antiboina 243
Antifirenana 92, 105
Antimahilaka 243
Antimaraha 243
Antimena 243
Antimilanja 243
Antiques 57
Antsahamanavaka 233
Antsahampano 16, 67, 211, 222, 225
Antsirabe 67, 76, 91, 92, 107, 127, 138–45, 150, 246, 248, 255
Antsiranana (Diego Suarez) 5, 9, 16, 31, 47, 60, 75, 174, 207, 209–17, 220, 221, 225, 230, 238, 261
Antsohihy 211, 260, 261
Arabs 5, 22, 199, 200, 223, 230, 245, 261
Arboretum d'Ivohitra 141
Arc-en-Ciel 264
Art Gallery Yerden 82
Art-Mad Souvenir Boutique 153
Artilux Location de Voiture 247
Artisanat 227
Arts Madagascar 227
Asabotsy 140, 145
Asabotsy market 145
Assik Photo 263
Atelier Dera 57
Au Coin de la Plage 232
Au Coin du Plaisir Bar and Restaurant 192
Au Gentil Pêcheur 186
Au Rendezvous des Pêcheurs 137
Au Rikiki Club 223
Auberge de Soleil Levant 133
Auximad Shipping 108, 174, 182, 191, 193, 238, 247, 261, 263
Aventours 68
Avenue of Baobabs 254

Avery, John 114, 167
Aye-Aye Island 182, 183

Bachmann, Rita 57
Backpacker 44
Baie d'Ambatozavavy 230
Baie d'Antongil 179, 181
Baie d'Ivondro 170, 175
Baie de Bombetoka 259, 270
Baie de la Mahajamba 60, 273
Baie de Mananivo 105
Baie des Dunes 214
Baie des Forbans 202, 203
Baie des Française 214
Baie des Galions 96, 99
Baie des Russes 231
Baie des Sakalava 214
Baie du Diego Suarez 220
Baie Lonkitsy 205
Baie Ste Luce 105
Bain Thermal et Piscine 141
Bamboo Club 118, 119
Baobab 20, 97, 259, 263
Bar Fleurs 229
Bar Mahavita Azy 112
Bar Niandipo 229
Bar Volatiana 147
Bara 13, 14, 92, 105, 119, 122
Bargaining 32, 43, 75, 85, 109, 134, 153, 226
Basse Ville 149
Bassin de Pisciculture 188
Batik Malagasy 134
Bavaratra 169
Beaches 230, 245, 268
Bealoka 95
Beef ranching 16, 17
Beer 52, 165
Beggars 32
Beheloka 113, 114, 115, 116
Bekijoly 124
Bekoaky Plateau 124
Bekopaka 256
Belle Vue 163, 205
Belo 257
Belo-Tsiribihina 253, 254–6
Beloha 103, 104
Bemapaza 233
Bemarivo River 238
Beraketa 92
Berenty Nature Reserve 71, 95, 96, 253
Beroroha 123

Beryl Hotel 178
Betafo 145, 147–8
Betanty (Faux Cap) 103
Betioky 116
Betroka 92, 95
Betsiboka River 60, 245, 259, 268, 269
Betsileo 13, 14, 127, 128, 129, 138, 148, 149, 153, 156, 163
Betsimisaraka 13, 14, 169, 185, 200, 201, 207, 240
Betty Plage 205
Bety, Princess 200
Bevato 124
Bezanozano 13, 169
BFV (Banky Fampandrosoana ny Varotra) 31, 77, 107, 139, 151, 173, 191, 194, 213, 225
Bibliomad 54
Bibliothèque Municipale 79
Bicycle 69, 113, 137, 139, 142, 143, 145, 146, 168, 203
Bight d'Antongil 241
Bijouterie Kalidas 176
Bijouterie Liladhar 176
Bijouterie M Kalidas 215
Bilharzia 38
Biosphere Reserve 182, 183
Birds 23, 116, 161, 162, 183, 187, 219, 221, 235, 241, 253, 254, 257, 258, 270, 271
Black market 30, 266
Blaise and Christine 215
Blue Moon 272
BMOI (Banque Malgache de l'Océan Indien) 30, 31, 77, 139, 173, 212, 222
BNI (Banque Crédit Lyonnais) 31, 79, 95, 107, 151, 173, 194, 213, 225, 262
BNPC (Banque Nationale pour le Commerce) 173
Boat 67, 168, 180, 193, 201, 225, 233, 235, 247, 260, 261, 263
Boating 60
Boina 245, 260, 269
Bon Bazar Store 226
Bongolava 261
Books 53
Bookshops 78
Boulangerie d'Ankaratra 138
Boulangerie Mimosa 138
Boulangerie Patisserie Bougheril-Charcuterie 252
Boulangerie Patisserie de l'Est 196

Bradt, Hilary 53
Brasseries Star Madagascar 53
Brillant 259
Britain 8
British 7, 8, 9, 157, 170, 194, 210, 245
BTM (Bankin' ny Tantsaha Mpamokotra) 31, 77, 94, 95, 107, 139, 151, 173, 191, 194, 213, 222, 262
Buccaneers 7, 210
Buddhists 18
Buses 47, 50, 64, 65, 73, 75, 84, 92, 94, 106, 120, 121, 127, 145, 147, 150, 168, 212, 214, 253, 254, 260, 261, 270, 273
Business hours 35
Butterflies 98, 219
Buvette l'Été Indien 217

Cafés 35
Cafeteria Al Bon Gout 229
Campement des Anglais 222
Camping 50, 103, 123, 125, 158, 163, 181, 188, 189, 192, 218, 220, 236, 258, 268, 272, 273
Cannabis 48, 249
Canoeing 60
Canyon des Singes 59, 122
Canyon du Rat 122
Cap Mine 209, 214
Car hire 68, 86, 173, 226, 247, 265
Carbit, Governor General 137
Carraccioli, Father 210
Carte Bleu 213
Carte Touristique de Madagasikara 55
Cascade del Riana 163
Casino 176, 233
Caves 113, 115, 269, 273
Caving 59
Central Hotel 107, 111, 251
Central Madagascar 127–65
Centre Medical 174
Centre Nautique 118
Cercle Mess Antsirabe 143
CFPF (Centre de Formation Professionelle Forestière) 252
Chameleons 22
Chez Abud 56, 227
Chez Alain 110, 111, 113
Chez Angeline 232
Chez Anita 102
Chez Babou 215
Chez Cloclo 228
Chez Cuccu 252

Chez Cuccu Restaurant 250
Chez Dépêche Mode 250
Chez Fazileabasse Hamid 217
Chez Gerard et Francine 231
Chez Henriette 102
Chez Hibiscus 192
Chez Jacqueline 101
Chez Jo 178
Chez Karon 265
Chez Loulou 233
Chez Marseilles 137
Chez Mme L'Aurence 228
Chez Napoleon 204, 206
Chez Papillon 94, 151, 154, 156
Chez Perline 102
Chez Rasalimo 256
Chez Renée (Arts Malagasy) 264
Chez Rogers 183, 184
Chez Thilan Restaurant 266
Chez Vavate 205
Chez Zou 232
Chief Tsimiharo 222
China 10
Christianity 18
Christians 8, 149
Church of Jesus Christ in Madagascar 79
Churches 83, 98, 108, 141, 147, 152, 165, 174, 194, 202, 262, 263, 267
Chute d'Antafofo 147
Cirque Rouge 260, 266, 272–3
Civilisation Museum (Anthropological) 152
Climate 12, 91, 127, 207, 218
Clothing 43
Club Sagittaire 142
Club Tahiti 142
Cocoa 16
Coconuts 16
Coffee 16, 56, 167
Col des Tapia 148
Cold drinks 53
Commissariat 26
Comoros 174, 260
Compagnie Balinere de Madagascar 213, 238
Copra 16
Costs 31
Cotton 16
Credit cards 30, 86, 191, 202, 225, 262
Crocodile Caves 60
Croisières, Pêche aux Gros and Hunting 263
Croissant d'Or Patisserie 179

Index

Cultural Centre 98
Culture 14
Curios 31, 82, 99, 109, 134, 153, 160, 165, 176, 181, 191, 215, 227, 232, 234, 249, 264
Customs 29
Cyclones 12, 13, 159, 168, 199, 207, 214

D'Andavaka 91
Davolo Hill 203
de Flacourt, Baron 93
De Gaulle 10
De Heaulme 96, 97, 99, 104, 253
De Mahajanga Lada 268
Defoe, Daniel 210
Delice Patisserie 102
Dentists 174, 226
Diamant Hotel 142
Diarrhoea 38
Diaz, Bartholomew 5
Diego Restaurant 217
Diego Suarez 207, 209
Dinosaurs 19
Direction des Eaux et Forêts 29, 262, 263, 270
Discothèque Harry's 249
Discothèque le Toukan 264
Discothèque Soavadia 249
Distilleries 226, 232
Dragon des Mers 179
Drinks 52
Drugs 47, 48, 174, 194, 266
Du Carrefour 112
Duke University 159, 161, 175
Dunes Hotel 119
Dutch 7, 22, 113, 157, 171, 245
Dysentery 38
Dzamandzary 232

East India Companies 7
Eastern Madagascar 4, 167–206
Eau de Vive 52
Ebony and Ivory Restaurant and Bar 252
Economy 15
Eden Hotel 177
Eden Sidi 195
Electricity 35
Elite Nautique 58, 62, 71, 72
Embassies and consulates 27, 80, 107, 173, 263
England, John 200
English 9, 24, 113, 225, 247, 256, 261

Étang de la Presqu'île 188
Étang Nympea 188
Étoile de Mer 112
Étoile Rouge Hotel, Restaurant and Snack Bar 177
Eugénie, Empress 202
Euro Rent 69
Evato 197
Evatra 104
Express Tours 107, 117

Fady (taboos) 14, 45, 92, 106, 113, 114, 116, 128, 129, 169, 198, 200, 209, 224, 240, 243, 245, 247, 248, 270
Fahafahana Memorial Park 83
Falanouc 219
Famadihana 15, 128, 129
Fanambana River 240
Fandriana 127
Fanilo Albrand 203
Farafangana 60, 167, 168, 169, 198–9
Farquhar, Robert 170
Fasambezo 248
Fauna 22
Fenoarivo 67, 172
Fenoarivo Atsinanana (Fenerive-Est) 182
Fenoarivo Atsinanana 175
Fenosoa 196
Ferries 172, 199, 201, 211, 215, 222, 225, 268
Fian-Tsilaka 216
Fianarantsoa 4, 31, 47, 67, 76, 91, 92, 94, 107, 119, 120, 127, 139, 148, 149–56, 158, 164, 189, 248
Fiherenana River 116
Filet, Jean-Onesime 200
First aid 42
"First Flower" festival 245
Fishing 17, 58, 97, 106, 108, 118, 157, 177, 186, 223, 225, 263
Fitsanganan'ny Maty 209
FLM Librairie 24, 54
Flora 20, 161, 181, 183, 218, 256, 271
Fofifa-Cendraderu 157
Foiben-Taosaritanin' i Madagasikara (FTM) 55
Fokonolona 248
Food 51
Forestry 16, 17
Forestry Office 225
Forests 19, 162, 167, 180, 184, 207, 209, 217, 240, 241, 252, 270, 271

Forts 202
Fossa (civet) 23, 97, 219, 258, 271
Fossils 258, 268
France 8, 9, 10, 69, 93, 147, 224
Free French 9
French 7, 8, 9, 10, 24, 73, 93, 105, 113, 127, 138, 140, 145, 164, 169, 170, 171, 194, 200, 210, 224, 225, 245, 247, 256, 259, 261, 272
French East India Company 200
Fruit 51, 167, 239

Gallieni, General Joseph 9
Gares routières 75
Gasikara Bazar and Bar de la Glace 156
Gemstones 47, 85, 140, 143, 149, 153, 176, 190, 194, 266, 268
Geography 11
German 171, 256, 261
Gina Village 100
Glace des As 112
Glass-bottomed boats 118
Gold 12, 47, 48, 109, 153, 176, 215
Gorges de la Tsiribihina 246, 255
Gorges du Mangoro 167
Government 11
Grand Hotel 149
Grand Mitsio 235
Grande Marche 249
Grande Marche de Mahajanga 263
Grandidier, Alfred 82
Grotte d'Andavaka 60, 116
Grotte de Mitaho 60, 115
Grotte de Sarondrano 112–13
Grottes d' Anjohibe (Zohin Andranoboka) 60, 260, 273
Grottes des Portugais 60
Groupements des Artisans d'Art d'Antsirabe 142
Guides 122, 160, 180, 181, 183, 184, 187, 203, 221, 238, 241, 242, 245, 248, 256, 257, 266, 269, 272, 273

Haba Gem Stones 85
Handicrafts 31, 227
Hashish 48
Hasina Chinese Hotel and Snack Bar 87
Haute Ville 149
Hauts plateaux 127
Health 37
Heat exhaustion 40
Heatstroke 40

Helena Salon de Thé and Bakery 145
Hell-Ville 15, 56, 71, 211, 261
Hell-Ville Marche 226
Hepatitis 39
Hiking 44, 58, 115, 123, 137, 146, 173, 189, 184, 220, 241, 242, 254, 269
Hilton Hotel 31, 33, 46, 49, 52, 55, 71, 76, 77, 80, 81, 84, 85–6, 255
Hinduism 259
Hindus 18
History 5
Hitchhikers 114
Hitchhiking 70, 113, 120, 134, 147, 163, 168, 190, 255, 258
HMS Gladstone 203
Hobman, Bob 5
Honey Salon de Thé 55, 88
Horse riding 137, 140, 142, 143
Hospitals 37
Hotel and Resto Baobab 143
Hotel Antongil 180, 181
Hotel Antsirabe 144
Hotel Antsiraka 184, 185
Hotel Atafana 205
Hotel Aye-Aye 184
Hotel Baby 149
Hotel Baobab 139, 258
Hotel Bemaraha 256
Hotel Berny 121
Hotel Bona 50, 266
Hotel Bon Voyage 143
Hotel Bons Amis 192
Hotel Calypso 239
Hotel Carrefour 238
Hotel Central 49
Hotel Chez Chabaud 266
Hotel Chinois 265
Hotel Coco Beach 180, 181
Hotel Colbert 36, 79, 84, 87
Hotel Continental (Mahajanga) 266
Hotel Continental (Morondava) 247, 250
Hotel Corsoyannis 49, 53, 155
Hotel Croix du Sud 259
Hotel Datier 258
Hotel de France (Antananarivo) 77, 87
Hotel de France (Mahajanga) 264, 273
Hotel de la Gare 49, 187, 188
Hotel de la Mer 49, 227, 228
Hotel de la Plage (Morondava) 251
Hotel de la Plage (Toamasina) 49
Hotel de la Poste 49, 215, 216, 217
Hotel de Madagascar 94, 151, 154

Hotel de Manakara 195
Hotel des Thermes 139, 142
Hotel du Centre 241
Hotel du Menabe 255
Hotel Escale 50, 155
Hotel Faneva 137
Hotel Foulpointe 186
Hotel Glacier 84
Hotel Ideal 155
Hotel Islamque 265
Hotel Jardin de la Mer 190, 191, 192
Hotel Joffre 177
Hotel Kaleta 96
Hotel l'Orchidée 216
Hotel la Plage 175, 177
Hotel la Rascasse 216
Hotel le Dauphin 95, 99
Hotel le Galion 95, 99
Hotel les Flamboyants 177
Hotel les Joyeux Lemuriens 121
Hotel les Lemuriens 234
Hotel les Orchidées 188
Hotel les Roches Rouges 265, 273
Hotel Libanona 100
Hotel Lito 139
Hotel Mahavoky 95, 98, 101, 103
Hotel Maki 234
Hotel Mamy 195
Hotel Manompana 184, 185
Hotel Manoro 107, 246
Hotel Menabe 247, 250
Hotel Miramar 95, 99, 105
Hotel Moderne 31, 53, 154
Hotel Morabe 195
Hotel Muraille de Chine 49, 87, 88
Hotel Nathalie 192
Hotel Nautilus 204
Hotel Neptune 176
Hotel Niavo 178
Hotel Niavo Fitsangantsanganana 141, 144
Hotel Océan Plage 241
Hotel Orange 206
Hotel Orchidea 238
Hotel Patricia 67, 223
Hotel Plazza 110, 111
Hotel Rainala 264, 266
Hotel Rakotozanany 189
Hotel Ravaka 121
Hotel Ravinala 160
Hotel Relais Bara 121
Hotel Restaurant Villa Blanche 232
Hotel Riviera 250

Hotel Rova 155
Hotel Rubis 143
Hotel Sidi 194, 195
Hotel Soafytel 143
Hotel Sofia Satrana 33
Hotel Stenny 192
Hotel Stop 144
Hotel Sud 50, 110
Hotel Tam Yock 240
Hotel Thermal 160
Hotel Trianon 143
Hotel Tropical 181
Hotel Valiha 49
Hotel Venance 178
Hotel Verger 165
Hotel Violette 149
Hotel Voanio 206
Hotely Malala 148
Hotelys 138, 145, 147, 160, 165, 179, 192, 196, 198, 199, 217, 232, 239, 240, 252, 255, 258

Iakora 91
Ianaboty 123
Iandratsay River 145
Ifanadiana 18, 158, 159
Ifaty 110, 117
Iharana (Vohemar) 212
Ihosy 43, 76, 94, 107, 119, 127, 150, 198
Ihotry 257
Ilafy 129
Île aux Forbans 203
Île aux Nattes (Nosy Nato) 204, 206
Île aux Prunes 173
Île Bourbon (Réunion) 93
Île Lokaro 104
Imaloto River 59
Imerina 7, 8, 13, 14, 73, 127, 128, 129, 131, 136, 138, 146, 148, 170, 222, 224, 245
Indonesians 5
Indra Nightclub 85
Indra Restaurant 88
Insects 42, 236
Institute of Tropical Diseases (Madagascar) 262
International Certificate of Vaccination 37
Ionaivo River 91
Irondo 158, 190, 193
Isalo Massif 58
Isalo National Park 60, 71, 107, 119
Isesy 238
Islam 18, 259

Island of lemurs 72, 233
Italy 91
Itampolo 114, 116
Ivato 26, 33, 73
Ivohibe 127, 198
Ivondro River 173
Ivongo 67

Jardin d'Amour 260
Jardin d'Essai 175
Jersey Wildlife Preservation Trust 97, 175, 272
Jewellery 56, 85, 109, 142, 215, 264
Joffre, Colonel 210
Joffre, General Joseph 214
Joffreville (Ambohitra) 213, 214, 218
Jupiter Hotel and Restaurant 177

Kaleidoscope Bar and Nightclub 84
Kaleta Reserve 100
Kalizy Bar and Café 267
Katsepy 263, 266, 268
Keliambahatsy Plateau 122, 124
Kelyhorombe Plateau 123
Kianjasoa 152, 153
Kinahandro 169
Kirindy Nature Reserve 248, 252–3
Kismat Chambres 251
Kismet Restaurant 267
Kodak 226
Kodak Express Photo Supplies 79
Kopf-mad 66

L'Artisan Galerie d'Art 109
L'Escale Hotel 178
L'Étranger 71
L'Extreme Orient 217
L'Hotel Marlin Club 231
L'Oasis 125
L'Oasis Salon de Thé 229
La Baleine 206
La Barachois Salon de Thé 206
La Bouffe 77
La Buffet 84
La Cabane Arts Malagasy 134
La Cantonaise Restaurant Chinoise 251
La Capital Art 134
La Cirque 205
La Cocoteraie 205
La Colline Bleue 134
La Cotonniere d'Antsirabe 264
La Fleuve Parfum Restaurant 144

La Gourmandise Salon de Thé 196
La Halte 144
La Hutte Canadienne 88
La Librairie de Madagascar 24
La Maison de Tourisme de Madagascar 3, 20, 32, 54, 76, 81, 84
La Potiniere Patisserie 88
La Rascasse Hotel 217
La Regina 50
La Reine (The Queen) 124
La Rotonde 89
La Sirene 247
La Sirene Bar and Restaurant 252
La Taverne Disco 215
La Vahinee 49
La Vahinee Nightclub 215
La Vahinee Snack Bar 217
Lab' Art Studio 80
Laborde, Jean 132
Lac Ambavarano 104
Lac Amparihibe 233
Lac Amparihimirahavavy 233
Lac Andraikiba 145
Lac Andranobe 147
Lac Andranotsara 240
Lac Anjavibe 233
Lac Anony 102
Lac Anosy 49, 76, 81, 84
Lac Antanavo 209, 220, 238
Lac Antsidihy 233
Lac de la Coupe Verte 220
Lac Froid 136
Lac Ihotry 258
Lac Kinkony 71, 268
Lac Lanirano 104
Lac Maintimaso 233
Lac Mandrozo 11
Lac Namonta 258
Lac Ranomafana 140, 141
Lac Sahambavy 156
Lac Sambalahitsara 122, 124
Lac Tritriva 145, 146
Lac Tsimanampetsotsa 60, 71, 91, 115
Lac Vert 188
Lakana 205
Lakana Vezo 119
Lakana Vezo Hotel 118
Lamba oany 56, 163, 249, 264
Land of Mu 5
Language 24
Lapidary 140
Las Palmas 239

Lavanono 103, 104
LCR Car Hire 173
le Vasseur, Olivier (La Buse) 7, 114, 167, 181, 200
Le Bambou 206
Le Buffet du Jardin 77, 88
Le Caveau 84
Le Dauphin 49, 102
Le Galion 105
Le Gourmet Restaurant 179
Le Grand Orient 88
Le Gras Salon de Thé 112
Le Jean Laborde 87
Le Maharadjah 111
Le Muriens Boutique 227
Le Panda 49, 156
Le Papillon 229
Le Paradis du Nord 50, 216
Le Pave 71
Le Rainala Nightclub 247, 264
Le Relais Normand 89
Le Shanghai 88
Le Synchro Restaurant and Hotel 144
Le Vanilla Restaurant and Bar 217
Le Vieux Port 227
Le Zebu Grill 89
Leatherwork 57
Lemurs 22, 23, 59, 97, 98, 100, 116, 124, 161, 162, 169, 175, 181, 183, 186, 187, 219, 221, 230, 234, 241, 253, 254, 256, 258, 268, 271
Lepidoptera 22
Les Bougainvilliers 250
Les Cannes d'Orgue 235
Les Cocotiers 232
Les Mangroves 113
Libabona Beach 99
Libanona 98
Libertalia 207, 210, 217
Librairie Avotra 79
Librairie Chez Shabir 247
Librairie de Madagascar 54, 79, 262
Librairie Ekena 213
Librairie GM Fakra 174
Librairie Mamy 151
Librairie Mixte 54, 79
Librairie Naima 226
Librairie Ny Fandro Soana 107
Librairie Sud 151
Librimad 96
Linda Garcia Arts 153
Lohatanjona Antsiraikiraiky 205

Lokaro Peninsula 104
Lokobe 71
Longo Hotel 111
Lotus Rouge 155, 179
Lotus Rouge Chinese Restaurant 196
Lou Midjou Pizzeria 89
Louis XIV 93

Ma Constance 216
Mad Airtours 212
Madagascar Airtours 31, 33, 47, 55, 68, 78, 86, 255, 256
Madagascar Dive School 231
Madagascar Tourist Board 197
Madagascar Tourist Bureau 20
Madame Chabaud's 268
Madame Chan Fah 231
Madame Madio's 234
Madirokely 231
Maevatanana 211
Mafio 66
Maha Bus Company 262
Mahabo 248
Mahafaly 13, 15, 92
Mahafaly Plateau 91, 114, 116
Mahajamba River 270
Mahajanga (Majunga) 8, 16, 20, 33, 56, 60, 65, 75, 174, 225, 247, 259–68, 270, 272
Mahalevona 241, 242
Mahambo 67
Mahanoro 171, 172, 190
Maharadjah Salon de Thé 112
Mahatalaky 104
Mahatsinjo 235
Mahavavy River 268
Mahavelo 11, 204, 206
Mahavelona (Foulpointe) 167, 185–6
Mahavoky Disco 99
Mahavoky Restaurant 95, 102
Maintirano 76
Maison de l'Artisant 176, 215
Maison du Syndicat d'Initiative 136
Majunga Press 262
Makoa 13, 207
Malagasy 14, 24
Malagasy Art Centre 82, 85
Malagasy Embassies and Consulates 27
Malagasy Tourist Board 48
Malaimbandy 247
Malaria 39
Malayo-Polynesians 5
Manafiafy (Ste Luce) 93, 105

Manakara 18, 67, 95, 150, 158, 167, 192–6, 198
Manakara River 193
Manambolo River 25,
Mananara 171, 180, 182–4
Mananara National Park 173, 182, 183, 185
Mananara River 91, 167, 183, 198
Mananarabe River 238
Manangotry 96
Mananjary 18, 95, 150, 158, 167, 168, 189–92, 193, 228
Manantenina 104, 105, 241
Manda Beach Hotel 186
Mandabe 258
Mandraka Reptile and Butterfly Farm 70
Mandrare delta 102
Mandrare River 96
Mangoky River 91, 95
Mangoro River 127, 138
Manguiers 123
Mania River 127, 148
Manja 257, 258
Manja Ranch 137
Manombo 110, 118
Manompana 67, 182, 184–5, 201
Manoro Hotel 142
Maps 3, 54, 77, 95, 151, 173, 261, 269
Marechal de France 213
Mariany River 124
Marine life 21
Marine reserves 182, 234
Markets 35, 98, 102, 108, 139, 140, 144, 145, 147, 148, 152, 153, 159, 174, 175, 176, 191, 194, 214, 226, 240, 248
Marlin Club 33, 49, 57
Maroantsetra 59, 71, 167, 168, 174, 179–81, 242,
Marodoka 223, 229
Marojezy 59
Marojezy Reserve 209, 238, 240
Marolambo 190
Maromandia 179, 204, 206, 242
Maromokotra 11
Marotia Restaurant and Bar 229
Marovato 104
Marovoalavo Peninsula 184
Marovoay 260, 261, 269–70
Marthe Ravaozanany 215
Masinandraina 145
Masoala Peninsula 13, 167, 241, 242
Massage 141

Massif de l'Isalo (Isalo National Park) 91, 114, 121, 122, 150
Massif du Makay 258
Matitanana River 196
Matsaborimanga 222
Mboahangy Gallery and Souvenir Shop 85
Media 36
Medical attention 80, 96, 136, 152, 174, 194, 202, 213, 248, 262
Mediterranean Shipping Company 62, 193, 213, 238
Memorials 214
Menabe 245, 269
Menamaty River 123
Menarano 159
Mermix and Co. 225
Miandrivazo 246, 255, 256
Miary 116
Mifankatiavatsara 196
Miladial 148
Ministère des Affaires Étrangeres (L'Immigration) 26
Ministère du Commerce 29
Ministère du Tourisme 58
Ministry of Agriculture 16, 240
Ministry of Industry and Mines 85
Ministry of Tourism 75, 78, 117
Mission 210
Mitaho 91
Mitsinjo 268–9
Mitsinjoroy 122, 124
Mitsio archipelago 72
Monastery 148
Money 30
Monoliths 147
Mont Ambondrombe 129
Mont Androhibe 145
Mont Beanjada 242
Mont Ibinty 148
Mont Marojezy 240
Mont Passot 231, 233
Mont Trafonomby 96
Montagne d'Ambre 71, 207, 212
Montagne d'Ambre National Park 214, 217–20
Montagne des Libre Française 211
Monument aux Morts 81
Mora Mora Hotel 118, 119
Mora Mora Restaurant 232
Moramanga 187, 189, 190
Morarano 124
Morombe 110, 246, 257–9

Morondava 20, 65, 76, 110, 120, 139, 150, 243, 245–52, 253, 255, 256, 257, 258
Morondava River 245, 247, 257, 258
Mosque Khoja Chid 249
Mosques 152, 249, 259, 263
Motel Capricorn 33, 49, 107, 109, 111, 116, 120
Motel Coco Plage 231
Motel Gina 33, 49, 50, 95, 100, 102, 103, 105
Motorcycle hire 226
Motorcycles 69, 203, 212
Mozambique Channel 12, 63, 117, 207, 259
Mozambique Current 17
Mozambique Pharmacy 108
Mpihira Gasy 15
Musée de l'Art et Archéologie 197
Musée Océanographique 108
Musée Ranomafana 161
Museum of Art and Archaeology 81
Museums 108, 129, 130, 148, 152, 197, 230
Music 15
Musical instruments 56
Muslims 18, 197, 239

Namonta 257
Namorona River 158, 159, 162, 163
Navana 167, 181–2
New Harlem Nightclub 227
Newspapers 151, 247, 262
Nightclubs and discos 15, 35, 84, 86, 98, 106, 109, 142, 174, 177, 188, 194, 195, 215, 216, 227, 233, 249, 264
Nina Glace Salon de Thé 217
Nintsika Hotely 229
Nirado 148
No. 1 Night Club 227
Northern Madagascar 4, 207–42
Norwegian Missionary Service 138, 194
Nosauto 226
Nosivarika 169
Nosy Alanana 176
Nosy Antaly Be 215
Nosy Bar 229
Nosy Be 15, 16, 18, 21, 31, 33, 47, 57, 58, 62, 67, 70, 71, 207, 211, 222, 235, 261
Nosy Be and surroundings 223–33
Nosy Be Subaqua Club 57
Nosy Boraha (Île Ste Marie) 18, 21, 57, 58, 67, 70, 71, 167, 172, 174, 182, 185, 199–206
Nosy Boutique 227

Nosy Diego 215
Nosy Iranja 58, 71, 72, 231, 236
Nosy Kely 250
Nosy Komba 72, 231, 233–4
Nosy Lonja 210
Nosy Mangabe 180
Nosy Mitsio 222, 231
Nosy Mitsio archipelago 235
Nosy Nato 58
Nosy Sakatia 72, 231, 236
Nosy Suarez 215
Nosy Tanikely 58, 231, 234–5
Nosy Tsarabanjina 72, 235
Nosy Varika 190
Nosy Ve 114
Nouvel Hotel 216, 264
Nouvelle Ville 151
Ny Antsika 148
Ny mahalala isan taona 170

Oil palms 16, 194
Onilahy River 91, 105, 114, 116
Operation Ironclad 210
Opticam Photo Supplies 79
Orchidées Bungalows 205
Orchids 20, 71, 98, 162, 183, 188, 219, 236

Palace Bar 185
Palais de Lambahoany 249
Palm Beach Hotel 232
Pangalanes Canal 50, 60, 168, 172, 173, 189, 190, 191, 196, 198
Panorama Bar 97
Panorama Disco 98
Panorama Hotel 87
Panorama Salon de Thé and Restaurant 102
Papier Antaimoro Soierie 163, 164
Papillon restaurant 53
Paradis du Peuple 179
Paradis Hotel 223
Parasailing 57
Parc Botanique et Zoologique de Tsimbazaza 84
Parc de l'Est 140, 141
Parc National de Ranomafana 4, 23, 151, 158, 159, 160–63, 190,
Paroisse Cathedral 98
Parque Zoologique et Botanique 175
Parson's chameleon 187
Parthenay Club Bungalows 195
Parti Social Démocrate 10
Patisserie Suisse 54, 79, 88

286 *Madagascar*

Pax Hotel 177
Perfumed flowers 16
Permit 151, 162, 180, 187, 218, 221, 230, 241, 256, 262, 269, 270
Perroquet restaurant 232
Petain, Marshal 210
Pharmacie Communautaire 159
Pharmacie d'Isoraka 80
Pharmacie de l'Espoir 248
Pharmacie de l'Hôtel de Ville 262
Pharmacie de l'Océan Indien 80
Pharmacie du Bazarbe 174
Pharmacie du Levant 194
Pharmacie Finaritra 194
Pharmacie Hasina 80
Pharmacie Havana 136
Pharmacie Lam Seck Roland 152
Pharmacie Nora 213
Pharmacie Tony 139
Pharmacie Tsarajoro 226
Pharmacies 37
Photo Lumiere 194
Photo Star 174
Photography 45, 79, 152, 174, 194, 213, 225, 263
Pic Boby 198
Pic d'Ambre 217, 220
Pic St Louis 93, 97, 98
Pierger Restaurant 143
Pirate Coast 167
Pirates 114, 167, 170, 181, 182, 199, 200, 202, 207
Piscine Naturelle 122
Pitcher plant 20, 97
Plateau de l'Anjafy 127
Plateau de Makira 180
Plateau du Bemaraha 255
Pluchard, Pascal 200
Pointe de Sable 263
Pointe Itaperina 105
Pointe Laree 199, 202
Poisson d'Or restaurant 240
Population 13
Port du Cratere 230, 231
Port-Berge (Boriziny) 261
Portuguese 5, 22, 93, 124, 171, 209, 210
Post office 33, 78, 95, 107, 121, 136, 139, 151, 159, 173, 190, 193, 194, 212, 225, 247, 262
Poste restante 34, 78, 247
Pousse-pousse 138, 142, 262

Presqu'île Masoala (Masoala peninsula) 70, 179, 180
Prickly heat 41
Primary tribes 13
Prisunic 15
Produits Artisanaux du Sud 99
Pronis, Governor Sieur 93, 105
Prostitutes 174, 177, 266
Protestantism 18
Protestants 9
Public transport 4, 32, 64, 66, 103, 106, 120, 127, 129, 158, 171, 215, 237, 243, 253, 260, 261
Publitours 77

Quatro Evasion 212
Qui Qui Clothing 227
Quotbi Photo 213

Radama Hotel 33, 52, 76, 77, 80, 84, 86–7, 88, 154, 255
Radama I 7, 8, 170, 185, 224, 245
Radama II 8, 130
Rade de Toamasina 171, 175
Rafting 238, 255
Railroad of Orchids (Chemin de Fer des Orchidées) 193
Rain 168, 180, 199, 218, 243, 245
Rainiharo 82
Rainilaiarivony, Hononaire 8
Rajerison, Docteur Irene 213
Rakotonirina, Angelo 94, 151, 246
Ralaimongo, Jean 24, 82
Ramantsoa 10
Ramarline, General 171
Ramena beach 214
Ranavalona I, Queen 8, 18, 129, 132, 149, 170
Ranavalona II, Queen 83, 145
Ranavalona III, Queen 9, 132
Ranitrarivo, Jean-René 170
Ranohira 58, 59, 107, 121
Ranomafana 158–63, 190
Ranovao 159
RAP Madagascar 235
Rasoherina, Queen 8, 73, 83, 132
Rasolafo Guesthouse 121, 122
Ratinola 206
Ratsimandrava, Colonel 10
Ratsimilaho, King 200
Ratsiraka, Didier 10
Ravinala 20

Ravinala hotely 112
Ravoraha 205
Rebobd Manambien 91, 95, 99
Reefs 117
Regional Museum (Musée Mahafaly-Sakalava) 108
Relais de la Reine Hat Soarano 124
Relais de Miandrivaz 256
Religion and Holidays 18
Reptiles 22, 97, 116, 161, 162, 181, 187, 219, 236, 241, 257, 270, 271
Réseau National des Chemins de Fer Malagasy 68
Réserve Spéciale d'Ankarana 221
Réserve Spéciale d'Lokobe 230
Réserve Forestière et Piscicole de Manjaktompo 136
Residence d'Ambatoloaka 231
Restaurant Abou 217
Restaurant and Bar le Loreol 178
Restaurant Asiatique 88
Restaurant au Bon Coin 206
Restaurant Boina 267
Restaurant Chabaud 267
Restaurant Chez Lilie 196
Restaurant Chez Nana 229
Restaurant Chinoise 178
Restaurant Classic Salon de Thé 229
Restaurant d'Ambohimanga 134
Restaurant de la Grand Île 88
Restaurant Degustation 229
Restaurant Fiaremana 88
Restaurant la Romance 179
Restaurant le Pousse-pousse 178
Restaurant Maharajah 156
Restaurant Maharani Salon de Thé 251
Restaurant Razafimamonjy 139, 144
Restaurant Sud 112
Restaurant Vietnamien 179
Resto Rak Malagasy Restaurant 156
Resto Tsarafandray 196
Reve Dile 77, 88
Rex Cinema 85, 154, 214
Rice 16, 51
Ritz Cinema 139
RNCFM Tananarive 172
Rock climbing 58
Roger's Reserve 183
Roman Catholicism 18
Rommy Snack Bar and Café 88
Rope-making 263
Rosaas, TG 140

Rose Rouge 198
Roussettes Forestry Station 220
Roux, Sylvain 170
Rova 8, 71, 76, 83, 129, 131, 185
Rova-soa 251
Rova-soa Bar-Épicerie 251
Rovan 'Ilafy 129
Roxy Cinema 77
Roxy Cinema Hall 229
Roxy Hotel 223
Royal Hotel 50, 215, 216
Royal Marche 80
Rum (rhum) 53, 113, 145, 156, 165, 169, 197, 232, 269
Russia 10

Sadjoavato 238
Safari Vezo 111, 114, 116
Saga Océan Indien 213
Sagatrans Travel Agents 173
Sahafatra 169
Sahambavy 156–8
Sahambavy lake 157
Saharerana River 238
Sahasifotra 203
Sakafihitra River 242
Sakafo 155
Sakalava 4, 7, 13, 14, 81, 92, 108, 197, 207, 223, 230, 243, 247, 254, 257, 259, 264, 268
Sakaleona River 148, 190
Sakatia Dive Lodge 236
Salegy 15
Salle d'Exposition 160, 161
Salon de Thé Abou 156
Salon de Thé Au Plaisir 179
Salon de Thé Moderne 145
Salon de Thé Patisserie Saify 267
Salon de Thé Riminy 196
Saloon 229
Sambalahitsara 124
Sambatra 18
Sambatra Hotel 50, 228
Sambava 59, 71, 207, 211, 236–9, 240, 241
Sambava Voyages 238
Sambirano Domaine 71
Sambivinany 159
Sampan d'Or 267
Sandrakatsy 183, 185
Saonambo 204
Sarimanok 5
Sarondrano 112

Sarondravay Research Station 223, 227
Satrana Vietnamese Restaurant 266
Satruka harefo 197
SCAC Shipping 213
Schuurman, Derek 12, 53, 60
SCTT 213, 263
Scuba diving 57, 117, 186, 204, 233, 234, 235
Sea transport 62, 213, 238
Security 46
Select Hotel 80
Service de l'Élevage 29
Service Philatelique 57
Service Phytosanitaire 29
Service Provincial des Eau et Forêts Fianarantsoa 151
Service Topographique 261, 262
SETAM 33, 72, 78
Sexual diseases 41
Shakti Voyages 173
Shipping companies 62, 174, 182, 193, 213, 238, 261
Shop Daya Location Voiture 247
Shopping 55, 109, 142, 176, 264
SHTM (Société Hôtelière et Touristique de Madagascar) 97, 104, 105, 109, 119, 195, 253
Sihanaka 13, 169
Silamo 197
Silampiky 269
Silk-screening 57
Silver 176
Silver Palace 83
Sinclair, Ian 23
Singing Dunes 186
Sirama Rum Distillery 53, 232
Sisal 16, 96
Slaves 113, 170
Smart, John 113
Snack Mambo 112
Snacks 52, 102
Snakes 162, 181, 241
Snorkelling 58, 98, 199, 204, 234, 235
Soa 148
Soalala 269
Soamiamina River 169
Soanambo 49
Soanierana-Ivongo 182, 184, 202
Soavinimerina 133
Soavita 164
Société Auto Express 68
Société Produits de Madagascar 175

Société Rahariseta et Cie 68
Sodextour 202
Sofia Hotel 53, 151, 152, 154
Sofia Satrana Hotel 50, 262, 265, 273
Soft Line Co. 172
Sol et Mar Hotel 239, 240
Soleil et Découverte 231
Solima 69, 70, 97, 108, 147, 217
Solimotel 87, 191
Sonatra 66
Source Bina 113
South Equatorial Current 17
Southern Madagascar 4, 91–125
Spices 16, 56, 167, 176, 191, 227, 237, 239
Spiny Desert 91, 99
St-Joseph 202
Stamps 57
Stany's 205
Star Brewery 141
Starlight Cruises 62
Ste Camille 152
Ste Marians 200
Street vendors 50, 52, 112
Sud Voyages 150
Sugar cane 16
Sultan of Zanzibar 224
Sunburn 40
Super Sice 192
Survival International 163
Swiss Forest 252
Syndicat d'Initiative 139, 150
Syndicat d'Initiative de Manakara 194

Tafondro 230
Talata 145
Talatakely 162
Tampoketsa d'Antsiatsia 183
Tanala 13, 148, 158, 160, 161, 169
Tanambao 192
Tanandava 258
Tanjona Bobaomby 11
Tanjona Vohimena (Cap Ste Marie) 11, 103
Tantely Hotel 144
Taolankarana 93
Tatao restaurant 86, 88
Tavy (slash and burn agriculture) 16, 19, 161, 167, 184, 235
Tax 62, 64
Taxis 36, 47, 50, 64, 65, 73, 75, 94, 96, 104, 105, 106, 107, 112, 114, 117, 120, 121, 127, 129, 130, 135, 136, 137, 139, 145, 146, 147, 148, 150, 156, 157, 158, 163,

Index

168, 171, 174, 175, 180, 182, 184, 185, 186, 187, 189, 190, 193, 197, 198, 207, 211, 212, 214, 217, 218, 221, 222, 225, 237, 238, 240, 241, 242, 243, 246, 247, 253, 254, 255, 256, 257, 258, 260, 261, 262, 269, 270, 273
Taylor, George 114, 200
Tea 16, 156, 157
Telephone 34
Temples 259
Tenrec 22, 97, 128, 188, 219, 271
Thé de Sahambavy 157
Thermal spa 141
Thermal springs 138, 158, 159
Tiana 270
Time 34
Tipping 32
Toamasina (Tamatave) 16, 20, 60, 65, 67, 73, 75, 167, 168, 170–79, 180, 182, 185, 186, 190, 201, 238
Tolanaro (Fort Dauphin) 13, 16, 19, 33, 62, 65, 76, 91, 93–102, 104, 105, 119, 174, 253
Toliara (Tulear) 12, 31, 33, 47, 58, 65, 76, 91, 92, 105–12, 114, 116, 120, 150, 174, 246, 247, 253, 257, 261
Tongobory 116
Top Ten Confection 267
Topographical Service 174
Tour operators 33, 72, 94, 117, 122, 130, 154, 163, 182, 186, 212, 217, 225, 238, 247, 255, 256, 270, 272
Tourism 17, 223
Tourist information 32, 76, 95, 107, 136, 139, 150, 159, 173, 190, 194, 202, 212, 225, 247, 261
Tours 70, 265
Tout pour l'École 79
Train 67, 135, 136, 138, 150, 156, 157, 172, 186, 187, 193
Trans Tour 261
Travel agencies 78, 173
Travel Assistance 37
Traveller's cheques 30, 47, 77, 86, 151, 191, 202, 212, 213, 222, 225, 262, 265
Treaty of Paris 170
Tropic (Malagasy hotel) 266
Tropic Hotel 50
Tropical Touring 59
Tropique Snack 88
Tsakafara 209
Tsangantsainy 209, 222

Tsara Guesthouse 155
Tsara Hotel 223
Tsarafandray Bar Restaurant 179
Tsaratanana 71
Tsaratanana Massif 71, 207
Tsiafajavona 136
Tsikivy 165
Tsimanampetsotsa Nature Reserve 115
Tsimbazaza 84
Tsimialonjafy Hotel 206
Tsimiavona 229
Tsimihety 13, 207, 240
Tsingy de Bemaraha 256–7
Tsingy de Namoroka Reserve 262, 269
Tsiombe 103, 104
Tsiomeko 224
Tsiranana, Philibert 10, 16
Tsiribihana River 60, 254, 255
Tulipes Rouge 198
Typhoid 41

UNESCO 183, 227, 256
Unusual Destinations 70

Valiha 56
Valiha Hotel 216, 217
Vanilla 16, 56, 167, 237, 239
Vanilla Coast 167
Vatolahy 147
Vatomandry 190
Vazimba 106, 115, 116, 113, 124, 240
Vegetarians 51, 102, 142, 143, 156, 178, 217, 249, 263
Venus Hotel and Restaurant 50, 228
Vezo 58, 91, 105, 106, 108, 113, 115, 243
Vichy French 194, 210
Vichy Government 9
Video Club Mahatama 195
Videos 194
Vieux Port Dance Hall 15, 72
Villa Fleuri Hotel 232
Villa Nirina 144
Village Petit Bonheur 95
Visas 26, 95, 107, 151, 174, 213, 226, 248
Vohemar (Iharana) 237, 239–40
Vohipeno 196–8
Vohitsara 177
Volcanoes 11
Vondrozo 169, 198
Vonea Bijoux 153
Voyages Bourdo 173
Voyages Bourdon 55, 68, 225

Wallace, Alfred Russel 19
Water sports 117, 118, 205
Waterfalls 147, 198, 219
Western Madagascar 4, 243-74
Whales 117
Wildlife 19
Wine 53, 164, 204
Winslow, Jonas 114
Women visitors 44
Women's health 41
World Heritage Site 256
Wright, Dr Patricia 161
WWF (World Wide Fund for Nature) 17, 96, 161, 163, 180, 212, 218, 221, 223, 230

Yachts 63
Yachy 217

Ylang-ylang 16, 20, 56, 23, 223, 226
Ylang-ylang Boutique 227
Ynayat Photo and Postcards 225

Zafimaniry 81, 148
Zafimbolafotsy 222
Zafitsimahito 220
Zafy, Albert 10
Zahamena Nature Reserve 173
Zahamotel 120
Zam Zam Snack Bar 267
Zana malata 200
Zanahary (gods) 104
Zaza Club 106, 109
Zohin' i Tenika (Caves of the Portuguese) 59, 122, 123
Zoma 31, 43, 55, 71, 75, 82, 85, 88
Zomandao River 94
Zoological Park 71

REFERENCE

	Airfield	————	Main road
	Places of interest	————	Secondary road
	Bus terminal	·····v·····	Road or track
	Police station	═══════	City street
	Spot height	·····~·····	Coral reefs
	Hotel		Hospital
	Restaurant		Information bureau
	Port		Post office